8051 Microcontrollers

8051 Microcontrollers

Hardware, Software and Applications

David M Calcutt
Frederick J Cowan
G Hassan Parchizadeh

University of Portsmouth

A member of the Hodder Headline Group
LONDON • SYDNEY • AUCKLAND

Co-published in North, Central and South America by
John Wiley & Sons Inc., New York • Toronto

First published in Great Britain in 1998 by
Arnold, a member of the Hodder Headline Group,
338 Euston Road, London NW1 3BH

http://www.arnoldpublishers.com

Co-published in North, Central and South America by
John Wiley & Sons Inc., 605 Third Avenue,
New York, NY 10158–0012

Whilst the advice and information in this book is believed to be true and
accurate at the date of going to press, neither the authors nor the publisher
can accept any legal responsibility or liability for any errors or omissions that
may be made.

British Library Cataloguing in Publication Data
A catalogue record for this book is available from the British Library

Library of Congress Cataloging-in-Publication Data
A catalog record for this book is available from the Library of Congress

ISBN 0 340 67707 4
ISBN 0471 314269 (Wiley)

Publisher: Sian Jones
Production Editor: Rada Radojicic
Production Controller: Rose James
Cover Design: Terry Griffiths

Typeset in 10/12pt Times by Photoprint Typesetters, Torquay
Printed and bound in Great Britain by J. W. Arrowsmith, Bristol

Contents

Appendix   **241**

Index   **327**

Preface

Microcontrollers, especially the ubiquitous 80C51, have been around now for some time and several books have been published on the subject. The authors have long believed in the requirement for a text to explain the details and applications of not only the 8-bit 80C51 microcontroller but other important members of its family, including the 16-bit relatives.

This text attempts to meet the requirement by explaining the structure, operation and applications of the basic 80C51 together with the simpler, and cheaper, 87C750 and the more complex and more versatile 80C552. Also included is a chapter devoted to the use of the Philips XA (eXtended Architecture) 16-bit microcontroller. Several appendices complete the story with details on the 8-bit and 16-bit microcontroller instruction set, manufacturers' data on the devices and development systems used with the devices.

The book is intended to be read on a chapter by chapter basis for those new to the subject and in this format would be suitable for those on degree, including postgraduate, courses. The text would also be suitable for any reader familiar with the devices but requiring information that takes them somewhat deeper into the detail and applications. For those readers with some experience of programming the chapter on programming could be omitted while those new to the subject might find it useful to read the chapter on programming first, before venturing through the remaining chapters. Programming examples have been implemented using Assembly language and, in many cases, using C.

The authors have attempted to show throughout the text programming applications where relevant and the final chapter is devoted to practical applications that the authors have found to work. Notwithstanding this, the authors can accept no responsibility for any program that a reader might attempt and find unsatisfactory. A copy of the programs used in this text is available on a $3\frac{1}{2}$" floppy disk and may be obtained by contacting the authors at the Department of Electrical and Electronic Engineering, University of Portsmouth, Anglesea Road, Portsmouth PO1 3DJ, England (price on application). This would include a copy of the 80C51 cross-assembler; this cross-assembler is also available on the Internet, Philips' web page.

It should perhaps be mentioned at this point that the Department of Electrical and Electronic Engineering at the University of Portsmouth is a Philips Accredited Product Expert Centre, one of only five in England. Short courses relevant to industry are run at the Centre on a regular basis and the Centre is kept up to date on new developments relating to Philips Semiconductors Ltd devices.

The authors hope that all readers of this text will find the information therein of some use in their studies and/or as a reference text.

David M Calcutt, Frederick J Cowan and G Hassan Parchizadeh

Acknowledgments

The authors would like to take the opportunity to thank all those individuals and/or companies who have contributed or helped in some way in the preparation of this text. Particular thanks must go to Derek Wilsdon, Manager Higher Education Initiative, Philips Semiconductors Ltd for his encouragement and for permission to use so much information from Philips' sources. Thanks also are due to Ceibo* for their permission to use information relating to their development systems for the 8-bit and 16-bit microcontrollers; to HiTech** and to Macraigor† for the use of their software in the preparation of some of the programs developed in the book and to Maxim‡ for the use of some items from their range of devices.

Lastly, and by no means least, the authors would like to thank their respective wives for their understanding and forbearance shown when the preparation of the book took time that could have been spent with the family. Our thanks then to David's wife Daphne, Fred's wife Sheila and Hassan's wife Helen.

*Ceibo, 7 Edgestone Court, Florissant, MO 63033, USA
**Hi-Tech Software, PO Box 103, Alderley, QLD, Australia 4051
†Macraigor Systems Inc, PO Box 1008, Brookling Village, MA 02147, USA
‡Maxim UK Ltd, 21C Horsehoe Park, Pangbourne, Reading RG8 7JW, UK

Glossary of Abbreviations

A/D Analogue to Digital
A or ACC Accumulator
AA Assert Acknowledge
ACK Acknowledge
ADC Analogue-Digital Conversion
ADCON ADC Control register
ALE Address Latch Enable
ALU Arithmetic and Logic Unit
ASCII American Standard Code for Information Interchange
BCD Binary Coded Decimal
BCR Bus Configuration Register
BUSW Bus Width
C/T Counter/Timer
CD Compact Disc
CMH Compare High
CML Compare Low
CMOS Complementary Metal-Oxide Semiconductor
CPU Central Processing Unit
CS Code Segment
CTCON Capture Control register
CTH Capture High
CTL Capture Low
D/A Digital to Analogue
d.c. Direct current
DAC Digital-Analogue Conversion
DB Define Byte
DIL Dual-In-Line
DIP Dual-In-Plastic
DOS Disk Operating System
DPH Data Pointer High byte
DPL Data Pointer Low byte
DPTR Data Pointer register
DS Data Segment

DSP Digital Signal Processor
DTMF Dual-Tone Multi-Frequency
EA External Access
EEPROM Electrically Erasable Programmable Read-Only Memory
ENIAC Electronic Numerical Integrator and Computer
EPROM Electrically Programmable Read-Only Memory
ES Extra Segment
FEEPROM Flash EEPROM
FET Field-Effect Transistor
I²C Inter Integrated Circuit
I/O Input/Output
IBM International Business Machines
IC Integrated circuit
IE Interrupt Enable register
IEN Interrupt Enable register
IIC as for I²C
INT External interrupt
IP Interrupt Priority register
IPH Interrupt Priority High byte
IPL Interrupt Priority Low byte
ISO International Standards Organisation
LCD Liquid Crystal Display
LED Light Emitting Diode
LS Low power Schottky
LSB Least Significant Bit
LSI Large-Scale Integration
MICE Microcontroller In-Circuit Emulator
MOSFET Metal-Oxide Semiconductor Field Effect Transistor
MSB Most Significant Bit
NMOS N-channel Metal-Oxide Semiconductor
NVM Non-Volatile Memory
OE Output Enable
OTP One-Time Programmable
PC Program Counter
PC Personal Computer
pcb Printed circuit board
PCH Program Counter High byte
PCL Program Counter Low byte
PCON Power Control register
PIN Personal Identification Number
PLCC Plastic Leaded Chip Carrier
PLD Programmable Logic Device
PQFP Plastic Quad Flat Pack
PROG Program pulse input during EPROM programming
PROM Programmable Read-Only Memory
PSEN Program Store Enable
PSW Program Status Word register
PWM Pulse Width Modulation

PWMP PWM Prescale register
QFP Quad Flat Pack
R/W̄ Read/Write
RAM Random Access Memory
RD External data memory Read strobe
RF Radio Frequency
RI Receive Interrupt
ROM Read-Only Memory
RTE Reset/Toggle Enable register
RTH Timer High Reload
RTL Timer Low Reload
RxD Serial data input
S0BUF Serial 0 data Buffer register
S0CON Serial 0 Control register
S1ADR The SI01 slave Address register
S1BUF The SIO1 Buffer register
S1CON The SI01 Control register
S1DAT The SI01 Data register
S1STA The SI01 Status register
SBUF Serial data Buffer register
SCL Serial port Clock line for I^2C bus
SCON Serial Port Control register
SCR System Configuration register
SDA Serial port Data line for I^2C bus
SFR Special Function Register
SI Serial Interrupt
SIO0 The 8XC552 full duplex UART port
SI01 The 8XC552 I^2C bus port
SM System Mode
SP Stack Pointer
SSEL Segment Selection register
SSI Small-Scale Integration
SSP System Stack Pointer
STE Set Enable register
SWR Software Interrupt Request register
T/C Timer/counter
TCON Timer Control register
T2CON Timer 2 Control register
TH Timer High byte
TI Transmit Interrupt
TL Timer 0/1 low byte
TM2CON Timer 2 Control register
TM2IR Timer 2 Interrupt flag register
TMH2 Timer 2 high byte
TML2 Timer 2 Low byte
TMOD Timer Mode register
TTL Transistor-Transistor Logic
TV Television

TxD Serial data output
UART Universal Asynchronous Receiver/Transmitter
USP User Stack Pointer
VCR Video Cassette Recorder
VLSI Very Large-Scale Integration
WDCON Watchdog Control register
$\overline{\textbf{WE}}$ Write Enable
WFEED Watchdog Feed register
$\overline{\textbf{WR}}$ External data memory write strobe
$\overline{\textbf{WRH}}$ Write High
$\overline{\textbf{WRL}}$ Write Low
XA Extended Architecture

1

The Evolution of the Microcontroller

1.1 Introduction

The electronic technology of today effectively began in 1948 with the invention of the bipolar transistor; commercially made discrete junction transistors were available by 1951. By the late 1950s the concept of a complete circuit on a single semiconductor wafer was gaining ground and by the early 1960s Integrated Circuits (ICs or 'chips' as they are popularly known) were a commercial proposition. The early devices used Small-Scale Integration (SSI) with no more than 100 components per chip. The rate of progress was rapid and by the late 1960s Large-Scale Integration (LSI) allowed up to 10 000 components on a chip. Circuits produced were both digital, with Transistor–Transistor Logic (TTL) available by 1961 and analogue, with the development of the operational-amplifier by 1964. The field-effect transistor joined the ranks of the transistor family by 1958 and by the early 1960s the Metal-Oxide Semiconductor Field-Effect Transistor (MOSFET) was available in integrated circuit form.

The computer concept can be said to have started in a practical way with the mechanical 'analytic engine' designed by Babbage in 1822; work on this machine progressed until 1833 when the lack of precision engineering parts caused its abandonment (a machine was constructed many years later and lived up to Babbage's expectations by working well). The analytical machine was the forerunner of the digital computer, using punched cards for input and a printing block to provide the output, and had memory and an arithmetic unit. Babbage also envisaged that the machine should be able to follow alternative courses of action, a forerunner of today's 'conditional transfer' operation.

The machine thought to be the first programmable electronic computer was built in 1943 and operated at Bletchley Park, Buckinghamshire, England. The machine, called Colossus, contained about 1500 thermionic valves and was used to break the coding machine Enigma used by Germany in the Second World War.

A machine, called the Electronic Numerical Integrator And Computer (ENIAC), was produced in 1945 at the University of Pennsylvania. Used for specific scientific military purposes it consisted of several racks of equipment filling a large room and using about 18 000 thermionic valves as the active devices. The machine was successful and operated for nine years before being overtaken by new developments. ENIAC was not a general purpose computer in the modern sense, not being programmable in the way it is understood today; it was designed for a specific task and needed to be reconfigured for any other task. However, it was capable of performing addition, subtraction, division and multiplication and could be used for the solution of partial differential equations using punched cards for input and output.

Still using thermionic valves, various developments of ENIAC were produced and the first commercially available machine for worldwide sale was the UNIVAC 1 built by Remington Rand in 1951. International Business Machines (IBM) produced the first of a range of digital computers for commercial use in 1953; such machines were known as first generation computers. The first transistorised special purpose computer was developed by Cray in 1956 and this was followed by commercial second and third generation systems in the late 1960s and early 1970s. Fourth generation computers employ Very Large-Scale Integration (VLSI) with more than 10 000 components on a chip.

Early computers were known as mainframe machines and were physically large without possessing, by today's standards, great computational power or memory capacity. Mini-computers and microcomputers followed with enhanced computational power and memory capability brought about by the advances in chip technology. At the heart of the microcomputer is the microprocessor which contains, on a single chip, the arithmetic, logic and control systems required by a computer to perform the data processing and/or computational tasks.

The first microprocessor was the 4-bit 4004 produced by Intel between 1969 and 1971 and this was rapidly followed by the 8-bit 8080. Other manufacturers soon followed with their own versions, and devices with an 8-bit word length were for years the accepted standard. Today 16-bit or even 32-bit word lengths are in common usage. Early work on digital computers had established the use of binary numbers and Boolean algebra and this has continued. The word 'bit' is in fact a contraction of the words **bi**nary dig**it** and a stored bit can have the value of logic 1 or logic 0. The bits represent the number of data elements that can be processed at any one time and is known as the word length.

The first microcontroller, the 8048, was produced by Intel in 1976. The 8048 contains a CPU (Central Processing Unit), 1k bytes of EPROM (Electronically Programmable Read-Only Memory), 64 bytes of RAM (Random Across Memory), an 8-bit timer and 27 I/O (Input/Output) pins. The 8051 followed in 1980 and contains 4k bytes of ROM (Read-Only Memory), 128 bytes of RAM, a serial port, two 16-bit timers and 32 I/O pins. The 8051 family has seen many additions and improvements over the years and remains a powerful tool for the modern day circuit designer.

As stated earlier the microcomputer consists of a microprocessor chip plus other elements such as memory and I/O ports. These key elements are interconnected by a series of buses to produce the complete system. A microcontroller on the other hand is a complete system on a single chip. The essential differences between the two devices will be discussed in the next section.

1.2   Microprocessors and microcontrollers

A basic block diagram of a microprocessor is shown in Figure 1.1. The **ALU** is the Arithmetic and Logic Unit while the control unit undertakes the timing and sequence functions. Additionally there are registers which can hold data while data manipulation takes place. Registers also assist in the role of program execution. A register is simply a store which can contain a set of logic states, i.e. logic 1 and logic 0.

The ALU performs arithmetic manipulations such as binary addition, subtraction and, possibly, multiplication and division. Also the logical functions such as AND, OR, NOT

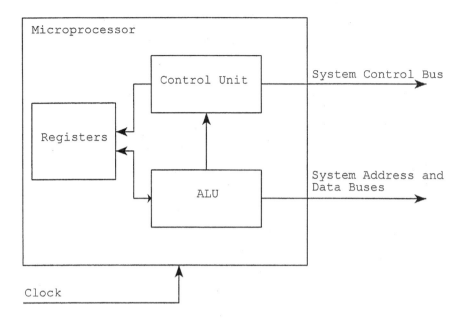

Figure 1.1 Block diagram of a microprocessor

and Exclusive-OR can be implemented. The ALU consists of gates which are organised to receive binary inputs and provide binary outputs according to the instruction code in force, i.e for the addition process the gates are arranged as an adder while for the AND process the gates are arranged as an AND gate, etc.

The **control unit** provides the essential timing of operations within the system including the process of **fetch and execute** whereby an instruction is fetched from memory and caused to be executed. This is known as the **instruction cycle**. Instrumental in this process is the **instruction decoder**, which determines which instruction code has been fetched and the action that must be taken to implement it, and the **Program Counter (PC)** which allows the processor to keep track of its position within the program.

The **register** group contains the data that the processor needs while performing the task of executing a program. The registers include the PC, the **Accumulator** (which is a storage register much used in specified data operations) and the **Stack Pointer (SP)** (used to indicate the position in memory where data may be stacked). There are many types of microprocessor available and the registers, and the names given to them, may vary from device to device.

Most modern microprocessors also incorporate a small amount of on-board memory and may well include clock circuitry.

1.3 Microcomputer

Essentially the microcomputer consists of three elements as shown in Figure 1.2.

MICROPROCESSOR

This has been dealt with earlier (see p. 2).

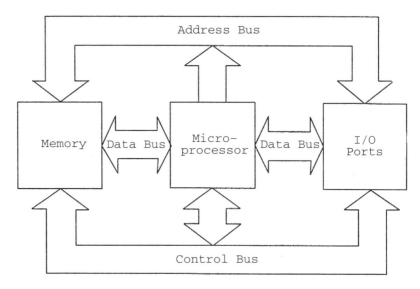

Figure 1.2 Basic microcomputer system

MEMORY

The memory element could be split into internal and external memory with the internal memory further sub-divided where applicable into **program storage memory** and **data storage memory**. Hard disks and/or flexible (floppy) disks can be used to store large amounts of memory. External memory could well be a floppy disk while internal memory would be RAM or ROM. RAM can be read or overwritten; RAM is volatile and its contents are lost once the power supply is switched off. ROM will keep its contents even if the power is removed.

A microcomputer system needs both RAM and ROM. A memory map will show how the memory locations are divided between the different types of memory. For a system operating with a 16-bit address bus the memory map could extend from location 0000 to location FFFF. This representation of the memory location is known as **hexadecimal** and provides a simple way of identifying a location without the need to specify all 16 bits of the actual address. There are 16 total variations represented by four bits (i.e. $2^4 = 16$), but only 0 (0000) to 9 (1001) can be represented by decimal numbers and the remaining six combinations (1010) to (1111) are represented by alphabetic figures A to F respectively. Thus 16 bits can be represented by four hexadecimal alphanumeric figures. Hence the first memory location is 0000 0000 0000 0000, represented in hexadecimal form by 0000, while the last is 1111 1111 1111 1111 represented by FFFF.

INPUT/OUTPUT

The system requires an interface with the 'outside world'. The I/O interface allows the connection of input data via, say, a keyboard and sensors which can transpose information such as movement, pressure, temperature, etc. into electrical signals; for output data there could be, say, a monitor to display instructions/data and outputs that can feed external devices such as relays, solenoids, LEDs (Light Emitting Diodes) etc.

It is possible to 'memory map' the I/O interface so that data read from the interface comes directly from the external device while data transferred to the interface is data fed directly to the external device. The I/O interfaces are usually referred to as **I/O ports**. Most microcomputer systems have ICs which perform the function of I/O ports and some are programmable which means that the operating mode may be changed to suit the particular system requirements. The ports may be serial, for moving data a bit at a time, or parallel where data is moved in a block with the rate of transfer determined by the system clock.

In addition to the three hardware elements there are three sets of connections, known as **buses**, that interconnect the chips. Details of each bus and its function are given below.

Data bus

Provides a path for the data which is to be processed. The data is usually in 'words' which can be anything from four bits to 32 bits in length; a combination of 1s and 0s in a word can represent specific data. It can be shown that for a 4-bit word there are 2^4 or 16 possible combinations ranging from 0000 through to 1111. Obviously with 8-, 16- or 32-bit words the number of combinations will be increased. A group of eight bits is known as a **byte** while four bits is a **nibble**. Thus two nibbles make a byte. A group of 16 bits is said to be made up of two bytes, etc.

Address bus

The memory device will consist of a number of memory cells which can be uniquely identified by an address. The memory cells can contain data or program instructions and each cell could contain several bits.

As an example, for a read operation the address of the memory location containing the data (or instruction) is placed on the address bus. The control bus carries a signal indicating that the process is a read operation; this signal allows the data in the specified memory location to be placed on the data bus. The data is read and stored in one of the internal registers or, where applicable, transferred to an output port.

As shown in Figure 1.2 the I/O chip is also accessed via the address bus. As stated earlier this arrangement is known as **memory-mapped I/O**. An alternative arrangement allows the microprocessor to be connected to the I/O with a dedicated bus structure giving what is known as **dedicated** or **port addressed I/O**.

The size of the address bus can vary; for an 8-bit system the address bus would be typically 16 bits wide giving 2^{16} or 65 536 (64k byte) address locations. The symbol k in computer terminology defines $2^{10} = 1024$; this is the closest binary number to 1000. For a 16-bit system the address bus is typically 20 bits wide giving 1M byte (one million) addressable locations. When an address is accessed by the microprocessor all other address locations are disabled so that the microprocessor communicates with only one address location at a time.

Control bus

This bus carries the signals required to synchronise the operations of the system. For example, as suggested earlier, if the microprocessor needs to read data from (or write data into) a memory location, the control bus carries the necessary signal. The signal in this case is the READ/WRITE (R/W̄) signal which is sent from the microprocessor to allow the necessary data movement to be carried out. The microprocessor would send a logic 1 via the control bus if a READ operation were to be performed from the memory location whose address was currently on the address bus. For a $\overline{\text{WRITE}}$ operation the signal would be a logic 0, as indicated by the bar over the letter W, i.e. $\overline{\text{W}}$ indicates an operation carried out with a signal that is **active low**.

Some I/O elements can send signals to the microprocessor via the control bus; such signals include interrupts, where the system is designed to respond to an external event, and RESET, where the system could be reset to a specified start condition.

The most important signal carried by the control bus is the system clock which, operating at frequencies in the range 1 to 30 MHz, provides the necessary synchronisation for the system to operate. The clock is crystal-controlled and, although not shown on the system diagram of Figure 1.2, is an integral part of the microprocessor block.

1.4   Microcontroller

The basic block diagram of a typical microcontroller is similar to the microprocessor but with the addition of I/0 ports, memory, counters, a clock and interrupt circuitry. A basic arrangement is shown in Figure 1.3.

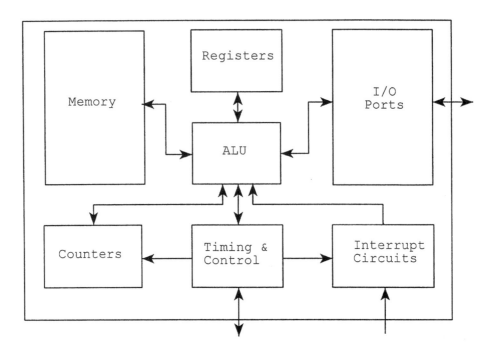

Figure 1.3 Basic microcontroller circuit

It is the additional circuitry, compared to the microprocessor, that makes the micro-controller such a unique device. The microcontroller is designed primarily to operate on data that is fed in through its serial or parallel input ports; the data is operated on, under the control of software stored in ROM, and external devices controlled through signals fed via the output ports. The incoming data may be from a variety of external devices and priority for receiving, and operating on, the data can be established using the interrupt control circuitry.

1.5 Comparison between microprocessors and microcontrollers

The microprocessor is designed to perform as the CPU in a microcomputer system. By configuring the microprocessor with other chips it is possible to produce a range of systems with the flexibility to provide for a range of customer requirements. The microprocessor instruction set is arranged to allow code and large amounts of data to be moved between the microprocessor and external memory using working registers and, where necessary, address pointers and offsets. Such instructions can operate on up to 32 bits of data and would usually operate on not less than four bits.

A microcontroller on the other hand is designed to operate with the minimum of external circuitry to perform control orientated tasks using a control program in ROM. The instruction set for the microcontroller is simpler than that of the microprocessor since most of its instructions will move code and data from internal memory to the ALU; the use of many I/O pins allows data to be moved between the microcontroller and external devices, often as single bits. The operation on single bits, such as logical operations, flag setting/ clearing, etc. is unique to the microcontroller since the microprocessor would generally operate on bytes or larger data groups.

The microcontroller architecture is designed to allow programming for single task operation which is ideal for applications requiring large product volumes. An example of the use of a microcontroller is the automatic washing machine where external parameters such as water level, water temperature, etc., can be monitored and controlled according to the requirements of the wash cycle. Such an application requires small amounts of RAM, to store transient data, and larger amounts of ROM to accommodate the control program. On the other hand, a microcomputer, employing a microprocessor as the CPU, is likely to require a large amount of RAM for user programs and a smaller amount of ROM for hardware interfacing routines. The amount of memory required for a microcomputer is obviously much greater than that required for a microcontroller because of the larger data handling requirements of the former.

1.6 Microcontroller types

The predominant family of microcontrollers are 8-bit types since this word size has proved popular for the vast majority of tasks the devices have been called upon to perform. The single byte word is regarded as sufficient for most purposes and has the advantage of easily interfacing with the variety of IC memories and logic circuitry currently available. The serial ASCII data is also byte sized making data communications easily compatible with the microcontroller devices. Because the type of application for the microcontroller may vary enormously most manufacturers provide a family of devices, each member of the family being capable of fitting neatly into the manufacturer's requirements. This avoids the use of a common device for all applications where some elements of the device would not be used; such a device would of necessity be complex and hence expensive. The microcontroller family would have a common instruction subset but family members differ in the amount of memory, timer facility, etc. possessed, thus producing cost effective devices for particular manufacturing requirements. Memory expansion is possible with off- chip RAM and/or ROM; for some family members there is no on-chip ROM or the ROM is EPROM. This latter arrangement allows for customer generated applications that can be tested before a final ROM version is ordered or for customer designs that can be changed 'in-house' to suit changing requirements. Additional on-chip facilities could include Analogue to Digital Conversion (ADC) and Digital to Analogue Conversion (DAC). Some family members include versions with a lower pin-count for more basic applications thus minimising costs. Many microcontroller manufacturers are vying in the market place and rather than try to list all types the authors have restricted the text to one manufacturer. This does not preclude the book from being useful for applications involving other manufacturers' devices; there is a commonality amongst devices from various sources so that explanations and descriptions within this text can in most cases be applied generally. The chapters that follow will deal with those microcontroller family members available from Philips Semiconductors and acknowledgment is due to the considerable assistance given by Philips Semiconductors in the production of this text. The Philips products are identified by the numbering system:

8XCXXX

where, in general since there are exceptions, the digit following the 8 is:

0 for a ROMless device
3 for a device with ROM
7 for a device with EPROM/OTP (one time programmable)
9 for a device with FEEPROM (flash).

Following the 'C' there may be two or three digits. Additional digits, not shown above, would indicate such factors as clock speed, pin-count, package code and temperature range.

Some members of the Philips 8-bit microcontroller family will be discussed briefly below. The devices mentioned are just a selection from an extensive list and are included so that an indication of the range and specification of the family of devices can be gauged. Details regarding device operation, architecture, instruction set, etc. will be dealt with in the chapters that follow.

- The 8XC51 is a 40-pin CMOS (Complementary Metal-Oxide Semiconductor) device with $4k \times 8$ ROM (80C51), $4k \times 8$ EPROM (87C51), 128×8 RAM, 32 I/O lines, two 16-bit counter/timers, a five-source two-priority level nested interrupt structure, on-chip oscillator, with speed range from 12 MHz to 33 MHz, and clock circuits. An 80C31 is a ROMless version of the device. Memory addressing capability is 64k ROM and 64k RAM. The device is TTL and CMOS compatible.

- The 8XC52 is a 40-pin CMOS device with $8k \times 8$ ROM (80C52), $8k \times 8$ EPROM (87C52), 256×8 RAM, 32 I/O lines, three 16-bit counter/timers, a full duplex serial channel, Boolean processor, on-chip oscillator, with speed range from 3.5 MHz to 24 MHz, and clock circuits. An 80C32 is a ROMless version of the device. Memory addressing capability is 64k ROM and 64k RAM. The device is TTL and CMOS compatible.

- The 8XC58 is a 40-pin CMOS device with $32k \times 8$ EPROM (87C58), $32k \times 8$ ROM (80C58), expandable externally to 64k bytes, 256×8 RAM, expandable externally to 64k bytes, four 8-bit I/O ports, three 16-bit counter/timers (one of which is an up/down counter), a full duplex enhanced UART (Universal Asynchronous Receiver/Transmitter), six interrupt sources and four level priority, on-chip oscillator and timing circuits. The device is TTL and CMOS compatible.

- The 8XC552 is a 68-pin CMOS device with 8k bytes mask programmable ROM (83C552), 8k bytes EPROM (87C552) and ROMless (80C552), expandable externally to 64k bytes, 256×8 RAM, expandable externally to 64k bytes, five 8-bit I/O ports plus one 8-bit input port shared with analogue inputs, three 16-bit counter/timers, one of which is coupled to four capture registers and three compare registers, a 10-bit ADC with eight multiplexed analogue inputs, a full duplex enhanced UART, on-chip watchdog timer, three speed ranges from 1.2 MHz up to 30 MHz and three ambient temperature ranges. The device is TTL and CMOS compatible. The device can function as an arithmetic processor with facilities for both binary and BCD (Binary Coded Decimal) arithmetic plus bit-handling capabilities.
- The 8XC750 is a low cost 24-pin CMOS device with $1k \times 8$ EPROM (87C750), $1k \times 8$ ROM (83C750), 64×8 RAM, 19 I/O lines, a 16-bit auto-reload counter/timer, a five-source fixed-priority level interrupt structure and an on-chip oscillator. The device is TTL and CMOS compatible.

All the devices listed would use the basic 8051 architecture with modifications to suit the device. Also the instruction set would use the basic 8051 instruction set with additions as required to suit the device. More detail on this point will be found in the chapters that follow.

Philips also produce families of 16-bit microcontrollers, some of which use the 68000 architecture and some the XA (eXtended Architecture). For the XA range Philips claim compatibility with the 80C51 at source code level with full support for the internal registers, operating modes and 80C51 instructions. Also claimed is a speed of operation that is three to four times faster than contemporary 16-bit architectures and 10 to 100 times faster than the 80C51.

The XA products are identified by the numbering system:

P51XA G3 XXXX

where:

P51XA is Philips 80C51 eXtended Architecture
G3 is the derivative name
next digit is memory option:
   0 = ROMless
   3 = ROM
   5 = bond-out (emulation)
   7 = EPROM/OTP
   9 = FEEPROM (flash)
next digit is speed:
   E = 16 MHz
   G = 20 MHz
   I = 24 MHz
   K = 30 MHz
next digit is temperature:
   B = 0°C to +70°C
   F = –40°C to +85°C
   H = –40°C to +125°C

final digit is package code:
A = Plastic Leaded Chip Carrier (PLCC)
B = Quad Flat Pack (QFP)
etc.

The XA architecture supports:

- 16-bit fully static CPU with a 24-bit program and data address range;
- eight 16-bit CPU registers each capable of performing all arithmetic and logic operations as well as acting as memory pointers;
- both 8-bit and 16-bit CPU registers, each capable of performing all arithmetic and logic operations;
- an enhanced instruction set that includes bit intensive logic operations and fast signed or unsigned 16×16 multiply and 32/16 divide;
- instruction set tailored for high level language support;
- multi-tasking and real-time executives that include up to 32 vectored interrupts, 16 software traps, segmented data memory, and banked registers to support context switching.

Specific features of the XA-G1, for example, are:

- 20-bit address range, 1M byte each program and data space (the XA architecture supports up to 24-bit addresses);
- 3.0 V to 5.5 V operation;
- 8k bytes on-chip EPROM/ROM program memory;
- 512 bytes of on-chip data RAM;
- three counter/timers with enhanced features;
- Watchdog Timer;
- two enhanced UARTS;
- four 8-bit I/O ports with four programmable output configurations;
- 44-pin PLCC and LQFP (Low profile Quad Flat Pack) packages.

XA-G2 devices are available with similar specifications to the XA-G1 except that there are 16k bytes on-chip EPROM/ROM program memory. In turn the XA-G3 is similar to the XA-G1 but has 32k bytes on-chip EPROM/ROM program memory.

The chapters that follow will deal with the operation and application of microcontrollers, especially the 80C51 and its family members. Chapter 10 is devoted entirely to the operation and application of the XA 16-bit microcontroller.

1.7   Microprocessor and microcontroller applications

The way in which the use of the microprocessor and, latterly, the microcontroller, has shaped our lives is breathtaking. Today these versatile devices can be found in a variety of applications which tend to be taken for granted because, in most cases, their use is transparent to the user. Such commercial applications as television sets, Video Cassette Recorders (VCRs), Compact Disc (CD) players, microwave ovens, washing machines, telephones, automobile engine management systems and smart cards are a few examples. Their use in such cases has made for versatile and user friendly, reliable operation.

As an example of the commercial use of a microcontroller consider Figure 1.4 which shows a simplified block diagram for a mobile telephone.

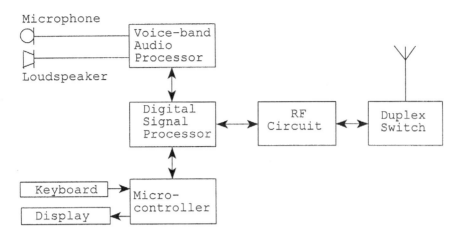

Figure 1.4 Block diagram of a mobile telephone arrangement

In this circuit arrangement the input circuit is a voice-band audio processor which interfaces between the analogue world of the telephone user and the Digital Signal Processor (DSP) chip. The voice-band audio processor uses two-way circuitry to provide for transmit and receive signals which operate under the control of an internal clock.

For transmission the analogue speech signal is converted into digital code, via an ADC, which is passed to the DSP. The DSP uses the coded signal to modulate a suitable RF (Radio Frequency) carrier for radio transmission purposes. The duplex switch allows the RF signal to be transmitted at the same time as an incoming RF signal is received from a distant transmitter.

For reception, the received signal from the duplex switch is passed through the RF circuits where demodulation recovers the wanted signal, in digital form, from the RF carrier and passes it to the receive section of the voice-band audio processor. The received signals are passed to a DAC for conversion back to analogue form and the resulting signal is used to produce speech via the loudspeaker. The microcontroller interfaces with the DSP and allows for the provision of input data, such as the required dialled number, via the keyboard and output data, such as a visual indication of the dialled number, via the display.

Another commercial application of the microcontroller is the smart card. Such cards are manufactured according to the ISO (International Standards Organisation) specification for IC cards and possess certain advantages compared to the 'ordinary' magnetic stripe card. The magnetic stripe card possesses personalised/security data information but this is fixed at source and is limited in terms of data capacity; the advantage of such a card is that it is cheap to produce but it does have a low security rating. The smart card on the other hand has built-in computational capacity that allows reconfiguration in use and has a high security rating. It is, however, more costly to produce than the magnetic stripe card.

The main uses for smart cards are:

- financial transactions where the user is identified by the use of a PIN (Personal Identification Number) code and transactions can be logged and balances stored, etc.;
- security applications allowing access to defined areas provided the user is identified by the smart card software as being eligible to enter such areas.

Smart cards are already numbered in millions and their use is likely to increase with the development of digital television. The advent of digital television, with channel capacity measured in the hundreds, will probably require a smart card to be used to select, and pay for, channels or specific programs as required by the user. The versatility of the smart card is that such transactions can be loaded on to the card when it is connected to a main computer and the user requirements changed in a manner that is transparent to the user.

The microcontroller arrangement for a smart card in block diagram form is shown in Figure 1.5. The microcontroller is inserted into ISO standard plastic cards with contacts that interface with external voltage supply, clock, input/output etc. As indicated in Figure 1.5 the on-chip memory is divided into distinct groups namely RAM, ROM and NVM (Non-Volatile Memory). RAM is used to temporarily store information and is volatile, i.e. it loses its contents when power is switched off. Non-volatile memory consists mainly of three distinct types each with the ability to retain data in the absence of electrical power. ROM is the simplest type of NVM and has its contents defined, according to customer requirements, during manufacture; the contents are then fixed for life and cannot be changed.

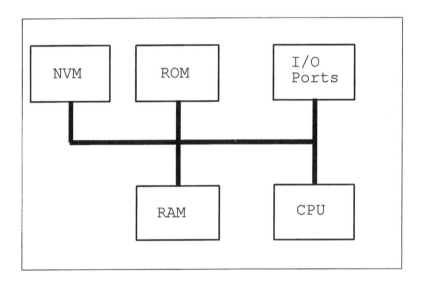

Figure 1.5 Block diagram of a smart card microcontroller

The other main types of NVM are EPROM and EEPROM:

- **EPROM** (Erasable Programmable ROM). This type of memory can store a '1' or a '0' in each cell depending on the level of stored charge. Each cell can be programmed by the use of a relatively high voltage to change the state of the cell from a '0' to a '1'. By exposure to UV (Ultra-Violet) light the contents of the entire memory can be erased causing all cells to lose their stored charge and return to the '0' state. Individual cells can then be reprogrammed as required.
- **EEPROM** (Electrically Erasable Programmable). This ROM operates in a similar manner to EPROM but has the ability to individually alter the contents of each cell, i.e.

each cell can be returned to the 'normal' '0' state by the application of a suitable voltage level.

The voltage levels required for programming both these non-volatile memories can be provided internally or by a power supply external to the chip. NVM has to be included since individual data is required for each user and this must be written into the card before issue. Such data must be retained even when the card is not in use and not powered up.

The main uses of NVM are for storing data that is frequently updated (results of individual cash transactions, etc.) and for the less frequent changes (personal details such as new PIN code, credit limit, changes in status, etc.) Whether EPROM or EEPROM, or both, are included in the smart card depends on the customer requirements and will be dictated mainly by cost and required flexibility of use.

1.8   Development systems for microcontrollers

To enable a microcontroller to be programmed to perform a task requires the software necessary for the task to be entered and tested to ensure it is 'bug' free. Microcontroller manufacturers will provide support tools for customer use and also assist other vendors who provide a similar service. Generally development systems are available in two versions for ROM and ROMless applications. The ROM emulation products can support all versions of a given device, including EPROM, ROM and ROMless devices, whereas the ROMless emulator can only support applications designed for a ROMless micro-controller. Most development systems are designed to connect to a PC. The PC could be fitted with an inexpensive EPROM programmer or dedicated, but more expensive, EPROM programming support could be provided by specialist suppliers. Software support is needed on the PC for the development system; the minimum software requirement would be a machine language assembler. More expensive software would provide high level language compilers and debuggers.

Microcontroller manufacturers will provide details of development system contacts and EPROM programming support contacts for customer use. Details of the development systems for the 80C51 and XA microcontrollers are included in the appendices at the end of this book.

Summary

- Modern VLSI techniques have made microprocessor and microcontroller devices possible.
- A microprocessor consists essentially of an ALU, a control unit and a bank of registers all on a single chip.
- A microcomputer comprises a microprocessor, memory and I/O chips interconnected via lines known as buses.
- A typical microcontroller is similar to the microprocessor but with the addition of I/O ports, memory, counters, a clock and interrupt circuitry on a single chip.
- The microprocessor is designed to perform as the CPU in a microcomputer system whereas the microcontroller is designed to operate with the minimum of external circuitry to perform control orientated tasks using a control program in ROM.
- Microcontrollers are available in various data sizes, the most popular of which is 8-bit although 16-bit is popular for higher performance specifications.

- Microprocessor and microcontroller applications are increasingly prevalent for modern electrical/electronic appliances, providing greater flexibility in the use of such appliances.
- Development tools are available to customers to assist in programming the micro-controller for specific applications.

Exercises

1. Write a brief account of the development of today's electronic technology starting with the design of the bipolar transistor.
2. What are the basic components of a microprocessor chip and what functions do they perform?
3. What are the basic building blocks of a microcomputer system?
4. What is meant by the terms RAM, ROM and EPROM?
5. What are the basic components of a microcontroller device?
6. What are the essential differences between a microprocessor and a micro-controller?
7. When was the first 8051 microcontroller produced and by which company?
8. Compare the specification of the first 8051 microcontroller and its modern day counterpart.
9. Suggest modern volume applications for microcontrollers likely to be seen in domestic use.
10. Why are development tools required as back up for a microcontroller?

2
8051 Microcontroller Structure

2.1 Introduction

The previous chapter gave an introduction to the various members of the 8051 family using Philips devices as the basis. The description given was merely to highlight, for the purposes of comparison, the various features of each device in terms of the number of pins, memory capacity, number of counter/timers, etc. This chapter will consider the 80C51 architecture and hardware arrangements and examine the devices in more detail. Three devices, namely the 80C51 itself, the 8XC552 and the 8XC750, will be considered in more depth in order to show the spread of attributes of the 80C51 family. The 80C51 can be considered as the 'core' device which has been expanded to produce the extra facilities of the 8XC552 and contracted to produce the low-cost 8XC750 device. Each microcontroller has been designed in order to provide the customer with a device to suit their particular requirements.

Device functions such as I/O ports, timer/counters, serial interfacing and interrupts will be discussed with the differences between the 80C51, 8XC552 and 8XC750 highlighted. Finally the chapter will look at 80C51 addressing modes which are common to all members of the 80C51 family. Pertinent data regarding the devices is included in appendices found at the end of the book. Appendix A details the 80C51 opcode mnemonics while Appendices C, D and E look at the 80C51, 8XC552 and 8XC750 devices respectively.

As described in Chapter 1, the 80C51 is a 40-pin device with the following architecture:

- $4k \times 8$ ROM
- 128×8 RAM
- four 8-bit I/O ports
- serial interface
- two 16-bit counter/timers
- a five-source two-priority level nested interrupt structure
- on-chip oscillator.

The arrangement for the 80C51 device is shown in Figure 2.1.

Variations exist according to the family member, i.e. the on-chip program memory could be ROM or EPROM and the memory size could vary (the 80C52 has 8k ROM while

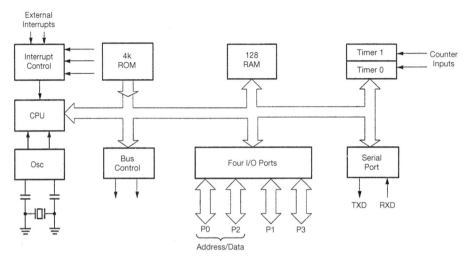

Figure 2.1 80C51 block diagram (courtesy Philips Semiconductors)

the 87C52 has 8k EPROM). Also the on-chip data memory size could vary (both the 80C52 and 87C52 devices have 256 bytes of RAM). Additionally the device could have a third counter/timer (as is the case for the 80C52). However, the block diagram of Figure 2.1 will serve to illustrate the hardware arrangements in a general way.

2.2   Pin-out diagram for the 80C51

The 80C51 microcontroller is available in a 40-pin DIL (Dual-In-Line) package; the arrangement is shown in Figure 2.2. Other packages are available and although the device pin functions are the same regardless of package configuration, pin-out numbers vary. Other packages are shown in appendix C together with the logic symbol for the device. The pin-out numbers referred to in the description that follows are valid only for the DIL package. A brief description of the function of each of the pins is as follows:

Supply voltage (V_{cc} and V_{ss})

The device operates from a single + 5V supply connected to pin 40 (V_{cc}) while pin 20 (V_{ss}) is grounded.

I/O ports

32 of the pins are arranged as four 8-bit I/O ports P0–P3. 24 of these pins are dual purpose (26 on the 80C52/80C58) with each capable of operating as a control line or part of the data/address bus in addition to the I/O functions. Details are as follows.

- **Port 0**. This is a dual purpose port occupying pins 32 to 39 of the device. The port may be used with external memory to provide a multiplexed address and data bus.
- **Port 1**. This is a dedicated I/O port occupying pins 1 to 8 of the device. For the 80C52 and 80C58 pins P1.0 and P1.1 could also function as external inputs for the third timer/ counter.

Figure 2.2 80C51 pin-out layout (courtesy Philips Semiconductors)

- **Port 2**. This is a dual purpose port occupying pins 21 to 28 of the device. The port may be used to provide the high-order byte of the address bus for external program memory or more than 256 bytes of external data memory.
- **Port 3**. This is a dual purpose port occupying pins 10 to 17 of the device. These pins, in addition to the I/O role, serve the special features of the 80C51 family; the alternative functions are summarised in Table 2.1.

Table 2.1 Port 3 alternative pin functions

Port	Symbol	Function
P3.0	RxD	Serial data input port
P3.1	TxD	Serial data output port
P3.2	$\overline{\text{INT0}}$	External interrupt 0
P3.3	$\overline{\text{INT1}}$	External interrupt 1
P3.4	T0	Timer/counter 0 external input
P3.5	T1	Timer/counter 1 external input
P3.6	$\overline{\text{WR}}$	External data memory write strobe
P3.7	$\overline{\text{RD}}$	External data memory read strobe

Reset *(pin 9)*

The 80C51 is reset by holding this input high for a minimum of two machine cycles before returning it low for normal running. An internal resistance connects to pin 20 (V_{ss}) allowing a power-on reset using an external capacitor connected to pin 40 (V_{cc}). The device internal registers are loaded with selected values prior to normal operation.

XTAL1 *and* **XTAL2** *(pins 19 and 18 respectively)*

The 80C51 on-chip oscillator is driven, usually, from an external crystal. The XTAL1 input also provides an input to the internal clock generator circuits.

$\overline{\text{PSEN}}$ *(Program Store Enable) (pin 29)*

This pin provides an output read strobe to external program memory. The output is active low during the fetch stage of an instruction. The signal is not activated during a fetch from internal memory.

ALE/$\overline{\text{PROG}}$ *(Address Latch Enable/PROGram Pulse) (pin 30)*

The ALE signal is an output pulse used to latch the low byte of an address during access to external memory. The signal rate is 1/6 the oscillator frequency and can be used as a general purpose clock/timing pulse for the external circuitry. The pin also provides the program pulse input ($\overline{\text{PROG}}$) during EPROM programming.

$\overline{\text{EA}}$/V$_{\text{pp}}$ *(External Access/programming voltage) (pin 31)*

This pin is tied either high or low according to circuit requirements. If tied high the device will execute programs from internal memory providing the address is not higher than the last address in the internal 4k bytes ROM (80C51) or the internal 8k bytes ROM (80C52). For the 80C51/80C52 devices the $\overline{\text{EA}}$ pin **may** be tied low, thus disabling the internal ROM, and program code accessed from external ROM. For a ROMless device (80C31/ 80C32) the $\overline{\text{EA}}$ pin **must** be tied low permanently and program code accessed from external ROM could be as much as 64k bytes. EPROM versions of the device also use this pin for the supply voltage (V_{pp}) necessary for programming the internal EPROM.

2.3   80C51 family hardware

The 80C51 architecture is shown in Figure 2.3. Although not numbered, the 40 pins and the pin functions as described earlier for the DIL package can be seen. The basic architecture is the same for all members of the 80C51 family (80C31/80C51/87C51, 80C32/80C52/87C52, 80C58/87C58, etc.) although there are differences for devices such as the 80C552/83C552 which have five 8-bit ports, comparators, ADC circuit, etc. and the 83C750/87C750 which have only two 8-bit ports plus a third 3-bit port. Block diagrams for the 8XC552 device can be seen in Appendix D while that for the 8XC750 can be found in Appendix E.

Reference has already been made in general terms to the 80C51 ports, timer/counters, internal RAM and ROM/EPROM (where applicable). Specific features include:

- 8-bit CPU with Registers A (Accumulator) and B
- 16-bit PC
- 16-bit Data PoinTeR register (DPTR)
- 8-bit Program Status Word register (PSW)
- 8-bit Stack Pointer (SP)

It is clear from the above that the 80C51 has a collection of 8-bit and 16-bit registers and 8-bit memory locations. The internal memory of the 80C51 can be shown by the programming model of Figure 2.4.

The programming model will be referred to again later in this chapter when addressing modes for device programming are discussed.

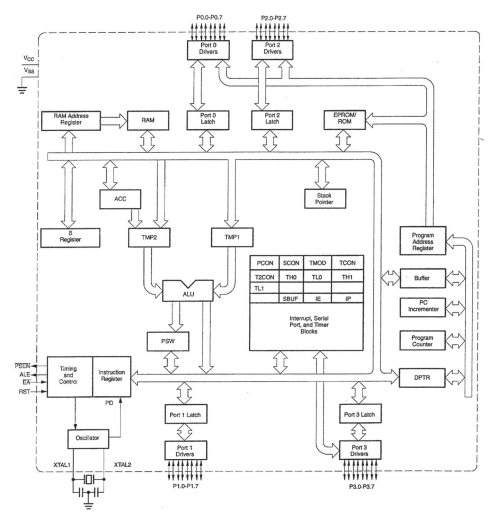

Figure 2.3 80C51 architecture (courtesy Philips Semiconductors)

2.4 Memory organisation

INTERNAL RAM

The 80C51 has 128 bytes of on-chip RAM plus a number of Special Function Registers (SFRs). Including the SFR space gives 256 addressable locations but the addressing modes for internal RAM can accommodate 384 bytes by splitting the memory space into three blocks, namely the lower 128, the upper 128 and the SFR space. The lower 128 bytes use address locations 00h to 7Fh and these can be accessed using Direct and Indirect Addressing. The upper 128 bytes use address locations 80h to FFh and may be accessed using Direct Addressing only; locations in this space with addresses ending with 0h or 8h are also bit addressable. Some members of the 80C51 family have 256 bytes of on-chip RAM and the upper 128 bytes in this case would be accessible only using the Indirect Addressing mode.

For the 80C51 device, the internal RAM of 128 bytes is broken down into:

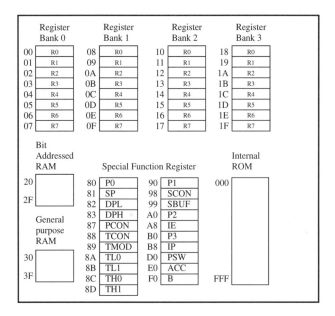

Figure 2.4 80C51 programming model

- four register banks 0 to 3, each of which contains eight registers R0 to R7. The 32 bytes occupy addresses from 00h to 1Fh. Each register can be addressed specifically when its bank is selected or an address can identify a particular register regardless of the bank, i.e. R2 of bank 2 can be specified if bank 2 is selected or the same location can be specified as address 12h. The register banks not selected can be used as general purpose RAM. Bits 3 and 4 of the PSW register determine which bank is selected when a program is running. Reset will cause bank 0 to be selected.
- 16 bytes that are bit addressable in the address range 20h to 2Fh giving 128 addressable bits. The bits have individual addresses ranging from 00h to 07h for byte address 20h, to 78h to 7Fh for byte address 2Fh. Thus a bit may be addressed directly, say bit 78h, which is bit 7 of byte address 2F.
- a general purpose memory range from 30h to 7Fh which is addressable as bytes.

In addition there are 21 SFRs in the address range 80h to FFh. This address range actually gives 128 addresses but only 21 are defined for the 80C51; the number defined varies according to device, being much larger for the 80C552/83C552 and less for the 83C750/ 87C750. Details of the SFRs for the 80C51, 8XC552 and 8XC750 devices are shown in Appendices C, D and E respectively.

For the 80C51 the SFRs of the internal RAM are described in more detail as follows.

- **Accumulator**. This 8-bit register, usually referred to as Register A, is the major register for data operations such as addition, subtraction etc. and for Boolean bit manipulation. The register is also used for data transfers between the device and external memory, where applicable. The Accumulator is both bit and byte addressable with the byte address at E0h and the bit addresses from E0h to E7h.
- **B Register**. This 8-bit register is used for multiplication and division operations. For other instructions it can be considered another 'scratch pad' register. The B Register is

both bit and byte addressable with byte address at F0h and bit addresses from F0h to F7h.
- **PSW**. This 8-bit register at address D0h contains program status information as shown below:

MSB							LSB
CY	AC	F0	RS1	RS0	OV	-	P
D7h	D6h	D5h	D4h	D3h	D2h	D1h	D0h

with the bit functions defined in Table 2.2.

Table 2.2 Program status word bit functions

Bit	Symbol	Function
PSW.7	CY	Carry flag
PSW.6	AC	Auxiliary Carry flag (for BCD operations)
PSW.5	F0	Flag 0 (available for general purpose use)
PSW.4	RS1	Register bank select control bit 1
		Set/cleared by software to determine working register bank (see Note)
PSW.3	RS0	Register bank select control bit 0
		Set/cleared by software to determine working register bank (see Note)
PSW.2	OV	Overflow flag
PSW.1	-	User definable flag
PSW.0	P	Parity flag
		Set/cleared by hardware each instruction cycle to indicate an odd/even number of 1 bits in the Accumulator

Note: The contents of (RS1, RS0) enable the working register banks as follows:

(0,0) – Bank 0 addresses 00h to 07h
(0,1) – Bank 1 addresses 08h to 0Fh
(1,0) – Bank 2 addresses 10h to 17h
(1,1) – Bank 3 addresses 18h to 1Fh

- **SP**. This 8-bit register at address 81h is incremented before data is stored during PUSH and CALL executions. The SP is initialised to RAM address 07h after a reset which causes the stack to commence at location 08h.
- **DP**. This 16-bit register is intended to contain the two bytes that make a 16-bit address, with the high byte (DPH) at address 83h and the low byte (DPL) at address 82h. It may also be used as two independent 8-bit registers.
- **Ports 0 to 3**. P0, P1, P2 and P3 are the 8-bit SFR latches of Ports 0, 1, 2 and 3 respectively. The addresses are 80h, 90h, A0h and B0h respectively. Writing a '1' to any bit of any of the port SFRs causes the corresponding port output pin to go high; writing a 0 causes the corresponding port output pin to go low. When used as an input, the external state of any port pin will be held in the port SFR.
- **Serial data BUFfer (SBUF)**. This 8-bit register at address 99h is used for serial data in both transmit and receive modes. Moving data to SBUF loads the data ready for transmission while moving data from SBUF allows access to received data.

- **Timer registers**. The 80C51 contains two 16-bit timer/counters. Timer 0 has a low byte TL0 at address 8Ah and a high byte TH0 at address 8Ch while Timer 1 has a low byte at address 8Bh and a high byte at address 8Dh.

  In addition to the two timer/counters described above, the 80C52 and 80C58 family contain an extra timer/counter; this timer can also operate as an event timer or event counter. An extra SFR register, the T2CON register, controls this timer.
- **Control registers**. Certain Control registers are required to provide control and status bits for the serial ports, timer/counters and the interrupt system. The 8-bit Control registers are:

      TCON (Timer/counter CONtrol) at address 88h
      TMOD (Timer/counter MODe control) at address 89h
      SCON (Serial port CONtrol) at address 98h
      IE (Interupt Enable) at address A8h
      IP (Interrupt Priority) at address B8h

  The effect of the control registers will be discussed later in this chapter.

The SFRs vary according to the device. The 8XC552 for example is a much more complicated device than the 80C51 and has considerably more SFRs. The SFRs of the 8XC552 are a mixture of those found in the 80C51 plus those that are either modified versions of the 80C51 SFRs or additional registers. The 8XC750 on the other hand is designed as a low cost device with fewer features than the 80C51 and operates with a reduced number of SFRs compared to the 80C51. As mentioned earlier in the chapter, the 80C51 operates with 21 SFRs; the 8XC552 has 56 SFRs while the 8XC750 has just 16.

INTERNAL ROM

As can be seen from Figure 2.4, the 4k of ROM in the 80C51 occupies the address range 0000h to 0FFFh. The ROM in a microcontroller is provided so that the control program can be resident on-chip. If the control program can be accommodated within the 4k (or 8k in the case of the 80C52 device) then no external program memory is required; if, however, the control program needs greater memory capacity external memory can be added up to 64k. The program counter (PC) can access program memory in the range 0000h to FFFFh so that any program address higher than 0FFFh will have to be located in external program memory. As stated earlier in this chapter, program memory can be exclusively external (and would have to be for the ROMless devices 80C31/80C32, etc.) by connecting to ground the external access pin EA. The read strobe for external program memory is PSEN (see Section 2.2 on pin-out functions).

The 8XC552 device has 8k bytes of on-chip program memory and will fetch instructions from internal memory unless the address exceeds 1FFFh. Thus any instructions in the range 2000h to FFFFh will be in external memory and can be fetched if the EA pin is held low in a manner similar to that for the 80C51. ROM locations 0003h to 0073h are utilised for interrupt service routines and are discussed further under interrupts.

The 8XC750 device has 1k byte of program memory (ROM on the 83C750, EPROM on the 87C750) which is not externally expandable. Thus certain 80C51 instructions, such as LJMP, MOVX and LCALL, cannot be implemented. There are fixed locations in program memory for addresses that contain instructions for interrupts and reset (Table 2.3).

The device also has only one 16-bit counter/timer, known as Counter/timer 0, whereas the 80C51 has two, i.e. Counter/timer 0 and Counter/timer 1.

Table 2.3

Event	Program memory address
Reset	000
External $\overline{\text{INT0}}$	003
Counter/timer 0	00B
External $\overline{\text{INT1}}$	013

On reset the CPU begins operations from memory location 0000h. Figure 2.5 shows that for the 80C51 there are five interrupt sources located at memory addresses starting at 0003h, each consisting of eight bytes (Table 2.4).

Table 2.4

Interrupt source	Vector address
External 0	0003h
Timer 0 overflow	000Bh
External 1	0013h
Timer 1 overflow	001Bh
Serial port	0023h

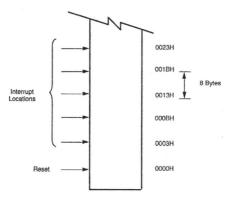

Figure 2.5 80C51 program memory and interrupt locations (courtesy Philips Semiconductors)

For each of the interrupts the eight bytes may be sufficient to accommodate the interrupt servicing routine but if not the programmer should provide a jump to the service routine. Whether or not an interrupt is enabled depends on the bit settings of the IE register. If no interrupts are used the programmer could establish the program from location 0000h; but with interrupts the programmer should enter a jump instruction from location 0000h to the starting address of the main program. Interrupts are dealt with later in this chapter.

EXTERNAL MEMORY

The 16-bit program counter of the microcontroller will allow program memory addresses of up to 64k; similarly the 16-bit data pointer allows data memory addresses of up to 64k.

Both address ranges are well beyond the capability of the microcontroller on its own but, if required, both data and program memory can be extended beyond the available on-chip values up to the 64k limit. Also involved with accessing external memory are certain control pins and I/O ports. In the sections that follow memory extension for program and for data are dealt with separately although in practice they could occur simultaneously.

External program memory access

For the 80C51, if extra program memory is required a circuit arrangement as shown in Figure 2.6 could be used. It can be seen from Figure 2.6 that Ports 0 and 2 are not available for I/O functions in this configuration but are used instead for bus functions during external memory fetches. Port 0 acts as a multiplexed address/data bus, sending the Low byte of the Program Counter (PCL) as an address and then waiting for the arrival of the code byte from external memory. The signal ALE clocks the PCL byte into the address latch during the period of time that the PCL byte is valid on Port 0. The latch will hold the low address byte stable at the input to the external memory while the multiplexed bus is made ready to receive the code byte from the external memory. Port 2 sends the Program Counter High byte (PCH) directly to the external memory; the signal $\overline{\text{PSEN}}$ then strobes the external

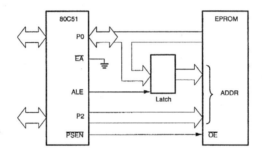

Figure 2.6 Use of external program memory (courtesy Philips Semiconductors)

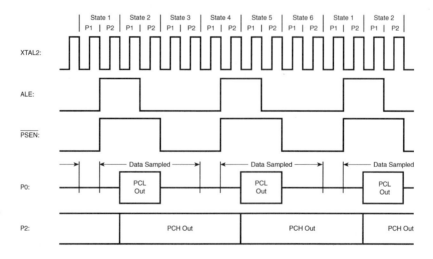

Figure 2.7 External memory program fetches (courtesy Philips Semiconductors)

memory allowing the code byte to be read by the microcontroller. The timing diagram for a program fetch from external memory is shown in Figure 2.7.

External data memory access

Up to 64k of read/write memory may be accessed by the 80C51 with the connections for the data and address lines the same as for program memory. The $\overline{RD}$ output from the microcontroller connects to the output enable ($\overline{OE}$) pin on the RAM while the $\overline{WR}$ output line connects to the RAM write enable ($\overline{WE}$) pin on the RAM. A possible arrangement is shown in Figure 2.8. In this arrangement three lines of Port 2 are being used to page the RAM. Memory addresses can be one or two bytes wide. One byte addresses are often used in conjunction with one or more other I/O lines to page the RAM as shown in Figure 2.8. Using port lines to page RAM is an economical way to use external memory since any port lines not used for paging can be used for normal I/O functions. A page consists of 256 bytes of RAM so that two port lines are needed for accessing four pages and three port lines, as shown in Figure 2.8, to access eight pages (which is 2k RAM). If two byte

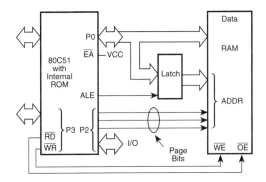

Figure 2.8 Access of external data memory (courtesy Philips Semiconductors)

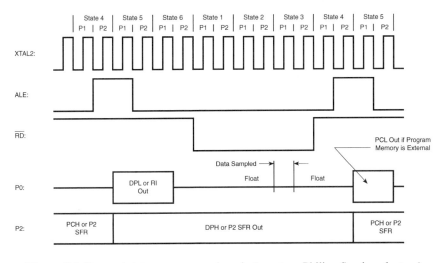

Figure 2.9 External data memory read cycle (courtesy Philips Semiconductors)

addresses are used the high address byte is connected via Port 2 in the same way as for accessing program memory. A typical timing diagram for a read cycle from external memory is shown in Figure 2.9. The timing for a write cycle is similar except that the $\overline{\text{WR}}$ line pulses low, $\overline{\text{RD}}$ stays high and data is placed on Port 0 lines as an input to the microcontroller.

2.5 I/O port configurations

80C51

As described elsewhere the four ports of the 80C51 differ slightly in that Ports 0 and 2 may be used for address/data lines while Port 3 has other functions. The structure of a port pin circuit varies according to the port but each port pin will have a bit latch and I/O buffer. The arrangement for a Port 1 pin is shown in Figure 2.10.

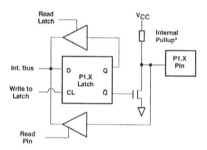

Figure 2.10 80C51 Port 1 bit latch (courtesy Philips Semiconductors)

The bit latch, shown as a D-type flip-flop, is one bit in the port's SFR. The latch will clock in a value from the internal bus in response to a 'write to latch' signal from the CPU or place its output level on the bus in response to a read signal from the CPU. The instructions that can be used to read a port can activate the 'read latch' signal or the 'read pin' signal. The requirement to read a latch rather than read a pin involves instructions known as 'read-modify-write'. These instructions would read the latch value, possibly modify the value and write it back to the latch. The reason for reading the latch rather than the pin under these circumstances is to avoid misinterpreting the pin voltage level when the pin is heavily loaded as would be the case if driving the base of an external transistor. Suppose, for example, the port bit is connected to an external transistor base and a 1 is written to the bit turning the external transistor on; the CPU reading the pin would find the base-emitter voltage level of the on transistor and read this as 0 while reading the latch output would register the correct level 1.

Ports 1, 2 and 3 have internal pull-up resistances. If a 1 is placed on the internal bus and the write signal applied to the D-type clock input, Q goes low and the Field-Effect Transistor (FET) goes off, allowing the pin value to go high via the pull-up resistor. Conversely a 0 on the bus latched into the flip-flop will switch the FET on and connect the output pin to ground.

For Ports 1, 2 and 3, to read the signal level on the pin a 1 is written to the flip-flop which as before switches the FET off and connects the output pin via the pull-up resistor to V_{cc}, i.e logic 1; this level can be pulled low by an external source. For the output pin to go low the driving circuit must sink the current which flows via the pull-up resistor from V_{cc}; a read signal on the lower buffer will cause the pin signal to appear on the internal bus. The output buffers for Port 1 (and Ports 2 and 3) can each drive four Low Power Schottky (LS) TTL inputs. Port 0 has open drain outputs and each output buffer can drive eight LS TTL inputs.

For simplicity Figure 2.10 does not show the alternate functions for Ports 0, 2 and 3. The alternate functions are:

    Port 0 – Address/data
    Port 2 – Address
    Port 3 – Alternate I/O function

The output drivers of Ports 0 and 2 are switchable using an internal control signal. During external memory accesses, the P2 SFR remains unchanged but the P0 SFR has 1s written into it.

Also if a P3 bit latch contains a 1 the output level is controlled by an 'alternate output function' signal while the actual Port 3 pin level is always available to the pin's 'alternate input function' if any.

8XC552

The 8XC552 device has five 8-bit I/O ports and one 8-bit input port. Each port has a latch (SFRs P0 to P5), an input buffer and an output driver for ports P0 to P4 only. Details are as follows.

- Port 0 operates in the same way as for the 80C51, i.e. bidirectional I/O port which additionally handles the multiplexed low-order address and data during access to external program and data memory.
- Port 1 is an 8-bit I/O port with alternate functions as follows:

    P1.1-P1.5: Quasi-bidirectional port pins
    P1.6, P1.7: Open drain port pins
    P1.0-P1.3: Capture timer input signals for Timer T2
    P1.4: T2 event input (T2)
    P1.5: T2 timer reset signal; rising edge triggered (RT2)
    P1.6: Serial port clock line for I²C bus (SCL)
    P1.7: Serial port data line for I²C bus (SDA).

Lines connected to pins P1.6 and P1.7 may be used via the Philips I²C bus to transfer data between devices connected to the bus. Details of the use of the I²C bus with the 8XC552 device are covered in some detail in Chapter 9. Port 1 is also used to input the lower-order address byte during EPROM programming and verification.

- Port 2 is the same as for the 80C51. An alternate function is to provide the high-order address byte for external memory.
- Port 3 is the same as for the 80C51. Alternate functions include:

    P3.0: Serial input port (RxD)
    P3.1: Serial output port (TxD)
    P3.2: External interrupt (INT0)
    P3.3: External interrupt (INT1)
    P3.4: Timer 0 external input (T0)
    P3.5: Timer 1 external input (T1)

P3.6: External data memory write strobe ($\overline{\text{WR}}$)

P3.7: External data memory read strobe ($\overline{\text{RD}}$).

- Port 4 is an 8-bit quasi-bidirectional I/O port. Alternate functions include:

    P4.0-P4.5: Timer T2 compare and set/reset outputs on a match with timer T2

    P4.6, P4.7: Timer T2 compare and toggle outputs on a match with timer T2.

- Port 5 may only be used as an input port and could be used to input up to eight analogue signals to the 8XC552 device ADC.

8XC750

The 8XC750 device has only three ports, namely Ports 0, 1 and 3.

- Port 0 is a 3-bit bidirectional port which can be used for data transfer and, where the device with EPROM (87C750) is concerned, provide alternate functions for programming the EPROM memory.
- Port 1 is an 8-bit bidirectional I/O port with internal pull-up resistors. The pins that have 1's written to them are pulled high by the internal pull-ups and can be used as inputs; under these conditions any pins that are pulled low externally will, because of the internal pull-ups, source current. Port 1 also serves to output the addressed EPROM contents in the verify mode and, during the program mode, will accept as inputs the value to be programmed into the selected address. Additionally Port 1 pins perform certain input functions as follows:

    P1.5 and P1.6; external interrupts

    P1.7; Timer 0 external input.

- Port 3 is an 8-bit bidirectional I/O port that functions in a similar manner to Port 1. Port 3 also operates as the address input for the EPROM memory locations that need to be programmed or verified.

2.6   Timer/counters

80C51

The 80C51 has two 16-bit Timer/counter registers known as Timer 0 and Timer 1. These registers are up-counters and may be programmed to count internal clock pulses (timer) or count external pulses (counter). Each counter is divided into two 8-bit registers to give Timer Low and Timer High bytes, i.e. TL0, TH0 and TL1, TH1.

    TL0 is at address 8Ah

    TL1 is at address 8Bh

    TH0 is at address 8Ch

    TH1 is at address 8Dh

None of these registers is bit addressable.

The operation of the timer/counters is controlled by the TMOD and TCON registers of the SFRs. TMOD is the Timer Special Function register and is in effect two identical 4-bit registers, one each for the two timers. TCON consists of control bits and flags. Details of these two registers are shown below.

TMOD

MSB							LSB
GATE	C/$\overline{T}$	M1	M0	GATE	C/$\overline{T}$	M1	M0

89h
- - - - - - - - - TIMER 1 - - - - - - - -   - - - - - - - TIMER 0 - - - - - - - - -

The bit functions are as follows.

GATE – When set Timer/counter x is enabled when INTx pin is high and TRx (see TCON) is set.
When clear Timer x is enabled when TRx bit set.

C/$\overline{T}$ – When clear, timer operation (input from internal clock).
When set, counter operation (input from Tx input pin).

The M1 and M0 bit functions depend on the bit assignment as shown in Table 2.5.

Table 2.5

M1	M0	Operation
0	0	8048 8-bit timer TLx serves as 5-bit prescaler
0	1	16-bit timer/counter. THx and TLx are cascaded. No prescaler
1	0	8-bit auto-reload timer/counter. THx contents loaded into TLx when it overflows
1	1	TL0 is 8-bit counter controlled by Timer 0 control bits
		TH0 is 8-bit timer controlled by Timer 1 control bits
1	1	Timer 1 off

The TMOD byte is not bit addressable.

TCON

MSB							LSB
TF1	TR1	TF0	TR0	IE1	IT1	IE0	IT0
8Fh	8Eh	8Dh	8Ch	8Bh	8Ah	89h	88h

The eight bits of the TCON register are duplicated pairs of four as shown in Table 2.6.

Table 2.6

Bit	Function
TF1/0	Timer 1/0 overflow flag
	Set by hardware on timer/counter overflow
	Cleared when CPU vectors to interrupt routine
TR1/0	Timer 1/0 run control bit
	Set/cleared by software to turn timer/counter on/off
IE1/0	Interrupt 1/0 edge flag
	Set by hardware when external interrupt edge detected
	Cleared when interrupt processed
IT1/0	Interrupt 1/0 control bit
	Set/cleared by software to specify falling edge/low level triggered external interrupts

When the timer/counter is performing the counter function the register is incremented in response to a falling edge transition at its external input pin (T0 or T1). The TMOD bit C/$\overline{\text{T}}$ must be set to 1 to enable the pulses from the Tx pin to reach the control circuit. To count a certain number of internal or external pulses a number is put into one of the counters; the number inserted represents the maximum count, less the desired count, plus one. It takes two machine cycles (24 oscillator periods) to recognise a 1-to-0 transition; the maximum count rate is 1/24 of the oscillator frequency. There are no restrictions on the duty cycle of an external input cycle but to ensure a given level is sampled at least once before it changes it should be held for at least one full cycle. The counter will increment from the initial number to the maximum and then resets to zero on the last pulse, setting the timer flag. Testing the flag state allows confirmation of the completion of the count or, alternatively, the flag may be used to interrupt the program.

When the timer counter is performing the timer function the register is incremented every machine cycle. Thus with 12 oscillator periods per machine cycle the count rate is 1/12 of the oscillator frequency.

The timer/counters have four operating modes (Mode 0, 1, 2 and 3) which are determined by the status of the bits M0 and M1 in the TMOD register. Modes 0, 1 and 2 are the same for both timer/counters but this is not the case for Mode 3. Some information has already been shown in abridged form under the TMOD register description and is described below in more detail.

Mode 0

Setting the timer mode bits to 0 in the TMOD register provides an 8-bit counter (THx), preceded by five bits of (TLx) which gives a divide-by-32 prescaler. The pulse input is thus divided by 32 in TLx giving the oscillator frequency divided by 384. The arrangement is shown in Figure 2.11 for Timer 1. The arrangement for Timer 0 is similar.

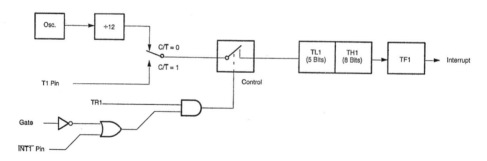

Figure 2.11 Timer/counter Mode 0 configuration (courtesy Philips Semiconductors)

As the count rolls over from all 1s to all 0s the Timer Interrupt flag TFx is set. Figure 2.11 shows that the input is passed to the timer when TRx = 1 AND GATE = 0 OR INTx = 1. TRx is a control bit in the TCON register while GATE is in the TMOD register. Setting the run flag TRx does not clear the registers.

Mode 1

This is provided when the TMOD register mode bits M1 = 0, M0 = 1 and gives the same effect as Mode 0 except that the Timer register runs using all 16 bits.

Mode 2

This occurs when TMOD register mode bits M1 = 1, M0 = 0 and configures the Timer register as an 8-bit counter (TLx) with automatic reload. The arrangement is shown in Figure 2.12 for Timer 1. The arrangement for Timer 0 is similar.

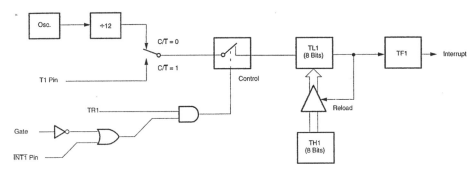

Figure 2.12 Timer/counter Mode 2 configuration (courtesy Philips Semiconductors)

Only the register TLx is used as an 8-bit counter while THx holds a value, set by software, that will be loaded into TLx every time TLx overflows. The overflow also sets the timer flag. This facility provides an initial count value for TLx that can be changed by software giving a predetermined time delay before overflow occurs.

Mode 3

This occurs when TMOD register mode bits M1 = 1, M0 = 1. Under these conditions Timer 1 is off and its count is inhibited. The control bit TR1 and timer flag TF1 are then used by Timer 0. Timer 0 has TL0 and TH0 as two separate counters with the arrangement shown in Figure 2.13. TL0 sets timer flag TF0 whenever overflow occurs while TH0 is controlled by TR1 and sets the timer flag TF1 whenever it overflows.

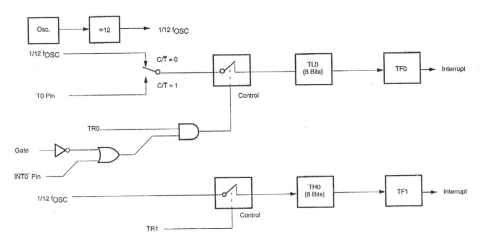

Figure 2.13 Timer/counter 0 Mode 3 configuration (courtesy Philips Semiconductors)

Mode 3 is provided for applications that require an extra 8-bit timer on the counter. With Timer 0 in Mode 3 the 80C51 can appear to have three timer/counters. When Timer 0 is in Mode 3, Timer 1 can be switched in and out of its own Mode 3 (switching Timer 1 to Mode 3 will hold whatever count it had reached prior to the switch) or it can be used by the serial port as a baud rate generator or any other Mode 0, 1 or 2 application not requiring an interrupt (or any other use of the TF1 flag).

8XC552

The 8XC552 device has Timers T0 and T1 but additionally has a Timer T2 which is a 16-bit timer consisting of two registers TMH2, which is the Timer 2 high byte at address EDh, and TML2 which is the Timer 2 low byte situated at address ECh.

The timer may be left off or clocked via a prescaler from one of two sources:

- an external signal
- frequency of oscillation divided 12, i.e. $f_{osc}/12$.

With the Timer T2 configured to be a counter, a rising edge on the external signal applied to pin P1.4 (T2) will increment the prescaler. The repetition rate has a maximum value of one count per machine cycle, i.e. 1 MHz with a 12 MHz oscillator. Timer T2 is controlled by an SFR TM2CON situated at address EAh.

TM2CON

MSB   LSB

T2IS1	T2IS0	T2ER	T2BO	T2P1	T2P0	T2MS1	T2MS0
7	6	5	4	3	2	1	0

Table 2.7

Bit	Symbol	Function
7	T2IS1	Timer T2 16-bit overflow interrupt select
6	T2IS0	Timer T2 byte overflow interrupt select
5	T2ER	Timer T2 external reset enable*
4	T2BO	Timer T2 byte overflow interrupt flag
3	T2P1	Timer T2 prescaler select defined by pin assignment as shown below
2	T2P0	

T2P1	T2P0	Timer T2 clock
0	0	Clock source
0	1	Clock source/2
1	0	Clock source/4
1	1	Clock source/8

1	T2MS1	Timer T2 mode select defined by pin assignments as shown below
0	T2MS0	

T2MS1	T2MS0	Mode selected
0	0	Timer T2 off
0	1	T2 clock source = $f_{osc}/12$
1	0	Test mode; do not use
1	1	T2 clock source = pin T2

*When this bit is set, Timer T2 may be reset by a rising edge on input P1.5 (RT2).

Timer T2 has no read latches so care must be taken since reading errors could occur if the timer is being read when an overflow from least to most significant byte occurs. This problem could be overcome with suitable software.

Timer T2 is not loadable and may be reset either by the RST signal or by a rising edge on the input signal on P1.5 (RT2) if enabled. RT2 is enabled by the setting of bit T2ER (bit 5 of the TM2CON register).

The timer may be used to generate an interrupt request when:

- the least significant byte of the timer overflows
- a 16-bit overflow occurs.

Either, or both, of these events could be programmed to request an interrupt and in both cases the interrupt vector will be the same. When the least significant byte (TML2) overflows the flag T2BO (bit 4 of the TM2CON register) is set. When the high byte (TMH2) overflows a flag is set in the Interrupt Flag register TM2IR (see later). The flags are set one cycle after an overflow occurs. A Timer T2 Interrupt ENable register (IEN1) is used to enable the overflow interrupts.

IEN1

MSB   LSB

ET2	ECM2	ECM1	ECM0	ECT3	ECT2	ECT1	ECT0
7	6	5	4	3	2	1	0

The IEN1 register bit functions and symbols are shown in Table 2.8.

Table 2.8 IEN1 register bit functions

Bit	Symbol	Function
7	ET2	Enable Timer 2 overflow interrupt(s)
6	ECM2	Enable T2 Comparator 2 interrupt
5	ECM1	Enable T2 Comparator 1 interrupt
4	ECM0	Enable T2 Comparator 0 interrupt
3	ECT3	Enable T2 Capture register 3 interrupt
2	ECT2	Enable T2 Capture register 2 interrupt
1	ECT1	Enable T2 Capture register 1 interrupt
0	ECT0	Enable T2 Capture register 0 interrupt

To enable byte overflow, bits ET2 (IEN1.7) and T2IS0 (TM2CON.6) must be set. Bit T2BO (TM2CON.4) is the Timer T2 byte overflow flag. To enable a 16-bit overflow interrupt, bits ET2 (IEN1.7) and T2IS1 (TM2CON.7) must be set. Bit T2OV (TM2IR.7) is the timer 2 16-bit overflow flag (see Interrupt Flag Register TM2IR).

All interrupt flags must be reset by software. To enable the byte and 16-bit overflow, T2IS0 and T2IS1 must be set and two interrupt service routines are necessary. The overflow flags may be tested to determine which routine should be executed. Whichever routine is invoked only the corresponding overflow flag should be cleared.

If the Timer T2 external reset enable bit (T2ER) in TM2CON is set then Timer T2 may be reset by a rising edge on pin P1.5 (RT2). This reset also clears the prescaler.

Timer T2 capture and compare logic

Timer T2 is connected to four 16-bit Capture registers and three 16-bit Compare registers. The function of the Capture register is to capture the contents of Timer T2 when a transition occurs on its corresponding input pin. The Compare register is used to set, reset or toggle Port 4 output pins at defined pre-programmable time intervals. The combination of Timer T2 and the capture and compare logic is used for specified applications which include automotive injection systems, etc.

Capture logic

The four 16-bit Capture registers connected to Timer T2 are labelled CT0, CT1, CT2 and CT3 (each register is divided into two byte size registers, i.e. CT0 is divided into CTH0 and CTL0). The registers are loaded with the contents of T2, and an interrupt is requested upon receipt of the input signals on input pins P1.0 to P1.3 (CT0I to CT3I). The four interrupt flags are in the Timer T2 Interrupt register (TM2IR). If the capture facility is not required, these inputs can be regarded as additional external interrupt inputs.

Compare logic

Whenever Timer T2 is incremented the value of the timer is compared with the contents of the three 16-bit Compare registers CM0, CM1 and CM2. A match will cause the corresponding interrupt flag in the register TM2IR to be set at the end of the following cycle. The sequence is different for each Compare register and will depend on the state of bits in other SFRs, namely the SeT Enable (STE) register and the Reset/Toggle Enable (RTE) register.

Interrupt Flag register TM2IR

There are nine timer T2 interrupt flags, eight of which are in the TM2IR SFR at address C8h. The ninth flag is TM2CON.4.

TM2IR

The TM2IR register bit functions and symbols are as shown in Table 2.9.

T2OV	CMI2	CMI1	CMI0	CTI3	CTI2	CTI1	CTI0
7	6	5	4	3	2	1	0

Table 2.9 TM2IR register bit functions

Bit	Symbol	Function
7	T20V	Timer T2 16-bit overflow Interrupt flag
6	CMI2	CM2 Interrupt flag
5	CMI1	CM1 Interrupt flag
4	CMI0	CM0 Interrupt flag
3	CTI3	CT3 Interrupt flag
2	CTI2	CT2 Interrupt flag
1	CTI1	CT1 Interrupt flag
0	CTI0	CT0 Interrupt flag

The CT0I and CT1I flags are set during S4 of the cycle in which the contents of Timer T2 are captured. CT0I is scanned by the interrupt logic during S2 and CT1I during S3. CT2I and CT3I are set during S6 and are scanned during S4 and S5. The associated interrupt requests are recognised during the following cycle. If the flags are polled, a transition at CT0I or CT1I will be recognised one cycle before a transition on CT2I or CT3I since registers are read during S5.

The CMI0, CMI1 and CMI2 flags are set during S6 of the cycle following a match. CMI0 is scanned by the interrupt logic during S2 while CMI1 and CMI2 are scanned during S3 and S4. A match is recognised by the interrupt logic (or by polling the flags) two cycles after the match occurs. The 16-bit overflow flag (T20V) and the byte overflow flag (T2BO) are set during S6 of the cycle in which the overflow occurs. These flags are recognised by the interrupt logic during the following cycle.

SFR Interrupt Priority IP1, at address F8h, is used to determine the Timer T2 interrupt priority:

IP1

PT2	PCM2	PCM1	PCM0	PCT3	PCT2	PCT1	PCT0
7	6	5	4	3	2	1	0

The IP1 register bit functions and symbols are as shown in Table 2.10.

Table 2.10 IP1 register bit functions

Bit	Symbol	Function
7	PT0	Timer T2 overflow interrupt(s) priority level
6	PCM2	Timer T2 Comparator 2 interrupt priority level
5	PCM1	Timer T2 Comparator 1 interrupt priority level
4	PCM0	Timer T2 Comparator 0 interrupt priority level
3	PCT3	Timer T2 Capture register 3 interrupt priority level
2	PCT2	Timer T2 Capture register 2 interrupt priority level
1	PCT1	Timer T2 Capture register 1 interrupt priority level
0	PCT0	Timer T2 Capture register 0 interrupt priority level

Setting a bit high in the IP1 register gives that function a high priority, while setting the bit low gives a low priority.

Watchdog Timer T3

As well as the standard timers and Timer T2, the 8XC552 device includes a watchdog Timer T3. The function of the Timer T3 is to generate a reset condition unless the user program reloads the Watchdog Timer within a specified time period (the 'watchdog interval'). The user program must therefore continually execute sections of code which reload the Watchdog Timer at a rate which has a period smaller than the watchdog interval. The Watchdog Timer comprises an 8-bit timer with an 11-bit prescaler; the prescaler is fed with a signal at a frequency of 1/12th of the oscillator frequency f_{osc}. The 8-bit timer is incremented every t seconds where:

$$t = 12 \times 2048 \times 1/f_{osc}$$

If Timer T3 overflows an internal reset pulse is generated which resets the device. The watchdog action will occur if the external pin $\overline{EW}$ is kept low. Under these conditions the Watchdog Timer cannot be disabled by software.

8XC750

The 8XC750 has only a single 16-bit timer/counter, the operation of which is similar to that of the 80C51 Mode 2 operation, but extended to 16 bits. The timer/counter is clocked by either:

- a signal at $f_{osc}/12$
- transitions on pin P1.7 (T0).

The mode to be used is selected by the C/T pin in the TCON SFR (TCON.6). The timer/counter is enabled when the TR bit in the TCON register (TCON.4) is set. The timer is composed of a High Byte register TH and a Low Byte register TL and the register pair is incremented by the clock source. There is a register reload pair: Reload Timer Low (RTL) and Reload Timer High (RTH), both single byte registers. An overflow on the register pair TH and TL will cause the register pair to be reloaded with the contents of RTH and RTL without changing the contents of the reload registers. The TF1 bit in the TCON register (TCON.5) is set on counter overflow and, if the interrupt is enabled, will generate an interrupt. The SFRs of the 8XC750 are the same as for the 80C51 except that for the former there is no TMOD register, no Port 2 (P2) and no Interrupt Priority (IP) register. Also the 8XC750 registers RTH and RTL replace the 80C51 registers TH1 and TL1 respectively. For the 8XC750 the arrangement for the TCON register is as follows.

MSB

Gate	C/T	TF	TR	IE0	IT0	IE1	IE0
7	6	5	4	3	2	1	0

The pin functions are as follows.

- Gate 1 — Timer/counter is enabled only when $\overline{INTO}$ pin is high, and TR = 1
  - 0 — Timer/counter is enabled when TR = 1
- C/T 1 — Counter/timer from P1.7 (T0)

- TF
  - 0 — Timer operation from internal clock
  - 1 — Set on overflow of TH
  - 0 — Cleared when processor vectors to interrupt routine and by reset
- TR
  - 1 — Timer/counter enabled
  - 0 — Timer/counter disabled
- IE0 1 — Edge detected in $\overline{\text{INT0}}$
- IT0
  - 1 — $\overline{\text{INT0}}$ is edge triggered
  - 0 — $\overline{\text{INT0}}$ is sensitive to level
- IE1 1 — Edge detected in $\overline{\text{INT1}}$
- IT1
  - 1 — $\overline{\text{INT1}}$ is edge triggered
  - 0 — $\overline{\text{INT1}}$ is sensitive to level

These flags are functionally identical to the corresponding 80C51 flags but because there is only one timer on the 83C750 the flags are combined into one register.

2.7 Serial interface

80C51

The 80C51 possesses an on-chip serial port to enable serial data transmission between the device and external circuits. The serial port is full duplex so that it can receive and transmit data simultaneously. The port is also buffered in receive mode so that it can receive a second data byte before the first data byte has been read from the register. The Serial Port register is SBUF at address 99h in the SFR. SBUF is actually two registers, one to handle receive data from the external source via RxD (P3.0) and one to hold transmit data for outward transmission via TxD (P3.1). Writing to SBUF loads data for transmission while reading SBUF accesses received data in the physically separate receive register. Register SCON at address 98h controls data communication while register PCON at address 87h controls data rates.

Details of the Serial port CONtrol (SCON) register are as follows.

MSB   LSB

SM0	SM1	SM2	REN	TB8	RB8	TI	RI
9F	9E	9D	9C	9B	9A	99	98

Bits SM0 and SM1 specify the serial port mode as shown in Table 2.11.

- SM2 In Modes 2 and 3, if SM2 set to 1 then RI will not be activated if the received 9th data bit RB8 is 0.
  In Mode 1 if SM2 = 1, RI will not be activated if a valid stop bit is not received.
  In Mode 0, SM2 should be 0.
- REN Set by software to enable serial reception.
  Clear by software to disable reception.
- TB8 The 9th data bit that will be transmitted in Modes 2 and 3.
  Set/clear by software.
- RB8 In Modes 2 and 3, is the 9th data bit received.
  In Mode 1 if SM2 = 0, RB8 is the stop bit that was received.
  In Mode 0, RB8 is not used.

Table 2.11 Serial port mode options

SM0	SM1	Mode	Description	Baud rate
0	0	0	Shift register	$f_{osc}/12$
0	1	1	8-bit UART	Variable
1	0	2	9-bit UART	$f_{osc}/32$ or $f_{osc}/64$
1	1	3	9-bit UART	Variable

- T1 Transmit interrupt flag.
    Set by hardware at the end of the 8th bit time in Mode 0, or at the start of the stop bit in other modes, in any serial transmission.
    Must be cleared by software.
- R1 Receive interrupt flag.
    Set by hardware at the end of the 8th bit in Mode 0, or halfway through the stop bit time in the other modes, in any serial reception (except see SM2).
    Must be cleared by software.

The serial port can operate in four modes.

Mode 0

Serial data enters and leaves via RXD. Pin TXD outputs the shift clock and this is used to synchronise data transmission/reception. Data is in the form of eight bits with the LSB first. The rate of transmission (baud rate) is 1/12 of the oscillator frequency. Transmission is initiated by any instruction that uses SBUF as a destination register. The 'write to SBUF' signal will also load a 1 into the 9th position of the Transmit Shift register. Reception is initiated by the condition REN = 1 and R1 = 0. A generalised diagram of the serial data format is shown in Figure 2.14. This format is applicable to all modes with modification, i.e the ninth data bit is shown but is not present on Modes 0 and 1.

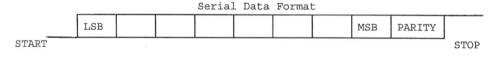

Serial Data Format

| | LSB | | | | | | | MSB | PARITY | |
START   STOP

Figure 2.14 Generalised serial data format

Mode 1

Ten bits are transmitted/received through TxD/RxD respectively. There is a start bit (low), eight data bits (LSB first) followed by a stop bit (high). For transmission the interrupt flag T1 is set after all 10 bits have been sent. The time for which each bit is at level 1 or 0 depends on the period set by the baud rate frequency. For received data, reception is initiated by the falling edge of the start bit and each bit is sampled in the centre of the bit time interval. The data word will be entered into the SBUF register provided:

    R1 = 0 AND
    SM2 = 0 OR stop bit = 1

If R1 = 0 then the program has read any previous data and is ready for the next byte. The stop bit set to 1 will complete data transfer to the SBUF register regardless of the state of SM2. For SM2 = 0 the byte will be transferred to SBUF regardless of the stop bit level.

On receive the start bit is discarded, the data bits are in SBUF and the stop bit is placed in RB8 of the SCON register to indicate a data byte has been received. Note that if R1 is set at the end of reception of a data byte, it suggests that the previously received data byte has not been read by the program; this would cause the new data to be lost since it will not be loaded. Transmission is again initiated by any instruction that uses SBUF as a destination register. In this mode however the bit times are synchronised to the divide-by-sixteen counter and not the 'write to SBUF' signal as was the case for Mode 0. Reception is initiated by the detection of a high-to-low transition at RxD.

Mode 2

Eleven bits are transmitted/received through TxD/RxD respectively. There is a start bit (low), eight data bits (LSB first), a programmable 9th data bit and a stop bit (high). For transmission the 9th data bit (TB8 in SCON) can have the value 0 or 1 or the parity bit (P in the PSW) could be moved into TB8. On receive the 9th data bit goes into RB8 in the register SCON, while both the start and stop bits are ignored. The conditions for received data are similar to Mode 1, i.e.:

> R1 = 0 AND
> SM2 = 0 OR 9th data bit = 1

If either of these conditions is not met the received frame is irretrievably lost.

Mode 3

This is identical to Mode 2 in all respects except that the baud rate is not fixed (as it is for Mode 2) but variable using Timer 1 to provide the required communication frequencies.

Baud rates

This has been described under the details of the SCON register. For Mode 0 the baud rate is fixed at oscillator frequency/12. For Mode 2 the baud rate depends on the value of the bit SMOD in the PCON SFR. If SMOD = 0 (which is the value on RESET), the baud rate is oscillator frequency (f_{osc})/64. If SMOD = 1, the baud rate is oscillator frequency/32, i.e.:

$$baud\ rate = \frac{2^{SMOD}}{64} \times f_{osc}$$

In the 80C51 the baud rates in modes 1 and 3 are determined by the Timer 1 overflow rate and the value of SMOD as follows:

$$baud\ rate = \frac{2^{SMOD}}{32} \times (Timer\ 1\ overflow\ rate)$$

The Timer 1 interrupt should be disabled in this application. The timer can be configured for timer or counter mode and if used in timer operation in the auto-reload mode the baud rate is given by:

$$baud\ rate = \frac{2^{SMOD}}{32} \times \frac{f_{osc}}{12 \times [256 - (TH1)]}$$

The oscillator frequency should be chosen to generate the required range of baud rates. Table 2.12 shows various commonly used baud rates and how they can be obtained from Timer 1. Applications involving baud rates and the use of Timer 1 can be found in Chapter 9.

Table 2.12 Typical baud rates generated by Timer 1 (courtesy Philips Semiconductors)

Baud rate	f_{osc} (MHz)	SMOD	Timer 1 C/T	Mode	Reload value
Mode 0 Max: 1.67 MHz	20	X	X	X	X
Mode 2 Max: 625k	20	1	X	X	X
Mode 1, 3 Max: 104.2k	20	1	0	2	FFH
19.2k	11.059	1	0	2	FDH
9.6k	11.059	0	0	2	FDH
4.8k	11.059	0	0	2	FAH
2.4k	11.059	0	0	2	F4H
1.2k	11.059	0	0	2	E8H
137.5	11.986	0	0	2	1DH
110	6	0	0	2	72H
110	12	0	0	1	FEEBH

8XC552

The 8XC552 device has two serial ports which can operate independently of each other. The ports are SIO0, which is a full duplex UART port identical to the 80C51, and SIO1 which is used for the I²C bus.

- **SIO0**. This port operates in the same way as the 80C51 serial port and also uses Timer 1 as a baud rate generator.
- **SIO1**. The I²C bus operates with two lines, SDA (Serial DAta line) and SCL (Serial CLock line) in order to transfer data between the microcontroller and other devices connected to the bus. For this port to be enabled, the output latches of P1.6 (the SCL line) and P1.7 (the SDA line) must be set to logic 1.

The microcontroller interfaces to the I²C logic using four of the 8XC552 SFRs:

S1CON

The SIO1 CONtrol register. This is an 8-bit register which can be read or written into. The S1CON register is at address D8h.

CR2	ENS1	STA	STO	SI	AA	CR1	CR0
7	6	5	4	3	2	1	0

CR2, 1, 0 are used to define the serial clock speed when SIO1 is in master mode. Details of the clock rates are not shown here but can be seen in Chapter 9 which deals with applications involving the I²C bus.

- **ENS1** The SIO1 ENable bit.
  ENS1 = 0. The SDA and SCL outputs are in a high impedance state and input signals are ignored. SIO1 is in the 'not addressed' slave state and bit 4 of the S1CON register (STO) is forced to 0. P1.6 and P1.7 may be used as open drain I/O ports.
  ENS1 = 1. SIO1 is enabled and P1.6 and P1.7 port latches must be set to 1.
- **STA** The STArt flag.
  STA = 1. In this state the SIO1 hardware checks the status of the I²C bus and generates a START condition if the bus is free. If the bus is not free then SIO1 waits for a STOP condition, which will free the bus, and then generates a START condition after a delay. The delay is half the clock period of the internal serial clock generator.
  STA = 0. In this state no START condition will be generated.
- **STO** is the STOp flag.
  STO = 1. A STOP condition will be transmitted to the I²C bus with the STO flag set while in the master mode. The STO flag is cleared by SIO1 hardware when the STOP condition is detected on the bus. In the case where the STA and STO bits are both set it is the STOP condition that is transferred to the I²C bus if SIO1 is in master mode. SIO1 then transmits a START condition. In the slave mode SIO1 will generate an internal STOP condition which is not transferred to the I²C bus.
  STO = 0. No STOP condition will be generated.
- **SI** The Serial Interrupt flag.
  SI = 1. In this state a serial interrupt is requested provided the EA and ES1 (Interrupt Enable register bits) are also set. SI is set by hardware when all but one of the 26 possible SIO1 states is entered. The only state that does not cause SI to be set is state F8h which indicates that no relevant state information is available.
  SI = 0. In this state no serial interrupt is requested.
- **AA** The Assert Acknowledge flag.
  AA = 1. In this state an acknowledge (low level to SDA) will be returned during the acknowledge clock pulse on the SCL line for the following conditions.

  (a) A data byte has been received while SIO1 is in the master receiver mode.
  (b) A data byte has been received while SIO1 is in the addressed slave receiver mode.
  (c) The 'own slave address' has been received.
  (d) The general call address has been received while the General Call bit (GC) in the S1ADR register is set.

  AA = 0. In this state a not acknowledge signal (high level to SDA) will be returned during the acknowledge clock pulse on SCL when:

  (a) Data has been received while SIO1 is in the master receiver mode.
  (b) A data byte has been received while SIO1 is in the addressed slave receiver mode.

S1STA

The SIO1 STAtus register. This is an 8-bit read-only register. The five most significant bits contain status information while the three least significant bits are always zero. There are 26 possible status codes with only one state (F8h) indicating that no relevant state information is available and no serial interrupt is requested. All other S1STA values will correspond to defined SIO states and when each of these states is entered a serial interrupt is requested (SI = 1). A valid status code is present in S1STA one machine cycle after SI is set by hardware and is still present one machine cycle after SI has been reset by hardware.

S1DAT

The SIO1 DATa register. This is an 8-bit register which contains a byte of data which is ready for transmission or has just been received. Providing the SFR is not in the process of shifting a byte, the register can be written into or read. This occurs when SIO1 is in a defined state and the serial interrupt flag is set. The data in S1DAT remains stable as long as SI is set. S1DAT always contains the last data byte present on the bus. Data in S1DAT is always shifted from right to left so that the first bit to be transmitted is the MSB (bit 7) and after the receipt of a data byte the first bit of the data is the MSB. While data is being shifted out, data from the bus is being shifted in.

SD7	SD6	SD5	SD4	SD3	SD2	SD1	SD0
9F	9E	9D	9C	9B	9A	99	98

$\longleftarrow$ —————————— shift direction ————————————

The eight bits (SD7 to SD0) are either those to be transmitted or those just received. Figure 2.15 shows how data in S1DAT is serially transferred to and from the SDA line. The S1DAT register together with the ACK flag forms a 9-bit shift register which comprises an 8-bit data byte followed by an acknowledge bit. The ACK flag is controlled by the SIO hardware. As shown in Figure 2.15, the rising edges of the serial clock pulses on the SCL line allow serial data to be shifted through the ACK flag to the S1DAT register. When S1DAT contains the data byte, the acknowledge bit is returned by the control logic during the ninth clock pulse. Serial data may be shifted out from S1DAT via the buffer BSD7 on the falling edges of the clock line SCL. When data is to be transmitted BSD7 is loaded with the contents of S1DAT.7, the MSB of the data byte and the first bit to be transmitted to the SDA line. After nine serial clock pulses the eight bits in S1DAT will have been transferred to the SDA line and the acknowledge bit will be present in the ACK flag. The eight transmitted data bits will also be shifted back into S1DAT.

S1ADR

The SIO1 slave ADdRess register. This is an 8-bit register which contains the micro-controller's slave address. Only the most significant seven bits are required for this; the LSB is the general call (GC) bit.

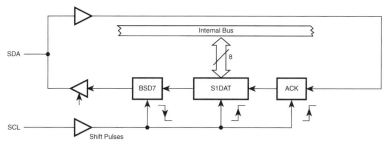

Figure 2.15 8CX552 Serial input/output arrangement

X	X	X	X	X	X	X	GC
7	6	5	4	3	2	1	0

$\longleftarrow$ ———————— own slave address ——————————$\longrightarrow$

S1ADR is not affected by the SIO1 hardware and the contents of S1ADR are irrelevant when SIO1 is in master mode. In slave modes the most significant seven bits must be loaded with the microcontroller's own slave address and, if bit 0 (GC) is set, the general call address (00h) is recognised; otherwise it is ignored.

SIO1 MODES OF OPERATION

There are four modes.

- **Master Transmitter mode** Pins P1.6 and P1.7 are outputs (Serial Data on P1.7 (SDA) and Serial CLock on P1.6 (SCL)). The first byte transmitted contains the address of the slave receiving device (seven bits) and the data direction bit which in this case is logic 0 (data direction bit R/W determines data direction and is logic 1 for read and logic 0 for write). Serial data is transmitted eight bits at a time and after each byte an acknowledge bit is received. START and STOP conditions are also output to indicate the beginning and end of a serial transfer.
- **Master Receiver mode** Similar to 1 above except that P1.6 (SCL) and P1.7 (SDA) are inputs and the data direction bit is logic 1 (for read). Serial data is received through SDA while SCL outputs the serial clock. Serial data is received a byte at a time and after each byte an acknowledge bit is transmitted. START and STOP conditions are also output to indicate the beginning and end of a serial transfer.
- **Slave Receiver mode** Serial data and serial clock are received through pin P1.7(SDA) and P1.6 (SCL) respectively. After each byte is received an acknowledge bit is transmitted. START and STOP are recognised as the beginning and end respectively of the serial transfer. Recognition of the address is performed by hardware after reception of the slave address and direction bit.
- **Slave Transmitter mode** The first byte is received and handled as in the Slave Receiver mode. However, in this mode, the direction bit will show that the direction of data transfer is reversed. As before serial data is through P1.7 (SDA) and serial clock through P1.6 (SCL). START and STOP conditions are also output to indicate the beginning and end of a serial transfer.

SIO1 can operate as a master or a slave. As a slave the SIO1 hardware looks for its own slave address and the general call address and if one of these addresses is detected, an interrupt is requested. If the microcontroller wishes to become the master, the hardware waits until the bus is free before the master mode is entered in order not to interrupt a possible slave action. If bus arbitration is lost in the master mode, SIO1 switches to the slave mode immediately and can detect its own slave address in the same serial transfer.

Chapter 9 deals with serial data transfer and includes a section on the use of the 8XC552 with the I²C bus. Application software is also included in that chapter.

2.8   Interrupts

Whenever a computer program is running it can be forced to respond to external conditions either by software techniques or the use of hardware signals called interrupts. Software techniques involve checking flags or the status of port pins and could take up valuable processor time, while the interrupt signals only stop the main software program when necessary. Interrupts may be generated internally or externally; whatever the source of the interrupt request it causes the device to switch to an interrupt subroutine that is located at predetermined addresses in program memory (see under Internal ROM on page 22).

80C51

There are five interrupt sources provided by the 80C51 and these are shown in Figure 2.16.

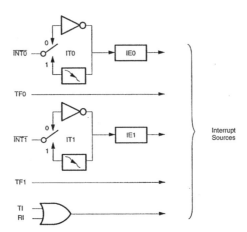

Figure 2.16 80C51 interrupt sources (courtesy Philips Semiconductors)

There is a sixth interrupt source in the 80C52/80C58 family of devices. Also the 8XC58 devices have an extra SFR associated with interrupts. In addition to the IE and IP registers, available as with the 8XC51 device, there is the IPH (Interrupt Priority High) register that provides a four-level interrupt routine. IPH is situated at address B7h.

In the 80C51 two of the interrupts are triggered by external signals via $\overline{INT0}$ and $\overline{INT1}$ while the remaining three interrupts are generated by internal operations: Timer 0, Timer 1 and the Or-ed output of R1 and T1. All of the bits that generate interrupts can be set or cleared by software. Each interrupt source can be enabled/disabled by the setting/clearing of a bit in the SFR IE. This register, details of which are shown below, also has a global disable bit EA which disables all interrupts at once.

MSB   LSB

EA	X	X	ES	ET1	EX1	ET0	EX0
AF			AC	AB	AA	A9	A8

IE register bit functions and symbols are shown in Table 2.13.

Table 2.13 IE register bit functions

Bit	Symbol	Function
IE.7	EA	Disables ALL interrupts if EA = 0 If EA = 1 each interrupt source is individually enabled/disabled by setting/clearing its enable bit
IE.6	–	Reserved
IE.5	–	Reserved
IE.4	ES	Enables/disables the serial port interrupt If ES = 0, the serial port interrupt is disabled
IE.3	ET1	Enables/disables the Timer 1 overflow interrupt If ET1 = 0 the Timer 1 interrupt is disabled
IE.2	EX1	Enables/disables external interrupt 1 If EX1 = 0, external interrupt 1 is disabled
IE.1	ET0	Enables/disables the Timer 0 overflow interrupt If ET0 = 0 the Timer 0 interrupt is disabled
IE.0	EX0	Enables/disables external interrupt 0 If EX0 = 0, external interrupt 0 is disabled

Each interrupt source can also be individually programmed to one of two priority levels by setting/clearing a bit in SFR register IP. A low priority interrupt can be interrupted in turn by a high priority interrupt but not by another low priority interrupt. A high priority interrupt cannot be interrupted by any other interrupt source. If requests of different priority level are received simultaneously the higher priority level is serviced first. If requests of the same priority level are received simultaneously an internal polling sequence is invoked which determines a second priority level as shown in Table 2.14.

Table 2.14

Priority	Source	Address
1	IE0	0003h
2	TF0	000Bh
3	IE1	0013h
4	TF1	001Bh
5	R1/T1	0023h

The address given is the starting address of the relevant interrupt subroutine. If the routine cannot be fitted into the available 8 bytes a jump instruction should route the routine elsewhere in memory. The interrupt will cause the main program to stop while the interrupt is serviced, with the PC address being saved on the stack. A RETurn from Interrupt (RETI) instruction at the end of the service routine restores the address reached by the PC prior to the interrupt back to the PC and resets the interrupt logic so that another interrupt, should it occur, can be serviced.

Details of the IP register are as follows.

MSB   LSB

X	X	X	PS	PT1	PX1	PT0	PX0
			BC	BB	BA	B9	B8

IP register bit functions and symbols are shown in Table 2.15.

Table 2.15 IP register bit functions

Bit	Symbol	Function
IP.7	-	Reserved
IP.6	-	Reserved
IP.5	-	Reserved
IP.4	PS	Defines serial port interrupt priority level
		PS = 1 programs it to higher priority level
IP.3	PT1	Defines Timer 1 interrupt priority level
		PT1 = 1 programs it to the higher priority level
IP.2	PX1	Defines external interrupt priority level
		PX1 = 1 programs it to the higher priority level
IP.1	PT0	Enables/disables Timer 0 interrupt priority level
		PT0 = 1 programs it to the higher priority level
IP.0	PX0	Defines the external interrupt 0 priority level
		PX0 = 1 programs it to the higher priority level

Internal interrupts

When a timer/counter overflows the corresponding timer flag TF0 or TF1 is set to 1. The flag is cleared by on-chip hardware when the service routine is vectored.

The serial port interrupt is generated by the logical OR of R1 (set to 1 in the SCON register when a data byte is received) and T1 (set to 1 in the SCON register when a data byte has been transmitted). Neither flag is cleared by hardware when vectoring to the service routine. In practice the service routine will have to determine whether it was R1 or T1 that generated the interrupt and the bit cleared by software.

External interrupts

The external interrupts INT0 and INT1 can be level-activated or transition-activated depending on the value of the bits IT0 and IT1 in the TCON register. The interrupts are actually generated by the flags IE0 and IE1 in TCON. When an external interrupt is generated the flag that caused it is cleared by hardware when the service routine is vectored only if the interrupt was transition-activated. Any level-activated interrupt must be reset by the programmer when the interrupt is serviced by the service subroutine. The low level must be removed from the external circuit before a RETI instruction is executed otherwise an immediate interrupt will occur after the execution of the RETI instruction.

Reset

The reset input is the RST pin and taking this pin high for at least two machine cycles while the oscillator is running will cause the CPU to generate an internal reset. Reset is a form of interrupt since the action of the RST pin overrides any software which the 80C51 may be running at the time. Unlike other interrupts the value of the address on the PC is not saved but is reset to 0000h. In fact the internal reset algorithm writes 0s to all SFRs except the port latches, SP and SBUF. The 80C51 reset values are shown in Table 2.16.

Table 2.16 80C51 reset values

Register	Reset value
PC	000h
ACC	00h
B	00h
PSW	00h
SP	07h
DPTR	0000h
P0–P3	FFh
IP	xxx00000b
IE	0xx00000b
TMOD	00h
TCON	00h
TH0	00h
TL0	00h
TH1	00h
TL1	00h
SCON	00h
SBUF	indeterminate
PCON	0xxxxxxxb

Internal RAM is not affected by reset. However, on power up the RAM values are indeterminate.

8XC552

The 8XC552 device has 15 interrupt sources, each of which can be assigned two priority levels. The subsystems which generate the interrupts are routed through Interrupt ENable registers (IEN0 and IEN1) and Interrupt Priority registers (IP0 and IP1). IEN1 and IP1 have been dealt with earlier in this chapter (under Timer T2 of the 8XC552, page 32); details of the registers IEN0 and IP0 will be covered later in this chapter.

The interrupt sources are:

• External interrupt request 0 (INT0)

- I²C serial port
- ADC
- Timer 0 overflow
- Timer 2 capture 0 (CT0I)
- Timer 2 compare 0
- External interrupt request 1 ($\overline{\text{INT1}}$)
- Timer 2 capture 1 (CT1I)
- Timer 2 compare 1
- Timer 1 overflow
- Timer 2 capture 2 (CT2I)
- Timer 2 compare 2
- UART serial port (transmit and receive)
- Timer 2 capture 3 (CT3I)
- Timer 2 overflow

There are five interrupt sources common to the 80C51, namely the external interrupts ($\overline{\text{INT0}}$ and $\overline{\text{INT1}}$), the Timer 0 and Timer 1 interrupts (IT0 and IT1 respectively) and the serial I/O interrupt (RI or TI). The standard serial interrupt in the 8XC552 is the SIO0. The eight Timer T2 interrupts are generated by flags CTI0 to CTI3, CMI0 to CMI2 (Interrupt Flag register TM2IR) and by the logical OR-ing of flags T2OV (TM2IR.7) and T2BO (control register TM2CON bit 4). The flags CTI0 to CTI3 are set by input signals CT0I to CT3I. Flags CMI0 to CMI2 are set when a match occurs between Timer T2 and the Compare registers CM0, CM1 and CM2. Flag T2BO is set when an 8-bit overflow occurs and T2OV is set when a 16-bit overflow occurs. The nine flags are not cleared by hardware and require a reset using software to avoid repeated interrupts.

All flags that generate interrupts may be set or cleared by software (except for the ADCI flag which can be reset by software but cannot be set by software). The ADC interrupt is generated by the ADCI flag which is bit 4 of the ADCON register at address C5h. This flag is set when an ADC conversion is ready to be read. ADCI is not cleared by hardware and must be reset by software to prevent recurring interrupts.

The SIO1 (I²C) interrupt is generated by the SI flag in the SIO1 Control register (S1CON); this flag is set when the S1STA register is loaded with a valid status code.

Interrupt ENable registers

Each interrupt source can be individually enabled/disabled by setting/clearing a bit in the Interrupt ENable SFRs IEN0 and IEN1. The interrupt enable register IEN1 has already been described (page 33); details of the IEN0 register, at address A8h, are as follows.

IEN0

MSB   LSB

EA	EAD	ES1	ES0	ET1	EX1	ET0	EX0
7	6	5	4	3	2	1	0

Bit functions and symbols are shown in Table 2.17.

Table 2.17 IEN0 register bit functions

Bit	Symbol	Function
7	EA	Global enable/disable control 0 = no interrupt enabled 1 = any individually enabled interrupt will be accepted
6	EAD	Enable ADC interrupt
5	ES1	Enable SIO1 (I^2C) interrupt
4	ES0	Enable SIO0 (UART) interrupt
3	ET1	Enable Timer 1 interrupt
2	EX1	Enable external interrupt 1
1	ET0	Enable Timer 0 interrupt
0	EX0	Enable external interrupt 0

As shown above global enabling/disabling of interrupt sources can be achieved by setting/clearing IEN0.7.

Interrupt priority structure

Each interrupt source may be assigned one of two priority levels determined by the interrupt priority SFRs IP0 and IP1. The interrupt priority levels are 0 for low priority and 1 for high priority. IP1 has been described earlier (page 35). Details of register IP0 are as follows.

IP0

MSB   LSB

-	PAD	PS1	PS0	PT1	PX1	PT0	PX0
7	6	5	4	3	2	1	0

Bit functions and symbols are shown in Table 2.18.

Table 2.18 IP0 register bit functions

Bit	Symbol	Function
7	-	Unused
6	PAD	ADC interrupt priority level
5	PS1	SIO1 (I^2C) interrupt priority level
4	PS0	SIO0 (UART) interrupt priority level
3	PT1	Timer 1 interrupt priority level
2	PX1	External interrupt 1 priority level
1	ET0	Timer 0 interrupt priority level
0	PX0	External interrupt 0 priority level

High priority interrupts will always take precedence over low priority interrupts. A low priority interrupt may itself be interrupted by a high priority interrupt. If two requests occur simultaneously then if one is high priority and the other low priority, the high priority interrupt will take precedence. If two requests of the same priority level occur

simultaneously an internal polling sequence will decide which interrupt receives precedence. This second priority structure which exists within each priority level is shown in
Table 2.19.

Table 2.19 Interrupt priority structure

Source	Name	Priority within level
External interrupt 0	X0	highest
SIO1 (I²C)	S1	⇑
ADC completion	ADC	‖
Timer 0 overflow	T0	‖
T2 capture 0	CT0	‖
T2 compare 0	CM0	‖
External interrupt 1	X1	‖
T2 capture 1	CT1	‖
T2 compare 1	CM1	‖
Timer 1 overflow	T1	‖
T2 capture 2	CT2	‖
T2 compare 2	CM2	‖
SIO0 (UART)	S0	‖
T2 capture 3	CT3	⇓
Timer 2 overflow	T2	lowest

Interrupt handling

The interrupt sources are sampled during S5P2 of every machine cycle and the samples are
polled during the following machine cycle. If one of the flags was in a set condition during
sampling, the polling cycle will find it and the interrupt system will generate an LCALL
to the appropriate service routine. This will occur provided that the hardware generated
LCALL is not blocked by any of the following conditions.

• An interrupt of higher or equal priority is already in progress.
• The current machine cycle is not the final cycle in the execution of the instruction in
  progress (i.e. a current instruction must be completed before an interrupt request can be
  serviced).
• The instruction in progress is a RETI or any access to the Interrupt Enable or Interrupt
  Priority registers (at least one other instruction must be executed subsequent to RETI
  instruction or a read/write to either Interrupt Enable register or either Interrupt Priority
  register).

The polling cycle is repeated with every machine cycle and the polled values are those
present at S5P2 of the previous machine cycle. The processor acknowledges an interrupt
request by the execution of a hardware generated LCALL to the appropriate service
routine. The flag which generated the interrupt may not always be cleared, i.e.:

• Timer 0, Timer 1 and external interrupt flags will be cleared;
• external interrupt flag IE0 or IE1 is cleared only if it was transition-activated;
• all other interrupt flags are not cleared by hardware and require resetting using
  software.

The LCALL pushes the contents of the PC on to the stack but does not save the PSW register contents; the PC is loaded with an address that depends on the source of the interrupt being vectored. The interrupt vector addresses are shown in Table 2.20.

Table 2.20 Interrupt vector addresses for the 8X552 device

Source	Name	Address
External interrupt 0	X0	0003h
Timer 0 overflow	T0	000Bh
External interrupt 1	X1	0013h
Timer 1 overflow	T1	001Bh
SIO0 (UART)	S0	0023h
SIO1 (I^2C)	S1	002Bh
T2 capture 0	CT0	0033h
T2 capture 1	CT1	003Bh
T2 capture 2	CT2	0043h
T2 capture 3	CT3	004Bh
ADC completion	ADC	0053h
T2 compare 0	CM0	005Bh
T2 compare 1	CM1	0063h
T2 compare 2	CM2	006Bh
T2 overflow	T2	0073h

Execution proceeds until the RETI instruction is encountered. The RETI instruction will clear the 'priority level active' flip-flop that was set when the interrupt was acknowledged. Then the top two bytes from the stack are popped back into the PC and execution of the interrupted program continues from the point of interruption. It is obvious from the above that if the interrupts are likely to be used the starting address for user programs must start after 0073h.

8XC750

For the 8XC750 device the IP register and two level interrupt system of the 80C51 is not present. The occurrence of simultaneous interrupt requests is dealt with on a single level fixed-priority basis as follows:

highest priority: pin $\overline{\text{INT0}}$
                    counter/timer flag 0
                    pin $\overline{\text{INT1}}$

2.9   On-chip oscillators

The 8051 device is available in an NMOS (N-channel Metal-Oxide Semiconductor) version and a CMOS version, with the latter having lower power consumption. In either case, although the circuitry differs, the on-chip oscillator circuit is a positive reactance intended to provide crystal-controlled resonance with externally connected capacitors. The arrangement is shown in Figure 2.17.

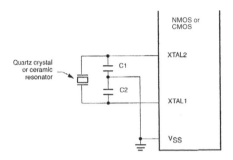

Figure 2.17 80C51 on-chip oscillator (courtesy Philips Semiconductors)

The crystal specifications and capacitance values are not critical and 30pF can be used at any frequency with good quality crystals. Where cost is critical ceramic resonators may be used and in this case the capacitor values should be higher, typically 47pF. To drive the device with an external clock source it is usual, for the CMOS device, to drive the XTAL1 input with the external clock and leave the input XTAL2 floating. This is shown in Figure 2.18.

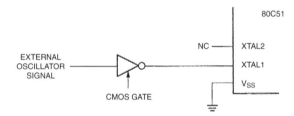

Figure 2.18 Using external clock source (courtesy Philips Semiconductors)

For the NMOS device the external clock is connected to XTAL2 input and XTAL1 is grounded. The reason for the difference is that in NMOS devices the internal timing circuits are driven by the signal at XTAL2 whereas in the CMOS devices they are driven by the signal at XTAL1.

MACHINE CYCLES

The oscillator formed by the crystal and associated circuit generates a pulse train at the crystal frequency f_{osc}. This pulse train sets the smallest interval of time P that exists within the microcontroller. The minimum time required by the microcontroller to complete a simple instruction, or part of a more complex instruction, is the machine cycle. The machine cycle consists of a sequence of six states, numbered S1 through to S6 with each state time lasting for two oscillator periods. Thus a machine cycle takes 12 oscillator periods. Each state is divided into a phase 1 half (P1) and a phase 2 half (P2). Figure 2.19 shows the fetch/execute sequences in states and phases for various kinds of instructions.

Normally two program fetches are generated during each machine cycle even if the instruction being fetched does not require it. If the instruction being executed does not need extra code bytes the CPU ignores the extra fetch and the PC is not incremented.

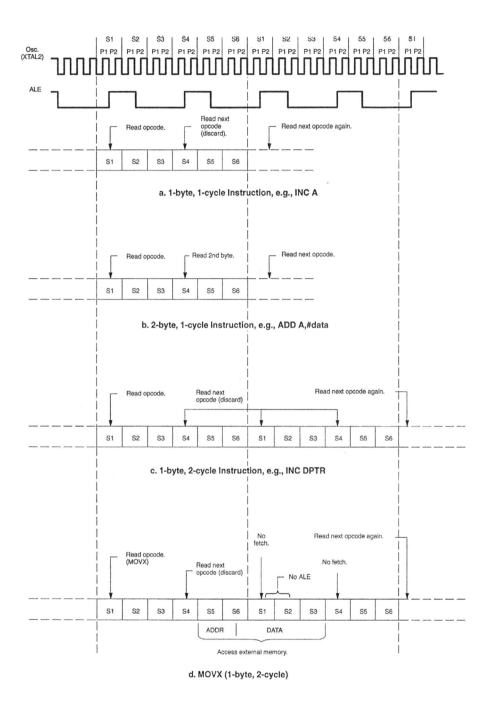

Figure 2.19 80C51 family state sequences (courtesy Philips Semiconductors)

Execution of a one cycle instruction begins during state 1 of the machine cycle with the opcode latched into the instruction register. A second fetch occurs during S4 of the same machine cycle and execution is completed at the end of S6 of the machine cycle.

The MOVX instructions take two machine cycles to complete and no program fetch is generated during the second cycle of the instruction. This is the only time that program fetches are skipped.

The sequences described are the same regardless of whether the program memory is internal or external to the chip since execution times do not depend on the location of code memory.

2.10   80C51 addressing modes

Addressing modes determine the way in which data is manipulated by the instruction. Each instruction contains a destination, and in most cases a source. The way the destination and the source are accessed is determined by the addressing mode. There are six different addressing modes available with the 80C51 family of microcontrollers and these are discussed below. A programming model of the 80C51 microcontroller is shown in Figure 2.4 which contains all the internal registers which will be referred to in the discussions which follow.

IMMEDIATE ADDRESSING

The destination register is loaded with a constant value immediately. The source is part of the data opcode. The Immediate Addressing mode is shown for data transfer, logical operations, and arithmetic operations below. Note that the data to be used is always preceded by a # character.

Moving data

MOV	A,	#F1h	[A]	< – – –	F1h
MOV	R3,	#1Ch	[R3]	< – – –	1Ch

In the examples above the data F1h is copied into the Accumulator and the data 1Ch is copied into R3 of the selected register bank. The square brackets around A and R3 are symbolic notation to refer to contents of the register, i.e. [A] refers to the contents of A.

Logical operations

ORL	A,	#33h	[A]	< – – –	[A] OR 33h
ANL	15h,	#88h	[15h]	< – – –	[15h] AND 88h

For the first example, the data 33h is OR-ed with the contents of the Accumulator and the result is stored in the accumulator.

In the second example the data 88h is AND-ed with the contents of RAM location 15h (which is R7 of the register bank 1) and the result of this operation is stored in R7.

Arithmetic operations

ADD	A,	#10h	[A]	< – – –	[A] + 10h
ADDC	A,	#10h	[A]	< – – –	[A] + 10h + C*

For these ADD operations the data 10h is immediately ADDed to the contents of the Accumulator and the result is stored in the Accumulator. The second example includes a carry which is to be included in the addition process.

DIRECT ADDRESSING

In Direct Addressing, the operand is specified by an 8-bit address field in the instruction. Only internal data RAM and SFRs can be directly accessed.

Moving data

| MOV | R5, | A | [R5] | < − − − | [A] |
| MOV | A, | R0 | [A] | < − − − | [R0] |

The first MOV instruction copies the contents of the Accumulator into the destination register, which in this case is R5 of the register bank selected. In the second instruction the R0 of the selected register bank is the source and the accumulator is the destination to which the contents of the source are copied.

Logical operations

| ANL | A, | R5 | [A] | < − − − | [A] AND [R5] |
| XRL | R5, | A | [R5] | < − − − | [R5] EX-OR [A] |

In a similar manner to the moving data examples, the logical operation examples show the source and destination, which in these cases are the registers indicated. In these examples after the logical operations their results are stored in the destination registers.

Arithmetic operations

| ADD | A, | R3 | [A] | < − − − | [A] + [R3] |
| ADDC | A, | R3 | [A] | < − − − | [A] + [R3] + C* |

These examples of Direct Addressing are the arithmetic operations. In the same way as described earlier for arithmetic operations with Immediate Addressing, the results of the operations are stored in the destination register, which in these cases is the accumulator.

INDIRECT ADDRESSING

For all addressing modes covered so far, the source or destination of data is an absolute number or name. In Indirect Addressing, the instruction specifies a register which contains the address of the operand. The address register for 8-bit addresses can be R0 and R1 of the selected banks. The address register for 16-bit addresses can only be the 16-bit data pointer or DPTR. Examples shown below should make this addressing mode clearer.

Moving data

| MOV | @R1, | A | [R1{M}] | < − − − | [A] |
| MOV | A, | @R0 | [A] | < − − − | [R0{M}] |

In the first instruction the Accumulator is the source and its contents are copied into the destination which is the memory location pointed to by the contents of R1. For the second instruction the source is the memory location pointed to by R0, the contents of which are copied into the Accumulator which is the destination register.

Logical operations

ORL	A,	@R0	[A]	< – – –	[A] OR [R0{M}]
XRL	@R1,	A	[R1]	< – – –	[R1{M}] EX-OR [A]

The first example is a logical OR instruction performed between the contents of the memory location, the address of which is held in Register R0, and the contents of the Accumulator. The destination of the result is the Accumulator. The second example is a logical Exclusive-OR instruction performed between the contents of the Accumulator (source) and the contents of the memory location, the address of which is held in Register R1. Register R1 is the destination of the result of the operation.

Arithmetic operations

ADD	A,	@R0	[A]	< – – –	[A] + [R0{M}]
ADDC	A,	@R1	[A]	< – – –	[A] + [R1{M}] + C*

In these examples the Accumulator is the destination which stores the results of the ADD operations and the source registers are locations pointed to by R0 and R1 of the selected banks respectively. Once again the second example shows the addition of the Carry flag to the source data.

REGISTER-SPECIFIC ADDRESSING

Some instructions are specific to certain registers. For example, some instructions always operate on the Accumulator, so no address byte is needed to point to it since the opcode itself does it. Also some instructions perform several operations while only one instruction is required, such as the one in the 'moving data' example below.

Moving data

PUSH TCON	[SP]	< – – –	[SP] + 1
	[SP{M}]	< – – –	[TCON]
POP DPL	[DPL]	< – – –	[SP{M}]
	[SP]	< – – –	[SP] – 1

For the PUSH TCON instruction, the SP is incremented by 1 and the contents of the TCON, which is the source here, is PUSHed (copied into) the memory location pointed to by the SP, which is the destination for this operation.

For the POP DPL instruction, the contents of the internal RAM location addressed by the SP is read, and the SP is decremented by 1. In this case the contents of the memory location initially read by the SP, which is the source, is copied into the DPL register which is the destination register.

Logical operations

RR	A	$[A_n]$	< – – –	$[A_{n+1}]$, n = 0 – 6
		$[A_0]$	< – – –	$[A_7]$
RRC	A	$[A_n]$	< – – –	$[A_{n+1}]$, n = 0 – 6
		$[A_0]$	< – – –	C*
		C*	< – – –	$[A_7]$

With this type of addressing mode the source and the destination are the same (i.e. the Accumulator). For the rotate right, RR A, instruction the contents of the Accumulator are shifted right by one bit, and bit zero is copied into bit seven of the Accumulator. For the case of rotate right with carry, RRC A, the rotation is done through the carry bit, i.e. the bit zero is copied into the Carry bit while the original value of the Carry bit is copied into bit seven.

Arithmetic operations

INC	A	$[A]$	< – – –	$[A] + 1$
INC	@R0	$[R0\{M\}]$	< – – –	$[R0\{M\}] + 1$

Here, as in the previous case, the source and the destination are the same register. INC A increments the contents of the Accumulator by one, while INC @R0, increments the contents of the memory location pointed to by R0 of the selected register bank.

EXTERNAL MEMORY ADDRESSING

The external memory can be as large as 64k bytes for both RAM and ROM memory areas. The data transfer instructions that move data to/from external memory use Indirect Addressing to specify external address.

MOVX A, @R0	$[A]$ < – – – $[R0\{M_{ext}\}]$	8-bit
MOVX @DPTR,A	$[DPTR\{M_{ext}\}]$ < – – – $[A]$	16-bit

The second method is faster but has the disadvantage that the eight bits of Port 2 are used for the high byte of the address so that Port 2 cannot be used for I/O purposes.

INDEXED ADDRESSING (CODE MEMORY READ-ONLY)

There are times when access to a pre-programmed mass of data is needed, such as tables of pre-defined bytes. This must be permanent to be of use for repeated access and is stored in the program ROM using assembler directives. Access to this data point is made possible by using Indirect Addressing and Register A in conjunction with either PC or DPTR.

In this addressing mode the destination is the Accumulator and the address of the source is calculated by addition of the contents of the Accumulator and the PC or the DPTR depending on the instruction used.

MOVC A, @A + PC   [A]   < – – –   [[[A] + [PC]]{M}]]
MOVC A, @A + DPTR   [A]   < – – –   [[[A] + [DPTR]]{M}]]

For the MOVC A, @A + PC, the source address is the internal ROM location whose address is calculated by adding the contents of the Accumulator to the contents of the PC. The MOVC A, @A + DPTR uses the contents of DPTR to calculate the source address.

More detail on the operations specified above appears in the chapters that follow.

Summary

The 80C51 device has:

- internal RAM and, for some family members, ROM; I/O ports; counter/timers; serial interface; nested interrupt structure and an on-chip oscillator;
- 40 pin functions;
- 128 bytes of on-chip RAM plus SFRs.
- 4k bytes of on-chip ROM (family members may have EPROM instead or even no ROM at all);
- memory expansion capabilities for RAM and ROM;
- four I/O ports, with Port 1 purely for I/O while Ports 0, 2 and 3 have other functions;
- timer/counters with four modes of operation;
- serial interface for data transmission with four modes of operation;
- the ability to work at different baud rates;
- five interrupt sources, three internal and two external;
- an on-chip oscillator which can be crystal-controlled;
- six different addressing modes; an addressing mode determines the way in which data is manipulated by the instruction.

The 8XC552 device has:

- internal RAM and, for some family members, ROM or EPROM; I/O ports; counter/timers; serial interface; a 15 source, two priority-level, nested interrupt structure; an eight-input ADC; a dual DAC pulse width modulated interface; two serial interfaces (UART and I²C); a 'Watchdog' Timer and an on-chip oscillator;
- 65 pin functions;
- 256 bytes of on-chip RAM plus SFRs;
- 8k bytes of on-chip ROM (family members may have EPROM instead or even no ROM at all);
- memory expansion capabilities for RAM and ROM;
- five I/O ports plus one 8-bit input port shared with analogue inputs;
- two standard 16-bit timer/counters with an additional 16-bit timer/counter coupled to four Capture registers and three Compare registers; there is also a 'Watchdog' Timer;
- serial interface for data transmission with full duplex UART and I²C capability;
- a 10-bit ADC with eight multiplexed analogue inputs;

- two 8-bit resolution, pulse width modulation outputs;
- the ability to work at different baud rates;
- an on-chip oscillator which can be crystal-controlled;
- six different addressing modes; an addressing mode determines the way in which data is manipulated by the instruction.

The 8XC750 device has:

- internal RAM and ROM (83C750)or EPROM 87C750); I/O ports; a counter/timer; serial interface; a five-source, fixed priority, nested interrupt structure and an on-chip oscillator;
- 24 pin functions;
- 64 bytes of on-chip RAM plus SFRs;
- 1k byte of on-chip ROM or EPROM;
- memory expansion capabilities for RAM and ROM;
- three I/O ports;
- a timer/counter with a single mode operation using 16 bits;
- serial interface for data transmission;
- three interrupt sources, operated at a single level with fixed priority;
- an on-chip oscillator which can be crystal-controlled;
- six different addressing modes; an addressing mode determines the way in which data is manipulated by the instruction.

Exercises

1. Identify the 40 pin functions of the 80C51 device.
2. Identify the 65 pin functions of the 8XC552 device.
3. Identify the 24 pin functions of the 8XC750 device.
4. For the 80C51 comment on the properties of the I/O ports P0, P1, P2 and P3.
5. For the 8XC552 comment on the properties of the I/O ports P0, P1, P2 P3, P4 and P5.
6. For the 8XC750 comment on the properties of the I/O ports P0, P1 and P3.
7. What is the size of internal RAM on the 80C51 and what are the location addresses?
8. Repeat question 7 for the 8XC552 device.
9. Repeat question 7 for the 8XC750 device.
10. How many SFRs are there in the 80C51?
11. Repeat question 10 for the 8XC552 device.
12. Repeat question 10 for the 8XC750 device.
13. Discuss the function of the bits in the 8-bit PSW register.
14. How many interrupt sources are there on the 80C51 and what are their vector addresses?
15. Repeat question 14 for the 8XC552 device.
16. Repeat question 14 for the 8XC750 device.

17. Suggest a possible circuit arrangement that would enable the 80C51 to access external program memory.
18. Suggest a possible circuit arrangement that would enable the 80C51 to access external data memory.
19. With reference to the Port 1 pin diagram of Figure 2.10 describe circuit action that occurs for a read or write signal from the 80C51 CPU.
20. For the 80C51, how many LS TTL inputs can be driven from the output buffers of (a) Port 1 and (b) Port 0?
21. For the 80C51 discuss the function of the TMOD and TCON registers on the operation of the Timer/counter registers.
22. For the 8XC552 device discuss the function of the Timer T2 TM2CON register.
23. For the 8XC552 device discuss the function of the Timer T2 capture and compare logic.
24. For the 8XC552 device discuss the function of the Interrupt Flag register TM2IR and interrupt Priority register IP1.
25. For the 8XC552 device what is the function of the 'Watchdog' Timer T3?
26. Discuss the operation of the 16-bit counter/timer of the 8XC750 device.
27. Discuss the four operating modes available to the 80C51 timer/counters. Which bits in the TMOD register determine the mode of operation?
28. What is the function of the 80C51 serial port SBUF and what is its address?
29. What is the function of the 80C51 register SCON and what is its address?
30. Discuss the four operating modes available to the 80C51 serial port.
31. If the on-chip oscillator frequency for an 80C51 is 11.059 MHz what would be the setting of TH1 to obtain a baud rate of 960 bits/sec with SMOD cleared to 0?
32. Repeat question 31 to obtain a baud rate of 1200 bits/sec.
33. Repeat question 32 with SMOD set to 1.
34. Discuss the operation of the SIO1 port on the 8XC552 device.
35. Name and discuss the modes of operation available with the SIO1 port.
36. List the five interrupt sources provided by the 80C51.
37. List the 15 interrupt sources provided by the 8XC552.
38. List the three interrupt sources provided by the 8XC750.
39. For the 80C51 device, which of the bits in the SFR IE disables all interrupts?
40. For the 80C51 device, discuss the function of the bits in the SFR IP.
41. List the priority level of the interrupts for the 80C51. What are the starting addresses of the interrupt subroutines for each interrupt?
42. For the 80C51, which of the SFRs has a reset value that is not 0000h?
43. For the 8XC552 device, discuss the interrupt priority structure. How does the device handle interrupts?
44. How many states are involved in a machine cycle and how many oscillator periods are involved?
45. If an 80C51 device operates from a 12 MHz crystal what is the duration of a machine cycle?
46. State what you understand by Immediate Addressing; give an example of this mode of addressing that involves an arithmetic operation.
47. State what you understand by Direct Addressing; give an example of this mode of addressing that involves a logical operation.
48. State what you understand by Indirect Addressing; give an example of this mode of addressing that involves moving data.

49. State what you understand by Register-specific Addressing; give an example of this mode of addressing that involves moving data.

50. State what you understand by External Memory addressing; give an example of this mode of addressing.

51. State what you understand by Indexed Addressing; give an example of this mode of addressing.

3

Arithmetic Operations

3.1 Addition

INTRODUCTION

There are 24 arithmetic operations within the 80C51 instruction set. Rather than simply list them, they have been broken up into groups with each operation explained within that group. Each operation is complete with illustrations to give a clearer picture of the action of the operation. It should be noted that unless otherwise stated, the address locations and memory contents given in the illustrated examples of this chapter are in decimal values. In practice a location content would be in binary, i.e. for an 8-bit register, say, the contents could be:

MSB   LSB

1	1	1	0	0	1	1	0

which corresponds to a decimal number of 230, i.e. 11100110b corresponds to 230d. The contents are more often expressed in hexadecimal form where a group of four bits would have a decimal value from 0 to 15 represented by 0h to Fh. In hexadecimal form therefore, a single term represents the four bits and the numbers 0 to 9 are represented directly and the numbers 10 to 15 are represented by the letters A to F respectively. Thus the register contents shown above would be represented in hexadecimal form as E6h.

The addition process contains four groups of operations, which are discussed individually below. These operations may affect some of the flag bits in the Program Status Word (PSW) register and, if so, this will be highlighted in brackets after each operation name. The flag bits are as shown in Table 3.1.

Table 3.1

Bit	Symbol	Function
7	CY	Carry flag
6	AC	Auxiliary carry flag
2	OV	Overflow flag

The full instruction set for the 80C51 microcontroller can be found in Appendix A.

INCREMENT

INC@R0 $[R0\{M\}] < - - - [R0\{M\}] + 1$

INC @R1 $[R1\{M\}] < - - - [R1\{M\}] + 1$

These instructions add one to the contents of the memory location pointed to by registers R0 and R1 respectively, using Indirect Addressing. Consider the example shown in Figure 3.1 which illustrates the instruction applied to both Register R0 and R1.

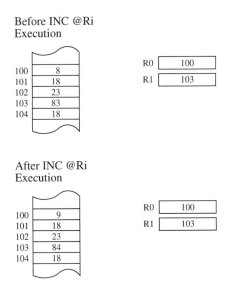

Figure 3.1 Use of the INC @Ri instruction

INC A $[A] < - - - [A] + 1$

This instruction adds one to the contents of the Accumulator directly, using Direct Addressing. An example is shown in Figure 3.2.

Before INC A   After INC A
Execution   Execution

A [100]   A [101]

Figure 3.2 Effect of the INC A instruction

INC direct $[direct] < - - - [direct] + 1$

Direct is an 8-bit internal data location address which could be an internal data RAM or an SFR, the content of which is incremented by one. These instructions use Direct

Addressing. Consider the example shown in Figure 3.3 where various direct addresses are specified including Register B, stack pointer (SP), Port 0 (P0) and internal RAM 1B.

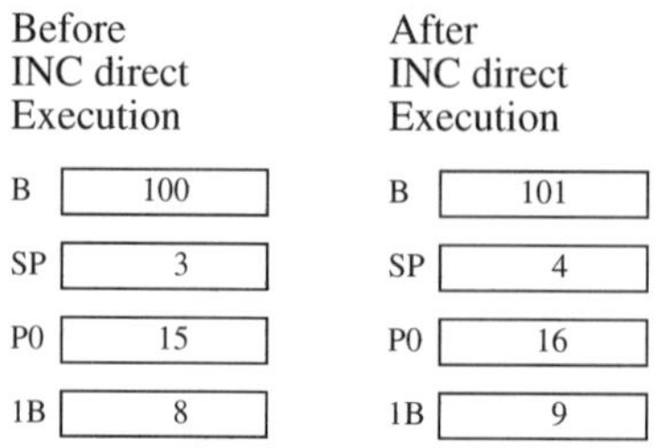

Before INC direct Execution		After INC direct Execution	
B	100	B	101
SP	3	SP	4
P0	15	P0	16
1B	8	1B	9

Figure 3.3 Use of the INC direct instruction

INC DPTR   [DPTR] < − − − [DPTR] + 1

This instruction adds one to the contents of the DPTR directly. It uses Direct Addressing. An example is shown in Figure 3.4.

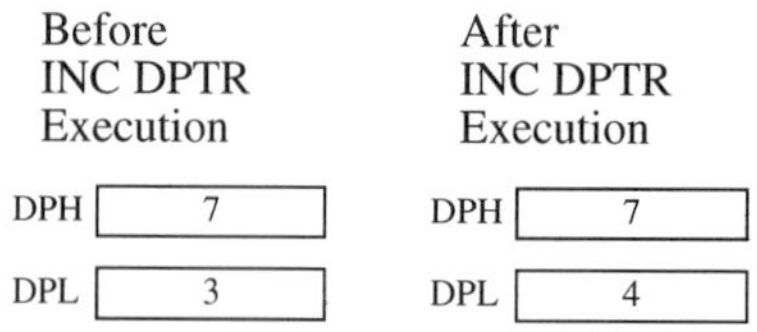

Before INC DPTR Execution		After INC DPTR Execution	
DPH	7	DPH	7
DPL	3	DPL	4

Figure 3.4 Effect of the INC DPTR instruction

INC Rn

These instructions add one to the contents of the register addressed (e.g. R3 of the register bank). They use Direct Addressing. The effect on each of the Rn registers is as shown in Table 3.2.

Table 3.2

Instruction	Effect of instruction
INC R0	[R0] < − − − [R0] + 1
INC R1	[R1] < − − − [R1] + 1
INC R2	[R2] < − − − [R2] + 1
INC R3	[R3] < − − − [R3] + 1
INC R4	[R4] < − − − [R4] + 1
INC R5	[R5] < − − − [R5] + 1
INC R6	[R6] < − − − [R6] + 1
INC R7	[R7] < − − − [R7] + 1

An example is shown in Figure 3.5 which illustrates the effect on Registers R0 and R4.

Before   After
INC Rn   INC Rn
Execution   Execution

R4 [7   ]   R4 [8   ]

R0 [3   ]   R0 [4   ]

Figure 3.5 Use of the INC Rn instruction

ADD(CY, AC, OV)

ADD A, @R0   [A] < − − −   [A] + [R0{M}]

ADD A, @R1   [A] < − − −   [A] + [R1{M}]

These instructions add the contents of the memory location pointed to by Registers R0 or R1 to the contents of the accumulator and store the result in the Accumulator. They use indirect Addressing. Consider the example shown in Figure 3.6 for both Registers R0 and R1.

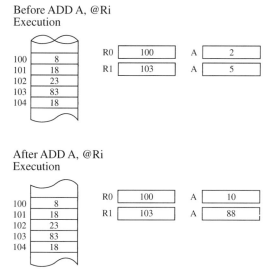

Before ADD A, @Ri
Execution

100	8	R0 [100]	A [2]
101	18	R1 [103]	A [5]
102	23		
103	83		
104	18		

After ADD A, @Ri
Execution

100	8	R0 [100]	A [10]
101	18	R1 [103]	A [88]
102	23		
103	83		
104	18		

Figure 3.6 Use of the ADD A, @Ri instruction

ADD A, #data   [A] < − − −   [A] + data

This instruction adds the constant value 'data' to the contents of the Accumulator and stores the result in the Accumulator. It uses Immediate Addressing. An example is shown in Figure 3.7.

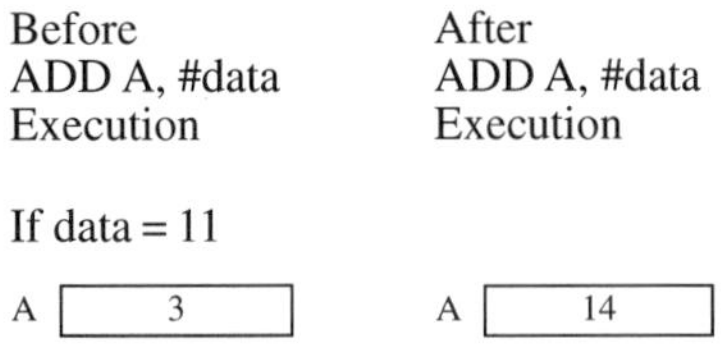

Before
ADD A, #data
Execution

After
ADD A, #data
Execution

If data = 11

A [3]   A [14]

Figure 3.7 Effect of the ADD A, #data instruction

ADD A,direct   [A] < − − −   [A] + [direct]

As before direct is an 8-bit internal data location address which could be an internal data RAM or an SFR, the contents of which are added to the contents of the accumulator and the result stored in the Accumulator. This instruction uses Direct Addressing. Consider the example shown in Figure 3.8 where the direct address is that of the SP.

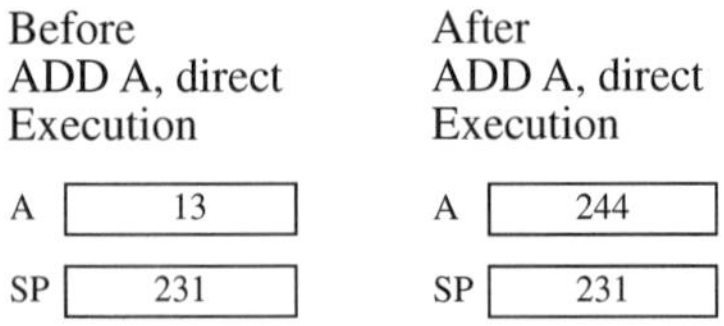

Before
ADD A, direct
Execution

After
ADD A, direct
Execution

A [13]   A [244]

SP [231]   SP [231]

Figure 3.8 Effect of the ADD A, direct instruction

ADD A,Rn

These instructions add the contents of the Register addressed (e.g. R3 of the register bank) to the contents of the Accumulator and store the result in the Accumulator. They use Direct Addressing. The effect on each of the registers Rn is shown in Table 3.3.

Table 3.3

Instruction	Effect of instruction
ADD A,R0	[A] < − − − [A] + [R0]
ADD A,R1	[A] < − − − [A] + [R1]
ADD A,R2	[A] < − − − [A] + [R2]
ADD A,R3	[A] < − − − [A] + [R3]
ADD A,R4	[A] < − − − [A] + [R4]
ADD A,R5	[A] < − − − [A] + [R5]
ADD A,R6	[A] < − − − [A] + [R6]
ADD A,R7	[A] < − − − [A] + [R7]

Consider the example shown in Figure 3.9 which uses Register R0.

Before
ADD A, Rn
Execution

After
ADD A, Rn
Execution

A   [3]   A   [14]

S0   [11]   S0   [11]

Figure 3.9 Use of the ADD A, Rn instruction

ADD WITH CARRY (CY, AC, OV)

ADDC A, @R0   [A] < – – –   [A] + [R0{M}] + [Carry Bit]

ADDC A, @R1   [A] < – – –   [A] + [R1{M}] + [Carry Bit]

These instructions add the contents of the memory location pointed to by Registers R0 or R1 and the contents of the Carry bit in the Status register to the contents of the Accumulator and store the result in the Accumulator. They use Indirect Addressing. An example is shown in Figure 3.10 using Register R0.

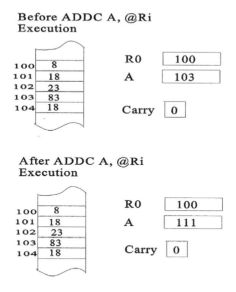

Figure 3.10 Use of the ADDC A, @Ri instruction

ADDC A, #data   [A] < – – –   [A] + data + [Carry bit]

This instruction adds the contents of the Carry bit and the constant value 'data' to the contents of the Accumulator and stores the result in the Accumulator. It uses Immediate

Addressing. Consider the example shown in Figure 3.11 which has a data value of 100 and a carry of 1.

Before ADDC A, #data
Execution

If data = 100

A   103

Carry 1

After ADDC A, #data
Execution

A   204

Carry 1

Figure 3.11 Effect of the ADDC A, #data instruction

ADDC A, direct   [A] < – – – [A] + [direct] + [Carry bit]

Again direct is an 8-bit internal data location address which could be an internal data RAM or an SFR, the contents of which and the contents of the Carry bit are added to the contents of the Accumulator, the result being stored in the Accumulator. This instruction uses Direct Addressing. An example is shown in Figure 3.12 where again the direct address is the SP.

Before   After
ADDC A, direct   ADDC A, direct
Execution   Execution

A   13   A   245

SP   231   SP   231

Carry 1   Carry 1

Figure 3.12 Effect of the ADDC A, direct instruction

ADDC A, Rn

These instructions add the contents of the register addressed (e.g. R3 of the register bank) and the contents of the Carry bit to the contents of the Accumulator and store the result in the Accumulator. They use Direct Addressing. The effect on each of the registers Rn is shown in Table 3.4.

Table 3.4

Instruction	Effect of instruction
ADDC A,R0	[A] < − − − [A] + [R0] + [Carry bit]
ADDC A,R1	[A] < − − − [A] + [R1] + [Carry bit]
ADDC A,R2	[A] < − − − [A] + [R2] + [Carry bit]
ADDC A,R3	[A] < − − − [A] + [R3] + [Carry bit]
ADDC A,R4	[A] < − − − [A] + [R4] + [Carry bit]
ADDC A,R5	[A] < − − − [A] + [R5] + [Carry bit]
ADDC A,R6	[A] < − − − [A] + [R6] + [Carry bit]
ADDC A,R7	[A] < − − − [A] + [R7] + [Carry bit]

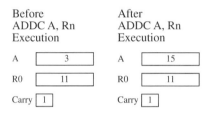

Figure 3.13 Use of the ADDC A, Rn instruction

Consider the example shown in Figure 3.13 which uses Register R0.

DECIMAL ADJUST FOR BINARY CODED DECIMAL BCD (CY)

DA A   [A(BCD)] < − − − [A(binary)]

This instruction adjusts the sum of two BCD numbers found in the Accumulator and stores the result in the Accumulator. The Carry flag is SET if the adjusted number exceeds 99 BCD and RESET otherwise. DA A only works with addition instructions and does not give correct adjustment for other arithmetic operations. This instruction uses Direct Addressing. An example is shown in Figure 3.14.

3.2 Subtraction

The subtraction operations contain two groups of operations, which are also discussed individually as before. Where these operations affect the flag bits in the Status register, they are highlighted in brackets after each operation name.

DECREMENT

DEC @R0   [R0{M}] < − − − [R0{M}] − 1

DEC @R1   [R1{M}] < − − − [R1{M}] − 1

These instructions subtract one from the contents of the memory location pointed to by Registers R0 and R1 respectively. They use Indirect Addressing. Consider the example shown in Figure 3.15 which shows the effect of the instruction on both Register R0 and R1.

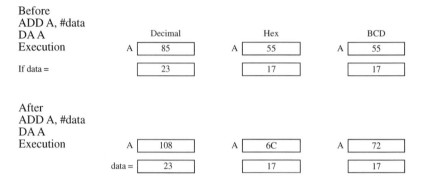

Figure 3.14 Use of the DA A instruction

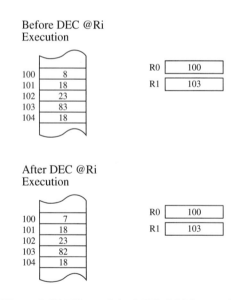

Figure 3.15 Effect of the DEC @Ri instruction

DEC A   [A] < – – – [A] – 1

This instruction reduces the contents of the Accumulator by one directly, using Direct Addressing. An example is shown in Figure 3.16.

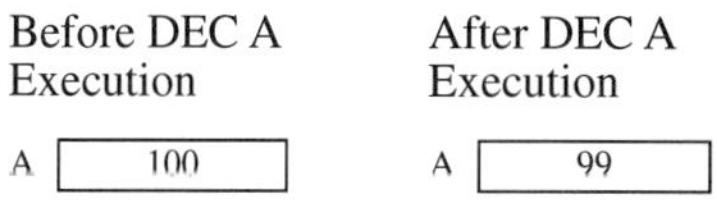

Before DEC A
Execution

After DEC A
Execution

A [100]   A [99]

Figure 3.16 Effect of the DEC A instruction

DEC direct   [direct] < − − − [direct] − 1

Again direct is an 8-bit internal data location address which could be an internal data RAM or an SFR, the contents of which is decremented by one. These instructions use Direct Addressing. Consider the example shown in Figure 3.17 where a variety of direct addresses are shown. The addresses shown are from the SFRs (Register B, SP and Port 0) and internal RAM (1B).

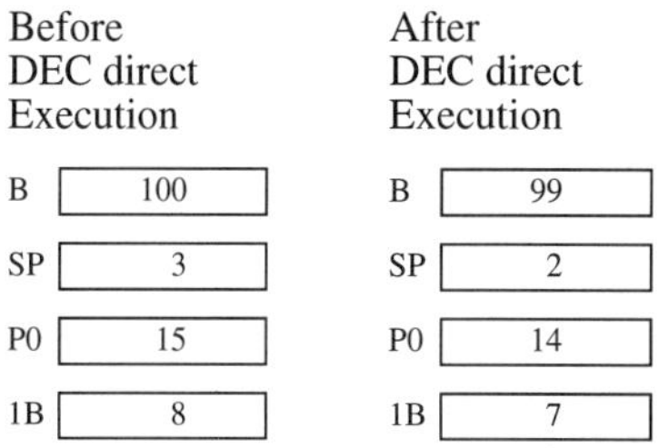

Before
DEC direct
Execution

After
DEC direct
Execution

B [100]   B [99]

SP [3]   SP [2]

P0 [15]   P0 [14]

1B [8]   1B [7]

Figure 3.17 Effect of the DEC direct instruction

DEC Rn

These instructions decrement by one the contents of the Register addressed (e.g. R3 of the register bank), using Direct Addressing. The effect on each of the Rn registers is shown in Table 3.5.

Table 3.5

Instruction	Effect of instruction
DEC R0	[R0] < − − − [R0] − 1
DEC R1	[R1] < − − − [R1] − 1
DEC R2	[R2] < − − − [R2] − 1
DEC R3	[R3] < − − − [R3] − 1
DEC R4	[R4] < − − − [R4] − 1
DEC R5	[R5] < − − − [R5] − 1
DEC R6	[R6] < − − − [R6] − 1
DEC R7	[R7] < − − − [R7] − 1

An example is shown in Figure 3.18 using Registers R0 and R4.

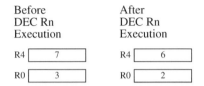

Figure 3.18 Use of the DEC Rn instruction

SUBTRACT WITH BORROW (CY, AC, OV)

SUBB A, @R0   [A] < − − −   [A] − [R0{M}] − [Carry bit]

SUBB A, @R1   [A] < − − −   [A] − [R1{M}] − [Carry bit]

These instructions subtract the contents of the memory location pointed to by Registers R0 or R1 and the contents of the Carry bit in the Status register from the contents of the Accumulator and store the result in the Accumulator. They use Indirect Addressing. Consider the example shown in Figure 3.19 which shows the effect of the instruction on Register R0.

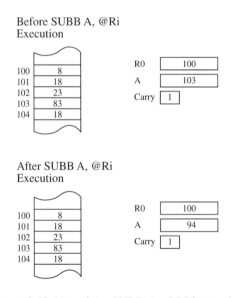

Figure 3.19 Use of the SUBB A, @Ri instruction

SUBB A, #data   [A] < − − −   [A] − data − [Carry bit]

This instruction subtracts the contents of the Carry bit and the constant value 'data' from the contents of the Accumulator and stores the result in the Accumulator. It uses Immediate Addressing. An example is shown in Figure 3.20.

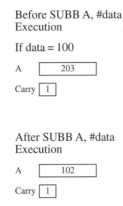

Before SUBB A, #data
Execution

If data = 100

A [203]

Carry [1]

After SUBB A, #data
Execution

A [102]

Carry [1]

Figure 3.20 Use of the SUBB A, #data instruction

SUBB A,direct [A] < – – – [A] – [direct] – [Carry bit]

As before direct is an 8-bit internal data location address which could be an internal data RAM or an SFR, the contents of which, together with the contents of the Carry bit, are subtracted from the contents of the Accumulator and the result stored in the Accumulator. This instruction uses Direct Addressing. Consider the example shown in Figure 3.21 which uses the SP as the direct address.

Before
SUBB A,direct
Execution

After
SUBB A,direct
Execution

A [250]   A [18]

SP [231]   SP [231]

Carry [1]   Carry [1]

Figure 3.21 Effect of the SUBB A, direct instruction

SUBB A, Rn

These instructions subtract the contents of the register addressed (e.g. R3 of the register bank) and the contents of the Carry bit from the contents of the Accumulator and store the result in the Accumulator. They use Direct Addressing. The effect on each of the Rn registers is shown in Table 3.6.

Table 3.6

Instruction	Effect of instruction
SUBB A,R0	[A] < – – – [A] – [R0] – [Carry bit]
SUBB A,R1	[A] < – – – [A] – [R1] – [Carry bit]
SUBB A,R2	[A] < – – – [A] – [R2] – [Carry bit]
SUBB A,R3	[A] < – – – [A] – [R3] – [Carry bit]
SUBB A,R4	[A] < – – – [A] – [R4] – [Carry bit]
SUBB A,R5	[A] < – – – [A] – [R5] – [Carry bit]
SUBB A,R6	[A] < – – – [A] – [R6] – [Carry bit]
SUBB A,R7	[A] < – – – [A] – [R7] – [Carry bit]

Consider the example shown in Figure 3.22, which applies to Register R0.

3.3   Multiplication

MUL AB $[A_{7-0}]$ < – – – [A] multiply [B]
$[B_{15-8}]$

This operation has only one instruction which could affect the Carry flag and Overflow bits. An example is shown in Figure 3.23.

3.4   Division

DIV AB $[A_{15-8}]$ < – – – [A] divide [B]
$[B_{7-0}]$

This operation also has only one instruction which could affect the Carry flag and Overflow bits. An example is shown in Figure 3.24.

Summary

All the arithmetic operations (addition, subtraction, multiplication and division) that can be performed by the 80C51 family of microcontrollers have been discussed in this chapter. The Immediate, Direct, Indirect, Register-specific (i.e. INC A) addressing modes are available which adds to the power of this microcontroller regarding the arithmetic operations.

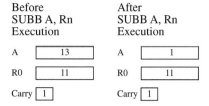

Figure 3.22 Effect of the SUBB A, Rn instruction

Before
MUL AB
Execution

	Decimal			Binary
A	85		A	0101 0101
B	23		B	0001 0111

After
MUL AB
Execution

	Decimal			Binary
A	163		A	1010 0011
B	7		B	0000 0111

Figure 3.23 Use of the MUL AB instruction

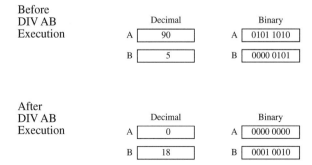

Before
DIV AB
Execution

	Decimal			Binary
A	90		A	0101 1010
B	5		B	0000 0101

After
DIV AB
Execution

	Decimal			Binary
A	0		A	0000 0000
B	18		B	0001 0010

Figure 3.24 Use of the DIV AB instruction

Exercises

1. If R0 contains 82h and A contains 23h, what would be the values in R0 and A after INC @R0 is executed?
2. Referring to question 1, what values would the register have after ADD A, @R0 is executed?
3. Referring to question 1, what changes are made after the execution of INC @R0?
4. Assume that the location 43h contains a value of 04h, accumulator A contains 23h, R0 contains 43h, and the Carry bit is RESET (i.e. Carry = 0). For the following program determine the contents of each register mentioned and the Carry bit after each instruction:

    > ADD A, @R0
    > INC A
    > ADC A, @R0
    > SUBB A, #12

5. Assuming Accumulator A contains a value of 60d and the Register B contains a value of 3d, what would each contain after the execution of MUL AB instruction?
6. For question 5, what would be contained in each register after execution of DIV AB?

4

Logical Operations

4.1 Introduction

There are 43 logical instructions of the 80C51 instruction set included in this chapter. Rather than simply list them they have been broken down into groups of operations. Logical operations are performed on bits and bytes and the bit operations are discussed first. Those operations that affect the Carry Flag bit in the Program Status Word (PSW) register are highlighted in brackets after each operation named. The instructions are set out with illustrated examples so as to more clearly show the effect of an operation on relevant bits, registers, etc. Unless otherwise indicated the illustrated examples use decimal values for locations, contents, etc. whereas hexadecimal values are more common. For more details on hexadecimal representation of decimal numbers refer to the introduction to Chapter 3.

The full instruction set for the 80C51 microcontroller can be found in Appendix A.

4.2 Bit operations

As discussed in Chapter 2, there are 16 bytes of RAM available as bit addressable locations giving 128 bits. This area of RAM has byte addresses from 20h to 2Fh. The bit addresses are numbered from 00h to 7Fh to represent the 128 bit addresses that exist in the range 20h to 2Fh. Thus bit 0 of byte address 20h is 00h and bit 7 of byte address 2Fh is 7Fh. These operations can only affect the individual bits of the bit addressable RAM (20h–2Fh) and SFR bits. Also conditional tests could be performed on bits for changing the flow of the program.

The following operations are available with the 80C51 family of microcontrollers.

CLR (AS TARGETED)

CLR C   Carry < – – – 0

This instruction clears the Carry bit in the PSW register. This is illustrated in the example shown in Figure 4.1.

Before
CLR C
Execution

PSW

CY	AC	F0	RS1	RS0	OV	–	P
1	0	0	0	0	0	0	1

After
CLR C
Execution

PSW

CY	AC	F0	RS1	RS0	OV	–	P
0	0	0	0	0	0	0	1

Figure 4.1 Example of the CLR C instruction

CLR bit   bit < – – – 0

This instruction clears the bit addressed in the internal RAM (20h-2Fh). Consider the example shown in Figure 4.2 where bit 10h is being accessed. This bit is thus bit 17 in the range of addresses from 20h to 2Fh, i.e. it is bit 0 at address 22h.

Before
CLR 10h
Execution

RAM Loc. 22 Hex

0	1	2	3	4	5	6	7
1	0	0	0	0	0	0	1

After
CLR 10h
Execution

RAM Loc. 22 Hex

0	1	2	3	4	5	6	7
0	0	0	0	0	0	0	1

Figure 4.2 Use of the CLR bit instruction

SETB (AS TARGETED)

SETB C   Carry < – – – 1

This instruction sets the Carry bit in the PSW register. An example is shown in Figure 4.3.

Before
SETB C
Execution

PSW

CY	AC	F0	RS1	RS0	OV	–	P
0	0	0	0	0	0	0	1

After
SETB C
Execution

PSW

CY	AC	F0	RS1	RS0	OV	–	P
1	0	0	0	0	0	0	1

Figure 4.3 Effect of the use of SETB C instruction

SETB bit   bit < – – – 1

This instruction sets the bit addressed in the internal RAM. Consider the example shown in Figure 4.4 which shows the opposite effect to that indicated by the CLR bit instruction in Figure 4.2.

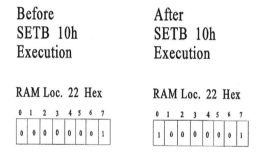

Figure 4.4 Effect of the SETB bit instruction

CPL (AS TARGETED)

CPL C   Carry < − − − /Carry

This instruction complements the Carry bit in the PSW register. An example is shown in Figure 4.5.

Before
CPL C
Execution

After
CPL C
Execution

PSW

CY	AC	F0	RS1	RS0	OV	--	P
1	0	0	0	0	0	0	1

PSW

CY	AC	F0	RS1	RS0	OV	--	P
0	0	0	0	0	0	0	1

Figure 4.5 Use of the CPL C instruction

CPL bit   bit < − − − /bit

This instruction complements the bit addressed in the internal RAM. Consider the example shown in Figure 4.6 where the bit operated on is the same as the one indicated in Figure 4.2.

Before
CLR 10h
Execution

After
CLR 10h
Execution

RAM Loc. 22 Hex

RAM Loc. 22 Hex

0	1	2	3	4	5	6	7
1	0	0	0	0	0	0	1

0	1	2	3	4	5	6	7
0	0	0	0	0	0	0	1

Figure 4.6 Use of the CPL bit instruction

ANL (CY)

ANL C,bit   Carry < – – –   Carry AND bit

This instruction ANDs the bit addressed with the Carry bit and stores the results in the Carry bit itself. Consider the example shown in Figure 4.7 where bit 1 of RAM location 20h (0 in this example) is ANDed with the Carry bit (1 in this example) and the result (0) is stored in the Carry bit.

Before
ANL C, 01h
Execution

After
ANL C, 01h
Execution

RAM Loc. 20 Hex

RAM Loc. 20 Hex

0	1	2	3	4	5	6	7
1	0	0	0	0	0	0	1

0	1	2	3	4	5	6	7
1	0	0	0	0	0	0	1

Carry 1

Carry 0

Figure 4.7 Example of the ANL C, bit instruction

ANL C,/bit   Carry < – – –   Carry AND /bit

This instruction ANDs the complement of the bit addressed with the Carry bit and stores the result in the Carry bit itself. An example is shown in Figure 4.8.

Before
ANL C, /01h
Execution

After
ANL C, /01h
Execution

RAM Loc. 20 Hex

RAM Loc. 20 Hex

0	1	2	3	4	5	6	7
1	0	0	0	0	0	0	1

0	1	2	3	4	5	6	7
1	0	0	0	0	0	0	1

Carry 1

Carry 1

Figure 4.8 Effect of the ANL C, /bit instruction

ORL (CY)

ORL C,bit   Carry < – – –   Carry OR bit

This instruction ORs the bit addressed with the Carry bit and stores the results in the Carry bit itself. Consider the example shown in Figure 4.9 where bit 0 of RAM location 20h (1 in this example) is ORed with the Carry bit (0 in this example) to give a result (1) which is stored in the Carry bit.

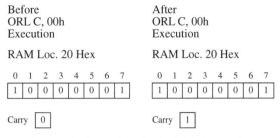

Figure 4.9 Use of the ORL C, bit instruction

ORL C,/bit   Carry < – – – Carry OR/bit

This instruction ORs the complement of the bit addressed with the Carry bit and stores the result in the Carry bit itself. An example is shown in Figure 4.10.

Before
ORL C, /03h
Execution

RAM Loc. 20 Hex

0	1	2	3	4	5	6	7
1	0	0	0	0	0	0	1

Carry 0

After
ORL C, /03h
Execution

RAM Loc. 20 Hex

0	1	2	3	4	5	6	7
1	0	0	0	0	0	0	1

Carry 1

Figure 4.10 Use of the ORL C, /bit instruction

MOV (AS TARGETED)

MOV C,bit   Carry < – – – bit

This instruction moves the bit addressed to the Carry bit in the PSW. Consider the case shown in Figure 4.11 where bit 07h (RAM location 20h bit 7) is moved to the Carry.

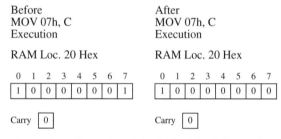

Before
MOV C, 07h
Execution

RAM Loc. 20 Hex

0	1	2	3	4	5	6	7
1	0	0	0	0	0	0	1

Carry 0

After
MOV C, 07h
Execution

RAM Loc. 20 Hex

0	1	2	3	4	5	6	7
1	0	0	0	0	0	0	1

Carry 1

Figure 4.11 Use of the MOV C, bit instruction

MOV bit,C   bit < – – – Carry

This instruction moves the Carry bit in the PSW into the bit addressed. A typical example is shown in Fig 4.12.

Before
MOV 07h, C
Execution

RAM Loc. 20 Hex

0	1	2	3	4	5	6	7
1	0	0	0	0	0	0	1

Carry 0

After
MOV 07h, C
Execution

RAM Loc. 20 Hex

0	1	2	3	4	5	6	7
1	0	0	0	0	0	0	0

Carry 0

Figure 4.12 Example of the MOV bit, C instruction

JMP

JC rel   [PC] < – – – [PC] + 2
              if Carry = 1 [PC] < – – – [PC] + rel

This instruction checks the Carry bit in the PSW and, if SET, the Program Counter (PC) would be loaded with 2 + rel, where rel is relative position with respect to present position of the PC. An example showing both of the carry possibilities is shown in Figure 4.13.

Before
JC rel
Execution

Carry 0

PC   100

After
JC rel
Execution

Carry 0

PC   100+2

Carry 1

PC   100

Carry 1

PC   100+2+rel

Figure 4.13 Use of the JC rel instruction

JNC rel   [PC] < – – – [PC] + 2
                    if Carry = 0 [PC] < – – – [PC] + rel

This instruction checks the Carry bit in the PSW and, if RESET, the PC would be loaded with 2 + rel, where rel is relative position with respect to present position of the PC. Consider the example shown in Figure 4.14 which shows the effect with either of the carry values.

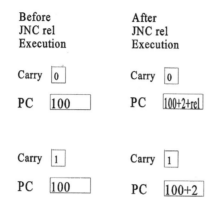

Figure 4.14 Example of the JNC rel instruction

JB bit,rel   [PC] < – – – [PC] + 3
                    if bit = 1 [PC] < – – – [PC] + rel

This instruction checks the RAM bit addressed and, if SET, the PC would be loaded with 3 + rel, where rel is relative position with respect to present position of the PC. If the RAM bit addressed is not SET the PC is loaded with PC + 3. An example is shown in Figure 4.15.

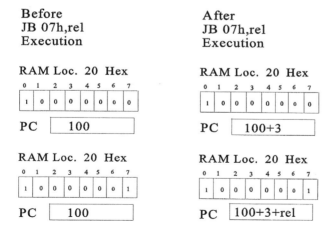

Figure 4.15 Effect of the JB bit,rel instruction

JNB bit,rel   [PC] < – – –   [PC] + 3
                    if bit = 0 [PC] < – – –   [PC] + rel

This instruction checks the RAM bit addressed and, if RESET, the PC would be loaded with 3 + rel, where rel is relative position with respect to present position of the PC. If not RESET the PC would be loaded with PC + 3. An example is shown in Figure 4.16.

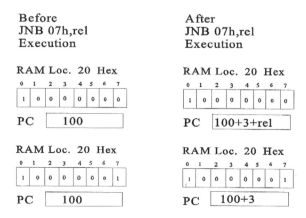

Before
JNB 07h,rel
Execution

RAM Loc. 20 Hex

0	1	2	3	4	5	6	7
1	0	0	0	0	0	0	0

PC   100

After
JNB 07h,rel
Execution

RAM Loc. 20 Hex

0	1	2	3	4	5	6	7
1	0	0	0	0	0	0	0

PC   100+3+rel

RAM Loc. 20 Hex

0	1	2	3	4	5	6	7
1	0	0	0	0	0	0	1

PC   100

RAM Loc. 20 Hex

0	1	2	3	4	5	6	7
1	0	0	0	0	0	0	1

PC   100+3

Figure 4.16 Effect of the JNB bit,rel instruction

JNZ rel   [PC] < – – –   [PC] + 2
                 if A ≠ 0 [PC] < – – –   [PC] + rel

This instruction checks the contents of the Accumulator A, and if it is not zero, then the PC would be loaded with 2 + rel, where rel is relative position with respect to present position of the PC. If the Accumulator contents are zero then the PC is loaded with PC + 2, as indicated in Figure 4.17.

Before
JNZ rel
Execution

A   0

PC   100

After
JNZ rel
Execution

A   0

PC   100+2

A   72

PC   100

A   72

PC   100+2+rel

Figure 4.17 Effect of the JNZ rel instruction

JZ rel   [PC] < – – –   [PC] + 2
         if A = 0 [PC] < – – –   [PC] + rel

This instruction checks the contents of the Accumulator A and, if it is zero, the PC would be loaded with 2 + rel, where rel is relative position with respect to present position of the PC. An example is shown in Figure 4.18.

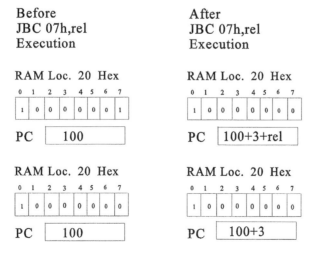

Before
JZ rel
Execution

A   23

PC   100

A   0

PC   100

After
JZ rel
Execution

A   23

PC   100+2

A   0

PC   100+2+rel

Figure 4.18 Effect of the JZ rel instruction

JBC bit,rel   [PC] < – – –   [PC] + 3
         if bit = 1 bit < – – –   0
              [PC] < – – –   [PC] + rel

This instruction checks the bit addressed and, if it is SET, it would RESET and the PC would be loaded with 3 + rel where, as before, rel is relative position with respect to present position of the PC. Otherwise PC would be incremented by 3. A possible case is shown in Figure 4.19.

Before
JBC 07h,rel
Execution

RAM Loc. 20 Hex

0	1	2	3	4	5	6	7
1	0	0	0	0	0	0	1

PC   100

RAM Loc. 20 Hex

0	1	2	3	4	5	6	7
1	0	0	0	0	0	0	0

PC   100

After
JBC 07h,rel
Execution

RAM Loc. 20 Hex

0	1	2	3	4	5	6	7
1	0	0	0	0	0	0	0

PC   100+3+rel

RAM Loc. 20 Hex

0	1	2	3	4	5	6	7
1	0	0	0	0	0	0	0

PC   100+3

Figure 4.19 Effect of the JBC bit, rel instruction

4.3 Byte operations

ACC CLR/COMPLEMENT

CLR A   [A] < – – – 0

This instruction clears the contents of the Accumulator A. See Figure 4.20.

Figure 4.20 Use of the CLR A instruction

CPL A   [A] < – – – [/A]

This instruction complements the contents of the Accumulator A. See Figure 4.21.

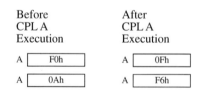

Figure 4.21 Use of the CPL A instruction

ROTATES

RL A $[A_{n+1}]$ < – – – $[A_n]$, n = 0 – > 6
          $[A_0]$ < – – – $[A_7]$

This instruction rotates all the bits of the Accumulator left by one bit and places bit 7 of the Accumulator into bit 0. The example of Figure 4.22 should make the action clear.

Before RL A Execution

A

7 6 5 4 3 2 1 0

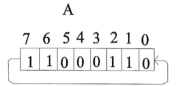

After RL A Execution

A

7 6 5 4 3 2 1 0

Figure 4.22 Example of the RL A instruction

RR A $[A_n] < - - - [A_{n+1}]$, n = 0 –>6
           $[A_7] < - - - [A_0]$

This instruction rotates all the bits of the Accumulator right by one bit and places bit 0 of the Accumulator into bit 7. This can be seen by referring to the example illustrated in Figure 4.23.

Before RR A Execution

A

7 6 5 4 3 2 1 0

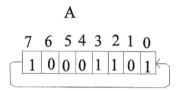

After RR A Execution

A

7 6 5 4 3 2 1 0

Figure 4.23 Example of the RR A instruction

ROTATE THROUGH CY (CY)

RLC A $[A_{n+1}] < - - - [A_n]$, $n = 0 -> 6$
$[A_0]$ $< - - -$ Carry
Carry $< - - -$ $[A_7]$

This instruction rotates all the Accumulator bits one place to the left. Bit 0 would be filled with the Carry bit and the Carry bit will take the value of bit 7 of the Accumulator. The example shown in Figure 4.24 illustrates this operation.

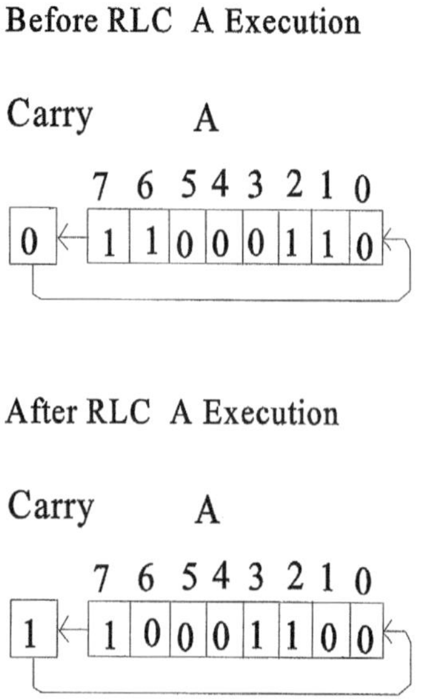

Before RLC A Execution

Carry   A

7 6 5 4 3 2 1 0
0 ← 1 1 0 0 0 1 1 0 ←

After RLC A Execution

Carry   A

7 6 5 4 3 2 1 0
1 ← 1 0 0 0 1 1 0 0 ←

Figure 4.24 Example of the RLC A instruction

RRC A

$[A_n]$ $< - - -$ $[A_{n+1}]$, $n = 0 -> 6$
$[A_7]$ $< - - -$ Carry
Carry $< - - -$ $[A_0]$

This instruction rotates all the bits of the Accumulator by one bit to the right and pushes bit 0 into the Carry bit and the Carry bit into bit 7 of the Accumulator. Figure 4.25 indicates the effect of the operation.

AND

ANL A, #data

$[A] < - - -$ $[A]$ AND data

This instruction ANDs the contents of the Accumulator with the immediate data and stores the result in the Accumulator. Figure 4.26 highlights this effect.

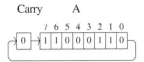

Figure 4.25 Example of the RRC A instruction

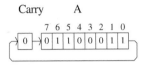

Figure 4.26 Use of the ANL A, #data instruction

ANL A,@Ri

[A] < – – – [A] AND [Ri{M}]

This operation ANDs the contents of the memory location pointed to by Register Ri (R0 or R1) with the Accumulator and stores the result in the Accumulator. Figure 4.27 illustrates an example with both R0 and R1.

ANL A,direct

[A] < – – – [A] AND [direct]

Direct is an 8-bit internal data location address which could be an internal data RAM or an SFR, the content of which is ANDed with the Accumulator with the result stored back in the Accumulator. Refer to Figure 4.28 for an example where the SP is the direct address.

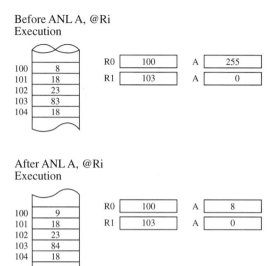

Figure 4.27 Use of the ANL A, @Rn instruction

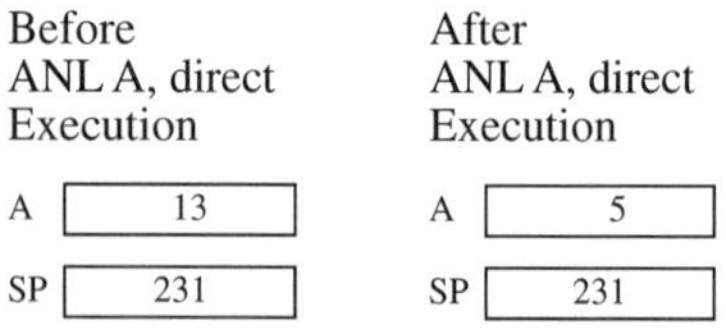

Before
ANL A, direct
Execution

After
ANL A, direct
Execution

A [13]   A [5]

SP [231]   SP [231]

Figure 4.28 Use of the ANL A,direct instruction

ANL direct,A   [direct] < – – – [direct] AND [A]

This is the same as the previous operation except that the result is stored into the direct location. Figure 4.29 highlights this operation, again with the SP as the direct address.

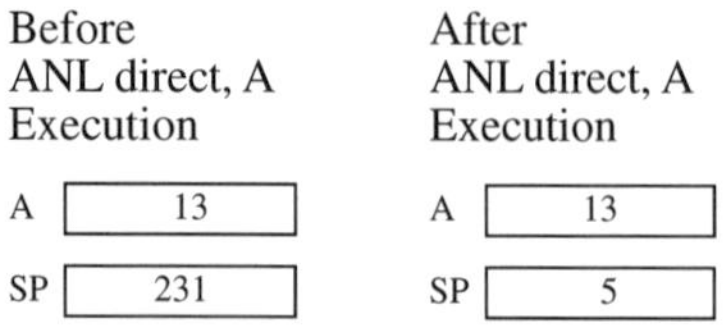

Before
ANL direct, A
Execution

After
ANL direct, A
Execution

A [13]   A [13]

SP [231]   SP [5]

Figure 4.29 Use of the ANL direct,A instruction

ANL A,Rn   [A] < – – – [A] AND [Rn]

In this operation the content of Register Rn (R0, R1, R2, R3, R4, R5, R6 or R7) is ANDed with the contents of the Accumulator and the result is stored in the Accumulator. Refer to Figure 4.30 for an example using Register R0.

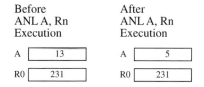

Before
ANL A, Rn
Execution

After
ANL A, Rn
Execution

A   13   A   5

R0   231   R0   231

Figure 4.30 Effect of the ANL A,Rn instruction

ANL direct,#data   [direct] < – – – [direct] AND data

Again direct is an 8-bit internal data location address which could be an internal data RAM or an SFR, the contents of which is ANDed with the immediate data and the result is stored in the direct location. Figure 4.31 illustrates the point using Port 0.

Before ANL direct, #data
Execution

	7	6	5	4	3	2	1	0
P0	1	1	0	0	1	1	1	0
Data	1	1	1	0	0	1	1	0

After ANL direct, #data
Execution

	7	6	5	4	3	2	1	0
P0	1	1	0	0	0	1	1	0
Data	1	1	1	0	0	1	1	0

Figure 4.31 Use of the ANL direct,#data instruction

OR

ORL A,#data   [A] < – – – [A] OR data

This instruction ORs the contents of the Accumulator with the immediate data and stores the result in the Accumulator. See Figure 4.32 which highlights this effect.

Before ORL A, #data Execution

	7	6	5	4	3	2	1	0
A	0	1	0	0	1	0	1	0
Data	1	1	1	1	0	1	1	0

After ORL A, #data Execution

	7	6	5	4	3	2	1	0
A	1	1	1	1	1	1	1	0
Data	1	1	1	1	0	1	1	0

Figure 4.32 Effect of the ORL A,#data instruction

ORL A,@Ri   [A] < – – –   [A] OR [Ri{M}]

This operation ORs the contents of the memory location pointed to by Register Ri (R0 or R1) with the Accumulator and stores the result in the Accumulator. Refer to Figure 4.33 for an example of this effect.

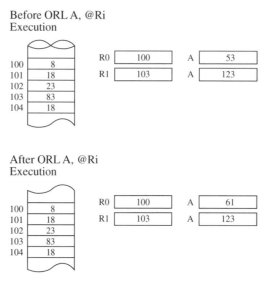

Figure 4.33 Effect of the ORL A, @Ri instruction

ORL A,direct   [A] < – – –   [A] OR [direct]

Direct is an 8-bit internal data location address which could be an internal data RAM or an SFR, the content of which is ORed with the Accumulator and the result stored in the Accumulator. Refer to Figure 4.34 for an example where the SP is the direct address.

Before ORL A, direct Execution		After ORL A, direct Execution	
A	13	A	239
SP	231	SP	231

Figure 4.34 Use of the ORL A,direct instruction

ORL direct, A   [direct] < – – –   [direct] OR [A]

This is the same as the previous operation except that the result is stored into the direct location. Figure 4.35 highlights this operation.

ORL A,Rn   [A] < – – –   [A] OR [Rn]

In this operation the content of Register Rn (R0, R1, R2, R3, R4, R5, R6 or R7) is ORed with the contents of the Accumulator and the result stored in the Accumulator. Refer to Figure 4.36 for an example using Register R0.

Before
ORL direct, A
Execution

| A | 13 |
| SP | 21 |

After
ORL direct, A
Execution

| A | 13 |
| SP | 29 |

Figure 4.35 Use of the ORL direct,A instruction

Before
ORL A, Rn
Execution

| A | 13 |
| R0 | 23 |

After
ORL A, Rn
Execution

| A | 31 |
| R0 | 23 |

Figure 4.36 Use of the ORL A,Rn instruction

ORL direct,#data   [direct] < – – – [direct] OR data

Again direct is an 8-bit internal data location address which could be an internal data RAM or an SFR, the content of which is ORed with the immediate data and the result stored back in the direct location. Refer to Figure 4.37 for an example using Port 0 as the direct address.

Before ORL direct, #data
Execution

	7	6	5	4	3	2	1	0
P0	1	1	0	0	1	1	1	0
Data	1	1	1	0	0	1	1	0

After ORL direct, #data
Execution

	7	6	5	4	3	2	1	0
P0	1	1	1	0	1	1	1	0
Data	1	1	1	0	0	1	1	0

Figure 4.37 Example of the ORL direct,#data instruction

XOR

XRL A,#data   [A] < – – – [A] XOR data

This instruction X-ORs the contents of the Accumulator with the immediate data and stores the result in the Accumulator. See Figure 4.38 which highlights this effect.

XRL A,@Ri   [A] < – – – [A] XOR [Ri{M}]

This operation X-ORs the contents of the memory location pointed to by Register Ri (R0 or R1) with the Accumulator and stores the result in the Accumulator. Refer to Figure 4.39 for an example.

Before XRL A, #data Execution

	7	6	5	4	3	2	1	0
A	0	1	0	0	1	0	1	0

Data   1 1 1 1 0 1 1 0

After XRL A, #data Execution

	7	6	5	4	3	2	1	0
A	1	0	1	1	1	1	0	0

Data   1 1 1 1 0 1 1 0

Figure 4.38 Use of the XRL A,#data instruction

Before XRL A, @Ri
Execution

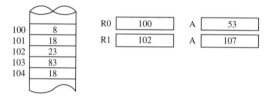

100	8
101	18
102	23
103	83
104	18

R0 | 100 | A | 53 |
R1 | 102 | A | 107 |

After XRL A, @Ri
Execution

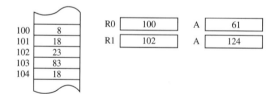

100	8
101	18
102	23
103	83
104	18

R0 | 100 | A | 61 |
R1 | 102 | A | 124 |

Figure 4.39 Example of the XRL A,@Ri instruction

XRL A,direct   [A] < − − − [A] XOR [direct]

Direct is an 8-bit internal data location address which could be an internal data RAM or an SFR, the content of which is X-ORed with the Accumulator and the result stored back in the Accumulator. Refer to Figure 4.40 which illustrates the effect of using Port 2 as the direct address.

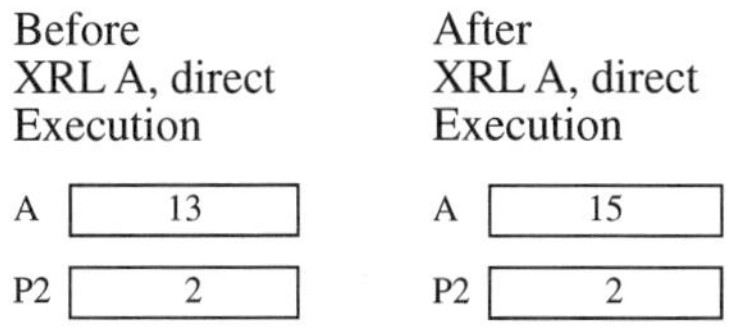

```
Before                    After
XRL A, direct             XRL A, direct
Execution                 Execution

A  [    13    ]           A  [    15    ]

P2 [     2    ]           P2 [     2    ]
```

Figure 4.40 Example of the use of the XRL A,direct instruction

XRL direct, A   [direct] < – – – [direct] XOR [A]

This is the same as the previous operation except that the result is stored into the direct register. Figure 4.41 highlights this operation with the SP as the direct address.

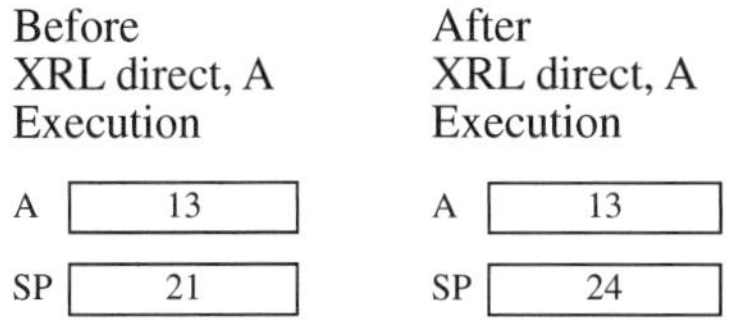

```
Before                    After
XRL direct, A             XRL direct, A
Execution                 Execution

A  [    13    ]           A  [    13    ]

SP [    21    ]           SP [    24    ]
```

Figure 4.41 Effect of the use of XRL direct,A instruction

XRL A,Rn   [A] < – – – [A] XOR [Rn]

In this operation the contents of Register Rn (R0, R1, R2, R3, R4, R5, R6 or R7) is X-ORed with the contents of the Accumulator and the result is stored in the Accumulator. Refer to Figure 4.42 for an example using Register R0.

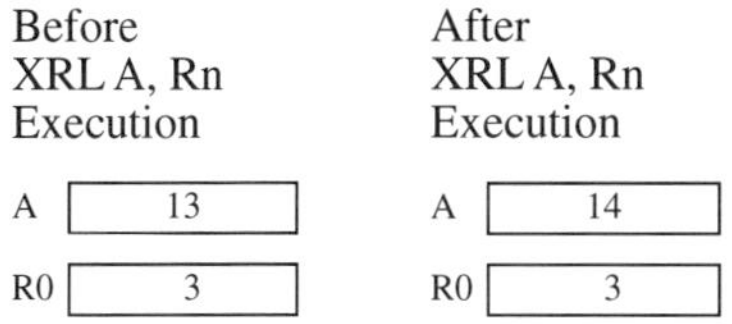

```
Before                    After
XRL A, Rn                 XRL A, Rn
Execution                 Execution

A  [    13    ]           A  [    14    ]

R0 [     3    ]           R0 [     3    ]
```

Figure 4.42 Use of the XRL A,Rn instruction

XRL direct,#data   [direct] < – – – [direct] XOR data

Again direct is an 8-bit internal data location address which could be an internal data RAM or an SFR, the content of which is X-ORed with the immediate data and the result stored back in the direct location. Refer to Figure 4.43 for an example using Port 0 as the direct address.

Before XRL direct, #data
Execution

	7	6	5	4	3	2	1	0
P0	1	1	0	0	1	1	1	0

Data   1   1   1   0   0   1   1   0

After XRL direct, #data
Execution

	7	6	5	4	3	2	1	0
P0	0	0	1	0	1	0	0	0

Data   1   1   1   0   0   1   1   0

Figure 4.43 Example of the effect of the XRL direct,#data instruction

Summary

The logical operations which can be performed on bits and bytes have been discussed. The fundamental logical operations such as AND, OR and XOR are used in applications for bit settings, maskings, etc., as required. The 80C51 provides a wealth of instructions in which various bits of various registers could be SET or RESET.

Exercises

1. If R1 contains 82h and A contains 3h, what would be the values in R0 and A after ANL A, @R1 is executed?
2. Referring to question 1, what values would the registers have after ORL A,R0 is executed?
3. Referring to question 1 what changes are made after the execution of XRL A, @R0?
4. Assume location 23h contains a value of 04h, Accumulator A contains 20h, R1 contains 23h, and the Carry bit is RESET (i.e. Carry = 0). For the following program, determine the contents of each register mentioned above and the Carry bit after each instruction.

```
        .
        .
        ANL A, @R0
        CPL A
        RRC A
        RR  A
        .
        .
```

5. Assuming Accumulator A contains a value of 60d and the Register B contains a value of 3d, what would each contain after the execution of the ANL A,B instruction?
6. For question 5, what would be contained in each register after execution of ANL B,A?

5

Data Transfer Operations

5.1 Introduction

There are 29 data transfer instructions of the 80C51 instruction set included in this chapter. Rather than simply listing them we have broken them down into groups of operations.

The data transfer operations are performed on bits and bytes and there are 12 groups of operations, which are discussed individually below. These operations do not affect any of the flag bits in the Program Status Word (PSW) register.

The instructions are set out with illustrated examples so as to more clearly show the effect of an operation on relevant bits, registers, etc. The illustrated examples mainly use decimal values for locations, contents, etc. whereas hexadecimal values are more common. For more details on hexadecimal representation of decimal numbers refer to the introduction to Chapter 3.

The full instruction set for the 80C51 microcontroller can be found in Appendix A.

5.2 Immediate

MOV A,#data   [A] < − − − data

This instruction moves the immediate data into the Accumulator A. See Figure 5.1 as an example.

Before MOV A, #data
Execution

	7	6	5	4	3	2	1	0
A	1	0	0	0	0	0	1	0

Data   1 1 1 1 0 1 1 0

After MOV A, #data
Execution

	7	6	5	4	3	2	1	0
A	1	1	1	1	0	1	1	0

Data   1 1 1 1 0 1 1 0

Figure 5.1 Use of a MOV A,#data instruction

MOV @Ri,#data   [Ri{M}] < – – – data

In this operation the immediate data is put into the memory location pointed to by the contents of the Register Ri (R0 or R1). Figure 5.2 shows an example of this operation using Register R0.

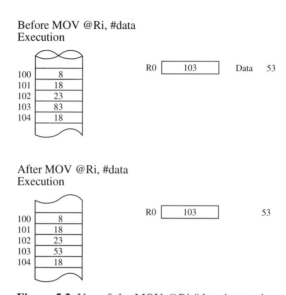

Figure 5.2 Use of the MOV @Ri,#data instruction

MOV direct,#data   [direct] < – – – data

Direct is an 8-bit internal data location address which could be an internal data RAM or an SFR, which is loaded with the immediate data. Figure 5.3 shows an example of this operation using Port 0 as a direct address.

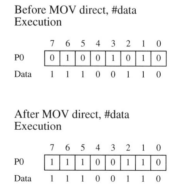

Figure 5.3 Example of the use of the MOV direct,#data instruction

MOV DPTR,#data   [DPTR] < – – – data (16-bit)

The DPTR is the pair of registers, Data Pointer High (DPH) and Data Pointer Low (DPL), put together to form a 16-bit register. This could be loaded individually or as a pair using the instruction above which puts the 16-bit immediate data into the DPTR. See Figure 5.4 for an example.

Before
MOV DPTR, #data
Execution

After
MOV DPTR, #data
Execution

DPH [23]   DPH [3E]

DPL [00]   DPL [25]

Data 3E25   Data 3E25

Figure 5.4 Effect of the MOV DPTR,#data instruction

MOV Rn,#data   [Rn] < – – – data

This instruction loads Register Rn (R0 to R7) with the 'data'. An example of this operation using Register R0 is shown in Figure 5.5.

Before
MOV R0, #data
Execution

After
MOV R0, #data
Execution

R0 [23]   R0 [E2]

Data E2   Data E2

Figure 5.5 Effect of a MOV Rn,#data instruction

5.3 Accumulator ↔ Register direct

MOV A,Rn   [A] < – – – [Rn]

The accumulator is loaded with the contents of Register Rn (R0 to R7). Figure 5.6 illustrates an example of this operation using Register R5.

Before
MOV A, R5
Execution

After
MOV A, R5
Execution

R5 [33]   R5 [33]

A [100]   A [33]

Figure 5.6 Use of the MOV A,Rn instruction

MOV Rn,A   [Rn] < – – – [A]

In this instruction the content of the Accumulator is copied into Register Rn (R0 to R7). Using Register R3, Figure 5.7 shows an example of this operation.

Before   After
MOV R3, A   MOV R3, A
Execution   Execution

R3 [233   ]   R3 [102   ]

A [102   ]   A [102   ]

Figure 5.7 Example of the MOV Rn,A instruction

5.4 Accumulator ↔ Register indirect

MOV @Ri,A   [Ri{M}] < − − − [A]

This instruction copies the contents of the Accumulator into the memory location pointed to by Register Ri (R0 or R1). An example of this instruction is shown in Figure 5.8.

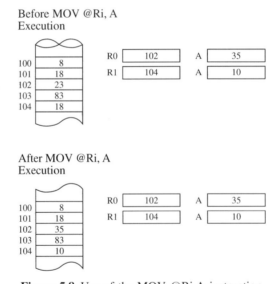

Figure 5.8 Use of the MOV @Ri,A instruction

MOV A,@Ri   [A] < − − − [Ri{M}]

With this operation the contents of the memory location pointed to by register Ri (R0 or R1) are copied into the Accumulator. See Figure 5.9 which gives an example of this operation.

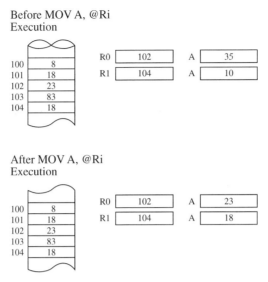

Figure 5.9 Use of the MOV A,@Ri,direct instruction

5.5 RAM ↔ Register indirect

MOV @Ri,direct   [Ri{M}] < − − − [direct]

With this operation the contents of direct, which is a data RAM or an SFR, is copied into the location pointed to by the contents of Register Ri (R0 or R1). Figure 5.10 shows an example of this operation using Register B and DPH as direct addresses.

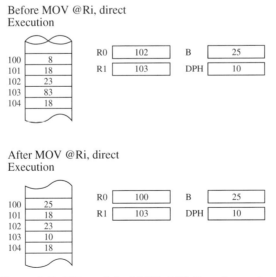

Figure 5.10 Effect of the MOV @Ri,direct instruction

MOV direct,@Ri   [direct] < – – – [Ri{M}]

This operation is the same as the operation above, except that the source and destination are swapped. See the example shown in Figure 5.11 which uses the Stack Pointer (SP) and Port 0 as the direct addresses.

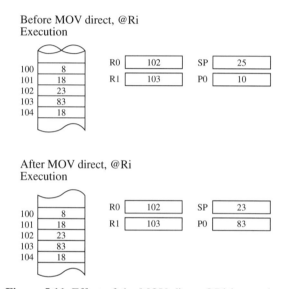

Before MOV direct, @Ri
Execution

100	8
101	18
102	23
103	83
104	18

RO [102]   SP [25]
R1 [103]   PO [10]

After MOV direct, @Ri
Execution

100	8
101	18
102	23
103	83
104	18

RO [102]   SP [23]
R1 [103]   PO [83]

Figure 5.11 Effect of the MOV direct,@Ri instruction

5.6   Accumulator ↔ RAM direct

MOV A,direct   [A] < – – – [direct]

With this operation the contents of direct, which is an internal RAM location or SFR, would be copied into the Accumulator. Figure 5.12 shows an example of this operation.

Before
MOV A, direct
Execution

A [13]

SP [21]

After
MOV A, direct
Execution

A [21]

SP [21]

Figure 5.12 Use of the MOV A,direct instruction

MOV direct,A   [direct] < – – – [A]

This operation is the same as before except that this time the contents of the Accumulator are copied into direct. Figure 5.13 shows an example of this operation using Register B as the direct address.

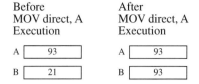

Before
MOV direct, A
Execution

After
MOV direct, A
Execution

| A | 93 |

| B | 21 |

| A | 93 |

| B | 93 |

Figure 5.13 Example of the use of the MOV direct, A instruction

5.7 RAM ↔ RAM

MOV direct,direct   [direct] < − − − [direct]

With this instruction the contents of source direct are copied into destination direct, both being internal RAM locations or SFRs. See Figure 5.14 which gives an example of such an operation using the 16-bit DPTR.

Before
MOV direct, direct
Execution

After
MOV direct, direct
Execution

Source
| DPH | 93 |

Destination
| DPL | 21 |

| DPH | 93 |

| DPL | 93 |

Figure 5.14 Example of the MOV direct,direct instruction

5.8 Register ↔ data MEM

MOV Rn,direct   [Rn] < − − − [direct]

This instruction copies the contents of source direct, which is an internal RAM location or SFR, into Register Rn (R0 to R7). An example of this is shown in Figure 5.15 using Register R5 as the destination address and Register B as the source address.

Before
MOV Rn, direct
Execution

After
MOV Rn, direct
Execution

| B | 3 |

| R5 | 121 |

| B | 3 |

| R5 | 3 |

Figure 5.15 Effect of the MOV Rn,direct instruction

MOV direct,Rn   [direct] < − − − [Rn]

With this instruction the contents of source Register Rn (R0 to R7) are copied into destination direct which is either an internal RAM location or an SFR. See Figure 5.16 for an example using Register R1 as the source address and the SP as the destination address.

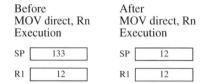

Figure 5.16 Use of the MOV direct,Rn instruction

5.9   Exchange Accumulator with RAM

XCH A,@Ri   [A] ⟷ [Ri{M}]

This instruction swaps the contents of the Accumulator with the contents of the memory location pointed to by Register Ri (R0 or R1). See Figure 5.17 for details.

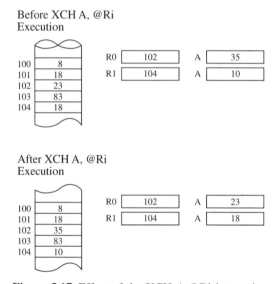

Figure 5.17 Effect of the XCH A,@Ri instruction

XCH A,direct   [A] ⟷ [direct]

This instruction swaps the contents of the Accumulator with the contents of Register direct which is either internal RAM locations or SFRs. Figure 5.18 is an example of this instruction.

XCH A,Rn   [A] ⟷ [Rn]

This instruction swaps the contents of the Accumulator with the contents of Register Rn (R0 to R7). Figure 5.19 shows the use of Register R7 to give an example of this operation.

Before
XCH A, direct
Execution

After
XCH A, direct
Execution

A | 13

A | 231

SP | 231

SP | 13

Figure 5.18 Effect of the use of the XCH A,direct instruction

Before
XCH A, Rn
Execution

After
XCH A, Rn
Execution

A | 132

A | 231

R7 | 231

R7 | 132

Figure 5.19 Use of the XCH A,Rn instruction

5.10 Program MEM table lookup

MOVC A,@A + DPTR $[A] < - - - [[[A] + [DPTR]] \{M\}]$

In this operation the contents of the DPTR are added to the contents of the Accumulator, so that together they form the address of the location in the PROM (i.e. a byte of code), the contents of which are then copied into the Accumulator. Figure 5.20 should make the sequence clear.

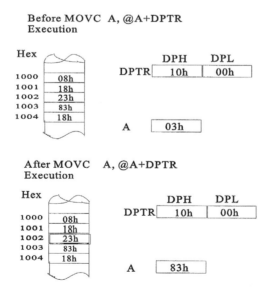

Before MOVC A, @A+DPTR
Execution

Hex

	DPH	DPL
DPTR	10h	00h

1000	08h
1001	18h
1002	23h
1003	83h
1004	18h

A | 03h

After MOVC A, @A+DPTR
Execution

Hex

	DPH	DPL
DPTR	10h	00h

1000	08h
1001	18h
1002	23h
1003	83h
1004	18h

A | 83h

Figure 5.20 Example of the MOVC A,@A+DPTR instruction

MOVC A,@A + PC $[A] < - - - [[[A] + [PC]] \{M\}]$

This is similar to the above operation, except that instead of using the DPTR, the PC is utilised. Figure 5.21 gives an example.

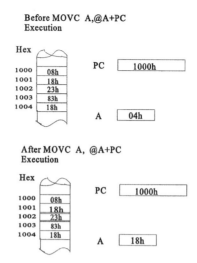

Figure 5.21 Use of the MOVC A,@A+PC instruction

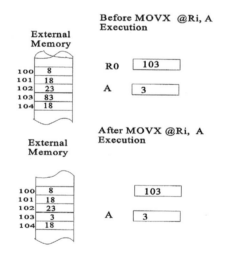

Figure 5.22 Effect of the MOVX @Ri,A instruction

5.11   Accumulator ↔ EXT data MEM

MOVX @Ri,A   [Ri {Ext_M}] < – – – [A]

This instruction copies the contents of the Accumulator to the 'external memory' pointed to by Register Ri (R0 or R1). See Figure 5.22 which gives an example of this operation using Register R0.

MOVX A,@Ri   [A] < – – – [Ri {Ext_M}]

With this instruction the contents of the 'external memory' pointed to by Register Ri (R0 or R1) are placed in the Accumulator. See Figure 5.23 for an example of such an operation using Register R0.

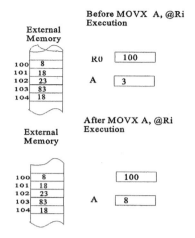

Figure 5.23 Effect of the MOVX A,@Ri instruction

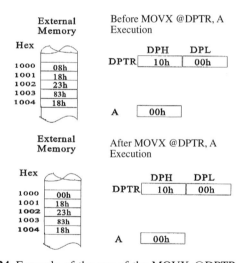

Figure 5.24 Example of the use of the MOVX @DPTR,A instruction

MOVX @DPTR,A   [DPTR{M}] < – – – [A]

This instruction copies the contents of the Accumulator to the 'external memory' pointed to by the DPTR. See Figure 5.24 for an example.

MOVX A,@DPTR   [A] < – – – [DPTR{Ext_M}]

With this instruction the contents of the 'external memory' pointed to by the DPTR are copied into the Accumulator. Figure 5.25 shows an example of this operation.

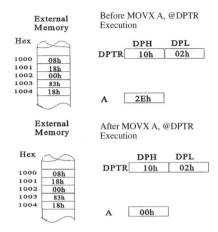

Figure 5.25 Example of the MOVX A,@DPTR instruction

5.12   Stack operation

POP direct   [direct] < – – – [SP{M}]
                       [SP]   < – – – [SP] – 1

With this operation the contents of the internal memory pointed to by the SP are copied into direct, which is an internal memory or SFR, and then the contents of the SP are decremented. Figure 5.26 shows a detailed example with Register B as the direct address.

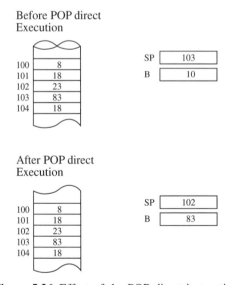

Figure 5.26 Effect of the POP direct instruction

PUSH direct   [SP]   < – – – [SP] + 1
                       [SP{M}] < – – – [direct]

With this operation the content of the SP is incremented and the contents of direct, which is internal memory or SFR, are copied into internal memory pointed to by the SP. Figure 5.27 shows a detailed example again using Register B as the direct address.

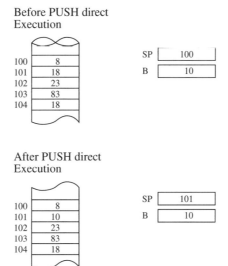

Before PUSH direct
Execution

100	8
101	18
102	23
103	83
104	18

SP | 100
B | 10

After PUSH direct
Execution

100	8
101	10
102	23
103	83
104	18

SP | 101
B | 10

Figure 5.27 Use of the PUSH direct instruction

5.13 Nibble swaps

SWAP A $\quad [A_{3-0}] \longleftrightarrow [A_{4-7}]$

In this operation the high nibble A_{4-7} is swapped with the low nibble A_{3-0}. The example shown in Figure 5.28 gives a detailed picture of this operation.

Before SWAP A Execution

	7	6	5	4	3	2	1	0
A	1	1	1	1	0	0	0	0

After SWAP A Execution

	7	6	5	4	3	2	1	0
A	0	0	0	0	1	1	1	1

Figure 5.28 Use of the SWAP A instruction

XCHD A,@Ri $\quad [A_{3-0}] \longleftarrow - - - \rightarrow [Ri\{M_{3-0}\}]$

The exchange operation allows an exchange of the low nibble A_{3-0} of the Accumulator with the low nibble of the memory location pointed to by the Ri Register (R0 or R1). An example of this is shown in Figure 5.29.

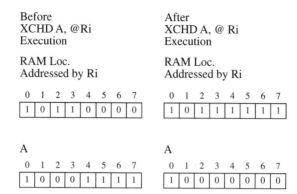

Figure 5.29 Use of the XCHD A,@Ri instruction

Summary

Data transfer operations have been discussed in detail and their addressing modes have also been mentioned. The fundamental data transfer operations such as MOV are used in applications for sending and receiving data to and from ports, registers, etc. as required. The 80C51 provides a wealth of data transfer instructions in which data can be sent and received even from external memories such as external ROM and RAM.

Exercises

1. If R0 contains 8Ah and A contains 3h, what would be the values in R0 and A after the MOV A,@R0 instruction is executed?
2. Referring to question 1, what values would the registers have after the MOV @R0,A instruction is executed?
3. Referring to question 1 what changes are made after the execution of the instruction XCH A,@R0?
4. Assume the location 13h contains a value of 04h, Accumulator A contains 1Eh, R1 contains 13h, and the Carry bit is RESET (i.e. Carry = 0). For the following program determine the contents of each of the registers mentioned above and the Carry bit after each instruction.

```
        .
        .
    MOV A,@R1
    SWAP A
    MOV @R1,A
        .
        .
```

5. Internal ROM contains the following:

Add (hex)	Data (hex)
20	A
21	B
22	C
23	D

Write a program to read the data in ROM and store the results in the registers R0–R3.

6. Repeat question 5 and assume that the data is placed in the external ROM.

6

Control Transfer Operations

6.1 Introduction

There are several control transfer operations within the 80C51 instruction set. These have been broken up into groups with each operation explained within that group. Each operation is complete with illustrations to give a clearer picture of its action. It should be noted as before that unless otherwise stated, the address locations and memory contents given in the illustrated examples of this chapter are in decimal values.

Some of the control transfer operations, such as 'bit operation' and 'conditional jumps on bits' have already been covered in the previous chapters. Here we cover the following groups of instructions: jumps, calls, compare jump not equal, and decrement jump not zero.

6.2 Unconditional

JUMPS

SJMP rel   [PC] < – – –   [PC] + 2
              [PC] < – – –   [PC] + rel

This instruction is jump short, which increments the Program Counter (PC) by 2, and then adds the relative value 'rel' (8 bits wide), which could be a positive or negative value, to the PC. This would give the address of the location where the program would continue to execute. Consider the example shown in Figure 6.1 which uses a relative value of 09h.

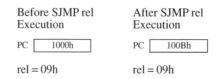

Before SJMP rel   After SJMP rel
Execution   Execution

PC [1000h]   PC [100Bh]

rel = 09h   rel = 09h

Figure 6.1 Use of the SJMP rel instruction

LJMP addr16   [PC] < – – – addr16

This is jump to absolute long range address (long range means 16-bit address). With this instruction the PC is loaded with the absolute 16-bit address 'addr16' from where the program will continue to be executed. An example is given in Figure 6.2.

Before LJMP addr16
Execution

After LJMP addr16
Execution

PC [A000h]   PC [3456h]

addr16 = 3456h   addr16 = 3456h

Figure 6.2 Use of the LJMP addr16 instruction

AJMP addr11   [PC] < – – – [PC] + 2
                   [PC] < – – – addr11

This is jump to absolute short range address (short range means 11-bit address). With this instruction the PC is loaded with the absolute 11-bit address 'addr11' from where the program will continue to be executed. The 'page address' will occupy the lower 11 bits of the PC. An example is given in Figure 6.3.

Before AJMP addr11
Execution

After AJMP addr11
Execution

PC [C011]   PC [C01F]

addr11 = C01Fh   addr11 = C01Fh

Figure 6.3 Example of the use of the AJMP addrll instruction

CALLS

When a 'call' is initiated via the software or hardware, the program is caused to jump to a location to execute a subroutine program. When the subroutine program is finished, indicated by RET or RETI, the execution of the program will continue from where it left off.

Also, there are LCALL and ACALL operations which are discussed below.

LCALL addr16   [PC]   < – – – [PC] + 3
                   [SP]   < – – – [SP] + 1
                   [SP{M}]   < – – – $[PC_{7-0}]$
                   [SP]   < – – – [SP] + 1
                   [SP{M}]   < – – – $[PC_{15-8}]$
                   $[PC_{15-0}]$ < – – – addr16

This is the long call operation, which when executed will cause the following to occur:

1. the PC is incremented by 3;
2. the Stack Pointer (SP) is incremented by 1;
3. the lower byte of the PC is pushed into the memory location pointed to by the SP;
4. the SP is incremented again by 1;

5.   the higher byte of the PC is pushed into the memory location pointed to by the SP;
6.   the PC is loaded with the value addr16, and the program continues to be executed from this new location.

Figure 6.4 shows an example of this operation.

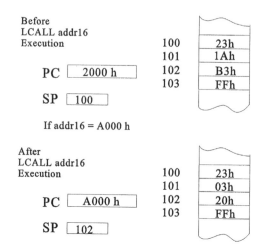

Figure 6.4 Effect of the LCALL addr16 instruction

ACALL addr11

$$
\begin{aligned}
[PC] &< --- [PC] + 2 \\
[SP] &< --- [SP] + 1 \\
[SP\{M\}] &< --- [PC_{7-0}] \\
[SP] &< --- [SP] + 1 \\
[SP\{M\}] &< --- [PC_{15-8}] \\
[PC_{10-0}] &< --- addr11
\end{aligned}
$$

This call operation is very similar to the LCALL, except that the address of the called routine is 11 bits wide, which places this routine in the same memory page for execution. When executed the following will occur:

1.   the PC is incremented by 2;
2.   the SP is incremented by 1;
3.   the lower byte of the PC is pushed into the memory location pointed to by the SP;
4.   the SP is incremented again by 1;
5.   the higher byte of the PC is pushed into the memory location pointed to by the SP;
6.   the PC is loaded with the value addr11, and the program executions continue from this new location.

Figure 6.5 shows an example of this operation.

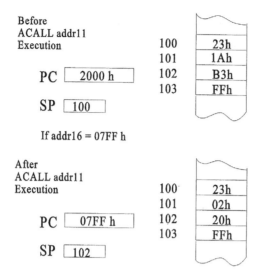

Figure 6.5 Effect of an ACALL addrll instruction

RETURNS

At the end of each subroutine which has been called by a call instruction there should be an opcode 'RET' to indicate to the controller that the execution of the program should resume from the location just after the 'call' instruction.

RET
$[PC_{15-8}]$ < − − − $[SP\{M\}]$
$[SP]$ < − − − $[SP] - 1$
$[PC_{7-0}]$ < − − − $[SP\{M\}]$
$[SP]$ < − − − $[SP] - 1$

When this instruction is encountered the following process occurs:

1. the contents of the memory location pointed to by the SP are pushed into the high byte of the PC;
2. the SP is decremented;
3. the contents of the memory location pointed to by the SP are pushed into the lower byte of the PC;
4. the SP is decremented again.

Figure 6.6 shows an example of this operation.

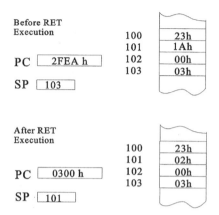

Figure 6.6 Use of the RET instruction

At the end of each interrupt routine there should be an opcode 'RETI'. This indicates to the controller that the interrupt routine has been served and program executions should recommence from the location just after the position where the interrupt occurred.

RETI $[PC_{15-8}]$ $< - - -$ $[SP\{M\}]$
            $[SP]$ $< - - -$ $[SP] - 1$
            $[PC_{7-0}]$ $< - - -$ $[SP\{M\}]$
            $[SP]$ $< - - -$ $[SP] - 1$

When this instruction is encountered the following process occurs:

1. the contents of the memory location pointed to by the SP are pushed into the high byte of the PC;
2. the SP is decremented;
3. the contents of the memory location pointed to by the SP are pushed into the lower byte of the PC;
4. the SP is decremented again.

Figure 6.7 shows an example of this operation.

TABLE JMP

JMP @A + DPTR

$[PC]$ $< - - -$ $[A] + [DPTR]$

When this opcode is used the contents of the Accumulator are added to the contents of the data page pointer and the sum loaded into the PC. For an example of this operation refer to Figure 6.8.

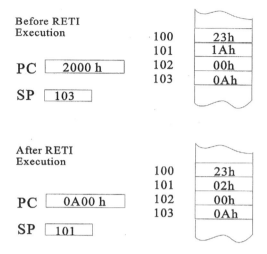

Figure 6.7 Example of the effect of the RETI instruction

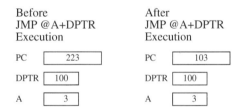

Figure 6.8 Use of the JMP@A+DPTR instruction

6.3 Conditional

COMPARE, JMP NOT EQUAL

CJNE @Ri,#data,rel

if [Ri{M}] <> data,
    [PC] < − − − [PC] + rel + 3
    C* < − − − 1
else,
    [PC] < − − − [PC] + 3
    C* < − − − 0

With this instruction the contents of the address contained in Register Ri (R0 or R1) are compared with the data value and if they are not equal the PC is loaded with the value of 'rel + 3'; this would cause the Carry flag to be set. Otherwise the PC would only be incremented by 3 and the Carry flag would be reset. An example of this instruction is shown in Figure 6.9 using Register R0.

CJNE A,#data,rel

if A <> data,
    [PC] < − − − [PC] + rel + 3

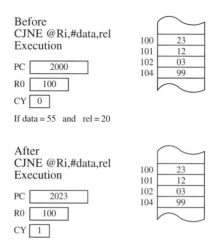

Figure 6.9 Use of the CJNE@Ri,data,rel instruction

   C* < − − − 1
  else,
   [PC] < − − − [PC] + 3
   C* < − − − 0

With this instruction the content of the Accumulator is compared with the data value, and if they are not equal the PC is loaded with the value of 'rel + 3'; this would cause the Carry flag to be set. Otherwise the PC would only be incremented by 3 and the Carry flag would be reset. An example of this instruction is shown in Figure 6.10.

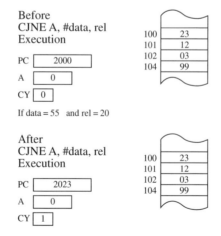

Figure 6.10 Effect of the CJNE A,#data,rel instruction

CJNE A,direct,rel

  if A <> direct,
   [PC] < − − − [PC] + rel + 3

$\quad$ C* < – – – 1

else,

$\quad\quad$ [PC] < – – – [PC] + 3

$\quad\quad$ C* < – – – 0

With this instruction the content of the Accumulator is compared with the content of the register 'direct', and if they are not equal the PC is loaded with the value of 'rel + 3'; this would cause the Carry flag to be set. Otherwise the PC would only be incremented by 3 and the Carry flag would be reset. An example of this instruction is shown in Figure 6.11.

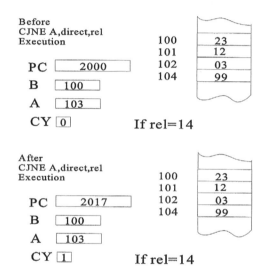

Figure 6.11 Effect of the CJNE A, direct,rel instruction

CJNE Rn,#data,rel

$\quad$ if Rn <> data,

$\quad\quad$ [PC] < – – – [PC] + rel + 3

$\quad\quad$ C* < – – – 1

$\quad$ else,

$\quad\quad$ [PC] < – – – [PC] + 3

$\quad\quad$ C* < – – – 0

This instruction operates the same as 'CJNE A,#data,rel', except that it compares the contents of Register Rn (R0 to R7) with the data. This is shown in Figure 6.12.

DJNZ Rn,rel $\quad\quad\quad\quad\quad\quad\quad\quad$ [PC] < – – – [PC] + 2

$\quad\quad\quad\quad\quad\quad\quad\quad\quad\quad\quad\quad\quad\quad\quad\quad$ [Rn] < – – – [Rn] – 1

$\quad\quad\quad\quad\quad$ if [Rn] > 0 or [Rn] < 0 [PC] < – – – [PC] + rel

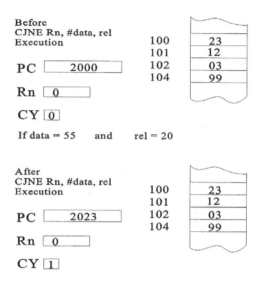

Before
CJNE Rn, #data, rel
Execution

	100	23
	101	12
PC [2000]	102	03
	104	99

Rn [0]

CY [0]

If data = 55   and   rel = 20

After
CJNE Rn, #data, rel
Execution

	100	23
	101	12
PC [2023]	102	03
	104	99

Rn [0]

CY [1]

Figure 6.12 Use of the CJNE Rn,#data,rel instruction

This instruction is 'decrement jump not zero'. First the PC is incremented by 2 and then the contents of Register Rn (R0 to R7) are decremented. If the result of the latter operation is not zero, the contents of the PC would be formed by the addition of the PC value and the 'rel' value. This operation is shown in Figure 6.13 using Register R5.

DJNZ direct,rel
$$[PC] \quad < --- \quad [PC] + 2$$
$$[direct] \quad < --- \quad [direct] - 1$$
$$\text{if } [direct] > 0, [PC] \quad < --- \quad [PC] + rel$$
$$[direct] \quad < --- \quad [direct] - 1$$
$$\text{if } [direct] < 0, [PC] \quad < --- \quad [PC] + rel$$

This is another version of the DJNZ instruction which in this case decrements the 'direct' register for the jump operation. This operation is shown in the example of Figure 6.14.

Summary

Control transfer operations mentioned here are the ones which only apply to the byte operations. There are control operations, which have been explained in the previous chapters, which only apply to the bit operations. These instructions are an important part of any microcontroller instruction set and the flow of the program is determined by such operations. These are the instructions used where a decision has to be made regarding the flow of the program.

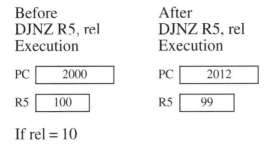

Figure 6.13 Example of the use of the DJNZ Rn,rel instruction

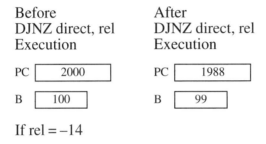

Figure 6.14 Example of the DJNZ direct, rel instruction

Exercises

1. Explain the differences between the 'JMP rel' and 'AJMP addr11' instructions.
2. Explain the differences between the 'LJMP addr16' and 'AJMP addr11' instructions.
3. What is the difference between a 'call' and a 'jump' instruction?
4. Explain when you would you use (a) a RET and (b) a RETI instruction.
5. The Accumulator contains the value 23d and the DPTR contains the value 1000d. After the execution of

    JMP @A + DPTR

   what would be contained in (a) A, (b) the DPTR, and (c) the PC?
6. If R0 contains 82d what would be the values in the PC and Carry flag after the following instruction?

    PC   opcode
    1000   CJNE @R0,#32,55

7

Programming

7.1 Introduction

When it comes to the moment of writing a program it is probable that the requirements of the engineering application the microcontroller system is to perform are reasonably well defined. There may be areas of uncertainty, but the programmer would wish to get started, to see if the system works. It may be that for large projects, programming in a high level language such as C is preferable because it makes the program more readable; this is important in industry where a team of engineers may be working on an application. It could be that each team member is responsible for part of the complete programming project and that each part can be more easily joined if the program is in a functional language such as C.

It is sometimes said that the ability to program in C makes it easier for the engineer to work with different microcontrollers since the programming level is above the machine code of the microcontroller. This is not altogether true since when using a C cross-compiler for a particular microcontroller the engineer must have a knowledge of the system architecture. For example when using 80C51 family devices the engineer must know about the Special Function Registers (SFRs) in order to configure them for particular applications. The competent engineer should have a knowledge of low level programming for the particular microcontroller, not only for confidence but also because of the final size of the compiled machine code. This is particularly relevant for the 87CXXX devices where the number 7 indicates that the device has on-board PROM and therefore a limited capacity.

The use of Assembly language programming can produce tight, minimal code and this could be an advantage. Really it is down to the skill and low level programming experience of the engineer who is familiar with the system that is being designed and would be aware of any possible programming short-cuts, for example using a short jump instruction instead of a long jump instruction. When using a C cross-compiler the engineer is handing over the task of program machine code size to the compiler designer. Cheap C cross-compilers tend to produce larger size machine code than if the program had been written in Assembly language, although it must be stated that a good quality C cross-compiler, albeit expensive, does produce minimal, tight machine code. Also the software debugging may be easier for an engineering team to comprehend if the program is written in C. Certainly it would be easier for the team manager to understand engineers' C programs and maintain an overall understanding of the project aims.

In this chapter we will investigate the low level Assembly language and the high level C language programming techniques as applicable to the microcontroller.

7.2 Assembly language programming

The cross-assembler ASM51.EXE used for programs in this book came from Philips Semiconductors' bulletin board system (bbs) on the Internet; the software originates from the Metalink Corporation. The Internet address used was

ftp://ftp.IBSystems.com/pub/Philips-MCU/bbs/

The same Internet address also has the XA_Tool.exe software, used in Chapter 11 which deals with 16-bit microcontrollers.

INTRODUCTION

The Assembly language program is generally referred to as the source program. Its name should be no more than eight characters long and it should have the extension

.ASM

for example

PROGNAME.ASM
PROG1.ASM
STEPPER.ASM

The program can be written using any convenient editor, even a word processor, so long as the file is saved in ASCII format.

After saving and exiting the program is cross-assembled, e.g.

ASM51   PROGNAME

There is no need to put the extension; the cross-assembler assumes that your program name ends with .ASM.

The cross-assembly process produces two extra files:

.LST   List file
.HEX   machine code file

The List file shows:

1. program addresses in hexadecimal numbers
2. program in hexadecimal numbers
3. syntax errors (i.e. typing mistakes)
   Corrections must be made in the .ASM file.

The machine code file consists of rows of hex (hexadecimal) numbers, each line preceded by a colon.

An example source program is shown below. If a system ran under this program then pin 4 of Port 1 would oscillate.

```
$MOD552                                  ; include file equating SFR addresses
          ORG          0                 ; reset address
          SJMP         START             ; jump over reserved addresses
          ORG          40H               ; program start address
START:    SETB         P1.4              ; set pin4 of port1 to logic 1
          CLR          P1.4              ; clear pin4 of port1 to zero
          SJMP         START             ; short jump back to start
          END                            ; end assembly
```

The corresponding List file is:

```
PROGNAME
                              PAGE 1
              1               $MOD552                ; include file equating SFR
addresses
0000          2               ORG        0           ; reset address
0000 803E     3               SJMP       START       ; jump over reserved addresses
0040          4               ORG        40H         ; program start address
0040 D294     5     START:     SETB       P1.4        ; set pin4 of port1 to logic 1
0042 C294     6                CLR        P1.4        ; clear pin4 of port1 to zero
0044 80FA     7                SJMP       START       ; short jump back to start
              8                END                    ; end assembly


VERSION 1.2h ASSEMBLY COMPLETE, 0 ERRORS FOUND
PROGNAME
                              PAGE 2
P1 ..................................... D ADDR 0090H PREDEFINED
START .................................. C ADDR 0040H
```

The corresponding machine code.file is:

```
:02000000803E40
:06004000D294C29480FA84
:00000001FF
```

This is the .HEX file, the code that would go into the system PROM (Programmable Read-Only Memory). It is clearly identified by the colon at the beginning of each line.

One of the instructions is altered, and shown below is the Progname List file, indicating the syntax error.

```
PROGNAME
                                        PAGE 1
              1          $MOD552              ; include file equating SFR addresses
0000          2          ORG    0            ; reset address
0000 803E     3          SJMP START          ; jump over reserved addresses
0040          4          ORG    40H          ; program start address
              5          START: SET P1.4      ; set pin4 of port1 to logic 1
****-----------------------------^
****ERROR #23: Illegal or missing directive
0040 C294     6          CLR P1.4            ; clear pin4 of port1 to zero
0042 80FC     7          SJMP START          ; short jump back to start
```

```
    8      END                    ; end assembly
```

VERSION 1.2h ASSEMBLY COMPLETE, 1 ERRORS FOUND
ERROR SUMMARY:
Line #5, ERROR #23: Illegal or missing directive
PROGNAME

                              PAGE 2
P1 .... D ADDR 0090H PREDEFINED
START .... C ADDR 0040H

The instruction to set a bit is SETB; the assembler points out the location of this syntax error and makes an attempt to describe the error type. The correction must be made in the source file (.ASM) which must then be re-assembled until no syntax errors remain. Note that this process only checks syntax errors; it does not check program errors. Program errors must be found by the engineer.

IMMEDIATE ADDRESSING

The small example program used Direct Addressing instructions and did not write any numbers into a location. The following is an example of Immediate Addressing (the # sign precedes the number):

```
MOV     R1,#33H            ; move the hex number 33 into register R1
MOV     R1,#51             ; move the decimal number 51 into register R1
MOV     R1,#00110011B      ; move the binary number 00110011 into R1
MOV     P1,#10H            ; a hex alternative to SETB P1.4
MOV     P1,#00010000B      ; a binary alternative to SETB P1.4
```

INDIRECT ADDRESSING

Indirect Addressing uses the sign @. It may be used with Registers R0 and R1, Program Counter (PC) and the Data PoinTeR (DPTR). The address destination is pointed to by the register used. The program lines shown below are taken from an RS232 program shown in Chapter 9. The first two lines use Immediate Addressing with the # symbol.

The first line gets the numerical address of the message (MSG1) and puts it into the DPTR. The second line clears the Accumulator by putting zero into it. The third line uses Indirect Addressing by moving the contents of the address, pointed to by the DPTR, into the Accumulator.

```
        MOV   DPTR,#MSG1      ; set Data Pointer to message address
NEXT:   MOV   A,#0            ; zeros the previous character
        MOVC  A,@A + DPTR     ; move ASCII character to accumulator A
```

In the high level C language the operator is actually called a Pointer.

ASM51.EXE is a two-pass cross-assembler. During the first pass, or scan, it builds a symbol table from the symbols and labels used. These are shown above at the end of the list file:

- P1 is the symbol for Port 1
- START is a loop label

During pass two the Source file is translated into machine code.

The 80C51 instruction set is given in Appendix A. Referring to it, it may be seen that the example program contains other symbols, consisting of labels, assembler controls and assembler directives.

ASSEMBLER CONTROLS

Assembler controls direct the flow of the program and allow program information to be given. For the cross-assembler used all assembler controls are prefaced with a dollar sign ($). Some common controls are:

        $TITLE(Port Pin Control Program)
        $PAGEWIDTH(80)

The example program shown earlier started with

        $MOD552

which for this cross-assembler is an include file listing all the SFR addresses, a very useful control since it removes the need for the programmer to remember the SFR hex addresses. Using this control the programmer can write source programs for the whole 80C51 microcontroller family, providing the number of ports and types of on-board SFRs are known.

A small part of the $MOD552 file is shown below. The full size of the include file is approximately two or three sides, but it can be seen from the size of the machine code file that all of this data is not included in the .HEX file, the two-pass assembler only uses the code requested by the program.

```
;            REV. 1.0    JUNE 13, 1988
;8xC552 REV. 1.1     January 14, 1993, G. Goodhue - Philips Semiconductors
P0          DATA       080H       ;Port 0
SP          DATA       081H       ;Stack Pointer
DPL         DATA       082H       ;Data Pointer - Low Byte
DPH         DATA       083H       ;Data Pointer - High Byte
PCON        DATA       087H       ;Power Control
TCON        DATA       088H       ;Timer Control
TMOD        DATA       089H       ;Timer Mode
TL0         DATA       08AH       ;Timer 0 - Low Byte
TL1         DATA       08BH       ;Timer 1 - Low Byte
TH0         DATA       08CH       ;Timer 0 - High Byte
TH1         DATA       08DH       ;Timer 1 - High Byte
P1          DATA       090H       ;Port 1
S0CON       DATA       098H       ;Serial Port 0 Control
S0BUF       DATA       099H       ;Serial Port 0 Buffer
P2          DATA       0A0H       ;Port 2
```

Loop label

The small example program also has a loop label START: The label name is chosen by the programmer; it must be terminated by a colon (:) and it points to a destination address.

Comments

Comments are preceded by a semicolon (;) and are used by the programmer to give a readable commentary to aid understanding of the program.

Assembler directives

These are used to:

- define symbols
- select memory spaces
- reserve memory space

The directives used in the small example program were:

- ORG 40h ; sets the program counter to address hex 0040
- END ;   means do not assemble anything after this point
- DATA ;   used in the INCLUDE file, assigns an internal memory address to a symbol

Other directives used in the book include:

- EQU   ;   EQUate labels to numbers
- COUNT EQU 100 ;   the label COUNT is equal to the number 100
- DB   ;   Define Byte, used in a serial transmission program
- MESSAGE   :   DB 'Jack and Jill' ; defined bytes corresponding to ASCII
                                       ; symbols Jack and Jill

Segment assembler directives may be used to set values in code and data memory. This cross-assembler has five segment selection directives:

- **CSEG** Program memory space,
            this is code memory or PROM.
- **BSEG** Bit memory space,
            microcontroller internal RAM between addresses 20h to 2Fh is bit addressable.
- **DSEG** Directly addressable internal data memory space,
            the lower 128 bytes of microcontroller internal RAM can be accessed by Direct and Indirect Addressing.
- **ISEG**   Indirectly addressable internal data memory space,
            the upper 128 bytes of microcontroller internal RAM, between addresses 80h and FFh, can only be indirectly addressed.
- **XSEG** eXternal data memory space,
            external memory space refers to memory space off the microcontroller which would mainly be extra RAM but could also be registers in other peripheral chips.

7.3 C program structure

A C program consists of one or more functions. Each has a name and one of these functions MUST be called main().

CONSTANTS AND VARIABLES

These can take many forms, examples of which are shown below.

```
void main(void)
{
    int event;          /* event is an integer variable */
    char heat;          /* heat is a character variable */
    float time;         /* time is a float variable */

    event = 5;
    heat = 'C';
    time = 27.25;

    printf("the winning time in heat %c",heat);
    printf("of the event %d was %f",event,time);
}
```

Initialising variables

Variables can be initialised as they are declared.

```
void main(void)
{
    int   event = 5;  ............................ /* const int event=5;*/
    char  heat = 'C';  ...................... /* const char heat = 'C';*/
    float time = 27.25;  .................. /* const float time = 27.25;*/

    printf("the winning time in heat %c",heat);
    printf("of the event %d was %f",event,time);
}
```

OPERATORS

Once variables are defined, some sort of manipulation must be performed using them. This is done by using operators. The C language has more operators than most languages. In addition to the usual assignment and arithmetic operators, C also has **bitwise** operators and a full set of logical operators.

Assignment operators

The most basic operator in C is the equal sign (=). The value on the right of the equal sign is assigned to the variable on the left, e.g.

> my_age = 22;

or stacked, e.g.

> my_age = your_age = 22;

Arithmetic operators

> * multiplication
> / division
> + addition
> – subtraction
> % modulus (integer remainder of division)

The first four operators listed are defined for all types of variable. The modulus operator is defined only for integer operand.

Arithmetic assignment operators

C allows operators to be combined with the assignment operator (=).

> e.g. x + = 3;   x = x + 3;
> e.g. x – = 3;   x = x – 3;
> e.g. x * = 3;   x = x * 3;
> e.g. x / = 3;   x = x / 3;

Increment and decrement operators

> ++   **x++;**   x + = 1;   x = x + 1;
> ––   **x––;**   x – = 1;   x = x – 1;

Relational operators

> <   less than   **if**(a < b) statement(s);
> >   greater than   **if**(a > b) statement(s);
> < = less or equal to   **if**(a < = b) statement(s);
> > = greater or equal to **if**(a > = b) statement(s);
> == equal to   **if**(a == b) statement(s);
> ! =   not equal to   **if**(a = = b) statement(s);

Logical operators

> ‖ logical OR   if(ch > 47 ‖ ch < 58)
>   digitcount ++;
> **&&** logical AND   if(ch > 47 **&&** ch < 58)
>   digitcount ++;
> ! logical NOT   if(!A) digitcount ++;

Bitwise operators

> **&**   bitwise AND   y = a **&** b;
> | bitwise OR   y = a | b;
> ^   bitwise EX-OR   y = a^b;
> ~   one's complement   y = ~ a;
> >>   shift right   a = a >> 2;
> <<   shift left   a = a << 4;

PROGRAM CONTROL

C has a complete set of program control features which allow conditional or repetition of statements based on the results of an expression.

Conditional execution

- **The if-else statement**. The 'if' statement is used to conditionally execute a series of statements based on the result of an expression. The 'if' statement has the following generic format:

```
if(results > 0)
{                                              /* positive output */
    out = 1;

    count ++;
}
else
{
    out = −1;
    count −−;
}
```

- **The switch statement**. When a program must choose between several alternatives, the 'switch' statement is used. The basic form of the 'switch' statement is as follows:

```
switch(i)
{
case 0: printf("\nError: i is zero);
        break;
case 1: send_data();
        break;
default: terminate();
}
```

Loop execution

C has three structures by which a statement or group of statements may be repeated a fixed or variable number of times.

- **The while loop**. Repeat the statements until an expression becomes false, or zero. The decision to go through the loop is made before a loop is ever started.

```
i = space_count = 0;

while(string[i])
{
if(string[i] = = ' ') space_count ++;
i ++;
}
```

- **The do-while loop**. This is used when a group of statements needs to be repeated and the exit condition should be tested at the end of the loop.

```
do{
    printf("\nEnter FFT length:");
    scanf("%d",&fft_length);
    } while(length < 1024);
```

- **The for-loop**. Combines an initialisation statement, an end condition statement and an action statement into a very powerful control structure.

```
for(i = 0 ; i<length ; i++) a[i] = 0;
```

Program jumps

The last three control statements, break, continue, and goto, allow for conditional program jumps.

- **The break statement**. This is already illustrated in conjunction with the switch statement and causes the program flow to break free of the SWITCH, FOR, WHILE control structure.
- **The continue statement**. Almost opposite BREAK, the continue causes the rest of the iteration to be skipped and the next iteration to be started.
- **The goto statement**. The goto statement in C uses a label rather than a number.

```
if(status = 0) goto error_exit;



error_exit:
```

FUNCTIONS

A function is defined by function type, a function name, a pair of parentheses containing an optional formal argument list, and a pair of braces containing the optional statements. An example of a function with one return value is shown below.

```
float average(array,size)
float array[];
int   size;
{
    int i;
    float sum = 0.0;  ....................................... /* initialise & declare */
    for(i = 0;i<size;i++)
        sum = sum + array[i];                              /*calculate sum*/
    return (sum/size);
}
```

ARRAYS AND STRINGS

Array declaration

Entering data into and reading from arrays

```
temp[2] = 24;                                    /* straight assignment */

today = temp[3];                                 /* reading from an array */
```

Initialising arrays

```
int table[7] = {50, 25, 10, 5, 1, 0, 99};

char my_name[]    = {'H', 'a', 's', 's', 'a', 'n', '\0'};
                         Null character
```

POINTERS AND ARRAYS

A Pointer is a variable that holds the address of some data, rather than the data itself.

Special Pointer operators

Two special Pointer operators are required to manipulate pointers: the **indirection operator (*)** and the **address operator (&)** . The indirection operator (*) is used whenever the data stored at the address pointed to by a Pointer is required, that is, whenever Indirect Addressing is required.

```
#include <stdio.h>
main()
{
  int i,*ptr;
  i = 7;                                         /* set the value of i */
  ptr = &i;                                      /* point to address of i */
  printf("\n%d",i);
  printf("\n%d",*ptr);
  *ptr = 11;                                     /* change i with pointer */
  printf("\n%d %d",*ptr,i);
}
```

Pointer arithmetic and manipulation of arrays

```
main()
{
  char *ptr_char;
  int *ptr_int;
    float *ptr_float;
    double *ptr_double;
  ptr_char ++;                                   /* ptr_char = ptr_char + 1 */
  ptr_int ++;                                    /* ptr_int = ptr_int + 2 */
}
```

Summary

- The chapter gives a first introduction to programming both in low and high level, initially covering Assembly language programming.
- It describes the process of writing a source program and describes the two extra files .LST and .HEX that result from the cross-assembly process, pointing out that successful completion only checks the syntax and not the program strategy.
- An introduction is made to the use of assembler controls and directives.
- It is pointed out that the program language C comprises functions, one of which must be called main().
- The method of defining constants, variables and operators is described.
- Program control structures are then described together with supporting examples.
- The use of the Pointer operator, so important when C is used for practical applications, is described. To increase the reader's understanding, the description of the C Pointer should be compared with the method of Indirect addressing as used in the Assembly language section.

Exercises

Low level

1. State the two file extensions following the successful cross-assembly of a program.
2. What is a source program?
3. What is a syntax error?
4. Does the successful cross-assembly of a program prove the program strategy or the program syntax?
5. What symbol is at the first line in a .HEX file?
6. Which file shows all the hex addresses?
7. Which file would indicate syntax errors?
8. What symbol precedes a comment?
9. What symbol identifies an Immediate instruction?
10. Which memory space does BSEG cover?
11. Can internal RAM address 92h be directly addressed?
12. State the memory address ranges covered by BSEG, DSEG and ISEG.
13. Briefly describe the method of Indirect Addressing, by example if necessary.
14. What would ORG 50H set if used in a program?
15. What information does $MOD552 give?
16. What is meant by a two-pass assembler? And what is the process in each pass?
17. What do you think $PAGEWIDTH(76) means?
18. How would you include a title into a program?

High level

19. What is the difference between the / and % operators?
20. What do += , −= , * = , and / = do?
21. What do the + + and −− operators do?
22. What are the differences between the && and & operators?
23. What are the differences between the || and | operators?

24. What are the differences between ! and ∼ ?

25. A variable is $A = 23$. What would its value be if $A = A >> 2$; is used ?

26. What are the differences between the while (condition) { } loop and the do { } while (condition) loop ?

27. If integer $A = 32$ and is placed in memory location 1000 and the integer pointer IP = &A; is used, what would be the value of A after the instruction *IP ++;?

28. If Port 1 address is pointed to by Pointer PI and data 25 is placed on the Pointer, how would you use the Pointer PI to send the data into the Accumulator A?

8

Switches, Motors and Displays

8.1 Introduction

Invariably switches and diodes are required for control and display purposes in a typical microcontroller system. The switches could be single manual on/off, or push-to-make, and used to start the system. Alternatively there could be a group of switches to select various system options. Transistors could be used as electronic switches to drive small inductive loads such as a relay or solenoid valve or in fact small electric motors.

Function displays could use single LEDs (Light Emitting Diodes) or LEDs manu-factured as seven segment displays, either single-digit or multi-digit. LCD (Liquid Crystal Diode) displays are quite common giving a better character definition with usually more characters and a much lower power consumption. The LED display is brighter than the LCD type although it is possible to obtain backlit LCD displays.

LEDs require a greater driving current than LCDs and it is important to ensure, when choosing the microcontroller for a particular application, that the port pin can actually supply the necessary current. If the device cannot supply the required current, and another microcontroller type is not wanted, then a device driver buffer, which could just be a common logic device, should be used.

Programs are included in this chapter to illustrate the application of switches, motors and displays using a microcontroller device. As an aid to the reader the program format is both Assembly language and C.

8.2 Manual switch

Typically a single switch could be manual on/off or push-to-make or a microswitch. Normally it would be connected to a dc supply to provide a particular logic level. Figure 8.1(a) and 8.1(b) shows typical resistor values for logic 0 and logic 1 switches.

In Figure 8.1(a), when the switch is not depressed the connection to the port is at logic 0 or 0 V. When the switch is pressed and held the switch circuit output would be directly connected to + 5 V dc, i.e. logic 1.

A small Assembly language routine that loops continuously until the switch is pressed is shown below; the program assumes the switch output is connected to Port 1 pin 0 (i.e. p1.0):

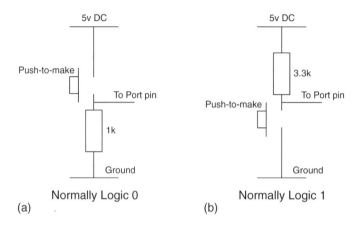

Figure 8.1 (a) Switch arrangement to give normally logic 0. (b) Switch arrangement to give normally logic 1

```
$MOD552                    ; include file for 80C552 microcontroller
       ORG 0               ; reset start address at 0
       SJMP START          ; short jump over reserved address field
       ORG 30H             ; program start address
START: JNB P1.0, START     ; jump to start if p1.0 is not bit (i.e. logic 0)
       END                 ; assembler directive
```

The C program routine for the above program is:

```
#include <reg552.h>        /* define 80552 registers */

main ()    {               /* main program */
    while (P1^0==0) {}      /* repeat forever while bit0 = 0 */
}
```

It should be stressed that this is not a complete program. It would be satisfactory until the switch is pressed. Then it would stop looping and run into whatever was in the rest of the EPROM, probably FFs.

If the normally high or logic 1 switch was used then the JNB operation shown in the above Assembly program should be changed for the JB operation.

The following Assembly language program is one that could be part of a dc motor speed control system. The program checks the logic level of three switches and if one is pressed it jumps to that speed control routine; if no switches are pressed then it keeps the dc motor turned off.

The three switches are connected to P1.0, P1.1 and P1.2, the dc motor is turned on by a logic 1 on P1.7 and off by a logic 0 on the same pin.

```
$MOD552                    ; include file for 80C552 microcontroller
       ORG 0               ; reset start address
       SJMP START          ; jump over reserved address field
       ORG 30H             ; program start address
```

```
START: JB P1.0,SPEED1   ; jump to speed1 routine if switch logic on p1.0 = 1
       JB P1.1,SPEED2   ; jump to speed2 routine if switch logic on p1.1 = 1
       JB P1.2,SPEED3   ; jump to speed3 routine if switch logic on p1.2 = 1
       CLR P1.7         ; turn motor off by clearing p1.7 to 0
       SJMP START       ; keep looping while switch not pressed
       END              ; assembler directive
```

The program would not run successfully if a switch were pressed. In fact, because the speed labels do not have destination addresses, the cross-assembly process would give syntax errors which would be identified in the .LST file.

The C program would be as follows:

```
#include <reg552.h>              /* define 80552 registers */
sbit MOTOR  = P1^7;              /* I/O pin : motor switch */
sbit SPEED1 = P1^0;              /* I/O pin : speed1 switch */
sbit SPEED2 = P1^1;              /* I/O pin : speed2 switch */
sbit SPEED3 = P1^2;              /* I/O pin : speed3 switch */

void speed1()    {/* the 'C' code for speed1 control */}
void speed2()    {/* the 'C' code for speed2 control */}
void speed3()    {/* the 'C' code for speed3 control */}

main ()     {                    /* main program */
    do{                          /* repeat forever */
    if     (SPEED1) speed1();/* speed1 routine */
    if     (SPEED2) speed2();/* speed2 routine */
    if     (SPEED3) speed3();/* speed3 routine */
    MOTOR = 0;                   /* turn off motor */
    } while (1);
}
```

Again the program is incomplete and is included for indicative purposes only.

8.3 Electronic switch

A transistor can be considered as an electronic switch. The device is very useful in this mode since it can be remotely turned on or off by voltages from the microcontroller. The necessary voltages are: logic 0 to turn the device off and logic 1 to turn it on. Figure 8.2 shows a typical circuit using a bipolar npn transistor.

With the correct choice of resistor R and a logic 1 (i.e. $+5$ V) on the port pin the transistor would be turned on, causing it to conduct. Under these conditions the transistor behaves like an on switch (i.e. passes a current with a low voltage drop across the device). Current would flow through the motor and, providing the current gain of the transistor was correct, the motor would rotate.

It is necessary to know the worst case motor current (which would be the start up current when the motor was mechanically loaded). Such information could be obtained from the motor specification sheet or by direct measurement. Placing a multi-meter in series with the dc motor supply, not forgetting to set the meter to amps, should provide the required current value. The value of the port current applicable to this circuit is given by equation 1,

$$I_{\text{port}} = \frac{I_{\text{motor}}}{h_{\text{FE}}} \tag{1}$$

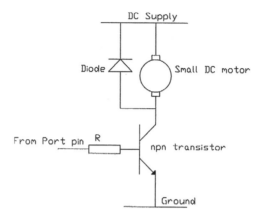

DC Supply

Diode

Small DC motor

From Port pin   R

npn transistor

Ground

Figure 8.2 Transistor used as a switch to drive a small inductive load

where h_{FE} is the transistor forward current gain.

Equation 1 indicates that the port current is equal to the worst case motor current divided by the transistor current gain. The transistor current gain value is usually given in component catalogues and is usually given either as a range of values or as a minimum value. If it is given as a range of values then the smallest value should be used to give the required worst case design. It is also necessary to ensure that the transistor can handle the motor current. Component catalogues normally give the transistor maximum current I_c. A transistor with a maximum I_c of twice the motor current should be chosen. To select a device with a maximum current value I_c equal to the motor current could cause the transistor to run hot.

Also it is necessary to check that the microcontroller port can supply the calculated port current; the 80C31, for example, is a very useful microcontroller but its port pins have a low current capability.

There are ways of dealing with the port current problem. One method is to use a Darlington transistor which usually has a very large current gain (could be at least 1000). Another method is to connect unused port pins together so that the total current supplied is the summation of these individual port pins. If these solutions are insufficient then a pair of inverter logic gates (e.g. 74LS04) could be connected in series between the resistance R and the microcontroller port pin. For this arrangement the transistor input current comes from the logic IC power supply.

The formula to find a suitable value of resistance (R) is given in equation 2:

$$R = \frac{(5V - V_{BE})}{I_{port}} \qquad (2)$$

The value of resistance is determined by the port pin logic 1 voltage (5 V) minus the transistor base emitter voltage, divided by the calculated port current. The base emitter voltage V_{BE} may be assumed to be 0.7 V.

The diode is included to reduce the induced back emf. A back emf is induced when currents are switched through inductive loads. This induced emf can be quite large, e.g. the spikes could be as high as 60 V for a dc supply of 12 V. Such spikes would impede the transistor action and could prevent the circuit from functioning correctly. This is certainly true when currents in the region of 1 A and above are switched and it is good practice to always include a diode when switching inductive loads.

Note that for normal, non-induced circuit, voltages the diode is connected in reverse bias, with its cathode towards the motor positive dc supply.

An Assembly language program to turn the motor on when a switch is depressed could be:

```
$MOD552                 ; include file for the 80C552
        ORG 0           ; reset address
        SJMP START      ; short jump over reserved addresses
        ORG 30H         ; program start address
START:  JB P1.0, MOTOR  ; if switch on p1.0 = 1 then jump to motor routine
        CLR P1.7        ; put logic 0 on p1.7 and turn motor off
        SJMP START      ; jump back to check switch
MOTOR:  SETB P1.7       ; put logic 1 (+5v) on p1.7 and turn motor on
        SJMP START      ; jump back to check switch
        END             ; assembler directive, do not cross-assemble after
                        ; this point.
```

The C program version would be:

```
#include <reg552.h>        /* define 80552 registers */

#define ON 1
#define OFF 0

sbit MOTOR = P1^7;          /* I/O pin : motor switch */
sbit SWITCH = P1^0;         /* I/O pin : switch */

main ()    {                /* main program */

    do{                     /* repeat forever */
      while(!SWITCH)        /* while switch is OFF, motor off */
      {MOTOR = OFF;}
      MOTOR = ON;           /* switch motor ON */
    }while(1);
}
```

This is a complete program. If the switch is not pressed then the motor remains turned off. If the switch is depressed continually the motor rotates. If the switch is push-to-make then if the finger is taken off the button the motor stops.

8.4 Mark/Space ratio

Figure 8.2 can be used for small inductive loads such as solenoid valves, relays, small stepper motors. It is not really a good arrangement for dc motors since the transistor is continually conducting and tends to get warm. This could be compensated for by the use of a heat sink to increase the effective surface area of the transistor.

A popular method of driving dc motors is to apply a variable Mark(on)/Space(off) rectangular wave signal. The advantage of this technique is twofold:

1. The transistor runs cooler because it is being turned on and off.

2. The method can be used to control the speed by varying the Mark/Space ratio.

The frequency of the Mark/Space signal should be much higher than the on/off response of the motor, e.g. at 2 kHz, the motor armature (rotor) has momentum and the angular speed is continuous.

A large Mark/Space ratio has a high average voltage and therefore a fast speed while a low Mark/Space ratio signal has a low average voltage and the motor rotation is slower. Care should be taken to ensure the average voltage is not too low otherwise the motor might not start. The principle is illustrated by Figure 8.3.

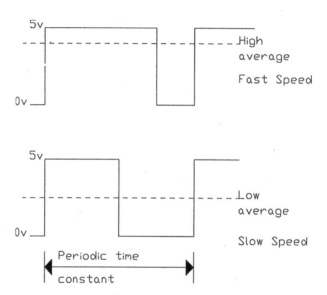

Figure 8.3 Examples of different Mark/Space ratios to give high and low speeds

An Assembly language program that will send a Mark/Space ratio signal to pin 7 on Port 1 is appended below:

```
$MOD552                         ; include file for 80C552
            ORG     0           ; reset address
            SJMP    START       ; jump over reserved address field
            ORG     30H         ; programme start address
START:      SETB    P1.7        ; set pin 7 port 1 to logic 1 (i.e. 5volts)
            ACALL   DELAYM      ; call subroutine delay mark
            CLR     P1.7        ; clear pin 7 port 1 to zero
            ACALL   DELAYS      ; call subroutine delay space
            SJMP    START       ; repeat the M/S routine
DELAYM:     MOV     R1,#0D0H    ; move hex number D0 into register 1
TAKEM:      DJNZ    R1,TAKEM    ; decrement r1 and repeat if r1 is not zero
            RET                 ; return from subroutine if r1=0
DELAYS:     MOV     R1,#2FH     ; move hex 2F into r1
TAKES:      DJNZ    R1,TAKES    ; decrement r1 and jump if not zero to takes
            RET                 ; return from subroutine if r1=0
            END                 ; assembler directive
```

There are two things to note about this program. The first point concerns the line:

MOV   R1,#0D0H

It is only hex D0 that is being put into Register r1 but in common with a lot of cross-assemblers it is necessary to precede the hex digit with a zero. If it is omitted then a cross-assembly syntax error will occur. It was not necessary for the line:

MOV   R1,#2FH

because the hex number started with a decimal digit.

The second point about this program is the use of a delay. Delay routines are very common and essential in many applications. Certainly it is true in this example where a logic level is being held. Delays can be made using the Timer/counter SFRs (Special Function Registers) or by using the method in this example where the delay depends on the time taken to reduce the number in r1 to zero. The method is:

```
DELAY MOV Rn,#hex number    ; mov hex number into register n (n = 1 to 7)
LOOP: DJNZ Rn, LOOP         ; keep decrementing rn until it becomes zero
      RET                   ; return from subroutine
```

The C version of the main program is:

```
#include < reg 552.h >       /* define 80552 registers */

#define MARK 1
#define SPACE 0

sbit MOTOR = P1^7;           /* I/O pin : motor switch */

void delay_M()
{
    int DELAY_M = 0xD0;      /* set mark delay value */
       while (- - DELAY_M);  /* repeat until is zero */
}
void delay_S()
{
    int DELAY_S = 0xD0;      /* set space delay value */
       while (- - DELAY_S);  /* repeat until is zero */

}

main ()    {                 /* main program */
   do{                       /* repeat forever */
     {MOTOR = MARK;}         /* motor ON */
     delay_M();              /* call MARK delay */
     MOTOR = SPACE;          /* motor OFF */
     delay_S();              /* call SPACE delay */
   }while(1);
}
```

8.5 Two-speed program

An Assembly language program that provides for a two-speed arrangement could be:

```
$MOD552                             ; include file for 80C552 microcontroller
        ORG     0                   ; reset address
        SJMP    START               ; jump over reserved address field
        ORG     30H                 ; programme start address
START:  JB      P1.0,SPEED1         ; jump to speed1 if button on p1.0 is pressed
        JB      P1.1,SPEED2         ; jump to speed2 if button on p1.1 is pressed
        CLR     P1.7                ; motor off if no button is pressed
        SJMP    START               ; keep checking switches
SPEED1: SETB    P1.7                ; motor on
        ACALL   DELAYM1             ; speed1 Mark hold delay for motor on
        CLR     P1.7                ; motor off
        ACALL   DELAYS1             ; speed1 Space hold delay for motor off
        SJMP    START               ; check switch is still pressed
SPEED2: SETB    P1.7                ; motor on
        ACALL   DELAYM2             ; speed2 Mark hold delay for motor on
        CLR     P1.7                ; motor off
        ACALL   DELAYS2             ; speed2 Space hold delay for motor off
        SJMP    START               ; check switch is still pressed
DELAYM1: MOV    R1,#0D0H            ; Speed1 Mark delay, put hex D0 into r1
TAKEM1: DJNZ    R1,TAKEM1           ; reduce r1 to zero
        RET                         ; return from subroutine to clr p1.7
DELAYS1: MOV    R1,#2FH             ; Speed1 Space delay, put hex 2F into r1
TAKES1: DJNZ    R1,TAKES1           ; reduce r1 to zero
        RET                         ; return from subroutine to clr p1.7
DELAYM2: MOV    R1,#0A0H            ; Speed2 Mark delay, put hex A0 into r1
TAKEM2: DJNZ    R1,TAKEM2           ; reduce r1 to zero
        RET                         ; return from subroutine
DELAYS2: MOV    R1,#5FH             ; Speed2 Space delay, put hex 5F into r1
TAKES2: DJNZ    R1,TAKES2           ; reduce r1 to zero
        RET                         ; return from subroutine
        END                         ; assembler directive
```

Speed1 Mark delay depends on hex D0 and the Space delay depends on hex 2F whereas Speed 2 Mark delay depends on hex A0 and the Space delay depends on hex 5F. Speed1 has the higher average and therefore the faster speed.

Note that in both cases the Mark number plus Space number have the same total:

$$D0 + 2F = FF$$
$$A0 + 5F = FF$$

So although their averages are different their frequencies are both the same and this is normal for the variable Mark/Space speed method.

The C version of the two-speed program is:

```
#include <reg552.h>        /* define 80552 registers */

#define MARK    1
#define SPACE   0
#define ON      1
#define OFF     0
```

```
sbit MOTOR  = P1^7;            /* I/O pin : motor switch */
sbit SPEED1 = P1^0;            /*I/O pin : speed1 switch */
sbit SPEED2 = P1^1;            /* I/O pin : speed2 switch */

void delay_M1()
{
    int DELAY_M1 = 0xD0;       /* set mark1 delay value */
       while(- - DELAY_M1);    /* repeat until is zero */
}
void delay_S1 ()
{
    int DELAY_S1 = 0xD0;       /* set space1 delay value */
       while(- -DELAY_S1);     /* repeat until is zero */
}
void delay_M2()
{
    int DELAY_M2 = 0xA0;       /* set mark2 delay value */
       while(- -DELAY_M2);     /* repeat until is zero */
}
void delay_S2()
{
    int DELAY_S2 = 0x5F;       /* set space2 delay value */
       while(- -DELAY_S2);     /* repeat until is zero */
}
void speed1()                  /* speed1 routine */
{
    MOTOR = ON;                /* put the motor ON */
    delay_M1();                /* call the delay for MARK1 */
    MOTOR = OFF;               /* turn motor OFF */
    delay_S1();                /* call the delay for SPACE1 */
}
void speed 2()                 /* speed 2 routine */
{
    MOTOR = ON;                /* put the motor ON */
    delay_M2();                /* call the delay for MARK2 */
    MOTOR = OFF;               /* turn motor OFF */
    delay_S2();                /* call the delay for SPACE2 */
}
main ()    {                   /* main program */
    do{                        /* repeat forever */
      if(SPEED1) speed1();     /* speed1 routine */
      if(SPEED2) speed 2();    /* speed2 routine */
      MOTOR = 0;               /* turn off motor */
    }while(1);
}
```

8.6 Stepper motor

Stepper motors are used extensively in electronic circuits. One possible application is for the disk drive in a computer that is stepped by a controlling program to a particular location where one of the user programs is stored.

Basically stepper motors are of two types. There is the relatively cheap type that rotates through 7.5 degrees per step or 48 steps per revolution. The more expensive type has a basic resolution of 1.8 degrees per step; it is possible to half step this type so that it has a resolution of 0.9 degrees per step. The resolution of both types can be improved by the addition of a step-down gearbox. A gearbox would also increase the torque, or turning force, of the motor shaft.

Compared in physical size to a dc motor, the stepper motor has a much lower torque; its advantage is in positional control.

The stepper motor has four sets of coils and when logic level patterns are applied to each set of coils the motor shaft steps through its angles. If a dc voltage is applied to a dc motor then it will begin to rotate at a very fast speed, rotating through many revolutions per second. The speed of the stepper motor shaft depends on how fast the logic level patterns are applied to the four sets of coils. The stepping motor drive circuit can be four sets of the circuit of Figure 8.2.

The stepping motor code is provided by the manufacturer in the motor specification data sheet; a very common stepping code is given by the hex numbers:

A	9	5	6

Each hex digit is equal to four binary bits:

1010	1001	0101	0110

These binary bits represent voltage levels to be applied to each of the coil driver circuits.

The steps are:

1010	5 V	0 V	5 V	0 V
1001	5 V	0 V	0 V	5 V
0101	0 V	5 V	0 V	5 V
0110	0 V	5 V	5 V	0 V

If the pattern is sent repeatedly then the motor shaft rotates.

An Assembly language program to continually rotate the stepper motor shaft could be:

```
$MOD552                         ; include file for 80C552
            ORG 0               ; reset address
            SJMP START          ; jump over reserved address field
            ORG 30H             ; program start address
START:      MOV P1,#0AH         ; move hex 0A into lower 4 bits of port 1
            ACALL DELAY         ; call subroutine step hold delay
            MOV P1,#09H         ; move hex 09 into lower 4 bits of port 1
            ACALL DELAY
            MOV P1,#05H         ; move hex 05 into lower 4 bits of port 1
            ACALL DELAY
            MOV P1,#06H         ; move hex 06 into lower 4 bits of port 1
            ACALL DELAY
            SJMP START          ; repeat stepping pattern
                                ;
                                ; Double loop delay
DELAY:      MOV R1,#0FFH        ; put hex FF into register 1
OUTER:      MOV R0,#0FFH        ; put hex FF into register 0
INNER:      DJNZ R0,INNER       ; decrement r0 until it is zero
            DJNZ R1,OUTER       ; decrement r1, go to outer until r1 = 0
            RET                 ; return from subroutine
            END                 ; assembler directive
```

Stepper motors cannot rotate as fast as dc motors and a larger step hold delay may be required. This program has a double loop delay and alteration of the number in r0 will give fine control over the speed whilst the number in r1 will give coarse variations in speed. It is assumed that the four lower pins of Port 1 (p1.0 to p1.3) are each connected to the four drive circuits of Figure 8.2.

The C program version would be:

```
#include < reg552.h>                  /* define 80552 registers */
#define STEPPER P1
void inner_delay()
{
    int INNER_DELAY = 0xFF;          /* set inner delay value */
      while(- -INNER_DELAY);         /* repeat until is zero */
}
void delay()
{
    int OUTER_DELAY = 0xFF;          /* set outer delay value */
      while(- -OUTER_DELAY)          /* repeat until is zero */
          inner_delay();             /* call inner delay */
}
main ()    {                         /* main program */
    do{                              /* repeat forever */
        STEPPER = 0x0A;              /* send the first byte to the motor */
            delay();
        STEPPER = 0x09;              /* send the second byte to the motor*/
            delay();
        STEPPER = 0x05;              /* send the third byte to the motor */
            delay();
        STEPPER = 0x06;              /* send the fourth byte to the motor */
            delay();
    }while(1);
}
```

The stepper motor will reverse if the code is sent in the opposite order:

      6   5   9   A

The following programs assume the stepper motor is still connected to pins p1.0 to p1.3 and in addition there are two push-to-make switches, one on p1.7 (forward) the other on p1.6 (reverse). When no button is pressed the stepping motor shaft is stationary.

```
$MOD552                                ; include file for 80C552
            ORG     0                  ; reset address
            SJMP    START              ; jump over reserved address field
            ORG     30H                ; program start
START:      JB      P1.7, FORWARD ; if p1.7 button pressed jump to forward
            JB      P1.6, REVERSE ; jump to reverse if p1.6 button pressed
            SJMP    START              ; check switches, motor will be off
```

```
FORWARD:    MOV     P1, #0AH        ; one step forward
            ACALL   DELAY           ; step hold delay
            MOV     P1,#09H         ; next step forward
            ACALL   DELAY
            MOV     P1,#05H         ; next step forward
            ACALL   DELAY
            MOV     P1,#06H         ; next step forward
            SJMP    FORWARD         ; keep rotating forward
REVERSE:    MOV     P1, #06H        ; one step back
            ACALL   DELAY           ; step hold delay
            MOV     P1,#05H         ; another step back
            ACALL   DELAY
            MOV     P1,#09H         ; another step back
            ACALL   DELAY
            MOV     P1,#0AH         ; another step back
            SJMP    REVERSE         ; stay in reverse
; First part of delay routine checks p1.7 and p1.6, if they are both at zero
; then the logic result of ANDing hex C0 will give zero and the program jumps
; back to testing the switches. This technique is known as masking and
; enables the simultaneous logic level testing of more than one pin.
; p1.7 and p1.6 will both be zero when both push-to-make switches are
; released; this would stop the motor.
DELAY:      MOV     A,P1            ; move the port 1 logic levels to
                                    ; accumulator
            ANL     A,#0C0H         ; AND logically Acc with the hex number C0
            JZ      START           ; if the result is zero then jump back to
                                    ; start.
            MOV     R1,#0FFH        ; put hex FF into register 1
OUTER:      MOV     R0,#0FFH        ; put hex FF into register 0
INNER:      DJNZ    R0,INNER        ; decrement r0 until it is zero
            DJNZ    R1,OUTER        ; decrement r1, go to outer until r1 = 0
            RET                     ; return from subroutine
            END                     ; assembler directive
```

The equivalent program in C would be:

```c
#include <reg552.h>             /* define 80552 registers */
#define STEPPER P1

sbit FORWARD = P1^7;            /* I/O pin : forward switch */
sbit REVERSE = P1^6;            /* I/O pin : reverse switch */

void delay()
{
    int OUTER_DELAY;
    int INNER_DELAY;

    OUTER_DELAY = 0xFF;          /* set outer delay value */
    while(--OUTER_DELAY)         /* repeat until is zero */
    {
    INNER_DELAY = 0xFF;          /* set inner delay value */
    while(--INNER_DELAY);        /* repeat until is zero */

    }
```

```
void forward()
{
    STEPPER  =  0x0A;              /* send the first byte to the motor */
        delay();
    STEPPER  =  0x09;              /* send the second byte to the motor */
        delay();
    STEPPER  =  0x05;              /* send the third byte to the motor */
        delay();
    STEPPER  =  0x06;              /* send the fourth byte to the motor */
        delay();
}

void reverse()
{
    STEPPER  =  0x06;              /* send the fourth byte to the motor */
        delay();
    STEPPER  =  0x05;              /* send the third byte to the motor */
        delay();
    STEPPER  =  0x09;              /* send the second byte to the motor */
        delay();
    STEPPER  =  0x0A;              /* send the first byte to the motor */
        delay();
}
main ()
{                                  /* main program */
    do{                            /* repeat forever */
      if(FORWARD) forward();
      if(REVERSE) reverse();
    }    while(1);
}
```

8.7   Illuminating an LED

It is necessary to provide the specified current in order for the LED to have the correct brightness so the current output of the microcontroller port pins must be checked.

Component catalogues normally give the forward bias current I_F and the forward bias voltage V_F of the LED; they are related by the following formula:

$$R = \frac{V - V_F}{I_F}$$

where:

V is the dc supply voltage, normally 5 V
R is the resistor in series with the LED.

Assuming the microcontroller port can supply the necessary current then there are two options, current source or current sink. Current sourcing occurs when the LED anode is driven from the port pin by a logic 1 (+ 5 V) with the LED cathode connected to the circuit ground.

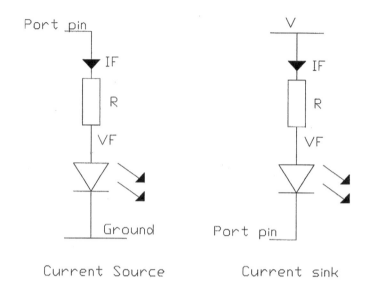

Current Source   Current sink

Figure 8.4 Driving an LED using current sourcing and current sinking

Current sinking occurs when the LED cathode is placed at logic 0 (0 V) by the microcontroller pin with the LED anode towards the circuit dc supply voltage. Figure 8.4 shows the two options.

Suitable programs are included below:

```
;Program to drive LED in current sink mode
$TITLE(Current sink LED driver program, flash on/off)
$DATE(10th December)
$MOD51
            ORG    0             ; reset start address
            SJMP   START         ; jump over reserved address space
            ORG    20H           ; program start address
; single LED, cathode connected to port 1 pin 1 (p1.1)
; anode connected via a resistor to + 5 volts.
START:      CLR    P1.1          ; puts cathode to logic 0, turns LED on
            ACALL DELAY          ; holding delay
            SETB   P1.1          ; puts cathode to logic 1, turns LED off
            ACALL DELAY          ; holding delay, sets flashing speed
            SJMP START           ; repeat
DELAY:      MOV    R3, #0FFH     ; triple loop holding delay
LOOP2:      MOV    R2, #0FFH
LOOP1:      MOV    R1, #0FFH
TAKE:       DJNZ   R1,TAKE
            DJNZ   R2,LOOP1
            DJNZ   R3,LOOP2
            RET
            END
```

Using C:

```
#include <reg552.h>            /* define 80552 registers */
sbit LED_Cathode = P1^1;       /* I/O pin : LED cathode */
```

```c
void inner_delay()
{
    int INNER_DELAY = 0xFF;          /* set inner delay value */
      while(- -INNER_DELAY);         /* repeat until is zero */
}
void middle_delay()
{
    int MIDDLE_DELAY = 0xFF ;        /* set inner delay value */
      while(- -MIDDLE_DELAY)         /* repeat until is zero */
             inner_delay() ;         /* call inner delay */
}

void delay()
{
    int OUTER_DELAY = 0xFF  ;        /* set outer delay value */
      while(- -OUTER_DELAY)          /* repeat until is zero */
             middle_delay() ;        /* call middle delay */
}

main ()       {                      /* main program */
  do{                                /* repeat forever */
    LED_Cathode = 0;                 /* turn LED ON */
    delay();
    LED_Cathode = 1;                 /* turn LED OFF */
    delay();
  }while(1);
}
```

```asm
;Program to drive eight LEDs connected in current source mode to port 1
$TITLE(Hex LED Flasher)
$MOD51
            ORG     0               ; reset start address
            SJMP    START           ; jump over reserved address space
            ORG     20H             ; program start address
START:      MOV     ACC, #0         ; clear the accumulator
            MOV     P1, #0          ; turn all LEDs off
AGAIN:      ACALL DELAY             ; call holding delay
            INC     ACC             ; increment the accumulator
; what happens when the accumulator eventually increments FF ?
            MOV     P1,ACC          ; contents of accumulator to port 1
            SJMP    AGAIN           ; continue
DELAY:      MOV     R3, #0FFH       ; triple loop delay
LOOP2:      MOV     R2, #0FFH
LOOP1:      MOV     R1, #0FFH
TAKE:       DJNZ    R1,TAKE
            DJNZ    R2,LOOP1
            DJNZ    R3,LOOP2
            RET
            END
```

While in C:

```
#include <reg552.h>                /* define 80552 registers */

void inner_delay()
{
    int INNER_DELAY = 0xFF;        /* set inner delay value */
      while(- -INNER_DELAY);       /* repeat until is zero */
}

void middle_delay()
{
    int MIDDLE_DELAY = 0xFF;       /* set inner delay value */
      while(- -MIDDLE_DELAY)       /* repeat until is zero */
          inner_delay();           /* call inner delay */
}

void delay()
{
    int OUTER_DELAY = 0xFF;        /* set outer delay value */

      while(- -OUTER_ DELAY)       /* repeat until is zero */
          middle_delay();          /* call middle delay */
}
main ()
{                                  /* main program */
    do{                            /* repeat forever */
              ACC = 0;             /* accumulator set to zero */
              P1 = ACC;            /* turn LEDs ON */
              delay();
              ACC ++;              /* increment Accumulator */
              P1 = ACC;            /* turn LEDs OFF */
              delay();
              }while(1);
}
```

Seven segment displays actually have eight LEDs in their package; the eighth LED is usually the decimal point. The arrangement is shown in Figure 8.5.

The segment LEDs could be connected to Port 1 in current source mode as shown by Table 8.1:

Table 8.1 Port 1 pin connections to seven-segment LED display

p1.7	P1.6	P1.5	P1.4	P1.3	P1.2	P1.1	P1.0
dp	g	f	e	d	c	b	a

To illuminate the number 3 the hex code segments dp, f and e should be off and therefore the hex code onto Port 1 would be 4Fh. For the number 4 the hex code on Port 1 would be 66h. It is left as an exercise for the reader to determine the required arrangement for the remaining decimal numbers.

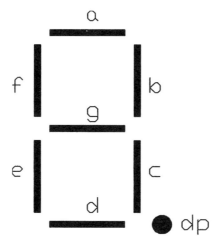

Figure 8.5 Seven segment display

Some ASCII characters are difficult to represent in seven segments so that upper and lower case letters have to be used. For example lower case letters would be required for n and b.

Some ASCII characters are not possible with seven segments. Characters such as K and X cannot be reproduced.

Consider the following programs:

```
; Program to display a repeated count from 0 to 4
$MOD51
            ORG 0                 ; reset start address
            SJMP START            ; jump over reserved addresses
            ORG 20H               ; program start address
START:      MOV P1,#3FH           ; hex for 0
            ACALL DELAY           ; hold delay
            MOV P1,#06H           ; hex for 1
            ACALL DELAY           ; hold delay
            MOV P1,#5BH           ; hex for 2
            ACALL DELAY           ; hold delay
            MOV P1,#4FH           ; hex for 3
            ACALL DELAY           ; hold delay
            MOV P1,#66H           ; hex for 4
            ACALL DELAY           ; hold delay
            SJMP START            ; start again
DELAY:      MOV R3,#0FFH          ; triple loop delay
LOOP 2:     MOV R2,#0FFH
LOOP 1:     MOV R1,#0FFH
TAKE:       DJNZ R1,TAKE
            DJNZ R2,LOOP1
            DJNZ R3,LOOP2
            RET                   ; return from subroutine
            END                   : assembler directive
```

Using C:

```
#include <reg552.h>                    /* define 80552 registers */

void inner_delay()
{
    int INNER_DELAY = 0xFF;            /* set inner delay value */
        while(- -INNER_DELAY);         /* repeat until is zero */
}

void middle_delay()
{
    int MIDDLE_DELAY = 0xFF ;          /* set inner delay value */
        while(- -MIDDLE_DELAY)         /* repeat until is zero */
            inner_delay()    ;         /* call inner delay */
}

void delay()
{
    int OUTER_DELAY = 0xFF  ;          /* set outer delay value */
        while(- -OUTER_DELAY)          /* repeat until is zero */
            middle_delay()   ;         /* call middle delay */
}

main ()
{                                      /* main program */ ·
    do{                                /* repeat forever */
        P1 = 0x3F;                     /* display 0 */
            delay();
        P1 = 0x06;                     /* display 1 */
            delay();
        P1 = 0x5B;                     /* display 2 */
            delay();
            delay();
        P1 = 0x6D;                     /* display 4 */
            delay();

        }while(1) ;
}
```

8.8   Four digit seven segment display

Figure 8.6 shows the seven segments driven from Port 1 and it may be seen from the diagram that the seven segment display is a common cathode type. A general purpose bipolar transistor is used as a switch to control the current through the LEDs.

This example presumes an 80C552 microcontroller is being used and the transistor is being switched from pin 5 of Port 3.

In the four digit display the seven segments of each of the four digits are all connected to one port, port 1 in this example.

The transistors for each digit are controlled from Port 3. The scheme is shown in Figure 8.7 where each digit block is similar to Figure 8.6.

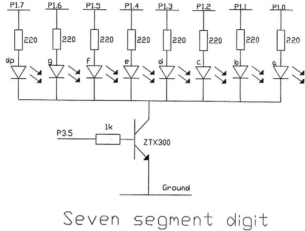

Figure 8.6 Seven segment display using common cathode

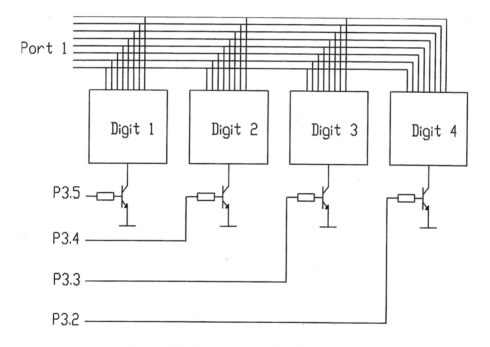

Figure 8.7 Seven segment four digit display

All the LED segments are connected together in this time-multiplexed display and each character is applied to all four digits. However, only one digit is turned on at any one time by the switching transistor.

Suppose the LEDs were to display:

FrEd

The hex numbers for each digit would be:

F	71H
r	50h
E	78h
d	5Ch

Each digit would be switched on from Port 3:

F	r	E	d
P3.5	P3.4	P3.3	P3.2

The digits are illuminated at a rate fast enough to deceive the human eye, so that all four characters would appear to be displayed simultaneously.

An example program could be:

```
$MOD552
               ORG 0                ; reset address
               SJMP START           ; jump reserved addresses
               ORG 20H              ; start address of program
START:         MOV P1, #71H         ; segment data for F to port 1
               SETB P3.5            ; first digit turned on
               ACALL DELAY          ; digit hold delay
               CLR P3.5             ; first digit turned off
               MOV P1, #50H         ; segment data for r to port 1
               SETB P3.4            ; second digit turned on
               ACALL DELAY          ; digit hold delay
               CLR P3.4             ; second digit turned off
               MOV P1, #78H         ; segment data for E to port 1
               SETB P3.3            ; third digit turned on
               ACALL DELAY          ; digit hold delay
               CLR P3.3             ; third digit turned off
               MOV P1, #5CH         ; segment data for d to port 1
               SETB P3.2            ; fourth digit turned on
               ACALL DELAY          ; digit hold delay
               CLR P3.2             ; fourth digit turned off
               SJMP START           ; repeat
; digit hold delay
DELAY:         MOV R1,#0FFH         ; hex FF into register r1
TAKE:          DJNZ R1, TAKE        ; decrement r1 until it is zero
               RET                  ; return from delay subroutine
               END                  ; assembler directive
```

Using C:

```c
#include <reg552.h>              /* define 80552 registers */
#define ON 1
#define OFF 0
sbit DIGIT1 = P3^5;             /* I/O pin : seven segment switch */
sbit DIGIT2 = P3^4;             /* I/O pin : seven segment switch */
sbit DIGIT3 = P3^3;             /* I/O pin : seven segment switch */
sbit DIGIT4 = P3^2;             /* I/O pin : seven segment switch */

void delay()
{
    int DELAY = 0xFF;           /* set delay value */
    while(- -DELAY);            /* repeat until is zero */
}
```

```
main ()          {                       /* main program */
         P3 = 0x00;                       /* All seven segs OFF */
    do{                                   /* repeat forever */
         P1 = 0x71;                        /* segment data for letter "F" */
             DIGIT1 = ON;                  /* first digit is turned ON */
                delay();
             DIGIT1 = OFF;                 /* first digit is turned OFF */

             P1 = 0x50;                    /* segment data for letter "r" */
             DIGIT2 = ON;                  /* second digit is turned ON */
                delay();
             DIGIT2 = OFF;                 /* second digit is turned OFF */

             P1 = 0x78;                    /* segment data for letter "E" */
             DIGIT3 = ON;                  /* third digit is turned ON */
                delay();
             DIGIT3 = OFF;                 /* third digit is turned OFF */

             P1 = 0x5C;                    /* segment data for letter "d" */
             DIGIT4 = ON;                  /* fourth digit is turned ON */
                delay();
             DIGIT4 = OFF;                 /* fourth digit is turned OFF */
    }while(1);
}
```

8.9 Liquid crystal display

LCDs are increasingly used. They take low power and their character matrix gives a much better definition than the seven segment display.

The LCD character matrix can be 35 points, seven high and five across.

Usually the LCD is driven by its own on-board microcontroller and this makes the display of ASCII characters much easier.

The main point to remember about LCDs is that they are much slower than the microcontroller and it is important when programming to wait for the Busy flag to clear.

Generally these intelligent LCDs have 14 pins as indicated in Table 8.2.

Table 8.2 Pin-out symbols and functions for 14-pin LCDs

Pin number	Symbol	Function
1	V_{SS}	0 V (ground)
2	V_{DD}	+ 5 V
3	V_o	Contrast adjustment voltage
4	RS	L: Instruction code input
		H: Char. data input
5	R/W	H: Data Read
		L: Data Write
6	EN	Enable signal
7–14	P1.0 to P1.7	8-bit data bus line

The LED display is inherently brighter although it is possible to purchase LCDs that are backlit. Such devices are, of course, more expensive.

The following example programs are for an LCD having two lines with 16 characters per line.

```
$TITLE(16 × 2 LCD display)
$MOD552                              ; Philips 80C552 Microcontroller 68 pin
                                     ; PLCC
; LCD 16 × 2 display
; P3.2 (/INT0) = RS    RS = 0 Command    RS = 1 Character Data
; P3.3 (/INT1) = R/W
; P3.4 (T0) = Enable
;
              ORG       0            ; origin 0
              SJMP      START        ; jump to start
              ORG       20H          ; new origin 0020
; Initialise LCD Commands
;

START:   CLR       P3.3       ; R/W = Write
         MOV       A, #38H    ; 8bits/ch,2 rows, 5 × 7 dots/ch
         ACALL     COMM       ; check if busy and write ch
         MOV       A, #0EH    screen on, cursor on, no blink
         ACALL     COMM
         MOV       A, #06H    ; cursor R/L, cursor
         ACALL     COMM
         MOV       A, #01H    ; clear LCD and memory, home cursor
         ACALL     COMM

; Messages, Top line
         MOV       DPTR, #MSG1 ; 'Good morning'
         ACALL     LCDATA
; Bottom line
; move cursor to bottom line
         CLR       P3.2       ; RS = 0 setting p1 to Control
         CLR       P3.3       ; RW = 0
         MOV       A, #0C0H   ; MOVe cursor to bottom line
         ACALL     COMM       ; command strobe
;
; bottom line message
         MOV       DPTR, #MSG2 ; 'everybody'
         ACALL     LCDATA
         MOV       A,ADCH
         ACALL     DISPL
;
; return cursor to start
         CLR       P3.2       ; RS = 0 setting p1 to Control
         CLR       P3.3       ; RW = 0
         MOV       A, #02H    ; Return display and cursor to start
         ACALL     COMM       ; Command strobe
; stop the program
HERE:    SJMP      HERE       ; a forever loop i.e. a stop
; set pointer and look for end of message
```

```
LCDATA:    MOV       A, #00H          ; beginning of table
           MOVC      A, @A+DPTR       ; setting data pointer
           CJNE      A, #7EH, MOD1    ; end of message. ASCII for ~ is 7E hex
           RET                        ; return from subroutine
; send character
MOD1:      ACALL     DISPL            ; display message
           INC       DPTR             ; next letter in display
           SJMP      LCDATA           ; jump to send character routine
; messages to be sent
MSG1:      DB    'Good morning~'      ; top line message
MSG2:      DB    'Everybody~'         ; bottom line message
; Command strobe, used when RS=0 and RW=0/1
COMM:      MOV       P1, #0FFH        ; set port 1 to FF
           SETB      P3.3             ; RS=1 Command busy check
           CLR       P3.2             ; R/W = write data
WAITC:     CLR       P3.4             ; Enable low
           SETB      P3.4             ; Enable high
           JB        P1.7, WAITC      ; Read data, back to waitc if busy
           CLR       P3.4             ; Enable low, end of check busy
           CLR       P3.3             ; RW=0 preparation for write command
           CLR       P3.2             ; RS=0
           MOV       P1, A            ; Acc A to port1, Control Reg on LCD
           SETB      P3.4             ; Enable high. Write LCD command
           CLR       P3.4             ; Enable low
           RET                        ; return from subroutine
; Display strobe, used when RS=1 and RW=0/1
DISPL:     MOV       P1, #0FFH        ; set port 1 to ff
           SETB      P3.3             ; RW=1 preparation for check busy flag
           CLR       P3.2             ; RS=0
WAITD:     CLR       P3.4             ; Enable low
           SETB      P3.4             ; Enable high
           JB        P1.7, WAITD      ; Read data, back to waitd if busy
           CLR       P3.4             ; Enable low, end of check busy
           CLR       P3.3             ; RW=0 preparation for write data
           SETB      P3.2             ; RS=1
           MOV       P1, A            ; Acc A to port 1
           SETB      P3.4             ; Enable high, write data when Enable hi/lo
           CLR       P3.4             ; Enable low
           RET                        ; return from subroutine
           END                        ; assembler directive
```

Using C:

```
/*******************************************************************
 *          this program is left for the reader to complete        *
 *******************************************************************/
#include <reg552.h>          /* define 80552 registers */
#define ON 1
#define OFF 0
```

```
#define WRITE 0
#define READ 1
sbit RS            = P3^2;      /* I/O pin : LCD RS pin */
sbit Read_Write    = P3^3;      /* I/O pin : LCD READ/WRITE pin */
sbit Enable        = P3^4;      /* I/O pin : LCD Enable pin */

char *message1 = "Good Morning";
char *message2 = "EveryBody~";

void Comm()
{

}

void Display()
{

}

main ()                                /* main program */
{
        Read_Write = WRITE;            /* set the write mode */
              ACC = 0x38;              /* 8 bits/ch, 2 rows, 5×7 dots/ch */
                  Comm();              /* check if busy and write ch */
}
```

Summary

This chapter:

- gives practical examples of how to apply logic level inputs using manual switches;
- introduces the bipolar transistor as an electronic switch and shows examples of the switching of small dc motors and other low current inductive loads;
- introduces the multi-loop delay which is based on decrementing registers down to zero. It should be emphasised at this point that an alternative delay is produced using the Timer/Counter registers (see chapter 11); both methods are in popular use;
- introduces the variable Mark/Space ratio as a method for variable speed drive of small dc motors which is convenient for microcontroller applications;
- confirms that the same transistor circuit may be used as the basic design for a stepper motor drive circuit and describes the method of driving this type of motor;
- gives programming examples and illustrated practical circuits on how to illuminate single LEDs and seven segment LED displays;
- gives an example on how to drive a two line dot matrix LCD.

Exercises

1. What do the letters LED and LCD stand for?
2. JNB P1.2,LOOP Does the program jump to LOOP if P1.2 is 1 or 0?
3. Using a transistor as a switch, the motor current is 400 mA and the Port pin current must not exceed 5 mA. What is the minimum h_{FE}?

4. (a) Using Assembly language write a triple loop delay using registers R1, R2, R3. Put hex FF in each register.
(b) Repeat using C language.
5. A Mark/Space ratio signal has 5 V on for 800 μs and 0 V for 200μs.
(a) What is the frequency of the signal?
4. (b) What is the average voltage?
(c) What Mark/Space ratio times would give an average of 3 V?
6. R1 contains hex FF and is incremented once. What hex number does it now contain?
7. Explain the action of the instruction DJNZ and give an example of its use.
8. A subroutine is called using ACALL. What instruction makes the program return from the subroutine?
9. Locate one example of Indirect Addressing in this chapter.
10. A stepper motor has a stepping angle of 7.5 degrees and rotates at a speed of 20 revolutions per minute. How long is each step held for?
11. Write a program in (a) Assembler, (b) C, that would rotate the stepper motor shaft three revolutions and then stop.
12. A 2 mA low current LED is directly driven from a microcontroller pin, and the LED V_F is 1.8 V. What suitable preferred value resistor should be used?
13. A seven segment display is connected to Port 1 as shown in the chapter. What hex numbers on port 1 would display d, A, V, E?
14. Draw a diagram of what you think would represent a common cathode seven segment display.
15. Give an example of where an LCD would be used in preference to an LED display.
16. Give an example of where an LED display would be preferable to an LCD.
17. Explain the action of the CJNE instruction and give an example of its use.
18. Which assembler directive in the last program of the chapter was used to define ASCII characters?
19. What does the instruction SETB P1.7 do, and what equivalent MOV instruction would perform the same function?
20. Which microcontrollers do $MOD552, $MOD51 and $MOD750 refer to?
21. How may the ANL instruction be used to detect a logic 1 on P1.4?

9

Serial Data Transmission

9.1 Introduction

This chapter covers two types of serial transmission.

- IIC or I²C (Inter Integrated Circuit) is designed primarily for data exchange between Integrated Circuits (ICs) on the same printed circuit board (pcb); it can also be used between boards or equipment where the joining cable length is no more than approximately 4 m.
- RS232, which is a common standard used for data exchange between different processor systems.

Both types of communication require supporting software but this can be minimal if the microcontroller has Special Function Registers (SFRs) to facilitate the data transfer. Initially each of the two sections will outline the hardware requirements necessary to effect the communication.

9.2 RS232 (hardware)

The voltage levels along an RS232 line are approximately -10 V for logic 1 and $+10$ V for logic 0 whereas the logic levels of the microcontroller are $+5$ V for logic 1 and 0 V for logic 0. Clearly one of the hardware requirements is for a device to convert these dc levels and the MAX232 from Maxim is extensively used. The alternative MAX233 is easier to use, in that it does not require external capacitors, but it is more expensive.

Figure 9.1 shows the connection of the MAX232 for a typical duplex connection. The capacitors are all the same value, typically 22 µF tantalum. Duplex refers to systems that can pass data in both directions. Half duplex communicates in one direction at a time whereas full duplex can pass data in both directions simultaneously. A simplex system can pass data in one direction only. The large voltage difference between the two logic levels, in an RS232 system, allows long cables to be used with reduced noise interference. Figure 9.2 shows an example circuit for a duplex connection between a microcontroller and a PC.

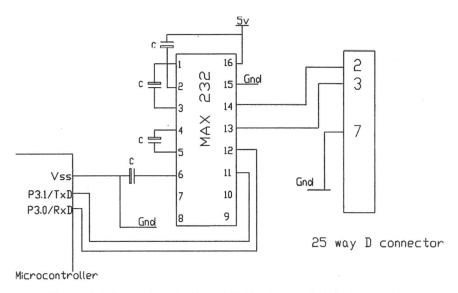

Figure 9.1 Connections for the MAX 232 for a typical duplex operation

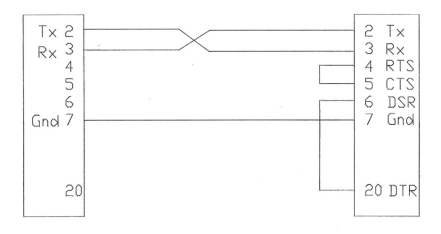

Figure 9.2 Typical arrangement for a duplex connection between a microcontroller and a PC

9.3   RS232 (software)

Some of the 80C51 family of microcontrollers have special registers to facilitate serial transmission. Such special registers are referred to as UART (Universal Asynchronous Receiver/Transmitter) registers. The 80C51 type microcontroller has many SFRs and the two associated with the RS232 serial transmission are:

SOCON   Serial 0 CONtrol
SOBUF   Serial 0 BUFfer

Both are 8-bit SFRs with the Control register SOCON being bit addressable. The 0 is used to distinguish between RS232 and IIC on microcontrollers capable of both types of serial communication; IIC uses 1. The 80C552 is an example of such a device, whereas the number is omitted when the microcontroller has only one type of serial transmission, i.e. the 80C51 has SCON and SBUF registers as described in Chapter 2.

There are three modes of UART operation in the 80C51 family, Modes 0, 1 and 2. Mode 0 is the Shift register mode; the Standard UART is Mode 1 while Mode 2 is the multi-processor mode. This chapter will concentrate on the Standard UART mode.

9.4 Baud rate

One of the first tasks to be undertaken is to set the speed of data transmission and this is defined by the baud rate. Baud rate refers to the speed at which bits are sent down the RS232 line, the number of transitions per second, and there are standard rates. Common baud rates are multiples of 75 bits per second (bit/s) and are typically:

75, 150, 300, 600, 1200, 2400, 4800, 9600, 19 200, 38 400 bit/s

In Mode 1, the Timer/counter registers of the microcontroller are used to set the baud rate. For a description of the baud rate in Modes 0 and 2, see Chapter 2.

The baud rate may be deduced from the formula:

$$\text{baud rate} = \frac{2^{SMOD}}{32} \times \frac{f_{osc}}{12 \times [256 - (TH1)]}$$

where f_{osc} is oscillator frequency.

SMOD is either 0 or 1 and is bit 7 in the PCON (Power CONtrol) register. This has been discussed in Chapter 2 and reference should be made to that chapter if more information on baud rate is required. The value put into TH1 (Timer High byte) will decide how quickly the up-counter rolls over. Re-arranging the equation gives:

$$TH1 = 256 - \frac{2^{SMOD} \times f_{osc}}{384 \times \text{baud rate}}$$

As an example, to set a baud rate of 9600 bit/s:

$$SMOD = 0, f_{osc} = 11.0592 \text{ MHz}$$

This gives TH1 = 253 decimal or FD in hexadecimal. Note that the microcontroller in this example used an 11.0592 MHz crystal which gave TH1 as a whole number and this would have been the case for any of the baud rates given above.

The example highlights the necessity of choosing the correct crystal value if it is required to use a standard baud rate for this, mode 1, operation.

EXAMPLE 9.1

An Assembly program that illustrates the concept is as follows:

```
; an example program transmitting one ASCII character, letter 'A'
;
$MOD552                             ; to fit an 80C552 microcontroller
          ORG    0                  ; reset address origin at 0
          SJMP   START              ; short jump to start of program
          ORG    40H                ; start address starts after reserved
                                    ; address space
;
; Initialise for serial transmission
;
START:    MOV    S0CON,#42H         ; hex 42 into SCON, for 8 bit UART Tx only
          MOV    PCON,#0            ; zero into PCON puts SMOD (PCON.7) = 0
          MOV    TH1,#0FDH          ; hex FD to Timer High byte for 9600 baud
          MOV    TMOD,#20H          ; hex 20 to Timer Mode reg for 8 bit auto-
                                    ; reload
          SETB   TR1                ; turn Timer on, running at baud rate, TR1 in
                                    ; TCON
;
; Send ASCII character
;
          MOV    S0BUF,#'A'         ; move ASCII character A into Serial Buffer
TXBUF:    JNB    TI,TXBUF           ; loop till Transmit Interrupt is set
          CLR    TI                 ; clear Transmit Interrupt (SCON.1)
FINISH:   SJMP   FINISH             ; continually loop i.e. a stop
          END                       ; assembler directive
```

Note the method of transmission; the data to be transmitted is loaded into the serial buffer S0BUF:

        MOV   S0BUF,#'A'

and then the program waits for the transmission to complete by continually branching until TI is set:

        TXBUF: JNB TI,TXBUF

A similar method is used for the I²C method of serial transmission.

This program sends a single character through the RS232 port.

For purposes of application the microcontroller RS232 was connected via a cable to the serial input of a PC. The PC was running Procomm, a common and popular communications software package, it was configured to run at 9600 baud, 8 data bits, 1 stop bit. Each time the microcontroller reset was pressed a letter A appeared on the PC screen.

For this first example it is useful to spend some time considering the initialisation since it will be similar for the following RS232 examples. Five SFRs are used:

SCON   Serial CONtrol
PCON   Power CONtrol
TH1   Timer 1 High byte
TMOD   Timer MODe control
TCON   Timer CONtrol

SCON

SM0	SM1	SM2	REN	TB8	RB8	TI	RI
bit 7	bit 6	bit 5	bit 4	bit 3	bit 2	bit 1	bit 0

Bits 7 and 6 are used to define the mode. This chapter will be concentrating on Mode 1, specified by:

> SM0 = 0
> SM1 = 1

which gives an 8-bit UART with variable baud rate.

SM2 is primarily for use with Modes 2 or 3 but if set to 1 in Mode 1 then it would affect the action of RI (the receive interrupt), so it will be left set to 0.

Receive ENable (REN), bit 4, is set by software to logic 1 to enable reception. A zero would disable receive. REN is set to zero in this program since the program's function is only to transmit. The first four bits are thus set to binary 0100 or decimal 4.

Bits 3 and 2 are used with Modes 2 or 3. Bit 1 is described in the manufacturer's handbook as a Transmit Interrupt (TI) flag, set by hardware.

Once the program is running TI will be set by the transition of the byte through the SBUF, the serial buffer, and yet the first line of the initialisation program apparently sets TI by software:

> MOV S0CON,#42h

Decimal 2 in binary is 0010. Regardless of this anomaly it is necessary to set the TI bit by software in order to get the transmit function to start.

It is not necessary to set RI, the Receive Interrupt, in the initialisation part of a program that uses the receive function since receive is initiated by an external signal, e.g. PC keyboard stroke.

> MOV PCON,#0

ensures that bit 7 in the Power Control register is zero.

The PCON bit 7 defines SMOD; if SMOD = 1 then the baud rate is doubled. This is not required in this example so SMOD is set to 0.

> MOV TH1,#0FDh

puts hex FD into the Timer 1 High byte register. This number was calculated earlier from the formula to give a baud rate of 9600 when an 11.0592 MHz crystal was used.

Note that some cross-assemblers give syntax errors if the zero is omitted (e.g. MOV TH1,#FDh).

> MOV TMOD,#20h

ensures that hex FD is automatically reloaded.

> SETB TR1

sets bit 6 in the register and this turns the timer on; the timer may be turned off by putting TCON.6 to zero.

As another example, consider the requirement to receive and transmit a single character.

EXAMPLE 9.2

The program below is designed to receive a keyboard character from the PC and re-transmit it back to the PC screen. Again the software was tried on a PC running Procomm.

- -

```
$MOD552                    ; include file equating labels to addresses
        ORG  0             ; reset to zero
        SJMP START         ; short jump over reserved address field
        ORG  40H           ; program start address
;
; Initialisation
START:  MOV  SOCON,#52H    ; mode 1, REN enabled, TI set to 1 for initial start
        MOV  PCON,#0        ; set SMOD to 0, no doubling of baud rate
        MOV  TH1,#0FDH      ; hex FD into timer high byte to define 9600 baud
        MOV  TMOD,#20H      ; automatically reload hex FD
        SETB TR1           ; turn the timer on
; receive character
RXBUF:  JNB  RI,RXBUF      ; check for received byte from PC
        CLR  RI            ; clear RI, ready for next PC character
        MOV  A,SOBUF       ; move character byte from buffer to ACC
; send received character
        MOV  SOBUF,A       ; move character into serial buffer and transmit
TXBUF:  JNB  TI,TXBUF      ; test for TX finished
        CLR  TI            ; clear TI, ready for next character to be
                             transmitted
        SJMP RXBUF         ; go back to receive a character
        END                ; assembler directive
```

Note the change to S0CON, the Serial Control register. As well as being set to mode 1, the receive bit REN has also been set to enable the receive function. The transmit check line is still in:

      TXBUF: JNB TI,TXBUF

looping until the transmit buffer is empty, setting TI.
   Earlier in the program there is a similar line for the receive buffer,

      RXBUF: JNB RI, RXBUF

looping until the keyboard character is received and then setting RI.
   Data is transmitted as soon as a byte is moved into the serial buffer. TI is set and must be cleared in order for another byte transmission to proceed.

EXAMPLE 9.3

Consider another example which will send a line of text. This program sends a string of ASCII characters to the PC screen.

```
$MOD552
          ORG       0                ; reset start address
          SJMP      START            ; jump over reserved address space
          ORG       40H              ; program start address
START:    MOV       S0CON,#42H       ; set 8 bit UART, enable Transmit Int flag
                                     ; (TI)
          MOV       PCON,#0          ; set SMOD = 0, i.e. K = 1 for baud rate
          MOV       TH1,#0FDH        ; hex FD into Timer High byte, 9600 baud
          MOV       TMOD,#20H        ; Timer 1, 8 bit auto-reload
          SETB      TR1              ; turn Timer on
; carriage return
CRTN1:    JNB       TI,CRTN1         ; stay here till TI is set
          CLR       TI               ; clear TI
          MOV       S0BUF,#0DH       ; carriage return hex into serial buffer
; line feed
LFEED1:   JNB       TI,LFEED1        ; stay here till TI is set
          CLR       TI               ; clear TI
          MOV       S0BUF,#0AH       ; line feed hex into serial buffer
; carriage return
CRTN2:    JNB       TI,CRTN2         ; another carriage return
          CLR       TI
          MOV       S0BUF,#0DH
LFEED2:   JNB       TI,LFEED2        ; another line feed
          CLR       TI
          MOV       S0BUF,#0AH
; send message (msg)
          MOV       DPTR,#MSG1       ; set Data Pointer to message address
NEXT:     MOV       A,#0             ; zeroes the previous character
          MOVC      A,@A + DPTR      ; move ASCII character to accumulator A
          CJNE      A,#7EH,TRX       ; checking end of string i.e. hex 7E is ASCII ~
          ACALL     DELAY            ; delay between message lines
          AJMP      CRTN1            ; goto line feed and carriage return
; send character
TRX:      JNB       TI,TRX           ; wait till TI is set
          CLR       TI               ; clear TI
          MOV       SOBUF, A         ; transmit message character
          INC       DPTR             ; point to next character
          AJMP      NEXT             ; get next character
MSG1:     DB        'Roses are red, violets are blue ~'
; double loop delay routine between lines.
DELAY:    MOV       R0,#0FFH         ; move hex FF into register R0
TAKE0:    MOV       R1,#0FFH         ; move hex FF into register R1
TAKE1:    DJNZ      R1,TAKE1         ; keep decrementing R1 until it is zero
          DJNZ      R0,TAKE0         ; keep decrementing R0 until it is zero
          RET                        ; return from subroutine
          END                        ; assembler directive
```

Note how the message is defined: DB define byte. Apart from the last one, the whole string of ASCII characters within ' ~ ' are passed to the PC screen; the character ~ is used to identify the end of the string. There is also carriage return and line feed control of the cursor. Note the use of the data pointer DPTR and MOVC to move program data.

9.5   Inter integrated circuit

The I²C bus or IIC bus was originally developed as a control bus for linking micro-controller and peripheral ICs for Philips' consumer products. The simplicity of a 2-wire bus that combined both address and data bus functions was quickly adopted in such diverse applications as:

* telecommunications
* automotive dashboards
* energy management systems
* test and measurement products
* medical equipment
* point of sales terminals
* security systems

This patented Philips method of serial data transmission uses two lines, one a Serial CLock (SCL) and the other for Serial DAta (SDA). The SDA line is bidirectional; data can go up it or down it.

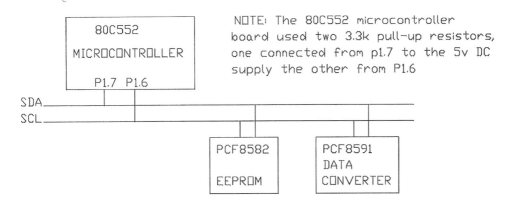

Figure 9.3 Typical hardware configuration with the 80C552 microcontroller as the master with two slave devices

A typical hardware configuration is depicted by Figure 9.3, which shows an 80C552 microcontroller as the master and the two slave devices, described in this chapter. The I²C can manage more than two slave devices and indeed can have a second microcontroller. Figure 9.3 shows that for the 80C552, pin 7 on Port 1 is the SDA line and that pin 6 is the SCL line. When used for I²C these two pins configure as open drain and it is necessary to have a pull-up resistor from each pin to 5 V. The 80C552 board used 3.3 kΩ resistors.

There are other microcontrollers belonging to the 80C51 family that have I²C SFRs, for example the 8XC652, 80CL410 and the 87C751.

It is important to note that there appear to be two classes of I²C, certainly as regards the hardware. The 8XC652, which is pin compatible with the 8XC51 has the same SFRs as the 80C552, also SDA is on Port 1 pin 7 and SCL is on Port 1 pin 6. This is also true for the 80CL410, which is pin compatible with the 8XC51 although if its low power option is pursued by using a 32 kHz clock crystal then probably the crystal decoupling passive component arrangement will be different.

The 87C751 and 87C752 are different; pin 1 on Port 0 is SDA and pin 0 on Port 0 is SCL, the I²C SFRs are I2DAT (DATa), I2CON (CONtrol), I2STA (STAtus) and I2CFG (ConFiGuration).

There are four modes of operation:

1   Master Transmitter
2   Master Receiver
3   Slave Receiver
4   Slave Transmitter

The master is the microcontroller while the slave is the device addressed by the microcontroller. However, in a system having two microcontrollers the master at a particular time is the one issuing the commands.

Philips manufacture a whole range of I²C slave devices. The range includes:

- memories, EEPROM and static RAM
- data converters
- LCD drivers
- I/O ports
- clock/calendars
- DTMF/tone generators
- TV decoders
- teletext decoders
- video processors
- audio processors

For purposes of explaining the IIC bus this chapter will deal with the 80C552 micro-controller and the slave devices:

PCF 8582   a 256-byte CMOS EEPROM
PCF 8591   an 8-bit A/D and D/A converter with four ADC channels.

The IIC bus serial interface block diagram is shown in Figure 9.4. As shown in Figure 9.4, the 80C552 has four IIC SFRs as follows:

S1CON   Serial 1 CONtrol
S1STA   Serial 1 STAtus
S1DAT   Serial 1 DATa
S1ADR   Serial 1 ADdRess

The S1ADR is used only in the Slave Transmitter mode, a mode that will not be covered in this chapter.

The S1DAT register is used to transmit a byte of data in much the same way as the S0BUF register was used for the RS232 UART operation. You may recall that when data was transmitted in the S0BUF the program waited, via a continuous loop, until the Transmit Interrupt (TI) bit was set. A similar method is used for the IIC bus; data is put into S1DAT and then the program continually loops until the Serial Interrupt (SI) bit is set. Data in S1DAT is stable as long as S1 is set. Data in S1DAT is always shifted right-to-left; the first bit to be transmitted is the MSB (bit 7). After a byte has been received the first bit of received data is located at the MSB of S1DAT. While data is being shifted out, data on the bus is simultaneously being shifted in; S1DAT always contains the last data byte present on the bus.

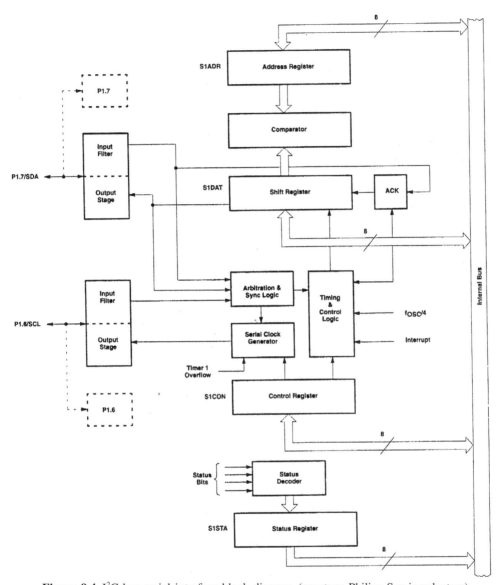

Figure 9.4 I²C bus serial interface block diagram (courtesy Philips Semiconductors)

Only the five most significant bits of the S1STA register are used and these are used to give information on the success or failure of each part of the IIC serial transmission.

The S1CON register is very important. It controls each part of the serial transmission and is worth looking at in some detail.

S1CON

CR2	ENS1	STA	STO	SI	AA	CR1	CR0
bit 7	bit 6	bit 5	bit 4	bit 3	bit 2	bit 1	bit 0

CR2,1,0 are used to define the serial clock speed (see Table 9.1).

Table 9.1 Bit assignment for CR2,1,0 to define the serial clock speed

CR2	CR1	CR0	f_{osc} divided by:
0	0	0	256
0	0	1	224
0	1	0	192
0	1	1	160
1	0	0	960
1	0	1	120
1	1	0	60
1	1	1	96 $\times$ (256 – reload value Timer 1)

The 80C552 experiment board used by the authors had a value of f_{osc} = 11.0592 MHz.

- ENS1 = ENable Serial 1
  = 1 to enable the IIC.

  When ENS1 is 0 the SDA and SCL outputs are in a high impedance state and SDA and SCL input signals are ignored. The ST0 bit (bit 4 of S1CON) is forced to 0. No other bits are affected. P1.6 and P1.7 may be used as open-drain I/O ports.

- STA = STArt and is used to generate Starts; refer to IIC protocol later.
- STO = STOp and is used to generate Stops; refer to IIC protocol later.
- SI = Serial Interrupt.
- AA = Assert Acknowledge.

These last four control bits are very important in the use of the IIC bus.

9.6   Use of the SI bit

SI is usually cleared by software and **SI is set when a function completes**.

EXAMPLE 9.4

Example of the use of SI:

```
; program to send a Start (STA = 1)
    SETB    STA         ; set STA = 1
    CLR     SI          ; clear SI
    JNB     SI,$        ; continually loop until SI = 1, then STA will = 1
```

```
; program to send a Stop (STO = 1)
    SETB    STO            ; set STO = 1
    CLR     SI             ; clear SI
    JNB     SI,$           ; continually loop until SI = 1, then STO will = 1
; program to send data e.g. #04h
    CLR     STA            ; clear start (STA = 0)
    MOV     S1DAT,#04H     ; put hex 4 into S1DAT
    CLR     SI             ; clear SI
    JNB     SI,$           ; continually loop until SI = 1, then S1DAT will
                           ; contain #04h
; program to set up transmission speed, send a stop, send a start, clear SI
; this is an example of the start of a typical IIC program
; the 80C552 f_osc is 11.0592 MHz, divide by 224 for clock cycle time
    MOV     S1CON,#51H     ; clock cycle time 20μs, set ENS1, set STOp, clear SI
    SETB    STA            ; set STArt
    CLR     SI             ; clear SI
    JNB     SI,$           ; continually loop till SI is set


; program to send Assert Acknowledge (AA)
; Note that AA is active low, a clear AA is sent to assert the acknowledge
    CLR     AA             ; clear AA to assert acknowledge
    CLR     SI             ; clear SI
    JNB     SI,$           ; continually loop till SI is set
```

The rest of the IIC explanation will be based on two design examples, using the slave devices mentioned previously.

9.7   Using the PCF8582 EEPROM

This 256-byte memory device can be written to by the microcontroller and retain the information even though the power is turned off. It is specified to have data retention for at least 10 years. It would be very useful for battery powered remote sensing devices and many more applications. It is in an 8-pin package as shown by Figure 9.5.

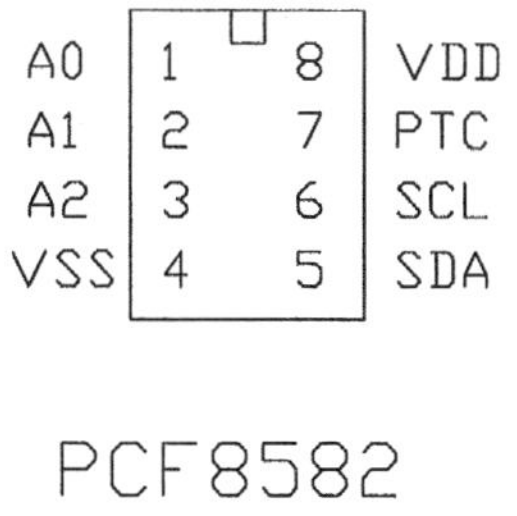

```
AO  | 1      8 | VDD
A1  | 2      7 | PTC
A2  | 3      6 | SCL
VSS | 4      5 | SDA
```

PCF8582

Figure 9.5 Pin-out diagram for the PCF 8582 EEPROM

Pins 1, 2 and 3 are hardwired by the engineer to define the slave address of the device. Being three definable address pins means that up to 2^3 or eight 8582 EEPROMs can be addressed on the I²C bus.

The first four address bits are internally configured; for the PCF8582 the address table is:

1	0	1	0	A2	A1	A0

In the following examples A2, A1 and A0 were all connected to ground or 0 V. The full slave address is:

1010000X

where the LSB X is 0 for Write data and 1 for Read data. The hex address for writing a byte is A0 and for reading a byte the address is A1.

In Figure 9.5:

- pin 4 is ground (0 V);
- pin 5 is SDA;
- pin 6 is SCL;
- pin 7 is Programming Timing Control (an output and may be left unconnected);
- pin 8 is the 5 V dc power supply.

The IIC bus has only two lines and therefore there is a certain protocol to be observed in order to store or retrieve data. Each device data sheet will have a block diagram to explain the necessary protocol and for the PCF8582 this is shown by:

S	SLAVE ADDRESS	0	A	WORD ADDRESS	A	DATA BYTE	A	P

1   Send a Start
2   Send the slave address + 0 for Write
3   Send word address
4   Send data byte
5   Send a Stop

A is the Acknowledge back from the slave PCF8582 and may be checked at the appropriate point by transferring the S1STA (status) to Port 4 using a routine such as:

```
LOOP: MOV    P4, S1STA
      SJMP   LOOP
```

The other functions, S, Slave Address, Word Address, Data byte and P are actioned by the microcontroller master and are completed when the SI flag is set. As indicated previously this occurs after:

```
JNB    SI,$
```

Look for this in the following program.

9.8   Program to write a byte into EEPROM

```
; program to write a hex byte 66 into a PCF8582 EEPROM
$MOD552
        ORG    0              ; reset
        SJMP   START          ; jump over reserved address space
        ORG    40H            ; start of the program
;
; set serial clock speed, set ENS1, set STOp, set STArt
```

```
START: MOV    S1CON,#51H    ; set clock speed, set ENS1, set STOp, clear SI
       SETB   STA           ; set STA after STO
       JNB    SI,$          ; continually loop till SI = 1
; at this point 08h would be in the S1STA (i.e. Status Register)
;
; EEPROM address is hex A0 = binary 1010 000 0 (LSBit = 0 for Write)
; send slave address + write (0)
       CLR    STA           ; clear start, don't want repeated start
       MOV    S1DAT,#0A0H   ; send EEPROM address + write to S1DAT
       CLR    SI            ; clear SI
       JNB    SI,$          ; continually loop till SI = 1
; at this point 18h would be in S1STA
;
; address location 04 in EEPROM, this is an arbitrary choice
; send word address
       CLR    STA           ; clear STA, don't want repeated start
       MOV    S1DAT,#04H    ; send EEPROM internal address to S1DAT
       CLR    SI            ; clear SI
       JNB    SI,$          ; continually loop till SI = 1
; at this point 28h would be in S1STA
;
; arbitrary choice of number hex 66 to store in EEPROM
; send data 66h
       CLR    STA           ; clear STA
       MOV    S1DAT,#66H    ; send hex 66 to S1DAT
       CLR    SI            ; clear SI
       JNB    SI,$          ; continually loop till SI = 1
; at this point 28h would be in S1STA
;
; send a stop
       SETB   STO           ; set STO = 1
       CLR    SI            ; clear SI
       JNB    SI,$          ; loop till SI = 1 and stop is set
;
AGAIN: SJMP   AGAIN         ; forever loop, a way of stopping
       END                  ; assembler directive
```

9.9   To read a byte of data

The protocol block diagram is given by:

S	SLAVE ADDRESS	WORD ADDRESS	S	SLAVE ADDRESS	DATA BYTE	P

The Acknowledges have been left out, **although the last acknowledge after Data byte and before P is sent by the microcontroller master.** The first Slave Address has 0 at the end for Write Word Address. The second slave address has 1 at the end for Read Data byte.

1   Send a Start
2   Send the slave address + 0 for Write
3   Send word address

4 **Send a repeated start**
5 Send the slave address + 1 for Read
6 Byte transfers to S1DAT
7 **Master generates acknowledge**
8 Send a Stop

Consider the following program to read a byte of data.

```
; program to read a byte
$MOD552
          ORG    0              ; reset start address
          SJMP   START          ; jump over reserved address space
          ORG    40H            ; program start address
START: MOV    S1CON,#51H     ; set speed, ENS1, set STO, clr SI
          SETB   STA            ; set STArt
          JNB    SI,$           ; wait till complete
; at this point 08h would be in S1STA
; send slave address + write (0)
          CLR    STA            ; ensure no repeated start
          MOV    S1DAT,#0A0H    ; write to PCF8582 slave address
          CLR    SI             ; clear SI
          JNB    SI,$           ; wait till complete
; at this point 18h would be in S1STA
; send word address 04h
          CLR    STA            ; ensure no repeated start
          MOV    S1DAT,#04H     ; data byte stored at address 04h
          CLR    SI
          JNB    SI,$           ; wait till complete
; send repeated start
          SETB   STA            ; generate a STArt
          CLR    SI
          JNB    SI,$           ; wait till start is complete
; send slave address + read (1)
          CLR    STA            ; ensure no repeated start
          MOV    S1DAT,#0A1H    ; send PCF8582 slave address to bus + Read
          CLR    SI
          JNB    SI,$           ; wait till complete
; send acknowledge
          CLR    AA             ; master sends acknowledge, recall acknowledge
          CLR    SI             ; is active low, clr sends acknowledge
          JNB    SI,$           ; wait till sent
; read data
          MOV    A,S1DAT        ; transfer data to accumulator
          MOV    P4,A           ; put data on port 4, check with logic pen
;
; send a stop
          SETB   STO            ; microcontroller master generates a stop
          CLR    SI
          JNB    SI,$           ; wait till stop is sent
;
AGAIN: SJMP   AGAIN          ; forever loop, a way of stopping
          END                   ; assembler directive
```

The 80C552 board used had Port 4 available and this was used to check the status at the end of each section in the previous program. The following two line program was inserted, checked and then moved along.

```
              MOV  P4, S1STA
      AGAIN: SJMP   AGAIN
```

This stopped the program at the end of each section allowing the logic level of Port 4 to be checked with a logic pen.

CHECKING THE SERIAL TRANSMISSION WITH A LOGIC ANALYSER

It is possible and convenient to check a byte of data by transferring it to a spare port, but it is difficult using the same method to display serial SDA and SCL trains of data. A logic analyser is very useful for observing serial data. Figure 9.6 shows the logic analyser traces resulting from running the program that writes a hex byte 66 into the EEPROM. The traces are triggered from a start condition (SDA going low when SCL is high). The logic analyser used was a Thandar 1000 and the internal clock was set to 1 MHz.

Figure 9.6 Logic analyser trace produced by the program that writes 66h into the EEPROM

There are nine SCL pulses to one data byte transfer, the first eight for the byte and the ninth pulse coinciding with the acknowledge from the slave. From Figure 9.6 it is possible to see that the first byte is binary 1010 0000 or hex A0 which is the EEPROM slave address plus 0 for write. Counting the SCL pulses it may be seen that the next byte is hex 04, which was chosen as the address to store the data. Finally the data byte hex 66 is transferred to the PCF8582 and a Stop is generated (SDA goes high when SCL is high).

Figure 9.7 Logic analyser trace produced by the program that reads a byte

Figure 9.7 shows a copy of the logic analyser traces when the program for reading a byte was run. The first two byte transfers are the same as for the previous program, because the data location address needs to be defined. Then a repeated Start is generated; check to see that SDA goes from high to low whilst SCL is high. The next hex byte sent is A1 (binary 1010 0001); this is the EEPROM slave address plus 1 for read. The hex data 66 is then read on the next transfer.

9.10 PCF8591 data converter

This device has the following data conversion facilities:

- four channels ADC
- one channel DAC

Figure 9.8 shows a pin-out of the PCF8591.

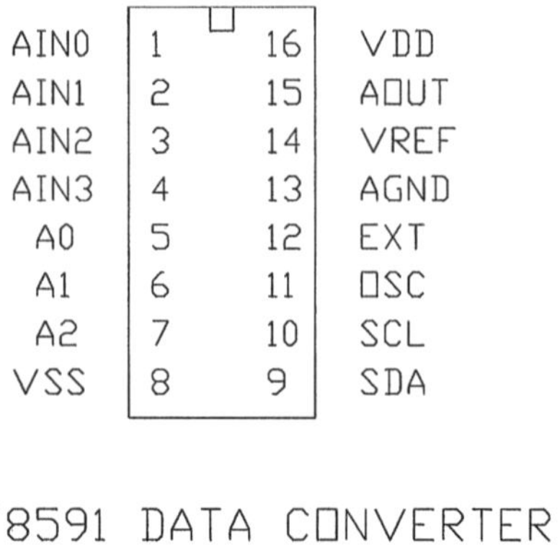

```
        AIN0  │ 1      16 │  VDD
        AIN1  │ 2      15 │  AOUT
        AIN2  │ 3      14 │  VREF
        AIN3  │ 4      13 │  AGND
         A0   │ 5      12 │  EXT
         A1   │ 6      11 │  OSC
         A2   │ 7      10 │  SCL
        VSS   │ 8       9 │  SDA
```

PCF8591 DATA CONVERTER

Figure 9.8 Pin-out diagram for the PCF 8591 data converter

Table 9.2 shows the pin functions and example connections for the PCF8591.

Table 9.2

Pin number	Function	Example connections
1 AIN0	Analogue INput 0	Input (0 to 5 V)
2 AIN1	Analogue INput 1	Input (0 to 5 V)
3 AIN2	Analogue INput 2	Input (0 to 5 V)
4 AIN3	Analogue INput 3	Input (0 to 5 V)
5 A0	Hardware address	Ground 0 V
6 A1	Hardware address	Ground 0 V
7 A2	Hardware address	Ground 0 V
8 V_{SS}	Ground	Ground 0 V
9 SDA	Serial DAta	Connect to P1.7 of 80C552
10 SCL	Serial CLock	Connect to P1.6 of 80C552
11 OSC	OSCillator output (optional use)	Not connected
12 EXT	EXTernal/internal switch for oscillator input	Ground 0 V
13 AGND	Analogue GrouND	Ground 0 V
14 V_{REF}	Voltage reference input	V_{DD} 5 V
15 AOUT	Analogue OUTput	Output
16 V_{DD}	Positive voltage supply	V_{DD} 5 V

DEVICE ADDRESS

A6	A5	A4	A3	A2	A1	A0	R/W
1	0	0	1	0	0	0	1/0

A6, A5, A4 and A3 are the same for all PCF8591 devices whereas A2, A1 and A0 are defined by the user and in Table 9.3 are indicated as being connected to ground. The R/W bit completes the slave address and is 1 for Read (e.g. using Analogue in) or 0 for Write (e.g. using Analogue out). For this application the PCF8591 Read address is 91h and the Write address is 90h.

CONTROL BYTE

Being a multi-function device the PCF8591 has a Control register.

C7	C6	C5	C4	C3	C2	C1	C0

- C7 and C3 are always = 0
- C6 = 1 Analogue out
- C6 = 0 Analogue out disabled
- C5 and C4 define single-ended inputs or differential inputs (Table 9.3):

Table 9.3

C5	C4	
0	0	4 single-ended inputs
0	1	3 differential inputs AIN0, AIN1, AIN2 with AIN3 common
1	0	2 single inputs (AIN0, AIN1) 1 differential input (AIN2, AIN3)
1	1	2 differential inputs

- C2 = 1 Channel auto increment switched on
- C2 = 0 Channel auto increment disabled
- C1 and C0 define ADC channels as follows (Table 9.4):

Table 9.4

C1	C0	
0	0	ADC channel 0
0	1	ADC channel 1
1	0	ADC channel 2
1	1	ADC channel 3

DAC MODE

The Control byte could be 40h enabling the analogue output. The bus protocol to write one byte is given by:

S	ADDRESS	0	A	CONTROL BYTE	A	DATA BYTE	A	P,S

- S = Start sent by Master (microcontroller)
- Address + 0 = 90h for our application
- A = Acknowledge from PCF8591
- Control byte = 40h for our application
- Data byte = the hex number that will be converted to analogue e.g. 99h
- P,S = stoP,Start sent by the Master to end the process

PROGRAM TO SEND 99H

```
$MOD552
        ORG    0               ; reset start address
        SJMP   START           ; jump over reserved address space
        ORG    40H             ; program start address


;
; define speed, ENS1, set stop, clear SI
START: MOV     S1CON,#51H
        SETB   STA             ; set start
        JNB    SI,$            ; wait till functions complete
; 08h should be in S1STA
;
; send PCF8591 address + write (0)
        CLR    STA             ; ensure no repeated start
        MOV    S1DAT,#90H       ; slave address of PCF8591 + 0
        CLR    SI
        JNB    SI,$            ; wait till functions complete
; 18h should be in S1STA
;
; send PCF8591 control byte
        CLR    STA             ; ensure no repeated starts
        MOV    S1DAT,#40H       ; enables DAC on PCF8591
        CLR    SI
        JNB    SI,$            ; wait till functions complete
;
; send data byte 99h to PCF8591
        CLR    STA             ; ensure no repeated starts
        MOV    S1DAT,#99H       ; convert 99h to analogue out
        CLR    SI
        JNB    SI,$            ; wait till functions complete
;
; send a stop
        SETB   STO             ; set stop
        CLR    SI
        JNB    SI,$            ; wait till stop is set
AGAIN: SJMP    AGAIN           ; forever loop, a way of stopping
        END                    ; assembler directive
```

PROGRAM TO READ A BYTE FROM THE ADC

It is necessary to write the Control byte prior to using the ADC and so initially the bus protocol is similar to that for the DAC.

S	ADDRESS	0	CONTROL BYTE	P	S	ADDRESS	1	DATA BYTE	A	P

1   Send a Start
2   Send slave (ADC) ADDRESS + 0 (for write, i.e. writing Control byte)
3   Send Control byte
4   Send a Stop
5   Send a Start
6   Send slave ADDRESS + 1 (for read, i.e. read Analogue byte)
7   Analogue byte is read
8   Send Acknowledge
9   Send a Stop

```
;program to read ADC byte
$MOD552
        ORG     0               ;reset start address
        SJMP    START           ;jump reserved address space
        ORG     40H             ;program start address
; set up speed, send ENS1, set stop, clear SI
START:  MOV     S1CON,#51H
        SETB    STA             ;send start
        JNB     SI,$
; 08h should be in S1STA
;
; send ADC slave address + 0 (0 for write control byte)
        CLR     STA             ;clear start
        MOV     S1DAT,#90H      ;90h = slave address + 0
        CLR     SI
        JNB     SI,$
; 40h should be in S1STA
;
; send control byte (disables DAC)
        CLR     STA             ;clear start
        MOV     S1DAT,#00H      ;00h = disables DAC
        CLR     SI
        JNB     SI,$            ;wait till functions complete
;
; send stop and then a start
        MOV     S1CON,#51H      ;includes stop, clr SI
        SETB    STA             ;send start
        JNB     SI,$
;
;send slave address + Read
```

```
        CLR     STA                 ;clear start
        MOV     S1DAT,#91H          ;91h = slave address + Read
        CLR     SI
        JNB     SI,$                ;wait till complete
;
; read byte
        CLR     STA                 ;clear start
        MOV     A,S1DAT             ;transfer byte into accumulator
        CLR     SI
        JNB     SI,$
        MOV     A,S1DAT             ;byte into accumulator
        MOV     P4,A                ;accumulator onto port 4
;
;send acknowledge
        CLR     AA                  ;master sends acknowledge
        CLR     SI
        JNB     SI,$
;
; send stop
        CLR     STA                 ;clear start
        SETB    STO                 ;send stop
        CLR     SI
        JNB     SI,$
;
AGAIN:  SJMP    AGAIN               ;forever loop, a way of stopping
        END                         ;assembler directive
```

Summary

- Two distinct methods of serial data transmission have been described; one asynchronous the other in synchronism with an SCL.
- The RS232 using the UART has two wires, send (Tx) and receive (Rx), three if ground is included. Although not described, an RS232 connection can have five wires, send, receive, ground and two handshake lines.
- Between systems the RS232 transmission voltages were larger in magnitude than the standard TTL levels of + 5 V and 0 V and this allowed greater connection lengths with reduced noise interference.
- The I^2C serial method is essentially for on-board connection of peripheral devices passing and receiving data between a master microcontroller.
- Increasingly the I^2C (IIC) method is being used for inter-board connection although the length of the connection cable should be no more than approximately 13 ft (4 m).
- Both methods used on-board SFRs, in particular the Serial Control registers, S0CON for RS232 and S1CON for IIC.
- For the IIC, S1CON is used to set the data transmission speed, enable the IIC and initialise the Start, Stop, Acknowledge and Interrupt conditions.
- The RS232 has more configurations than the IIC and the S0CON is used to define a particular protocol as well as setting the interrupt conditions.
- The speed of RS232 data transmission is set up by configuring the Timer/Counter register, where the time taken for the register to overflow is used to determine the baud rate.

- For both methods the data is passed by loading or retrieving it from a data buffer, S0BUF for the RS232 and S1DAT for the IIC.
- Similarly an interrupt bit is used to test when the transmission is complete, TI for the RS232 and SI for the IIC.

Exercises

1. An 80C552 microcontroller has an 11.0592 MHz crystal. What is the clock frequency?
2. For the microcontroller in question 1, determine the hex byte to be loaded into TH1 for a baud rate of 2400.
3. What conditions are set when hex 42 is put into S0CON?
4. (a) Which bit is set when the S0BUF has sent an ASCII character? (b) Give a one line programming example of how it may be tested.
5. What does the following instruction do?

    MOV   TMOD,#20H

6. (a) What effect does SMOD have on the baud rate? (b) Give a one line programming example of how it may be set to zero.
7. Give a one line programming example of how the timer may be turned on.
8. (a) What is RI? (b) How is it used to indicate the arrival of a byte?
9. What does IIC stand for?
10. How many modes of operation are associated with IIC? What are they?
11. What do SDA and SCL stand for?
12. How are Start and Stop conditions defined for IIC?
13. During a data transfer is SCL low or high when SDA changes?
14. Regarding voltage levels what is the essential difference between data transfer using IIC and that using RS232?
15. What do S0CON and S1CON refer to?
16. To which SFRs do TI and SI belong?
17. Briefly explain why TI and SI have similar functions.
18. Which bits of the S1STA are used?
19. An 80C552 microcontroller has a crystal frequency of 11.0592 MHz and during an initialisation program hex D1 is put into the IIC Control register. What is the I^2C transmission speed?
20. (a) What are the functions of STA and STO? (b) To which SFR do they belong?
21. What does the following one line program do?

    JNB   SI,$

22. Assuming the crystal frequency is 12 MHz, write a four line program routine that will set the IIC clock cycle time to 80 μs, enable the IIC, set STO, clear SI and after this set STA.
23. The full slave address of a PCF8582 is hex AE. Is the device being read or written to? What are the logic levels on pins 1, 2 and 3 of this EEPROM?
24. Write a program that will store two hex bytes A2 and 3C into consecutive addresses 34H and 35H of a PCF8582.
25. What is a PCF8591?
26. Sketch a small schematic circuit showing the hardware configuration for a PCF8591 having four single-ended inputs and one output.

27. How is the DAC in the PCF8591 disabled?

28. Write a program that will read in a voltage on channel 2 of the PCF8591 and then directly output it onto the DAC.

29. Write a program that will read in a voltage on channel 1 of the PCF8591 and then transmit it via an RS232 to a PC.

30. A program reads channel 0 on the PCF8591 and transfers the data to the Accumulator. Draw what you think would be the corresponding logic analyser traces for SCL and SDA.

10

16-Bit Microcontroller

10.1 Introduction

Large architecture microcontrollers with 32-bit registers have been available for some time. As a rule such devices tend to be in large packages with over 100 pins. However, there is a class of microcontrollers emerging from the 8-bit families that have 16-bit registers and yet are still housed in small packages. The Philips XA (eXtended Architecture) is a good example of such a device.

The XA is very fast since the clock rate is no longer one twelfth of the crystal frequency; instead it is the same as the crystal frequency and this can be as high as 30 MHz.

Not only does the XA have 16-bit registers but it also has a 16-bit data bus. The 16-bit registers, and there are 21 of them, are used in place of the Accumulator and are in the CPU core so that movement of data between them is very fast.

The XA is versatile in that it can be configured as an 80C51 compatible 8-bit microprocessor but retaining the fast speed of the XA.

The XA-G3 is the current derivative with a 16-bit data bus and 20 address lines. The first 16 of these address lines can be used to address a 64k byte block (i.e. 2^{16}), the same as for the current 80C51. However, the XA has some extra CPU core SFRs (Special Function Registers) that enable the top four address lines to be used to select 16 64k byte segment blocks (because $16 = 2^4$).

Future XA derivatives are planned having 24 address lines and they will be able to use eight top address lines to select 256 memory segment blocks. 64k byte per block and 256 blocks means that this small package device has the capability of addressing 16M bytes of memory which is quite amazing for a 40- or 44-pin package.

Although segmented, the arrangement of the extra SFRs ensures that the 16M byte of program memory would be auto-incremented and appear seamless to the user, assuming that the correct hardware is in place. This segmenting capability also means that the XA can easily implement multi-tasking.

The XA also has some interesting low power options suitable for NiCad and NiMh applications with the **P**ower **CON**trol (PCON) register really controlling the power.

It is possible to set the XA in IDLe mode, when it takes no more than 25 mA whilst still running at 30 MHz, or it can be set to Power Down mode when the oscillator stops and the

XA takes no more than 50 µA. The XA may be awakened and returned to normal operation by either a hard reset or a remote interrupt.

Apart from not being pin compatible another difference between the XA and the 80C51 is that the reset pin is active low as can be seen by reference to the schematic diagram in Figure 10.1.

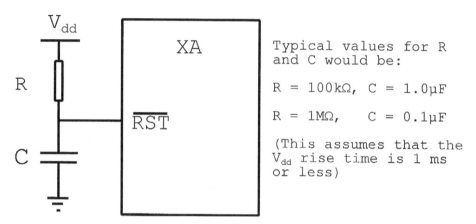

Figure 10.1 External reset circuit for the XA microcontroller

The XA has two stack pointers namely the User Stack Pointer (USP) and System Stack Pointer (SSP); unlike the 80C51 both stack pointers stack down. The use of two stack pointers, one having a higher priority than the other, enables quite sophisticated systems to be designed where access to system controlling functions can only be done in System Mode (SM), using the SSP. In System Mode when the SSP is selected all registers, instructions and memories are available to the system designer. This makes the XA suitable for use in secure systems, giving the system designer access to the hierarchy control without allowing this level of input to the system user.

Such secure systems could include:

- burglar alarms
- fire control alarms
- computer systems
- surveillance systems

The XA has a large space at the beginning of program memory reserved for exception interrupt vectors and in fact the start address of programs should not be below 11Ch. Table 10.4 (shown on p. 199) indicates the list of XA exception vectors.

Using Assembly language the start of an XA program could be:

```
$INCLUDE XA-G3.EQU              ;include file giving the hex addresses of the
                                ; SFRs
        ORG    0                ; reset start address
        DW     $8F00,START      ; define word hex($) 8F00
        ORG    $120             ; $120 clears $11B
;
; 8 = 1000 binary and puts XA in System Mode
; F = 1111 binary and sets the highest Interrupt Mask level.
```

The XA also has an enhanced instruction set (refer to Appendix B for a summary).

One of the fundamental differences between the XA instruction set and that of the 80C51 is that data may be moved in Byte (.B), Words (.W) or Double words (.D). The use of Double word instructions is restricted to some arithmetic operations.

Although the registers are 16 bits long (i.e. Word length) they can also be addressed as High or Low, to accommodate bytes. An example could be:

    MOV.B R3L,#$55

This instruction will move a hex number 55 into the Low byte of Register 3.

There are two things to be noted from this:

- If the extension .B was omitted then the instruction would default to Word (.W);
- $ has been used to signify a hex number although h can still be used.

Another example could be:

    MOV [R4],R1

Because the extension has been left off the Move instruction it defaults to Word. The instruction means: Move the Word contents of Register R1 into the address pointed to by Register R4. This is an example of Indirect Addressing. If R4 contained the hex number $1234 and R1 contained 55h then the operation would put 55h into the address $1234.

A modification could be:

    MOV [R4 +],R1

Using the same register contents as before, the instruction would increment the address $1234 to $1235 after the contents of R1 have been put into address $1234. This is a very useful instruction for moving data in a table.

The XA has three timers plus a Watchdog Timer. The Watchdog is used mainly when the timer/counters are being used and it will reset the XA, after a set time, if the Timer/counter register is not serviced. This may not appear to be of interest to the user who does not intend using the Watchdog, but in the XA the Watchdog Timer is on by default. In order to stop the XA resetting it is necessary to turn the Watchdog off. This would require a modification to the start of a typical XA program:

```
$INCLUDE XA-G3.equ          ; include file listing SFR addresses
        ORG     0           ; reset start address
        DF      $8F00,START ; set SM, Int Mask level and jump to start
        ORG     $120        ; program start address
; turn the Watchdog off
START:  MOV.B   WDCON,#0
        MOV.B   WFEED1,#$A5 ;
        MOV.B   WFEED2,#$5A ;
; rest of the program
```

The XA-G3 also has two UARTs that can be used in much the same way as the 80C51.

Future XA derivatives will match the on-board functions of the current 80C51 family although it is understood that the derivative with on-board ADCs (Analogue to Digital Converters) will have at least one fast ADC to match the speed of the XA.

10.2 Hardware

Figure 10.2 shows the pin-out for the XA-G3 44-pin PLCC package while Table 10.1 shows the pin-out functions for the XA-G3 device.

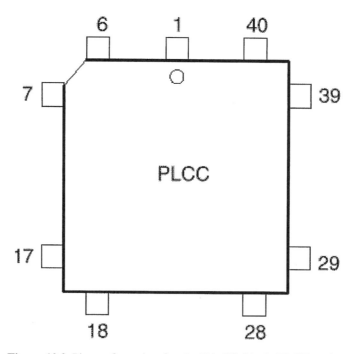

Figure 10.2 Pin configuration for the XA-G3 44 pin PLCC package

Table 10.2 compares the pin functions for the XA and 80C51 in both 44-pin PLCC and 40-pin DIP (Dual-In-Plastic) packages.

It may be seen from Table 10.2 that although the PLCC packages are similar, neither the XA 44-pin or the 40-pin package is pin compatible with the 80C51. In fact the first four address lines of the XA (A0 to A3) are not multiplexed with data and in a design they are connected directly to the memory or peripheral IC; they do not connect to an octal latch.

When the XA is used as an 8-bit data device, perhaps in an 80C51 system, then the upper address lines (A12 to A19) do not use an octal latch but are connected directly, as address lines, to the memory or peripheral.

If the device is used in a 16-bit data system then a second octal latch is needed to demultiplex data on D8 to D15 from the address lines A12 to A19.

Some of the 80C51 features are retained. Examples are given in Table 10.3.

Apart from dual grounds (V_{SS}), and dual supplies (V_{DD}), there are other additions.

Table 10.1 Pin-out functions for the XA-G3 device

Pin	Function	Pin	Function
1	V_{SS}	23	V_{DD}
2	P1.0/A0/$\overline{WRH}$	24	P2.0/A12D8
3	P1.1/A1	25	P2.1/A13D9
4	P1.2/A2	26	P2.2/A14D10
5	1.3/A3	27	P2.3/A15D11
6	P1.4/RxD1	28	P2.4/A16D12
7	P1.5/TxD1	29	P2.5/A17D14
8	P1.6/T2	30	P2.6/A18D14
9	P1.7/T2EX	31	P2.7/A19D15
10	$\overline{RST}$	32	$\overline{PSEN}$
11	P3.0/RxD0	33	ALE/$\overline{PROG}$
12	NC	34	NC
13	P3.1/TxD0	35	/EA/V_{PP}/WAIT
14	P3.2/$\overline{INT0}$	36	P0.7/A11D7
15	P3.3/$\overline{INT1}$	37	P0.6/A10D6
16	P3.4/T0	38	P0.5/A9D5
17	P3.5/T1/BUSW	39	P0.4/A10D4
18	P3.6/$\overline{WRL}$	40	P0.3/A7D3
19	P3.7/$\overline{RD}$	41	P0.2/A6D2
20	XTAL2	42	P0.1/A5D1
21	XTAL1	43	P0.0/A4D0
22	V_{SS}	44	V_{DD}

- Write High and Write Low ($\overline{WRH}$, $\overline{WRL}$) show that the XA has a 16-bit data bus. Along with the ReaD signal these may be used together with the high-order address lines the (A16 to A19) to address locations beyond the 16-address line 64k byte boundary.
- BUS Width (BUSW) is the hardware side of configuring an 8-bit data bus or 16-bit data bus. If BUSW is set to logic 0 then the XA is in 8-bit data mode and if BUSW is connected to logic 1 then the XA is in 16-bit data mode.
- Bus Configuration Register (BCR) is an XA SFR:

-	-	-	WAITD	BUSD	BC2	BC1	BC0

The binary reset default value of the BCR is 0000 0A11, where A is the hardware logic 0 or logic 1 set by BUSW.
- WAITD Disables the WAIT input (XA pin 35). A WAIT input would cause wait states to be introduced, extending the length of a data transfer bus cycle, and this would allow time for slower memory and peripheral devices to function in the fast XA environment.
- Setting BUSD would disable the XA bus functions; this may be useful to prevent an instruction pre-fetch when the XA is executing code near the end of the on-chip code memory.

10.3   Layout of 8-bit data XA minimum board

Figure 10.3 shows a minimum XA circuit configured by BUSW as an 8-bit data system and includes a UART. The layout of minimum XA board is shown in Figure 10.4.

Table 10.2 Comparison of pin-out functions for the XA and 80C51 in both 44-pin PLCC and 40-pin DIP packages
Pin listings:

44-pin PLCC XA-G3		44-pin PLCC 80C51		40-pin DIP XA-1		40-pin DIP 80C51	
1	V_{SS}	1	NC	1	P3.1/TxD0	1	P1.0
2	P1.0/A0/$\overline{\text{WRH}}$	2	P1.0	2	P3.2/INT0	2	P1.1
3	P1.1/A1	3	P1.1	3	P3.3/INT1	3	P1.2
4	P1.2/A2	4	P1.2	4	P3.4/T0	4	P1.3
5	P1.3/A3	5	P1.3	5	P3.5/T1/BUSW	5	P1.4
6	P1.4/RxD1	6	P1.4	6	P3.6/WRL	6	P1.5
7	P1.5/TxD1	7	P1.5	7	P3.7/RD	7	P1.6
8	P1.6/T2	8	P1.6	8	XTAL1	8	P1.7
9	P1.7/T2EX	9	P1.7	9	XTAL2	9	RST
10	$\overline{\text{RST}}$	10	RST	10	V_{SS}	10	RxD/P3.0
11	P3.0/RxD0	11	P3.0/RxD	11	V_{DD}	11	TxD/P3.1
12	NC	12	NC	12	P2.0/A12D8	12	$\overline{\text{INT0}}$/P3.2
13	P3.1/TxD0	13	P3.1/TxD	13	P2.1/A13D9	13	$\overline{\text{INT1}}$P3.3
14	P3.2/$\overline{\text{INT0}}$	14	P3.2/$\overline{\text{INT0}}$	14	P2.2/A14D10/RxD1	14	T0/P3.4
15	P3.3/$\overline{\text{INT1}}$	15	P3.3/$\overline{\text{INT1}}$	15	P2.3/A15D11/TxD1	15	T1/P3.5
16	P3.4/T0	16	P3.4/T0	16	P2.4/A16D12	16	$\overline{\text{WR}}$/P3.6
17	P3.5/T1/BUSW	17	P3.5/T1	17	P2.5/A17D13	17	$\overline{\text{RD}}$/P3.7
18	P3.6/$\overline{\text{WRL}}$	18	P3.6/$\overline{\text{WR}}$	18	P2.6/A18D14	18	XTAL2
19	P3.7/$\overline{\text{RD}}$	19	P3.7/$\overline{\text{RD}}$	19	P2.7/A19D15	19	XTAL1
20	XTAL2	20	XTAL2	20	PSEN	20	V_{SS}
21	XTAL1	21	XTAL1	21	ALE	21	P2.0/A8
22	V_{SS}	22	V_{SS}	22	EA/V_{PP}/WAIT	22	P2.1/A9
23	V_{DD}	23	NC	23	P0.7/A11D7	23	P2.2/A10
24	P2.0/A12D8	24	P2.0/A8	24	P0.6/A10D6	24	P2.3/A11
25	P2.1/A13D9	25	P2.1/A9	25	P0.5/A9D5	25	P2.4/A12
26	P2.2/A14D10	26	P2.2/A10	26	P0.4/A8D4	26	P2.5/A13
27	P2.3/A15D11	27	P2.3/A11	27	P0.3/A7D3	27	P2.6/A14
28	P2.4/A16D12	28	P2.4/A12	28	P0.2/A6D2	28	P2.7/A15
29	P2.5/A17D13	29	P2.5/A13	29	P0.1/A5D1	29	PSEN
30	P2.6/A18D14	30	P2.6/A14	30	P0.0/A4D0	30	ALE/$\overline{\text{PROG}}$
31	P2.7/A19D15	31	P2.7/A15	31	V_{DD}	31	$\overline{\text{EA}}$/V_{PP}
32	$\overline{\text{PSEN}}$	32	$\overline{\text{PSEN}}$	32	V_{SS}	32	P0.7/AD7
33	ALE/$\overline{\text{PROG}}$	33	ALE/$\overline{\text{PROG}}$	33	P1.0/A0/$\overline{\text{WRH}}$	33	P0.6/AD6
34	NC	34	NC	34	P1.1/A1	34	P0.5/AD5
35	/$\overline{\text{EA}}$/V_{PP}/WAIT	35	/$\overline{\text{EA}}$/V_{PP}	35	P1.2/A2	35	P0.4/D4
36	P0.7/A11D7	36	P0.7/AD7	36	P1.3/A3	36	P0.3/D3
37	P0.6/A10D6	37	P0.6/AD6	37	P1.4	37	P0.2/D2
38	P0.5/A9D5	38	P0.5/AD5	38	P1.5	38	P0.1/D1
39	P0.4/A8D4	39	P0.4/AD4	39	RST	39	P0.0/D0
40	P0.3/A7D3	40	P0.3/AD3	40	P3.0/RXD0	40	V_{CC}
41	P0.2/A6D2	41	P0.2/AD2				
42	P0.1/A5D1	42	P0.1/AD1				
43	P0.0/A4D0	43	P0.0/AD0				
44	V_{DD}	44	V_{CC}				

Table 10.3 XA pin functions that are common with the 80C51

Pin number	Symbol	Function
32	$\overline{\text{PSEN}}$	Program Strobe ENable
33	ALE/$\overline{\text{PROG}}$	Address Latch Enable and PROGramming
14	$\overline{\text{INT0}}$	External interrupt
15	$\overline{\text{INT1}}$	External interrupt
16	T0	Timer 0 external input
17	T1	Timer 1 external input
19	$\overline{\text{RD}}$	Read

The schematic of Figure 10.3 does not show the second octal latch and on an actual prototype board the direct connections of the address lines A12 to A19 can be made by inserting connecting wires in the latch socket terminals. The XA-G3 can be configured to have an external EPROM by grounding pin 35 on the XA (EA) and a PROM emulator may be used to develop the programs.

The Philips PLC42VA12FA PLD (Programmable Logic Device) can be used and the equations written using Philips SNAP software (rev 1.85) as shown below.

The PLD is pin compatible with a large number of other 24-pin skinnydip packages.

```
@PINLIST
a16      I;
a17      I;
a18      I;
a19      I;
ale      I;
wrl      I;
psen     I;
rd       I;
pld23    o;
pld22    o;
pld21    o;
pld20    o;
pld19    o;
pld18    o;
pld17    o;
pld16    o;
@LOGIC EQUATIONS
```

$$\text{pld23} = (\overline{a19}*\overline{a18}*\overline{a17}*\overline{a16}*wrl*psen*ale*rd + \overline{a19}*\overline{a18}*\overline{a17}*\overline{a16}*wrl*psen*ale*\overline{rd});$$
$$\text{pld22} = (\overline{a19}*\overline{a18}*\overline{a17}*\overline{a16}*wrl*psen*ale*\overline{rd} + \overline{a19}*\overline{a18}*\overline{a17}*\overline{a16}*wrl*psen*ale*\overline{rd});$$
$$\text{pld21} = (\overline{a19}*\overline{a18}*\overline{a17}*\overline{a16}*wrl*psen*ale*\overline{rd} + \overline{a19}*\overline{a18}*\overline{a17}*\overline{a16}*wrl*psen*ale*\overline{rd});$$
$$\text{pld20} = (\overline{a19}*\overline{a18}*\overline{a17}*\overline{a16}*wrl*psen*ale*rd + \overline{a19}*\overline{a18}*\overline{a17}*\overline{a16}*wrl*psen*ale*\overline{rd});$$
$$\text{pld19} = (\overline{a19}*\overline{a18}*\overline{a17}*\overline{a16}*wrl*psen*ale*rd + \overline{a19}*\overline{a18}*\overline{a17}*\overline{a16}*wrl*psen*ale*\overline{rd});$$
$$\text{pld18} = (\overline{a19}*\overline{a18}*\overline{a17}*\overline{a16}*wrl*psen*ale*rd + \overline{a19}*\overline{a18}*\overline{a17}*\overline{a16}*wrl*psen*ale*\overline{rd});$$
$$\text{pld17} = (\overline{a19}*\overline{a18}*\overline{a17}*\overline{a16}*wrl*psen*ale*rd + \overline{a19}*\overline{a18}*\overline{a17}*\overline{a16}*wrl*psen*ale*\overline{rd});$$
$$\text{pld16} = (\overline{a19}*\overline{a18}*\overline{a17}*\overline{a16}*wrl*psen*ale*rd + \overline{a19}*\overline{a18}*\overline{a17}*\overline{a16}*wrl*psen*ale*\overline{rd});$$
$$\text{pld15} = (a19*\overline{a18}*\overline{a17}*\overline{a16}*wrl*psen*ale*rd + a19*\overline{a18}*\overline{a17}*\overline{a16}*wrl*psen*ale*\overline{rd});$$
$$\text{pld14} = (a19*\overline{a18}*\overline{a17}*a16*wrl*psen*ale*rd + a19*\overline{a18}*\overline{a17}*a16*wrl*psen*ale*\overline{rd});$$

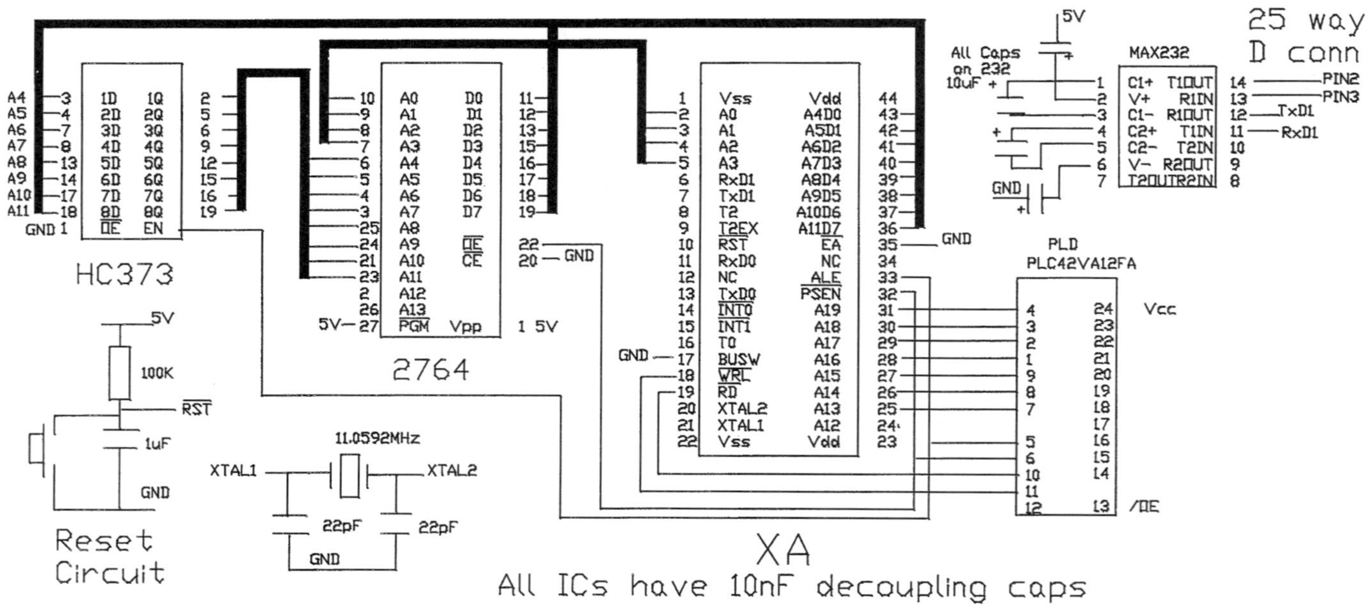

Figure 10.3 Minimum XA circuit

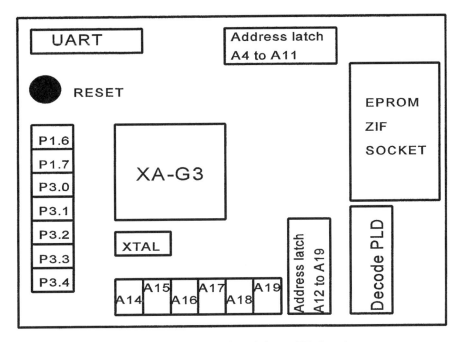

Figure 10.4 Layout of a minimum XA board

The first program written for the minimum XA board is shown below. This program is not too ambitious and the object is simply to make pin 4 on Port 3 send logic 1/logic 0 continuously. All programs are written using the Philips XA development tools, downloaded from the Internet, originating from Macraigor Systems Inc. This is quite a good introductory cross-assembler and simulator, although limited in this version to on-chip memory.

```
;Program 1
$PAGEWIDTH 80T                       ; optional
$INCLUDE XA-G3. EQU                  ; SFR addresses include file
         ORG    0                    ; reset start address
         DW     $8F00,START          ; set System Mode & Int Mask level
         ORG    $120                 ; program start address
; watchdog off
START:   MOV.B  WDCON,#0
         MOV.B  WFEED1,#$A5
         MOV.B  WFEED2,#$5A
; rest of program
LOOP:    SETB   P3.4                 ; pin4 port3 to logic 1
         CALL   DELAY                ; delay subroutine
         CLR    P3.4                 ; pin4 port3 to logic 0
         CALL   DELAY
         BR     LOOP                 ; branch to loop
DELAY:   MOV.W  R1,#$1234            ; move word $1234 into reg 1
TAKE:    DJNZ   R1,TAKE              ; keep decrementing if R1 not zero
         RET                         ; return from delay subroutine
         END                         ; assembler directive
```

Note the three program lines for turning the Watchdog Timer off. The XA has the Watchdog on by default and unless it is maintained it will automatically reset the microcontroller before the program can execute the CLR P3.4 instruction, in other words it will stop the program from functioning.

The same program is shown below using the HiTech C compiler for DOS:

```c
#include <xa.h>
/* ***************************************************************** /
/ *                      Program 1 for the P51XAG3                 */
/ * ***************************************************************** /

void delay (void);                          /* pre declaration */
main(){
            /* watchdog OFF */

            WDCON  = 0;
            WFEED1 = 0xA5;
            WFEED2 = 0x5A;

            /* rest of the program */
            do{     P3| = 0xFF;              /* pin4 port3 to logic 1 */
                    delay();                 /* delay subroutine */
                    P3| = 0xEF;              /* pin4 port3 to logic 0 */
                    delay();                 /* delay subroutine */
            }while(1);                       /* loop forever */
}
void delay(void)                            /* delay subroutine */
{
            int i,TIME = 0x1234;            /* this delay depends */
            For(I = 0;i<TIME;i++)           /* on the compiler */
                 ;                           /* call time too */

}
```

When the Watchdog is used the software will regularly feed the timer to ensure that the timer does not count down to zero. If a fault occurs and normal operation ceases then the timer will count down to zero and the next clock pulse to decrement the timer will result in a system reset.

The next program uses the UART and gives the example of sending what is perhaps a trivial message but the program shows an application of incremented indirect addressing to shift a table of message data.

```
; Program 2, RS232 connection using the UART:
$INCLUDE            XA-G3.EQU
          ORG   0
          DW    $8F00,START
          ORG   $120
; watchdog off
START:  MOV.B  WDCON,#0
        MOV.B  WFEED1,#$A5
        MOV.B  WFEED2,#$5A
; rest of program
```

```
; initialise serial SFRs
        MOV.B   SCR,#0          ; system config reg set to 0, puts N = 4
        MOV.B   SOCON,#$42      ; serial
        MOV.B   PCON,#$00       ; power control reg = 0
        MOV.B   TL1,#-18        ; timer low byte to 256-18 for 9600 baud
        MOV.B   RTL1,#-18       ; timer
        MOV.B   TMOD,#$20
        SETB    TR1             ; turn timer on
;
; send message "Jack and Jill went up the hill~"; ~ = ASCII $7E
MESSGE: MOV.W   R6,#MSG1        ; put message address into DPTR
NEXTCH: MOVC.B  R3L,[R6+]       ; contents of R6 into R31 and increment R6
        CJNE.B  R3L,#$7E, TRX   ; if not ASCII $7E then jump to send next ch
CR:     JNB     TI,CR           ; carriage return
        CLR     TI
        MOV.B   SOBUF,#$0A
LF:     JNB     TI,LF           ; line feed
        CLR     TI
        MOV.B   SOBUF,#$0D      ; short delay between lines
        MOV.W   R2,#$FFFF
TAKE:   DJNZ.W  R2,TAKE
        BR      MESSGE          ; send message again
;
; send single message ASCII character
TRX:    JNB     TI,TRX          ; loop till tx int bit is set, i.e. char sent
        CLR     TI              ; clear transmit interrupt
        MOV.B   SOBUF,R3L       ; ASCII character into serial tx buffer & send
        BR      NEXTCH          ; branch to get next character
;
; message listing
MSG1:   DB 'Jack and Jill went up the hill ~ ' ; define bytes in message
        END                     ; assembler directive
```

Again the program is included using the HiTech C compiler for DOS:

```
#include <xa.h>                      /* declare all internal registers */

/* ********************************************************************** /
/*                      Program 2 for the P51XAG3                      */
/* ********************************************************************** /

char *pointer;                       /* pointer to write to hardware */

char *msg1 = "Jack and Jill went up the hill~";/* the message to be sent */

long int DELAY;                      /* some variables to be used */

void trx(void);                      /* transmits one character */

main() {
        /* watchdog OFF */
```

```
        WDCON  =  0;
        WFEED1  =  0xA5;
        WFEED2  =  0x5A;
        /* rest of the program */
        /* initialise serial SFRs */

        SCR  =  0;                      /* system config reg set to 0, N = 4 */
        SOCON  =  0x42;                 /* serial */
        PCON  =  0;                     /* power control reg  =  0 */
        TL1  =  -18;                    /* timer low to 256-18 for 9600 baud */
        RTL1  =  - 18;                  /* timer */
        TMOD  =  0x20;
        TR1  =  1;                      /* turn timer ON */

        * send message 'Jack and Jill went up the hill' */

        pointer  =  msg1;               /* pointer address set */

        while (*pointer!  =  '~'){      /* check if reached end of message */
        trx();                          /* send the character */
Cr_rt:if(TI1) goto Cr_rt;              /* carriage return */
        TI1  =  0;

Ln_fd:if(TI1) goto Ln_fd;              /* line feed */
        TI1  =  0;

        SOBUF  =  0x0A;                 /* short delay between lines */
        DELAY  =  0xFFFF;
        while(DELAY--)
            ;
        pointer++;                      /* look at the next character */
        } ;                             /* loop forever */
        }
        void trx(void)
        {
Not_set:if(!TI1) goto Not_set;         /* loop until TI is set, i.e. ch sent */
        TI1  =  0;
        SOBUF  =  *pointer;             /* character into serial tx buffer */
        return;
}
```

10.4   Calculation of timer number

For a UART program, using UART in Mode 1 and Timer 1 in Mode 2:

$$\text{Baud rate} = \frac{Osc}{N \, 16 \, (256 - R)}$$

where:

Osc = crystal frequency
N = 4, 16 or 64 pre-scaler values set up in the System Configuration Register (SCR).

SCR3	SCR2	Pre-scaler
0	0	$N = 4$ (Reset value)
0	1	$N = 16$
1	0	$N = 64$
1	1	reserved

R = timer Reload value

Another form is:

$$X = \frac{Osc}{16\ N\ B}$$

where:

$X = 256 -$ Reload value
Osc, N and B are as above

X can be used directly in decimal form as a negative number, as shown in the following example. If

Osc = 11.0592 MHz
N = 4
B = 9600

then

$X = 18$

and can be used directly:

```
MOV.B TL1,# – 18      ; move –18 to Timer1 Low byte
MOV.B RTL1,# –18      ; move – 18 to Timer1 Reload Low byte
```

10.5 Using segmented memory

Addressing off-chip memory or peripherals is achieved using the Segment SELection register (SSEL) together with the Program Counter (PC), Code Segment (CS), Data Segment (DS) or Extra Segment (ES). Refer to Figure 10.5.

As Figure 10.5 shows the complete 24-bit address (XA derivative having 24 address lines) is made up from a 16-bit address (A0 to A15) placed in one of the registers plus the upper eight address bits (A16 to A23) assigned to either PC, CS, DS or ES. For the XA-G3 derivative having 20 address lines this would be A16 to A19.

PC and CS are used for program memory whilst DS and ES are used for data memory and peripherals. Figure 10.5 shows the use of DS and ES; it is similar for program memory where PC and DS are used instead. The PC is a 16-bit register in the CPU core and the

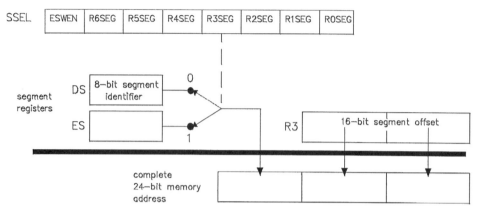

Figure 10.5 Using segmented memory to access a 24-bit address

SSEL, CS, DS and ES are all 8-bit SFRs in the CPU core and so the movement of data between them is very fast.

When addressing code memory the PC and CS segments are used with the SSEL; the PC being a 16-bit register is truncated to its higher eight bits.

Providing the correct hardware is in place the auto-incrementing of the PC would ensure that the program (or code) memory could automatically extend beyond the 16-bit address limits of 64k bytes. It may be required to move code memory when accessing a look-up table and the instruction MOVC is reserved for this. This would be an example of when the CS would be used with the SSEL.

When addressing data memory or peripherals the segments DS and ES are used with the SSEL. The ES is reserved for general use whilst the DS is normally used with the stack pointer.

SEGMENT SELECTION REGISTER (SSEL)

ESWEN	R6SEG	R5SEG	R4SEG	R3SEG	R2SEG	R1SEG	R0SEG

The logic status of ESWEN, the MSB of the SSEL register, defines which segment is used to make up the full address. When addressing data memory or peripherals:

- ESWEN = 0 defines DS
- ESWEN = 1 defines ES

When addressing code or program memory:
- ESWEN = 0 defines top byte of the PC
- ESWEN = 1 defines CS

When writing a byte into the SSEL the MSB chooses the segment register, as shown above. One of the remaining seven bits, in the SSEL, is used to select which of the CPU registers will hold the 16-bit address.

The following program shows an example of the ES being used. The minimum board described earlier does not have any external memory or peripheral but it does have a PLD used to decode the high-order address lines (A16 to A19). Therefore when this program is run on the minimum board the relevant PLD output pin corresponding to the segment selection address will oscillate high/low.

```
; Program 3. Write to External Segment device.
$INCLUDE          XA-G3.EQU
          ORG   0
          DW    $8F00,START
          ORG   $120
; watchdog off
START:    MOV.B WDCON,#0
          MOV.B WFEED1,#$A5
          MOV.B WFEED2,#$5A
; writing a hex number 55 into locations $061234 and $021234
          MOV.B SSEL,#$88     ; set ESWEN and select reg R3
          MOV.B R21,#$55      ; $55 into reg R2 low byte
          MOV.B R3,#$1234     ; pointer address into reg R3
AGAIN:    MOV.B ES,#$06       ; high order address nibble into ES
          MOV.B [R3],R21      ; indirect, $55 into $061234
          MOV.B ES,#$02       ; high order address nibble into ES
          MOV.B [R3],R21      ; indirect $55 into $021234
          BR    AGAIN         ; repeat
          END
```

This program is also included using the HiTech C compiler for DOS:

```
#include <xa.h>                       /* declare all internal registers */
/* ************************************************************************ /
/*                    Program 3 for the P51XAG3                          */
/* ************************************************************************ /
char *pointer;                        /* pointer to write to hardware */

main(){
        /* watchdog OFF */

        WDCON = 0;
        WFEED1 = 0xA5;
        WFEED2 = 0x5A;

        /* writing a hex number 55 into locations $061234 and $021234 */
        SSEL = 0x88;              /* set ESWEN and select reg R3 */
        Pointer = (char*) 0x1234; /* pointer address set */

    do {
        ES = 0x06;                /* high order address nibble into ES */
        *pointer = 0x55;          /* hex 55 into hex 061234 */
        ES = 0x02;                /* high order address nibble into ES */
        *pointer = 0x55;          /* hex 55 into hex 021234 */
    }while (1);                   /* loop forever*/
```

10.6   XA interrupts

The XA has four sets of interrupts and there is space at the bottom of program memory for their vector addresses. This reserved space stretches from $0000 to $011B and so the start of any program should not be below $011C. The types of interrupts are:

- exception
- event
- software
- trap

EXCEPTION INTERRUPTS

These are caused by important system events that must be serviced such as:

- stack overflow
- divide-by-zero
- trace instruction
- breakpoint
- non-maskable interrupt
- user RETurn from Interrupt (RETI)

EVENT INTERRUPTS

Generally these are caused by on- or off-chip peripherals such as the timers or UARTs or external interrupts.

SOFTWARE INTERRUPTS

These are similar to Event Interrupts in that they are caused by the actions of an SFR. The SoftWare interrupt Request register (SWR) has seven bits, each representing a level of priority. The Software Interrupt is activated by setting the relevant bit.

TRAP INTERRUPTS

These are caused by the TRAP instruction, the syntax being:

        TRAP #data4

The four bits may be encoded into any one of 16 levels of Trap Interrupt. The Trap instruction is a convenient mechanism to enter globally used routines. One of the main uses of the Trap instruction is to allow transitions between user mode and System mode. The Trap Interrupt only occurs if the Trap instruction is executed.

10.7   Exception vector table

The exception vector table is shown in Table 10.4.

    The following program gives an example of a timed interrupt; every time the interrupt occurs a program of this type could be used to perform a set of multi-task operations. When used on the minimum XA board the set of 'multi-task' sequences could be to

Table 10.4 XA exception vectors

```
org    0      ; Exception interrupts
$0000         Reset
$0004         Breakpoint
$0008         Trace
$000C         Stack overflow
$0010         Divide by zero
$0014         Return from interrupt

org    $40    ; Trap interrupts
$0040         Trap 0
$0044         Trap 1
$0048         Trap 2
$004C         Trap 3
$0050         Trap 4
$0054         Trap 5
$0058         Trap 6
$005C         Trap 7
$0060         Trap 8
$0064         Trap 9
$0068         Trap 10
$006C         Trap 11
$0070         Trap 12
$0074         Trap 13
$0078         Trap 14
$007C         Trap 15

org    $80    ; Event interrupts
$0080         External Interrupt 0
$0084         Timer 0 Interrupt
$0088         External Interrupt 1
$008C         Timer 1 Interrupt
$0090         Timer 2 Interrupt
$00A0         UART0 receive
$00A4         UART0 transmit
00A8          UART1 receive
$00AC         UART1 transmit

org    $100   ; Software Interrupts
$0100         SWI1
$0104         SWI2
$0108         SWI3
$010C         SWI4
$0110         SWI5
$0114         SWI6
$0018         SWI7
```

oscillate consecutively pins 1, 2 and 3 on Port 3. Note how the Interrupt Masking level is changed so that the Timer 0 interrupt has a higher priority than the system.

```
$PAGEWIDTH 80T
$INCLUDE          XA-G3.EQU
          ORG     0
          DW      $8600,START
          ORG     $84
          DW      $8900,MTASK
          ORG     $120
START:    MOV.W   R7,#$100         ; set stack pointer
          MOV.B   TMOD,#$02        ; select timer0
          MOV.B   TL0,#-50         ; load timer
          MOV.B   RTL0,#-50        ; reload
          MOV.B   IPA0,#$F0        ; set timer0 int priority
          MOV.B   PSWH,#$84        ; lower cpu exec priority
          MOV.B   IEL,#$82         ; enable timer0 int
          SETB    TR0              ; turn timer on
; normal routine
AGAIN:    SETB    P3.4
          CLR     P3.4
          BR      AGAIN
; Time0 Interrupt routine
MTASK:
; task1 is logic level change on pin1
          CLR     P3.1
          SETB    P3.1
; task2 is logic level change on pin2
          CLR     P3.2
          SETB    P3.2
; task3 is logic level change on pin3
          CLR     P3.3
          SETB    P3.3
          RETI                     ; return from interrupt
          END
```

Summary

- The XA is a 16-bit microcontroller having a data bus that can be set to eight bits or 16 bits.
- The XA also has general purpose 16-bit registers.
- The XA-G3 has 20 address lines giving it the capability to address 1M byte, which it does by addressing consecutive 64k byte blocks in a seamless method by using the SSEL register.
- The XA clock frequency is the same as the crystal frequency, not divided down as with the 8-bit 80C51 family.
- The XA retains the popular 80C51 instructions but includes extra ones that are similar to some Motorola 68000 instructions.
- The XA has two stack pointers, USP and SSP, and like the 68000 they stack down.
- The XA has a Watchdog Timer that is on by default and must be turned off by software if not required; failure to do so will result in continual reset.
- The XA is able to manipulate data in Bytes (.B), Words (.W) and in some instances Double words (.D). The default is Word, which again is similar to Motorola 68000.

Exercises

1. An XA microcontroller uses a 30 MHz crystal. What is the clock speed?
2. What is the XA programming line that replaces SJMP START?
3. How many 64k byte blocks can the XA-G3 address?
4. How many 64k byte blocks could the XA address if it had 24 address lines?
5. If not being used what problem would occur if the Watchdog Timer was not turned off?
6. A minimum XA microcontroller has a clock speed of 10 MHz. Write a small Assembly language routine that would cause pin 4 on Port 3 to oscillate at a frequency of 1 Hz.
7. What is the interrupt vector address for Timer 2?
8. What hardware modifications would be required before an XA-G3 44-pin PLCC IC could be slotted into the socket intended for an 80C51 44-pin PLCC IC?
9. Sketch a typical XA reset circuit, giving component values and describe how this circuit differs from an 80C51 reset circuit.
10. Describe what the program line MOVC.B R3L,[R6 +] does.
11. Determine the number that must be loaded into the Timer Low byte register in order to establish a baud rate of 4800.
12. Write an Assembly language routine that will store $33 into address $87654.

11

Debugging, Development and Applications

11.1 Introduction

Most of the programs described so far in this book have been tested using a Philips 80C552 minimum microcontroller based system, the circuit of which is shown in Figure 11.1. The zero in the chip number indicates that the device does not have on-board ROM, hence for development, and for the final system, external PROM must be used.

The ROM version is the 83C552 and the ultra-violet erasable Programmable ROM (PROM) version is the 87C552. This popular 68-pin Plastic Leaded Chip Carrier (PLCC) device, also available in Plastic Quad Flat Pack (PQFP), has numerous features including:

- three timer/counters
- 256 bytes of RAM

and the following interfaces:

- 8-channel multiplexed 10-bit ADC
- two 8-bit PWM (Pulse Width Modulation) outputs
- UART
- I^2C

which on the minimum system were brought out to suitable connectors.

11.2 Debugging and development

The advent of the microcontroller with its on-chip facilities has greatly reduced the complexity of small systems. Previously systems based on 8-bit microprocessors had to rely on external timer/counters, serial interfaces and peripheral ports; some had on-board RAM but many did not.

The microprocessor based system therefore required a greater degree of hardware design and debugging and the printed circuit was also more complex. When designing a microprocessor based system it is necessary to carefully inspect the timing diagrams of all the system devices including the processor to ensure that control signals' logic (e.g. address strobes, data strobes, etc.) conforms with these timing diagrams.

There are various methods of debugging the prototype hardware but knowledge of the system and previous experience of the system processor are a necessity. The use of a

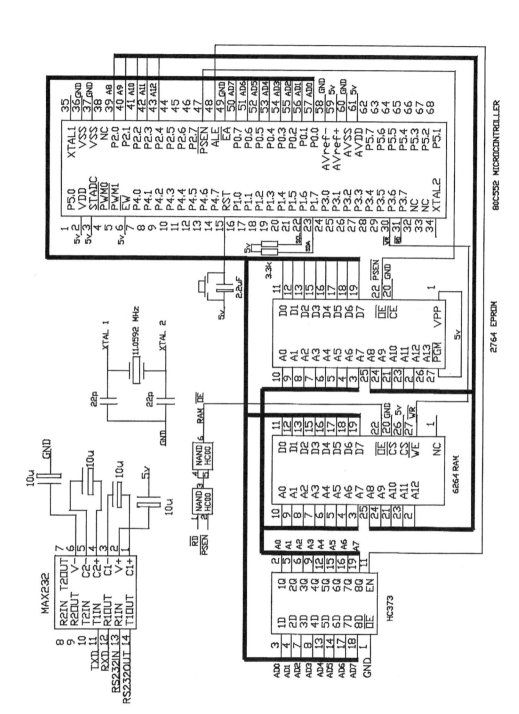

Figure 11.1 80C552 minimum microcontroller board

Microprocessor or Microcontroller In Circuit Emulator (MICE) greatly reduces prototype debug time. Such systems are extremely versatile; the minimum that is required when using a MICE is that the system clock is good and chip power supplies are correct. The processor or controller chip is removed and the header plug of the MICE takes its place. The MICE has on-board RAM, which may be referred to as overlay RAM, and some of it can be configured as read-only, acting as PROM.

The MICE is a very powerful hardware debug tool, usually connected to, and controlled from, a PC. One disadvantage of the MICE is that it usually supports only one processor or controller device although some MICE manufacturers produce a basic system having clip-on device pods. The MICE does tend to be expensive with current prices ranging from £2000 to £12 000.

The use of a logic pen and a PROM emulator is a cheaper alternative but it is certainly not as versatile or as satisfactory as a MICE. This method may be acceptable to the low volume user who is designing with microcontrollers where the circuit complexity is greatly reduced.

When testing an initial prototype a careful inspection of the pcb (printed circuit board) is recommended before any chips are placed in the circuit. The use of a magnifying glass may be useful for this purpose. Things to look for include breaks in the tracks, tracks shorting together or component legs and socket pins not soldered. When using a PLCC device particular attention should be paid to the possibility of tracks shorting together. Initially a multi-meter should be used to ensure that V_{DD} does not connect to ground. The meter should then be used to check that all the chip socket power pins are connected to V_{DD} and ground. Because of pin-out arrangements checking is difficult with a PLCC socket and easier with a DIP (Dual-In-Plastic) socket.

The header plug of the PROM emulator replaces the external PROM of the microcontroller system. The MICE has the advantage that it replaces the microcontroller which controls all of the external chips on the system.

The PROM does not have this function; instead it contains the system controlling program but it is the ability to quickly change this program that makes the PROM emulator an attractive, cheaper debug and development option.

When developing software for a prototype the engineer wants a development system that allows fast, smooth alteration and testing of program changes and the PROM emulator enables this. So also does the MICE but it is far more expensive than the PROM emulator. The use of a PROM emulator by low volume users means that their systems tend to use external PROMs rather than the microcontrollers having on-board EPROMs (e.g. 87C51) or ROMs (e.g. 80C51). The MICE is the ideal tool for this type of microcontroller.

Some users gain confidence by using evaluation boards. These are specially produced systems which usually comprise one pcb and host a particular microcontroller. Sometimes they support more than one microcontroller (e.g. CEIBO DB51). Details of some of the available CEIBO evaluation boards are given in the appendices. When these systems were first introduced they usually had a blank area with connectors allowing the user to patch small applications. Lately these evaluation systems (e.g. CEIBO DB 750) tend to have ribbon wire with a header plug, allowing the users to plug into their own target boards. These evaluation systems usually have their own software debug environment.

The CEIBO DB 750 is an evaluation system supporting the Philips 87C750 microcontroller. This is a 24-pin DIP device having 1k byte of on-board EPROM. A typical target circuit is shown in Figure 11.2.

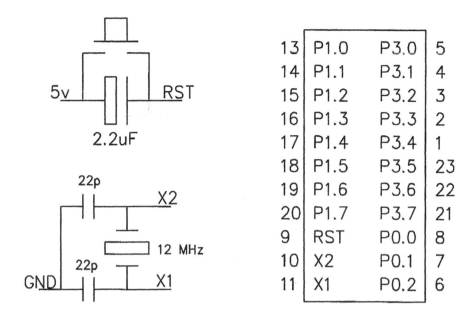

13	P1.0	P3.0	5
14	P1.1	P3.1	4
15	P1.2	P3.2	3
16	P1.3	P3.3	2
17	P1.4	P3.4	1
18	P1.5	P3.5	23
19	P1.6	P3.6	22
20	P1.7	P3.7	21
9	RST	P0.0	8
10	X2	P0.1	7
11	X1	P0.2	6

87C750

Figure 11.2 87C750 minimum microcontroller board

It may be seen that having the on-board EPROM, the 87C750 target circuit is relatively simple and there is no need for an octal latch (74HC373).

The evaluation system for the 87C750 is quite cheap currently costing around £50. Initially when setting up, a monitor program is fixed into an on-board 87C752 which is a larger capacity microcontroller belonging to the same family as the 87C750. The monitor program occupies a small space, at the low end of the 87C752 on-board EPROM, allowing the rest of the EPROM space to be used by the 87C750 program when the kit operates in Emulation mode.

Using the system with the header plug into the target allows the user to single step through the prototype program whilst SFR changes are displayed on the PC screen by the system debug software.

In this Simulation-plus mode the evaluation kit will run the target, albeit at a greatly reduced operating speed; it appears to run at approximately 1/100 of the normal clock operating speed. There are three modes to this evaluation kit:

- Simulation   software only
- Simulation-plus   header plug replacing the target 87C750
- Emulation   87C750 program runs at normal speed, whilst header plug still in target

The evaluation kit can also be used as a programmer for 87C750, 87C751 and 87C752 microcontrollers.

The 87C751 and the 87C752 both have 2k byte of on-board EPROM and I²C. The former is pin compatible with the 87C750 whereas the 87C752 is a 28-pin DIP part having a single channel PWM output and a five channel ADC.

The only way the emulated 87C750 can run at normal clock speed is to fix the program into the upper part of the kit's system 87C752 EPROM. It lacks the capability of the MICE but at the current price of £50 it is excellent value and provides the user with a convenient platform for familiarisation with the 87C750.

USING THE PROM EMULATOR

PROM emulators come in various sizes and prices. The one used to test the programs in this book currently costs about £100 and was purchased from Smart Communications. It has two sets of DIL switches, one for setting the size of emulated EPROM and the other for defining the data bus width. It is possible to gang these PROM emulators for varying bus widths; for example a 16-bit microcontroller system could use two of these PROM emulators.

The PROMulator, as it is named by Smart Communications, can draw its power from either the target board or an external power supply. The PROMulator is a convenient and cost effective piece of equipment since it replaces the EPROM and not the microcontroller. This means that it is not processor dependent and may be used for systems with different microcontrollers or microprocessors. The PROMulator connects to the PC printer port via a standard printer cable and the loader software is included in the equipment cost together with a small instruction manual. When used to test the programs described in this book the PROMulator was set to draw its power from the target board.

When initially hardware testing the microcontroller prototype a small program was written. Typically:

```
$MOD552                             ; include file of SFR addresses
          ORG       0               ; reset start address
          SJMP      START           ; jump over reserved space
          ORG       40H             ; program start address
START:    SETB      P1.1            ; set pin1 port 1 to logic 1
          ACALL     DELAY           ; call subroutine delay
          CLR       P1.1            ; reset pin1 port 1 to logic 0
          ACALL     DELAY           ; call subroutine delay
          SJMP      START           ; jump back to start
DELAY:    MOV       R1, #12H        ; start of double loop delay, hex 12 into R1
OUTER:    MOV       R0, #34H        ; hex 34 into R0
INNER:    DJNZ      R0, INNER       ; keep decrementing R0 till it becomes zero
          DJNZ      R1, OUTER       ; decrement R1 and go back to OUTER if R1 not
                                    ; zero
          RET                       ; return from subroutine
          END                       ; end of cross-assembly
```

This program produces an oscillating signal on pin 1, Port 1.

This source program was then cross-assembled to produce two extra files;

        progname.LST
        progname.HEX

The object code, progname.HEX is:

      : 02000000803E40
      : 10004000D291114AC291114A80F679127834D8FEC1

: 03005000D9FA22B8
: 00000001FF

The format for the object code is:

: BC AAAA RT HH HH HH HH HH .... HH CS

- :   precedes Intel type code
- BC   Byte Count, the hex number of data bytes in the line
- AAAA 16-bit address of the first data byte in the line
- RT   Record Type, 00 for data, 01 for end of file (eof)
- HH   hex data bytes
- CS   check sum, actually the two's complement of the summation of all previous bytes on the line

Compare this with the .LST file which shows both the object code and the source program:

```
               1 $MOD552                    ; include file of SFR addresses
0000           2              ORG   0        ; reset start address
0000 803E      3              SJMP  START    ; jump over reserved space
0040           4              ORG   40H      ; program start address
0040 D291      5 START:  SETB  P1.1          ; set pin1 port 1 to logic 1
0042 114A      6              ACALL DELAY     ; call subroutine delay
0044 C291      7              CLR   P1.1      ; reset pin1 port 1 to logic 0
0046 114A      8              ACALL DELAY     ; call subroutine delay
0048 80F6      9              SJMP  START     ; jump back to start
004A 7912     10 DELAY:  MOV   R1,#12H        ; start of double loop delay, hex 12
                                             ; into R1
004C 7834     11 OUTER:  MOV   R0,#34H        ; hex 34 into R0
004E D8FE     12 INNER:  DJNZ  R0,INNER       ; keep decremeting R0 till it becomes
                                             ; zero
0050 D9FA     13              DJNZ  R1,OUTER   ; decrement R1 and go back to OUTER if
                                             ; R1 not zero
0052 22       14              RET             ; return from subroutine
              15              END             ; end of cross-assembly
```

The header plug of the PROMulator replaces the EPROM and the target board power supply is turned on. From the PC the object code, progname.HEX is loaded into the PROMulator with the following command line:

LD progname.hex/i/8k/e

- /i means Intel type code
- /8k emulating an 8k EPROM
- /e go into edit mode when the hex file is loaded
- LD.EXE is the PROMulator loader file

When the procedure is complete the display on the PC screen is similar to that shown in Figure 11.3 which is the edit mode.

The cursor address is shown on the bottom line of the display and in Figure 11.3 it is pointing to the reset address 00000.

Pressing the Function key F1 displays the information given by Figure 11.4.

When Function key F3 is pressed the object code is transferred from the PC down to the PROMulator.

```
+----------------------------------------------------------------------+
¦  <F1> = INFO     <F2> = MENU        <F3> = SEND       <F10> =  EXIT    ¦
+----------------------------------------------------------------------+


+----------------------------------------------------------------------+
¦                                                                      ¦
¦   80 3E 00 00 00 00 00 00 00 00 00 00 00 00 00 00     Ç>             ¦
¦   00 00 00 00 00 00 00 00 00 00 00 00 00 00 00 00                    ¦
¦   00 00 00 00 00 00 00 00 00 00 00 00 00 00 00 00                    ¦
¦   00 00 00 00 00 00 00 00 00 00 00 00 00 00 00 00                    ¦
¦   D2 91 11 4A C2 91 11 4A 80 F6 79 12 78 34 D8 FE     -æ J-æ JÇ+y x4+_ ¦
¦   D9 FA 22 00 00 00 00 00 00 00 00 00 00 00 00 00     +·"            ¦
¦   00 00 00 00 00 00 00 00 00 00 00 00 00 00 00 00                    ¦
¦   00 00 00 00 00 00 00 00 00 00 00 00 00 00 00 00                    ¦
¦   00 00 00 00 00 00 00 00 00 00 00 00 00 00 00 00                    ¦
¦   00 00 00 00 00 00 00 00 00 00 00 00 00 00 00 00                    ¦
¦   00 00 00 00 00 00 00 00 00 00 00 00 00 00 00 00                    ¦
¦   00 00 00 00 00 00 00 00 00 00 00 00 00 00 00 00                    ¦
¦   00 00 00 00 00 00 00 00 00 00 00 00 00 00 00 00                    ¦
¦   00 00 00 00 00 00 00 00 00 00 00 00 00 00 00 00                    ¦
¦   00 00 00 00 00 00 00 00 00 00 00 00 00 00 00 00                    ¦
¦   00 00 00 00 00 00 00 00 00 00 00 00 00 00 00 00                    ¦
+----------------------------------------- Address = 00000 ------------+
```

Figure 11.3 PROMulator edit page

```
+----------------------------------------------------------------------+
¦       Object file.             promul.hex                            ¦
¦       Object file type.        Intel Hex                             ¦
¦       Target ROM size.         08K                                   ¦
¦       Object file offset.      $000000                               ¦
¦       Address offset.          $000000                               ¦
¦       Load ROM from.           $00000                                ¦
¦                    To.         $01fff                                ¦
¦       ROM fill.                Off                                   ¦
¦       Send to PROMulator #.    1                                     ¦
¦       Output to parallel port. LPT1:                                 ¦
¦       Split factor.            1                                     ¦
¦            Reset target.       No                                    ¦
¦                                                                      ¦
¦ Key F2:    Misc functions menu    1) Save ram contents to disc       ¦
¦                                   2) Load file from disc             ¦
¦                                   3) Jump to memory location.        ¦
¦                                                                      ¦
¦ Key F3:    Sends data to PROMulator(s).                              ¦
¦                                                                      ¦
¦ Key F10:   Exit to dos.                                              ¦
¦                                                                      ¦
¦ To move cursor use  up, down, right, left, pg up, and pg dn keys.    ¦
¦                                                                      ¦
+----------------------------------------------------------------------+
```

Figure 11.4 PROMulator information page

The PROMulator has a large reset button and when this is pressed the target board microcontroller accesses the program and the prototype runs, assuming there are no hardware problems.

HARDWARE CHECKING

The use of a logic pen may be preferable to an oscilloscope when hardware debugging the prototype, since it is not necessary to look up from the board. The logic pen or probe usually has some LEDs to indicate the presence of logic 1 or logic 0 or an oscillating signal such as an address or data line. Some logic pens also have an audible actuator giving a high pitched sound for logic 1 and a low pitched sound for logic 0. Check the power supply voltage levels of all the on-board ICs.

The test program is meant to oscillate pin 1 on Port 1 so check this point with the logic pen. If it is oscillating then this would indicate that the hardware is satisfactory and the other port pins could be checked. See *USING THE PROMULATOR EDITOR*, p. 213.

If the pin is not oscillating then the Address Latch Enable (ALE) and Program Store ENable (PSEN) should be checked, both at the microcontroller point and on the external chips to which they are connected. The ALE would go to pin 11 on the HC373 octal latch and PSEN might go to the EPROM socket. If one of these signals is oscillating on the microcontroller but not on the external IC then this would indicate a break in the connecting path; this could be a pcb track break or a connection not soldered.

If these two signals are oscillating both on the microcontroller and on the chips they connect to, then the other enable logic levels on these external chips should be checked. For example pins 1 and 27 on a 2764 EPROM must be connected to +5 V.

Also, on the 2764 if pin 20 is not controlled from logic chips then it should be connected to ground. If pin 1 on the HC373 octal latch is not controlled by other logic then it must be connected to ground since it is also an active low input. The schematic circuit of Figure 11.1 shows that pin 22 of the 8k RAM chip 6264 is enabled by a NAND logic combination of the READ (RD) and PSEN signals. Although not required for this test program pin 22 on the RAM should be oscillating and its connecting path from the microcontroller could be checked, using the logic pen.

If ALE or PSEN are not oscillating then this might indicate a fault with either the reset or the crystal oscillator circuit. On the 80C552 pin 34 is XTAL2, the crystal oscillator output. Check this point with the logic pen. If it is not oscillating then check the soldered connections and check that the small decoupling capacitors have no short circuits across them. It is essential that the oscillator works.

If your circuit has a reset switch then put the logic pen onto the microcontroller Reset pin and press the reset switch; it should be high when the switch is pressed and go low when the switch is released, for 8-bit microcontrollers in the 80C51 family.

Check that the capacitor is the correct value and also check that it is connected the right way. Being a large value capacitor it will be either a tantalum or an electrolytic and the polarity must be correct.

If the XTAL2, ALE and PSEN are all oscillating and the program is apparently still not working then this would point to a short circuit, maybe an open circuit, possibly between address lines or between data lines. These checks can be done using a multi-meter adjusted to the low resistance setting for continuity.

Testing for open circuits is easier; try this first, between the microcontroller and the EPROM to start with. If the fault is still not found then check for short circuits; try the data lines on the EPROM first, then the address lines.

USING THE PROMULATOR EDITOR

This PROMulator has the useful facility of enabling the hex code to be edited and changed. This allows program changes without having to make changes to the source program and repeating the process of cross-assembly. Compared to the use of a MICE this technique could be considered crude, but for the small volume PROMulator user it is quite convenient.

Referring to the .LST file it may be seen that the hex for SETB P1.1 is D291 and that the hex code for CLR P1.1 is C291. Hex 90 is actually the base address of the Special Function Register (SFR) Port 1. D290 is the hex code for set pin 0 on Port 1. D297 sets pin 7 on port 1.

It may be seen from the hex dump of Figure 11.3 that D291 is located at address 0040 and further along the line is C291. The method is to move the cursor to the 91 and change it to whichever pin number you wish to check. For example pin 3 would give the changes D293 and C293. Then return the cursor to the start address by pressing the PC key, Home and then press Function key F3 to send this modified data to the PROMulator. Press the PROMulator reset button and the microcontroller system runs. Use the logic pen to check that the revised pin is oscillating.

If the base addresses of the other ports are known then the hex dump can be modified accordingly. For example the base address of Port 4 is C0, so D2C2 would set pin 2 on Port 4.

The delay could also be altered, using the same technique. In this program a double-loop delay was used; hex 12 was used in the outer loop and hex 34 in the inner loop. Changing the hex 12 would give coarse control of the delay time while altering the hex 34 would give fine control.

11.3   8-bit microcontroller applications

Three microcontrollers from the Philips 80C51 family are used in this book, namely the 80C31, 80C552 and the 87C750. The 80C31 is the ROMless type of the basic core 80C51 controller whereas the 80C552 has many special features. The 87C750 is a basic, 24-pin skinnydip (0.3 in wide) microcontroller having an on-board EPROM.

It is probably true to say that most, if not all, microcontrollers have on-board timer/ counter registers and these are incremented by the microcontroller's clock signal, which for the 80C51 family is 1/12 of the crystal frequency. The XA 16-bit microcontroller described in the previous chapter is much faster having its clock and crystal frequencies the same.

TIMER/COUNTER

The timer/counter register structure has been described in Chapter 2. The following example program uses timer 0 in Mode 1, set in 16-bit mode by the line:

```
MOV TMOD, #01H
```

```
$MOD552                      ; include file listing SFRs for the 80C552
        ORG   0              ; reset start address
        SJMP  START          ; jump to start of program
        ORG   40H            ; program start
START:  MOV   TMOD,#01H      ; set timer 0 to mode 1, 16 bit
        CLR   P3.4           ; put pin4 port 3 to logic 0
        ACALL DELAY          ; call 1 minute delay
        SETB  P3.4           ; set pin4 port 3 back to logic 1
        SJMP  START          ; repeat the program
DELAY:  MOV   R6,#6          ; 6 times 10 sec = 60 sec delay
OUTER:  MOV   R7,#200        ; 200 times 50 ms = 10 sec delay
INNER:  MOV   TH0,#HIGH -46080 ; 50 ms delay, High byte of -46080 into TH0
        MOV   TL0,#LOW  -46080 ;              Low byte of -46080 into TL0
        SETB  TR0            ; turn Timer 0 on
        JNB   TF0,$          ; wait for Timer 0 Flag to set, indicates roll-over
        CLR   TF0            ; clear Timer over flow flag
        CLR   TR0            ; turn Timer 0 off
        DJNZ  R7,INNER       ; decrement R7, repeat 50 ms delay if R7 not zero
        DJNZ  R6,OUTER       ; decrement R6, refill R7 if R6 not zero
        RET                  ; return from delay subroutine
        END                  ; end of cross-assembly
```

Note the method of defining the base number to go into the Timer 0 16-bit register. In this example the Timer 0 delay is to be 50 ms or 50 000 μs.

The crystal frequency is 11.0592 MHz; this crystal value was chosen in order to obtain 9600 baud for the RS232 serial transmission. The clock frequency is 1/12 of 11.0592 MHz which is 0.9216 MHz and so the clock or machine cycle time is 1/0.9216 μs. This gives 1.085 069 4 μs. Dividing this machine cycle time into 50 000 μs gives 46 080.002, which for the program has been taken as 46 080.

Now a 16-bit register has a maximum of $2^{16} - 1$ which is 65 535, i.e. a count of 65 536 if started from zero. In order to achieve a 50 000 μs delay the timer has to be clocked 46 080 times.

We could subtract 46 080 from 65 536 to give 19 456 and then convert it to hex to give 4C00 and then in this hex form it would be easy to split the number into a high byte of 4C and a low byte of 00. 4C could be moved into the Timer High byte (TH0) and 00 could be moved into the Timer Low byte (TL0).

Instead the technique shown in the program removes the need to do this. Once it is known how many times the timer must be clocked to achieve the desired delay (46 080 in this example) then by using the High and Low additives it can be easily and conveniently programmed, using the decimal number. Remember the minus sign before the number.

MOV TH0, #HIGH − 46080 ; 50 ms delay, High byte of − 46080 into TH0
MOV TL0, #LOW − 46080 ;   Low byte of − 46080 into TL0

STEPPER MOTOR (SPEED)

A stepper motor program was described in Chapter 8 where the holding delay for each step would determine the speed of the motor shaft, but the microcontroller timer was not used for the delay. The delay routine was:

```
; Double loop delay
DELAY: MOV    R1,#0FFH   ; put hex FF into register 1
OUTER: MOV    R0,#0FFH   ; put hex FF into register 0
INNER: DJNZ   R0,INNER   ; decrement R0 until it is zero
       DJNZ   R1,OUTER   ; decrement R1, go to outer until R1 = 0
       RET              ; return from subroutine
```

The clock cycles for each operation would need to be considered when working out the time delay for this routine:

DJNZ   Rn,rel   takes 2 clock cycles
MOV   Rn, #data   takes 1 clock cycle

Therefore the total number of clock cycles for the delay routine would be:

$256 \times ((256 \times 2)+1)) \approx 256 \times 256 = 65\,536$

The clock frequency is 0.9216 MHz, giving a clock cycle time of 1.085 07 µs. Therefore the delay is:

$65\,536 \times 1.085\,07$ µs $= 71.1$ ms

This is the hold time for each step and the motor would perform 48 steps per revolution of the shaft. Therefore the time for one revolution is:

71.1 ms $\times$ 48 $= 3.41$ s

which gives a shaft speed of about 18 rev/min.

A formula could be contrived, when using this method for the step delay, perhaps something like:

Delay $= N_1 \times N_2 = T_C$

where: N_1 = number loaded into R1
       N_2 = number loaded into R0
       T_c = clock cycle time

Alternatively the Timer register could be used. Suppose this stepper motor is to be driven at 40 rev/min.

40 rev = 60 s
1 rev = 6/4 s = 1.5 s

The motor step angle is 7.5°, therefore the number of steps (and delays) per revolution is:

360/7.5 = 48 steps per rev

Every time the motor steps it is held for one delay so that there are 48 delays per rev, so:

48 delays = 1.5 s

1 delay = 1.5/48 s
1 delay = 0.03125 s

Clock frequency is 0.9216 MHz (i.e. 11.0592 MHz divided by 12) so that the clock cycle time T_c is 1/0.9216 MHz. Therefore the number of clock cycles for one delay is:

delay/T_c or
delay × clock frequency

For this example delay the number of clock cycles to reach roll-over in the 16-bit Timer register is:

$$0.03125 \times 0.9216 \times 10^6 = 28800$$

Therefore the delay routine could be:

```
DELAY: MOV    THO,#HIGH-28800   ; 31.25 ms delay, High byte of -28800 into THO
       MOV    TLO,#LOW-28800    ; Low byte of -28800 into TLO
       SETB   TR0               ; turn Timer 0 on
       JNB    TF0,$             ; wait for Timer 0 Flag to set, indicates
                                ; roll-over.
       CLR    TF0               ; clear Timer over flow flag
       CLR    TR0               ; turn Timer 0 off
       RET                      ; return from subroutine
```

Of course in the main body of the program the Timer would have to be set in the correct operating mode.

FOUR-CHANNEL SAMPLER

This application is based on an 80C31 system using a MAX154 4-channel ADC to sample analogue data on four channels and then transmitting the data to a remote PC using the 80C31 UART. The basic system is shown in Figure 11.5.

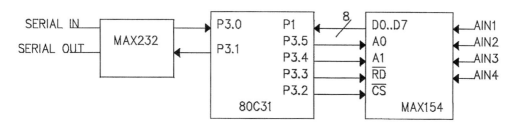

Figure 11.5 Block diagram of four-channel sampler

In this application a PC sends a request signal to the 80C31 UART whereupon the microcontroller reads four consecutive samples from the Maxim 4-channel ADC and sends the hex values back to the PC. The MAX154 is unipolar 4-channel ADC. Its minimum and maximum ranges are shown in Table 11.1.

Table 11.1 MAX154 unipolar 4-channel ADC range limits

ADC	Input	Output
Minimum	0 V	hex 00
Maximum	5 V	hex FF

Between these two extremes the relationship is linear. The MAX154 is a parallel ADC and the symbol 8/ on Figure 11.5 indicates that there is an 8-wire bus between D0..D7 on the ADC and P1 on the 80C31. The MAX154 pin-out is shown by Figure 11.6.

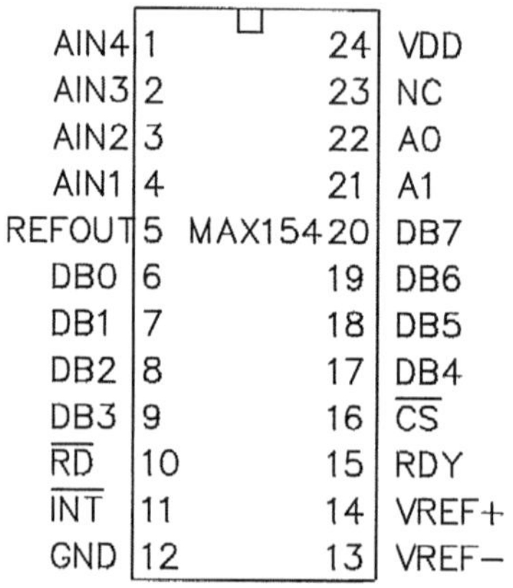

```
        AIN4 1          24  VDD
        AIN3 2          23  NC
        AIN2 3          22  AO
        AIN1 4          21  A1
      REFOUT 5  MAX154 20  DB7
         DB0 6          19  DB6
         DB1 7          18  DB5
         DB2 8          17  DB4
         DB3 9          16  CS
          RD 10         15  RDY
         INT 11         14  VREF+
         GND 12         13  VREF-
```

Figure 11.6 MAX154 pin-out

The MAX154 is an 8-bit device and its resolution is given by:

$$1\ LSB = \frac{V_{REF+} - V_{REF-}}{256}$$

In this application:

- V_{REF-} is set to 0 V at ground
- V_{REF+} is set to +5 V at V_{DD}

giving a bit resolution of approximately 19.5 mV.

Port 3 pins 4 and 5 of the 80C31 are used to select the ADC channels as shown in Table 11.2.

Table 11.2 MAX154 pin assignment for ADC channel selection

A0	A1	Selected channel	
0	0	Channel 1	AIN1
0	1	Channel 2	AIN2
1	0	Channel 3	AIN3
1	1	Channel 4	AIN4

The MAX154 pin functions are given in Table 11.3.

The schematic diagram for the sampling system is shown in Figure 11.7. It is based on the 80C31 microcontroller. The flow diagram is represented by Figure 11.8.

Port 3 Control

7	6	5	4	3	2	1	0
NC	NC	A0	A1	$\overline{RD}$	$\overline{CS}$	TXD	RXD

- NC = not connected, i.e. not used
- A0, A1 = channel control
- $\overline{RD}$ = ADC ReaD input
- $\overline{CS}$ = ADC Chip Select
- TXD = 80C31 serial output
- RXD = 80C31 serial input

The program is given by:

```
$MOD51
            ORG     0               ; reset start address
            SJMP    START           ; jump over reserved space
            ORG     40H             ; program start address
START:      MOV     SCON,#52H       ; set 8 bit UART
            MOV     PCON,#0         ; set SMOD=0, i.e. K=1 for baud rate
            MOV     TH1,#0FDH       ; hex FD into timer high byte, 9600 baud
            MOV     TMOD,#20H       ; timer 1, 8 bit auto-reload
            SETB    TR1             ; turn timer on
            MOV     P3,#0FFH        ; set all pins p3 high
; wait for input from PC
LOOP:       JNB     RI,LOOP         ; stay here until RI set
            CLR     RI              ; clear RI

; set Port 3 controls and goto sample
            MOV     P3,#0C3H        ; ch1 select +CS +RD low
            ACALL   SAMPLE          ; sample
            MOV     P3,#0D3H        ; ch2 select +CS +RD low
            ACALL   SAMPLE          ; sample
            MOV     P3,#0E3H        ; ch3 select +CS +RD low
            ACALL   SAMPLE          ; sample
            MOV     P3,#0F3H        ; ch4 select +CS +RD low
            ACALL   SAMPLE          ; sample
            LJMP    LOOP            ; repeat sampling loop
```

Table 11.3 Pin function table for the MAX154 device

Pin	Name	Function
1	AIN4	Analogue INput Channel 4
2	AIN3	Analogue INput Channel 3
3	AIN2	Analogue INput Channel 2
4	AIN1	Analogue INput Channel 1
5	REF OUT	REFerence OUTput (2.5 V)
6	DB0	Three-state output, bit 0 (LSB)
7	DB1	Three-state output, bit 1
8	DB2	Three-state output, bit 2
9	DB3	Three-state output, bit 3
10	$\overline{\text{RD}}$	ReaD input, controls conversions and data access
11	$\overline{\text{INT}}$	INTerrupt output, going low indicates end of conversion
12	GND	Ground
13	V_{REF-}	Lower limit of reference span, sets the zero-code voltage; Range: GND to V_{REF+}
14	V_{REF+}	Upper limit of reference span, sets the full-scale input voltage. Range V_{REF-} to V_{DD}
15	RDY	ReaDY output. Open-drain output with no active pull-up device. Goes low when $\overline{\text{CS}}$ goes low and high impedance at the end of a conversion
16	$\overline{\text{CS}}$	Chip-Select input, must be low for device to be selected
17	DB4	Three-state output, bit 4
18	DB5	Three-state output, bit 5
19	DB6	Three-state output, bit 6
20	DB7	Three-state output, bit 7 (MSB)
21	A1	Channel Address 1, input
22	A0	Channel Address 2, input
23	NC	Not Connected
24	V_{DD}	Power-supply voltage, +5 V

```
; check last sample gone, get new sample and send through serial buffer
SAMPLE:   ACALL   DELAY           ; pause
WAIT:     JNB     TI,WAIT         ; wait till last sample gone
          CLR     TI              ; clear TI
          MOV     SBUF,P1         ; move sample to buffer and send
          MOV     P3,#0FFH        ; RD and CS on ADC high
          RET
; pause delay
DELAY:    MOV     R0,#0FFH        ; move hex FF into register R0
TAKE0:    MOV     R1,#0FFH        ; move hex FF into register R1
TAKE1:    DJNZ    R1,TAKE1        ; keep decrementing R1 until it is zero
          DJNZ    R0,TAKE0        ; keep decrementing R0 until it is zero
          RET                     ; return from sub-routine
          END                     ; assembler directive
```

TIMED OPERATION OF THREE SOLENOIDS

In a project it was required to activate three solenoids at four hourly intervals, from a particular time, each day. Each solenoid tilted a trough which contained animal food, the

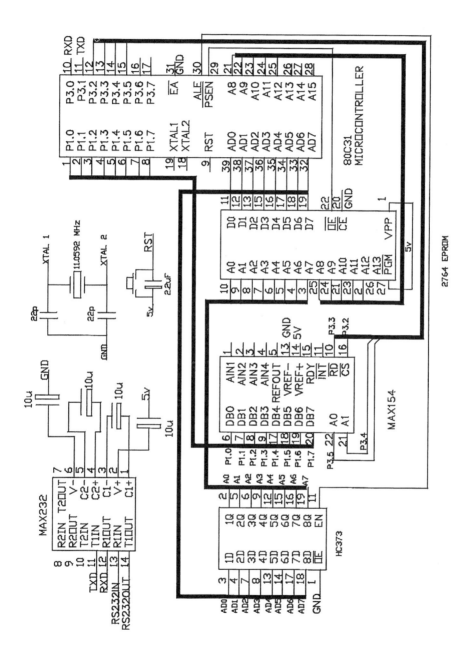

Figure 11.7 Schematic diagram of four channel sampler

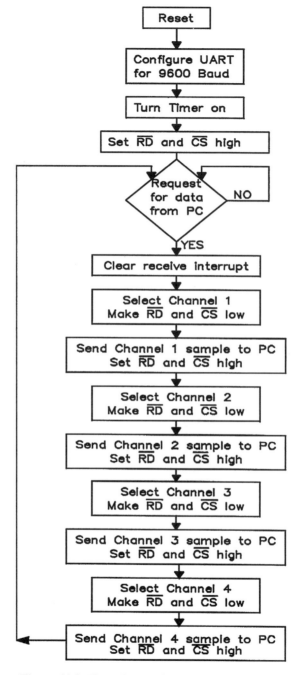

Figure 11.8 Flow diagram for four channel sampler

trough positions were reset manually. For the design an 80C31 microcontroller having a 12 MHz crystal was used, driving the solenoids through an appropriate drive circuit. The whole system was powered from a 12 V car type battery and so a 5 V regulator was required to supply the 80C31 board. The system is represented by Figure 11.9(a) and the schematic for the solenoid drive circuit is shown in Figure 11.9(b).

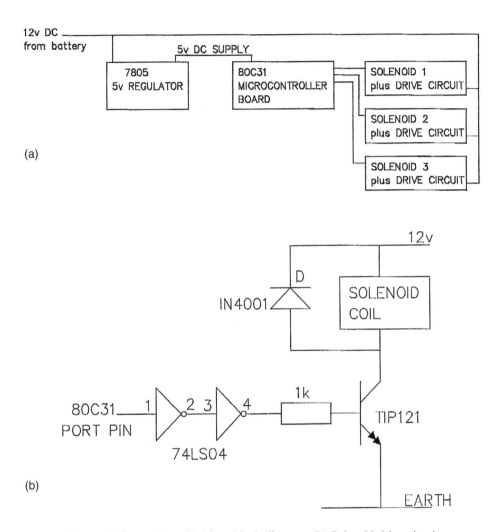

Figure 11.9 (a) Solenoid driver block diagram. (b) Solenoid drive circuit

The following program was used for the prototype:

```
$MOD51                      ; include file giving 80C31 (80C51 family) SFR
                            ; addresses
        ORG    0            ; reset start address
        SJMP   START        ; short jump over reserved space
        ORG    20H          ; program start address
```

```
START:  MOV     MOD,#01H    ; set Timer to mode 1, 16 bit
        CLR     P1.3        ; set pin 1.3 low to turn solenoid off
        CLR     P1.4        ; set pin 1.4 low to turn solenoid off
        CLR     P1.5        ; set pin 1.5 low to turn solenoid off
        ACALL   DELAY       ; call 4hr delay
        SETB    P1.3        ; set pin 1.3 high, first solenoid on after 4 hours
                            ; and
        ACALL   SOLON       ; hold for 1sec delay
        CLR     P1.3        ; set pin 1.3 low to turn first solenoid off
        ACALL   DELAY       ; call 4hr delay
        SETB    P1.4        ; set pin 1.4 high, second solenoid on after a
                            ; further 4 hours and
        ACALL   SOLON       ; hold for 1sec delay
        CLR     P1.4        ; set pin 1.4 low to turn second solenoid off
        ACALL   DELAY       ; call 4hr delay
        SETB    P1.5        ;setpin1.5high,thirdsolenoidonafterafurther
                            ; 4 hours and
        ACALL   SOLON       ; hold for 1sec delay
        CLR     P1.5        ; set pin 1.5 low to turn third solenoid off
LOOP:   SJMP    LOOP        ; stops program until reset at next daily visit
;
; 4 hour delay
; 80C31 has a 1 MHz clock therefore the clock cycle time is 1µs
;
DELAY:  MOV     R1,#8       ; 8 × half an hour = 4 hours
LOOP2:  MOV     R2,#180     ; 180 × 10 sec = 1800 sec = half of one hour
LOOP1:  MOV     R3,#200     ; 200 × 50 ms = 10 sec delay
AGAIN:  MOV     TH0,#HIGH -50000 ; 50000 ×  1µs = 50 ms
        MOV     TL0,#LOW -50000 ;
        SETB    TR0         ; turn timer0 on
WAIT:   JNB     TF0,WAIT    ; wait for roll over
        CLR     TF0         ; clear Timer0 flag
        CLR     TR0         ; turn Timer0 off
        DJNZ    R3, AGAIN   ; keep looping to AGAIN until R3 is zero
        DJNZ    R2, LOOP1   ; keep looping to LOOP1 until R2 is zero
        DJNZ    R1, LOOP2   ; keep looping to LOOP2 until R1 is zero
        RET                 ; return from subroutine
; SOLenoid ON for 1 second
;
SOLON:  MOV     R4,#200     ; 200 × 5 ms = 1sec delay
LOOP3:  MOV     TH0,#HIGH -5000 ; 5000 × 1µs = 5 ms
        MOV     TL0,#LOW -5000 ;
        SETB    TR0         ; turn Timer0 on
WAIT1:  JNB     TF0, WAIT1  ; wait until Timer0 flag is set
        CLR     TF0         ; clear Timer0 flag
        CLR     TR0         ; turn Timer0 off
        DJNZ    R4,LOOP3    ; keep looping to LOOP3 until R4 is zero
        RET                 ; return from subroutine
        END
```

TIMER INTERRUPTS

The previous programs have all had a similar start:

```
$MOD552
        ORG    0        ; reset start address
        SJMP   START    ; jump over reserved addresses
        ORG    40H      ; program start address
```

The comment regarding the jump over reserved addresses refers to the Interrupt Vector addresses at the beginning of PROM space.

In Chapter 2 this address range was given for the various microcontrollers, including the 80C552. Compared to the 80C51, the 80C552 controller has more SFRs and also has a greater range of Interrupt addresses; the addresses are given in Table 11.4.

Table 11.4 Vector addresses for the 80C552 microcontroller

Source	Priority (1 = highest)	Name	Vector address
Reset	1	RST	0000h
External Interrupt 0	2	X0	0003h
Timer 0 overflow	5	T0	000Bh
External Interrupt 1	8	X1	0013h
Timer 1 overflow	11	T1	001Bh
SIO0 (UART)	14	S0	0023h
SIO1 (I²C)	3	S1	002Bh
T2 capture 0	6	CT0	0033h
T2 capture 1	9	CT1	003Bh
T2 capture 2	12	CT2	0043h
T2 capture 3	15	CT3	004Bh
ADC completion	4	ADC	0053h
T2 compare 0	7	CM0	005Bh
T2 compare 1	10	CM1	0063h
T2 compare 2	13	CM2	006Bh
T2 overflow	16	T2	0073h

If all of these reserved addresses were being used in an 80C552 program then the program start address should be at least 007Bh or 7Bh instead of 40h that has been used in the previous programs.

The highest priority interrupt is the Reset and the lowest is the Timer 2 overflow. Timer 0 priority is higher than Timer 1 and so if a Timer 1 interrupt routine is running it can itself be interrupted by the demand for a Timer 0 interrupt routine.

The following is an example program, using the Timer 1 interrupt.

```
$MOD552                  ; include file containing 80C552 SFR addresses
        ORG    0         ; reset address
        SJMP   START     ; short jump over reserved addresses
        ORG    1BH       ; Timer 1 interrupt vector address
        LJMP   SERVICE   ; long jump to interrupt service routine
        ORG    40H       ; start of main program
;
```

```
;Initiate the Timer
START     MOV   TMOD,#10H   ; set Timer 1 to mode 1 (16 bit)
          MOV   TH1,#HIGH -46080 ; 50 ms delay, HIGH byte
          MOV   TL1,#LOW -46080 ; 50 ms delay, LOW byte
          SETB  TR1           ; turn Timer 1 on
          MOV   IE,#88H       ; enable Timer 1 interrupt
;

; Main program
FOREVER: SJMP  FOREVER        ; stay here
;
; Interrupt service routine
SERVICE: SETB  P1.1           ; set pin1 on port 1 to logic 1
         CLR   P1.1           ; set pin1 on port 1 to logic 0
         RETI                 ; return from interrupt routine
         END                  ; end of cross-assembly
```

This may seem to be a trivial program with the main part appearing to be stuck in a forever loop. However, once every 50 ms the program diverts to an interrupt sequence and toggles pin 1 on port 1.

Actually this forms the framework of a useful program. For example in a more complicated system the service routine, that occurs every 50 ms, could be used to check the analogue voltage levels using the ADCs of the 80C552 and perhaps send this data to a PC, using the 80C552 UART. For the remaining part of the 50 ms gap, after the service interrupt routine has completed (RETI), the main part of the program could update a microcontroller seven segment display.

PULSE WIDTH MODULATED OUTPUTS

The 80C552 microcontroller has two PWM outputs, PWM0 and PWM1, on pins 4 and 5 for the PLCC package. PWM was introduced in Chapter 8 as a method for controlling the speed of a small dc motor where the Mark and Space delays gave different average voltages with the delay time always adding up to the same total, giving a constant frequency.

The 80C552 has three PWM SFRs, PWMP, PWM0 and PWM1. PWMP is a Prescale register, which has the effect of reducing the PWM frequency. The PWM frequency (f_{PWM}) is given by the following formula:

$$f_{PWM} = \frac{f_{osc}}{2 \times (1 + PWMP) \times 255}$$

where:

f_{osc} = crystal oscillator frequency
PWMP = 8-bit Prescale value

PWM0 and PWM1 are also 8-bit registers. The number held in them relates to the length of the Space, the off part of the signal. A small number in a PWMn (n = 0 or 1) register establishes a signal with a large Mark/Space ratio and a large 8-bit number gives a small Mark/Space ratio signal.

The Mark/Space (M:S) ratio is given by:

$$M:S = \frac{255 - (PWMn)}{(PWMn)} \qquad n = 0 \text{ or } 1$$

The following example program is for an 80C552 using an 11.0592 MHz crystal. PWM1 is used with a value of decimal 85 and a prescale (PWMP) value of decimal 216 is used. From the above formulae this would give a Mark/Space ratio of 2:1 at a frequency of approximately 100 Hz. A Mark/Space ratio of 2:1 should give an average voltage of about 3.33 V, i.e. $(2\times5)/(2+1)$.

```
$MOD552                        ; include file giving SFR addresses
          ORG    0             ; reset address
          SJMP   START         ; short jump over reserved addresses
          ORG    40H           ; program start address
START:    MOV    PWMP,#216     ; decimal 216 into the prescale (PWMP) register
          MOV    PWM1,#85      ; decimal 85 into PWM1 register
AGAIN:    SJMP   AGAIN         ; repeat
          END                  ; end of cross-assembly
```

Note that the program does not need to keep looping to the PWM1 register. Both PWM outputs could be used, driving two motors at different speeds (i.e. using different averages) and at the same time the microcontroller could be servicing some other routine. This is illustrated in the following program:

```
$MOD552                        ; include file equating SFR addresses
          ORG    0             ; reset address
          SJMP   START         ; short jump over reserved address space
          ORG    40H           ; program start address
START:
; pwm M/S signals
          MOV    PWMP,#216     ; set M/S signal frequency to approximately 100 Hz
          MOV    PWM1,#85      ; gives an average of approximately 3.33 volts
          MOV    PWM0,#2       ; small number in PWM0 gives large Mark / Space
;
; port 1 pins pulsed by microcontroller
AGAIN:    MOV    P1,#0         ; turn all port 1 pins off
          MOV    R1,#88H       ; move hex88 into register R1
TAKE1:    DJNZ   R1,TAKE1      ; short delay while R1 is decremented to zero
          MOV    P1,#0FFH      ; turn all port 1 pins on
          MOV    R1,#88H       ; move hex88 into register R1
TAKE2:    DJNZ   R1,TAKE2      ; short delay while R1 is decremented to zero
          SJMP   AGAIN         ; repeat
          END                  ; end of cross-assembly
```

ANALOGUE TO DIGITAL CONVERTER

The 80C552 has an eight-channel multiplexed ADC, based on the successive approximation method. The ADC is essentially a 10-bit resolution converter but may also be used as eight bits. The ADC is unipolar only; the negative reference AV_{REF-} is connected to ground. One Least Significant Bit (LSB) is given by:

$$1 \text{ LSB} = \frac{AV_{REF+} - AV_{REF-}}{1024}$$

The positive reference (pin 59 on the PLCC package) could be connected to +5 V and the negative reference (pin 58 on the PLCC package) could be connected to 0 V at ground, giving a 1-bit resolution of approximately 5 mV.

This ADC has two SFRs associated with it:

ADCH ADC High byte (bits 2 to 9)
ADCON ADC control (also contains two LSBs 0,1)

ADCH

7	6	5	4	3	2	1	0

bit 9	bit 8	bit 7	bit 6	bit 5	bit 4	bit 3	bit 2

ADCON

bit 1	bit 0	ADEX	ADC1	ADCS	AADR2	AADR1	AADR0

The two MSBs are the two LSBs of the converted 10-bit result.

- ADEX = 0 Software only start conversion is done by putting ADCS = 1
  = 1 Software and hardware start conversion
     STADC (pin 3 PLCC) = 1 initiates hardware start of ADC conversion.
- ADCI   ADC interrupt flag, = 1 when ADC conversion result is ready to be read.
     ADC cannot start a new conversion whilst the ADCI flag is high.
     Flag can be cleared by software or an Interrupt service routine.
- ADCS   ADC Start and Status.
     Setting ADCS starts an ADC conversion.
     ADCS is reset immediately after ADCI is set.
     ADCS cannot be reset by software.
     A new conversion cannot start while either ADCS or ADCI is high.
- AADRn Analogue input channel select (n = 0, 1, 2)
     Refer to Table 11.5.

Table 11.5 Pin assignment for analogue input channel selection

AADR2	AADR1	AADR0	Selected Analogue Channel
0	0	0	ADC0 (P5.0)
0	0	1	ADC1 (P5.1)
0	1	0	ADC2 (P5.2)
0	1	1	ADC3 (P5.3)
1	0	0	ADC4 (P5.4)
1	0	1	ADC5 (P5.5)
1	1	0	ADC6 (P5.6)
1	1	1	ADC7 (P5.7)

An example program is shown below. In this program note the use of logic and byte functions to start the ADC conversion (ADCS = 1) and check for end of conversion (ΛDCI = 1).

The necessity for using logic functions to set or check bits is because the ADCON SFR is not bit addressable.

```
;
; Program reads an analogue voltage on channel 5 and puts the 10 bit output
; onto the ports 4 and 1
; bits 9 to 2 on port 4.7 to 4.0   bit 1 on P1.7   bit 0 on P1.6
;
$MOD552                             ; SFR addresses
        ORG     0                   ; reset start address
        SJMP    START               ; short jump over reserved addresses
        ORG     40H                 ; program start address
START:  ANL     ADCON,#05H          ; clear ADCI and choose channel 5
        ORL     ADCON,#0DH          ; set ADCS to start conversion
EOC:    MOV     A,ADCON             ; move ADCON to accumulator
        JNB     ACC.4,EOC           ; check ADCI set for End Of Conversion
        MOV     P4,ADCH             ; move upper 8 bits to port 4
        MOV     A,ADCON             ; move ADCON to accumulator
        ANL     A,#0C0H             ; mask all but two LSBits
        MOV     P1,A                ; ADC.1 to P1.7, ADC.0 to P1.6
AGAIN:  SJMP    AGAIN               ; stop here
        END                         ; end of cross-assembly
```

11.4 CEIBO 87C750 evaluation kit

This evaluation kit supports the Philips 87C750, a 24-pin DIL microcontroller. Details of the system are given in Appendix I. The system has three modes:

- Simulation
- Simulation-plus
- Emulation

The first mode, Simulation, is software only and allows assembler and C programs to be debugged. All the SFRs can be displayed in the Watches window; their contents are seen to be updated as the program is stepped through. Refer to Figure 11.10.

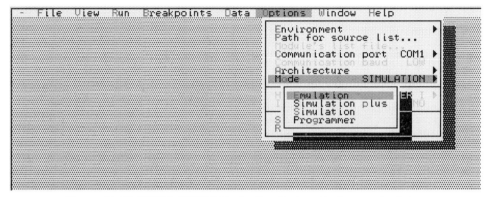

Figure 11.10 CEIBO 87C750 Evaluation System Environment window

The software will run in both a DOS and Windows environment although its windows are not the conventional type. Figure 11.10 shows the the main Menu window; the Option sub-menu is highlighted. It can be seen in this example that the COM1 serial port is chosen and that the system is in the Simulation mode. The example shown in Figure 11.10 also indicates that there is a Programmer mode; this low cost evaluation system may be used to program the 87C750 and also the 87C751 and 87C752.

The Menu choice View allows other windows to be shown as indicated by the list shown in Figure 11.11. Hex program files are loaded from the Files menu item. Figure 11.12 shows a small delay program listed below:

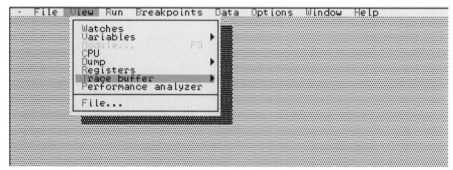

Figure 11.11 CEIBO 87C750 Evaluation System View menu window

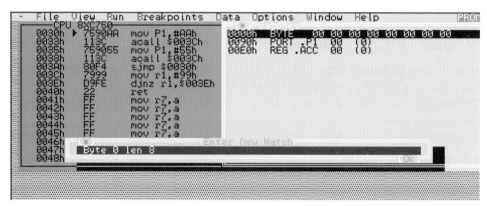

Figure 11.12 CEIBO 87C750 Evaluation System CPU and Watches window

```
$MOD750                        ; include file of 87C750 SFR addresses
        ORG    0               ; reset start address
        SJMP   START           ; short jump over vector addresses
        ORG    30H             ; program start address
START:  MOV    P1,#0AAH        ; move hex AA onto Port 1
        ACALL  DELAY           ; call a hold delay
        MOV    P1,#55H         ; move hex 55 onto Port 1
        ACALL  DELAY           ; call a hold delay
        SJMP   START           ; repeat
DELAY:  MOV    R1,#99H         ; move hex 99 into register R1
TAKE:   DJNZ   R1,TAKE         ; decrement R1 while it is not zero
        RET                    ; return from subroutine delay
        END                    ; cross-assembler directive
```

The CPU window shows the assembler program and next to it is the Watches window showing the SFRs used in the program. An overlay window strip shows the method in assigning the registers to the Watches window. The command line is:

    Byte 0 Len 8

This means show eight registers from address 0.

The Function key commands are shown at the bottom of the main screen as shown in Figure 11.13.

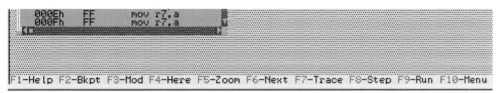

Figure 11.13 CEIBO 87C750 Evaluation System Function Key commands

F8 single steps through the program, avoiding subroutine delay calls; F7 also single steps and includes the subroutines.

The evaluation kit comes complete with a header plug clamped onto a short length of ribbon wire. This header plug may be pushed into the target board socket. The use of the header plug combines with the other two modes of operation, Simulation-plus and Emulation.

In Simulation-plus mode, logic levels may be written into the target and they may also be read from the target. In this mode it is possible to single step through the program, by pressing Function key F8, observing the effect on the target board using a logic pen or other instrument. At the same time any changes to the SFRs may be observed in the Watches window.

The software also has a line assembler and the program can be modified to try out ideas without having to return to the editor to modify the original source program.

The main disappointment with the Simulation-plus mode is the slow run speed, chosen when the Function key F9 is pressed. It seems to run at approximately one hundredth of the clock speed, which means that applications such as variable Mark/Space ratio are too slow to apply average voltages.

Of course the Emulation mode will run at normal clock speed, but this requires the main 87C752 system microcontroller to be programmed with the test routine and this breaks the smooth, continuous debugging routine. The authors believe it would have been more acceptable if the Simulation-plus mode had run at one tenth of normal clock speed.

The main system 87C752 microcontroller is configured with the evaluation system monitor program when the kit is initially set up. The 87C752 has more EPROM space than the 87C750, 2k byte as opposed to 1k byte and even though the system monitor routine is programmed into the 87C752 there is enough EPROM space remaining to run small 87C750 routines when using the Emulation mode.

Apart from the lack of speed the Simulation-plus mode gives a good level of hardware debugging versatility in what is effectively a low cost evaluation system.

11.5   XA cross-assembly and simulation

The XA Assembly language programs have been written using the Macraigor software which may be obtained from the Philips page on the Internet. It is quite a nice package working under Windows and it also has a cross-simulator. The software on the Internet is version 1.0; the software used for this book is version 2.0 which supports the Macraigor XA In-circuit Emulator/Simulator. Figure 11.14 shows the Edit window displayed; the example program is the serial XA application explained in Chapter 10.

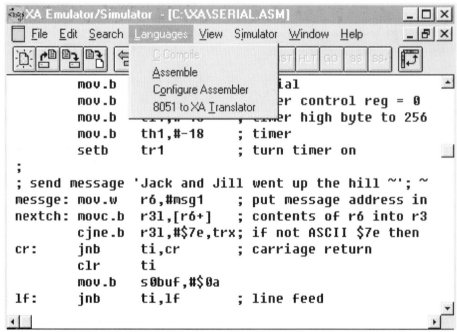

Figure 11.14 Macraigor XA System Exit window, showing Languages drop-down menu

The Languages drop-down menu is shown to have Assemble, Configure Assemble and an apparently useful option, 8051 to XA Translator. Assemble is available on one of the buttons covered by the drop-down menu. The Configure Assemble has the list of options: Generate Object Code, Debug File, Listing File, which are actioned for default.

The 8051 to XA Translator is somewhat disappointing, it seems to imply that an 8051 program is completely translated into a working XA program but this is not the case. It shows a lot of the differences but not all of them and it does not mention about turning the Watchdog Timer off!

It is possible when writing an XA program to move data into the Accumulator or into Register B. The XA allows for this by putting the Accumulator data into Register R4 Low byte and the B Register data into R4 High byte. DPTR data is put into Register R6.

It is the authors' opinion that when preparing to write software for the XA the device should be viewed as a new 16-bit microcontroller, not as an 80C51 upgrade. The XA is an interesting, fast and versatile microcontroller. It retains some of the favourite 80C51 instructions but it has a lot of new ones to try. The reader is advised to follow the basic rules given in Chapter 10 and to develop their own XA programming skill; the use of the Translator is not recommended.

On assembly any syntax errors are highlighted. For the purposes of demonstration the letter P was removed from PCON in the program and it can be seen from Figure 11.15 that the cross-assembler sees the result CON as an undeclared label. Double clicking the left hand mouse button on this error message takes the programmer back to the place in the Edit mode where the syntax error has occurred.

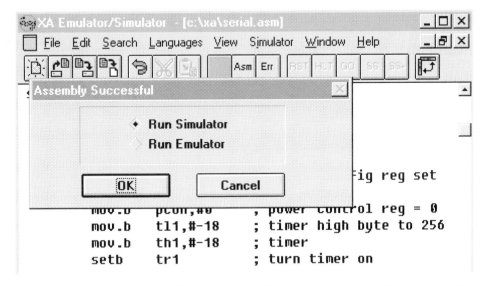

Figure 11.15 Macraigor XA System Syntax Error window

On successful cross-assembly there are two options, Simulate or Emulate. Simulate is a software function whilst Emulate drives the Macraigor In-circuit Emulator which is able to drive the target at normal speed and proves very useful. The Simulator is quite good although limited to on-chip memory. In Simulation mode the Option window is similar to the Edit window, the difference being that more of the options are available. Figure 11.16 shows the Simulation window.

Figure 11.16 Macraigor XA System window showing choice between Simulation and In-circuit Emulator

Figure 11.17 shows the Simulation window together with the View drop-down menu which indicates the possible options that can be displayed. Any of the Global or Banked registers can be changed so there is no need to get stuck in a long delay loop.

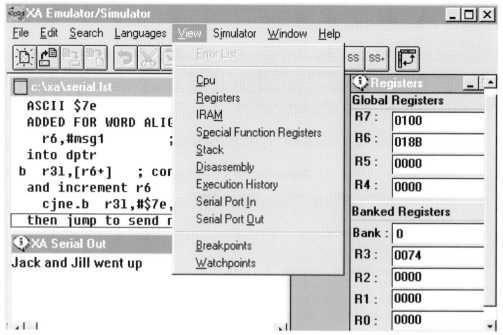

Figure 11.17 Macraigor XA System Simulation window and View drop-down menu

The Serial Port windows are a nice option; the Simulation can be Single Stepped by pressing the SS button or run at animation speed by pressing the SS+ button. It is quite a good cross-simulator although when displaying the SFRs it is necessary to know their addresses since the SFR identity names are not used.

Using the Emulator allows the hardware design to include the option of using the XA with on-board EPROM and this frees up the ports that were used to multiplex the address and data lines to an external EPROM. This can lead to a smaller minimum controller board, being far more self contained, and the ports can be used to interface other devices such as parallel data converters.

The Macraigor In-circuit Emulator pcb is already laid out to include an XA programmer; it just requires populating by the user.

11.6   16-bit (XA) application

Another practical requirement involved sampling a low frequency periodic waveform to establish whether each half cycle had the same amplitude. This application investigated the power absorption and reflective properties of a thin metallic film evaporated on to a specially prepared pyro-electric detecting element. The film was irradiated by a laser beam chopped by a rotating disc at approximately 80 Hz; thus the film received the heating effect of the laser during the half cycle that the beam was not blocked by the chopper. During the half cycle that the laser beam was prevented from reaching the film a dc heating signal was passed to the film; the amplitude of this heating signal could be controlled so that its heating effect should be the same as that of the laser. The pyro-electric element converts the heating effects to a voltage which is detected on a back contact of the modified pyro-electric detector and fed to a null amplifier. The amplitude and offset of the electrical heating signal was adjusted until the null amplifier gave an approximately zero output voltage. At this point the voltage across the film and the current through it were measured and these two values used to measure the absorbed power and the reflectivity of the metallic film. The arrangement is shown in Figure 11.18. The pyro-electric element is capacitive and before nulling the resulting voltage to the null amplifier is exponential. Figure 11.18 represents the analogue part of the application. The XA microcontroller application attempts to automate the system by using a microcontroller together with data converters. It was decided to use 12-bit ADC to read the analogue voltages but to get good offset control it was decided to use a 16-bit DAC.

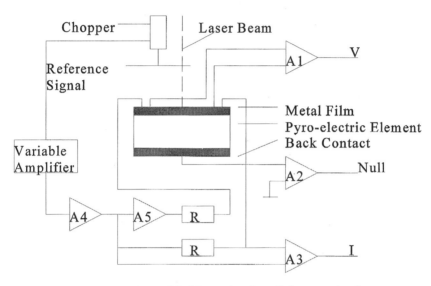

Figure 11.18 Modified Pyro-electric null detector circuit

An XA microcontroller has 16-bit registers which is convenient when reading, writing or manipulating data that is 12 or 16 bits long. Also the XA-G3 has an on-board UART which meant the calculations for power and resistivity could be made off-line, on a PC.

The PROM emulator was used to develop the software and therefore the XA was used in external EPROM mode. This meant that two ports were used for the address lines so the remaining port pins were at a premium. For this reason it was decided to use serial ADCs and DACs.

Maxim make a wide range of devices and provide the engineer with data in book and CD form. Maxim also supply engineering samples for prototyping purposes. After reading the Maxim *New Release Data Book* and checking the Maxim CD-ROM it was decided to use the MAX176 Serial 12-bit ADCs for reading the Null, Voltage and Current signals and the MAX542 Serial 16-bit DAC for producing the electrical heating signal with offset.

USING THE 16-BIT MAX542 DAC

The MAX542 was used in the bipolar configuration. The circuit is shown in Figure 11.19(a). It may be seen that two other MAXIM ICs are required:

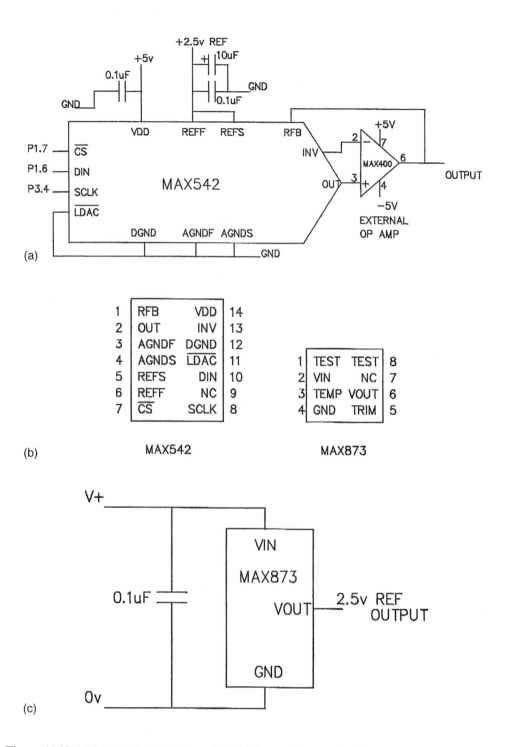

Figure 11.19 (a) MAX542 DAC schematic. (b) Pin-out diagrams for the MAX542 and MAX 873 devices. (c) MAX873 voltage reference schematic

- MAX873   2.5 voltage reference
- MAX400   operational amplifier

The pin-out diagram for the DAC and voltage reference are shown in Figure 11.19(b). The MAX400 is an 8-pin DIL IC and the pin numbers are as shown in Figure 11.19(a). The schematic for the MAX873 voltage reference is shown in Figure 11.19(c). The pins on the MAX873 that are not used are left unconnected. The pin functions for the MAX542 are shown in Table 11.6.

Table 11.6 Pin function table for the MAX542 device

Pin	Name	Function
1	RFB	FeedBack Resistor, connect to external op amp's output in bipolar mode
2	OUT	DAC OUTput voltage
3	AGNDF	Analogue GrouND (Force)
4	AGNDS	Analogue GrouND (Sense)
5	REFS	Voltage REFerence input (Sense). Connect REFS to external 2.5 V reference
6	REFF	Voltage REFerence input (Force). Connect REFF to external 2.5 V reference
7	$\overline{\text{CS}}$	Chip Select input
8	SCLK	Serial CLocK input. Duty cycle must be between 40% and 60%
9	NC	Not Connected, not internally connected
10	DIN	Serial Data INput
11	$\overline{\text{LDAC}}$	LDAC input, a falling edge updates the internal DAC Latch
12	DGND	Digital GrouND
13	INV	Junction of internal scaling resistors. Connect to external op amp's inverting input in bipolar mode
14	V_{DD}	+5 V supply voltage

The timing diagram to send one 16-bit sample is shown in Figure 11.20.

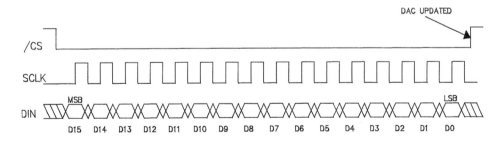

Figure 11.20 Timing diagram for the MAX542 DAC

The following trial program was written to check the resolution of the MAX542 DAC:

```
; program to drive the Maxim542 16-bit serial DAC
; 2.5 volt reference provided by the Max873
; Bipolar using a Maxim opamp, the Max400
;
```

```
; XA connections,
;
; T0            SCLK        P3.4        Max542(pin8)
; T2            DIN         P1.6        Data in MAX542(pin10)
; T2EX          CS          P1.7        used to frame the data Max542(pin7)
;
; DAC output is pin6 on Max400 op amp
;
; XA clock speed is 11.0592 MHz (periodic time is 90.42 ns)
; Maximum SCLK frequency is 6.25 MHz
; Data bit latched on rising edge of SCLK
;
$INCLUDE XA-G3.EQU
                ORG         0
                DW          $8F00,START
                ORG         $120
START:
;
; watchdog off
                MOV.B WDCON,#0
                MOV.B WFEED1,#$A5
                MOV.B WFEED1,#$5A
; main program
;
; trial number into register R2 for DAC output
                MOV.W       R2,#$AAAA
;
                CLR         P1.6        ; start with DIN low
                MOV.B       R1L,#16     ; clock pulse count
REPT:           CLR         P3.4        ; bring SCLK low
                CLR         P1.7        ; bring CS low
                RLC         R2,#1       ; rotate left
                BCS         SETDIN      ; jump to set DIN if C set
                CLR         P1.6        ; otherwise clear DIN
                BR          OVER        ; jump over set DIN
SETDIN:         SETB        P1.6        ; set DIN
OVER:           SETB        P3.4        ; bring clock high
                DJNZ        R1L,NEXT    ; decrement clock pulse count
                SETB        P1.7        ; CS high, frame data, update DAC
AGAIN:          BR          AGAIN       ; stop here if 16 clocks through
NEXT:           NOP                     ; no operations
                NOP
                NOP
                NOP
                BR          REPT        ; go back for another data bit
                END
```

The MAX 542 DAC was set by hardware to work in the range +2.5 V to −2.5 V and so the resolution was:

5 V/65536 $(65536 = 2^{16})$

Therefore the bit resolution was 76.2 μV.

The above program sends hex AAAA which is 43 690 decimal multiplied by 76.2 μV i.e., 3.329178 V. Subtracting 2.5 V gives 0.829178 V. Note that the range is effectively 5 V so that 3.329178 V is in the range 0 V to 5 V and needs to have 2.5 V subtracted to give the actual positive value. This can be seen from the range of voltages equivalent to a hex value shown below:

FFFF	+ 2.5 V	
AAAA	+ 0.83 V	↑
8000	0 V	3.329178 V
0000	− 2.5 V	↓

The program was run and a three-digit multi-meter used to measure the latched DAC output: it read 0.831 V. 5555, the complement of AAAA, measured –0.832 V.

Hex 8000 was the zero voltage point. Voltages close to zero required a more accurate instrument than a cheap three-digit multi-meter.

USING THE MAX176 12-BIT ADC

The MAX176 was chosen because it is a serial device with 12-bit resolution and has a bipolar input. It also has Track and Hold (T/H) and an on-chip voltage reference; it is in fact a very compact 8-pin DIL device. This project uses three ADCs and one drawback of using the MAX176 is the absence of a chip select pin so that the ADCs not being used could not be turned off. Nevertheless it was decided to use it in the prototype system, joining the clock inputs of all three ADCs together and also the convert-starts of all three ADCs together. Of course the data output devices from each device were kept separate.

The MAX176 was used as a bipolar ADC having an input range of + or –5 V and to achieve this V_{ss} was connected to –12 V (the possible range is –15 V to –12 V). The binary output described as two's complement has the range:

0111 1111 1111	+5 V
0000 0000 0001	0 V + 0.5LSB
1111 1111 1111	0 V – 0.5LSB
1000 0000 0000	–5 V

where: $1LSB = \dfrac{10\ V}{2^{12}} = 2.44\ mV$

A conversion is initiated by the convert (CONVST) start. Rising edge and clock edges typically appear after the convert start's rising edge. For this converter, data is latched on falling edges of the clock. The first bit appearing at the DATA pin on the MAX176 is always high followed by 12 data bits with the MSB first. The MSB is 0 for positive analogue inputs and 1 for negative analogue inputs. The connection diagram is shown in Figure 11.21.

It is unnecessary to show a separate pin-out diagram for the MAX176 since it is an 8-pin DIL IC and this information is shown in Figure 11.21. The function of each pin of the MAX176 is shown in Table 11.7. The timing diagram is shown in Figure 11.22.

Test inputs were set up using a separate dc power supply and the program below was used to read these set dc inputs. The binary coded signal transferred to the XA microcontroller from the MAX176 was detected using a logic analyser.

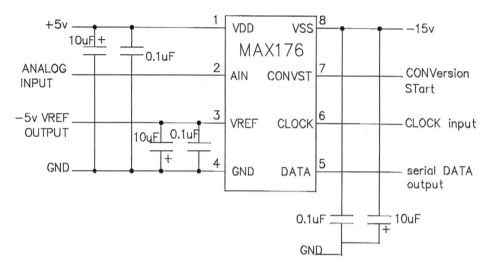

Figure 11.21 MAX176 connection diagram

Table 11.7 Pin function table for the MAX176 device

Pin	Name	Function
1	V_{DD}	Positive supply +5 V
2	AIN	Analogue INput +/–5 V bipolar input range
3	V_{REF}	REFerence voltage output –5 V
4	GND	Ground
5	DATA	Serial Data output
6	CLOCK	Clock input, TTL / +5 V CMOS compatible
7	CONVST	CONVersion STart input
8	V_{SS}	Negative supply, –11.4 V to –15.75 V

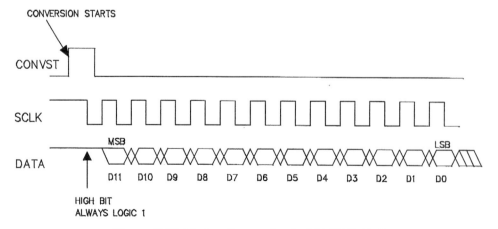

Figure 11.22 Timing diagram for the MAX176 ADC

```
; program to drive the Maxim176 Bipolar 12 bit serial ADC
;
;                     _  __
;           Vdd 1 |      | 8 Vss      Vss -15V DC
;           Ain 2 |      | 7 CONVST   CONVST Conversion start (High)
;          VREF 3 |      | 6 CLOCK    CLOCK 100 kHz to 3 MHz (from micro)
;           GND 4 |__    | 5 DATA     VREF output, approx -5V out
;                                     Ain analogue input +/- 5V range
;                                     Vdd +5V DC
; TO      CLOCK      P3.4
; INT1    DATA       P3.3            ____
; INT0    CONVST     P3.2      __ |      | __
;
; XA clock speed is 11.0592 MHz (periodic time 90.42 ns)
; Maximum conversion clock (CLK) speed is 3.0 MHz (4.0 MHz)
;
$INCLUDE XA-G3.EQU
            ORG    0
            DW     $8F00,START
            ORG    $120
START:
; watchdog off
;
            MOV.B  WDCON,#0
            MOV.B  WFEED1,#$A5
            MOV.B  WFEED2,#$5A
;
; main program
;
            MOV.W  R2,#$8000    ; used to set logic 1 into data store
            MOV.W  R1,#0        ; clear R1 to accept data in
            CLR    P3.2         ; start with convst low
            MOV.B  R0L,#16      ; allow for 16 bits in R0 Low byte
            SETB   P3.4         ; clock high
            SETB   P3.2         ; convst high, conversion starts
            NOP                 ; no operation
            NOP
            CLR    P3.4         ; clock low, data latches
            NOP
            CLR    P3.2         ; convst low
SAMPLE:     SETB   P3.4         ; clock high
            NOP
            NOP
            NOP
            CLR    P3.4         ; clock low
; Read serial sample bits into register R1 from P3.3 (DATA)
            JNB    P3.3,ZERO    ; jump next op if P3.3 = 0
            OR     R1,R2        ; set bit in DATA store
ZERO:       RR     R2,#1        ; Rotate Right logic 1 in R2 down one bit
            DJNZ   R0L,SAMPLE   ; check for 16 bits clocked through
            SETB   P3.2         ; set convst high
            SETB   P3.4         ; set clock high
AGAIN:      BR     AGAIN        ; a stop
            END                 ; cross-assembler directive.
```

Summary

- Initially some common development systems were described and compared, the advantages and disadvantages being highlighted and then a basic hardware checking methodology described.
- The use of the Timer/Counter was explained and its use in a delay routine compared to a previous method of decrementing registers to zero. The Timer/Counter counts up and sets a flag when it rolls over; this is when the Timer/Counter register is full and binary 1 is added as the LSB, causing the register to roll over to zero.
- Application examples were given, using the Timer/Counter followed by an example of how to set and initiate a Timer interrupt routine.
- The control of PWM signals, using an 80C552 microcontroller, was described. This method is used increasingly for driving small dc motors. The control technique is simplified by using the 80C552 SFRs.
- The 10-bit ADC, resident on the 80C552, was described. It was explained that this eight-channel, multiplexed ADC could be used with 8-bit or 10-bit resolution. In common with other microcontrollers having on-board ADCs, this one was unipolar meaning that in its basic configuration it cannot be used for analogue signals that go negative.
- The 87C750 microcontroller was given as an example of the type having an on-board EPROM and it was seen that because of this there was no need to use ports or an octal latch to direct address and data lines to an external EPROM and this greatly simplified the overall circuit design. The disadvantages included:
  - EPROM size limited to microcontroller type;
  - an expensive MICE required for serious prototype development.
  An inexpensive 87C750 evaluation system was described and its advantages and limitations were outlined.
- A laser power absorption application using the 16-bit XA microcontroller was described. The application used high bit resolution serial ADCs and DACs. The DAC was 16-bit, having a bit resolution of 76.2 μV.
  Serial data converters take longer to transfer data to or from the microcontroller but have the important advantage of needing fewer transfer lines, quite often just two or three.

Exercises

1. In computer terms briefly describe the uses of a mouse and a MICE.
2. What does PLCC stand for?
3. Using a logic pen during a hardware check two data lines stick at 5 V. What may be a possible cause?
4. The logic pen shows that ALE is pulsing but touching pin 11 on the HC373 octal latch indicates no voltage present. What fault do you suspect?
5. Before populating an 80C31 board, power is applied to the board. Pin 20 on the HC373 octal latch shows 5 V but pin 40 on the 80C31 shows no voltage. What may be the problem?
6. Power is applied to a populated 80C552 board and a logic pen shows that the ALE is not pulsing. What could be the problem?
7. What do the letters PWM stand for?

8. What is the type of memory used in a PROM emulator?
9. Why is a MICE preferred to a PROM emulator?
10. The following line shows the grouping of hex characters in a line of machine code. Identify and describe each block:

    BC AAAA RT HH HH HH .... HH CS
11. What does a .LST file show that a .ASM file does not?
12. A small program is required to be written so that the pulsing of the data lines of a prototype 80C552 board can be checked. Write a small program that loads Register R1 with hex 55 and continually loops on this instruction.
13. What do the letters PSEN stand for?
14. A minimum board has only the following ICs: 80C31, an EPROM and an HC373 octal latch. What signal from the microcontroller is used to select the EPROM?
15. Which signal from the microcontroller is active when a valid address is present? How is it used?
16. What are the active reset levels for the XA and the 87C750?
17. Sketch an XA reset circuit showing typical capacitor and resistor values; include a push-to-make reset switch.
18. On an 80C31 prototype board the $\overline{PSEN}$, ALE and XTAL2 pins are all pulsing; even the data lines are pulsing and yet a simple program to pulse the Port 1 pins does not function. What hardware problem would this suggest and how would you attempt to locate it?
19. The following is a small XA program intended to pulse pin 4 on Port 3. It compiles satisfactorily and also simulates, and yet in hardware the pin 4 seems to stick at 5 V. What is missing from the program that causes the pin to remain at 5 V?

```
     $INCLUDE              XA-G3.EQU
              ORG          0
              DW           $8F00,START
              ORG          $120
     START:   SETB         P3.4
              CALL         DELAY
              CLR          P3.4
              CALL         DELAY
              BR           START
     DELAY:   MOV          R1,#$1234
     TAKE:    DJNZ         R1,TAKE
              RET
              END
```

20. What decimal number is in the TH0 SFR following the program line MOV TH0, #HIGH –46080?
    Write an Assembly language program that will cause a delay of 4 hours.
21. What is the reset vector address number? In which IC is it located?
22. 22. What is the SI01 (I²C) vector address number for an 80C552?
23. Assuming all the vector addresses are to be used for an 80C552 system, what should be the program start ORG address?
24. Describe the use of a timer interrupt sequence in a multi-task system.
25. What do the letters PWMP stand for?
26. An 80C552 microcontroller system has an 11.0592 MHz crystal. Write a small routine that will create 100 Hz 4:1 Mark/Space signal at PWM1.

27.   What is the bit resolution of a 10-bit ADC?

28.   A joystick controller has two linear potentiometers each connected between 5 V dc and ground. The wiper of one potentiometer is connected to P3.4 of an 80C552 and the other potentiometer wiper to P3.5. Write an Assembly language routine that will use the ADC of the 80C552 in 8-bit mode and store the binary coded value of one potentiometer in Register R3 and the other in R4.

29.   At a particular joystick position there is 2 V on one potentiometer and 3 V on the other. What would be the corresponding hex numbers in Registers R3 and R4?

30.   An ADC is required for a particular application where an amplified transducer signal varies between plus and minus 2 V. What would be the preferred choice: an 80C552 with on-board ADC or an XA working with an external ADC?

Appendix A
8051 Instruction Set

A.1 Notes on instruction set

Rn   Registers R7-R0 of the currently selected register bank.

direct   8-bit internal data location address. This could be internal data RAM or an SFR.

@Ri   8-bit internal data RAM location addressed indirectly through Register Ri (R0 or R1).

addr 16   16-bit destination address. Used by LCALL and LJMP. A branch can be anywhere within the 64k byte program memory space.

addr 11   11-bit destination address. Used by ACALL and AJMP. The branch would be within the same 2k byte of program memory.

bit   Direct addressed bit in internal data RAM or SFR.

#data   8-bit constant included in the instruction.

#data 16   16-bit constant included in the instruction.

C*   Carry bit in the PSW register.

/   Complement byte or bit.

rel   Signed (two's complement) 8-bit offset byte.

A.2 Data transfer instructions

MOV A, Rn	[A]	< – – –	[Rn]
MOV A, direct	[A]	< – – –	[direct]
MOV A, @Ri	[A]	< – – –	[Ri{M}]
MOV A, #data	[A]	< – – –	data
MOV Rn, A	[Rn]	< – – –	[A]
MOV Rn, direct	[Rn]	< – – –	[direct]
MOV Rn, #data	[Rn]	< – – –	data
MOV direct, A	[direct]	< – – –	[A]
MOV direct, Rn	[direct]	< – – –	[Rn]
MOV direct, direct	[direct]	< – – –	[direct]
MOV direct, @Ri	[direct]	< – – –	[Ri{M}]
MOV direct, #data	[direct]	< – – –	data
MOV @Ri, A	[Ri{M}]	< – – –	[A]

MOV @Ri, direct	[Ri{M}]	< – – –	[direct]
MOV @Ri, #data	[Ri{M}]	< – – –	data
MOV DPTR, #data 16	[DPTR]	< – – –	data (16-bit)
MOVC A, @A + PC	[A]	< – – –	[[[A] + [PC]] {M}]
MOVC A,@A + DPTR	[A]	< – – –	[[[A] + [DPTR]] {M}]
MOVX A,@Ri	[A]	< – – –	[Ri{M}]
MOVX A,@DPTR	[A]	< – – –	[DPTR{M}]
MOVX @DPTR,A	[DPTR{M}]	< – – –	[A]
PUSH direct	[SP]	< – – –	[SP] + 1
	[SP{M}]	< – – –	[direct]
POP direct	[direct]	< – – –	[SP{M}]
	[SP]	< – – –	[SP] – 1
XCH A,Rn	[A]	← — →	[Rn]
XCH A,direct	[A]	← — →	[direct]
XCH A,@Ri	[A]	← — →	[Ri{M}]
XCHD A,@Ri	$[A_{3-0}]$	← — →	$[Ri\{M_{3-0}\}]$

A.3 Arithmetic instructions

ADD A,Rn	[A]	< – – –	[A] + [Ri]
ADD A,direct	[A]	< – – –	[A] + [direct]
ADD A,@Ri	[A]	< – – –	[A] + [Ri{M}]
ADD A,#data	[A]	< – – –	[A] + data
ADDC A,Rn	[A]	< – – –	[A] + [Ri] + C*
ADDC A,direct	[A]	< – – –	[A] + [direct] + C*
ADDC A,@Ri	[A]	< – – –	[A] + [Ri{M}] + C*
ADDC A,#data	[A]	< – – –	[A] + data + C*
SUBB A, Rn	[A]	< – – –	[A] – [Rn] – C*
SUBB A, direct	[A]	< – – –	[A] – [direct] – C*
SUBB A,@Ri	[A]	< – – –	[A] – [Ri{M}] – C*
SUBB A,#data	[A]	< – – –	[A] – data – C*
INC A	[A]	< – – –	[A] + 1
INC Rn	[Rn]	< – – –	[Rn] + 1
INC direct	[direct]	< – – –	[direct] + 1
INC @Ri	[Ri{M}]	< – – –	[Ri{M}] + 1
DEC A	[A]	< – – –	[A] – 1
DEC Rn	[Rn]	< – – –	[Rn] – 1
DEC direct	[direct]	< – – –	[direct] – 1
DEC @Ri	[Ri{M}]	< – – –	[Ri{M}] – 1
INC DPTR	[DPTR]	< – – –	[DPTR] + 1
MUL AB	$[A_{7-0}]$	< – – –	[A] × [B]
	$[B_{15-8}]$	< – – –	[A] × [B]
DIV AB	$[A_{15-8}]$	< – – –	[A] / [B]
	$[B_{7-0}]$	< – – –	remainder
DA A	if $[A_{3-0}]$	> 9 OR Aux C* = 1	
	then $[A_{3-0}]$	< – – –	$[A_{3-0}]$ + 6
	if $[A_{7-4}]$	> 9 OR C* = 1	
	then $[A_{7-4}]$	< – – –	$[A_{7-4}]$ + 6

A.4 Logical instructions

ANL A, Rn	[A]	$< - - -$	[A] AND [Rn]
ANL A, direct	[A]	$< - - -$	[A] AND [direct]
ANL A, @Ri	[A]	$< - - -$	[A] AND [Ri{M}]
ANL A, #data	[A]	$< - - -$	[A] AND data
ANL direct, A	[direct]	$< - - -$	[direct] AND [A]
ANL direct, #data	[direct]	$< - - -$	[direct] AND data
ORL A, Rn	[A]	$< - - -$	[A] OR [Rn]
ORL A, direct	[A]	$< - - -$	[A] OR [direct]
ORL A, @Ri	[A]	$< - - -$	[A] OR [Ri{M}]
ORL A, #data	[A]	$< - - -$	[A] OR data
ORL direct, A	[direct]	$< - - -$	[direct] OR [A]
ORL direct, #data	[direct]	$< - - -$	[direct] OR data
XRL A, Rn	[A]	$< - - -$	[A] EX-OR [Rn]
XRL A, direct	[A]	$< - - -$	[A] EX-OR [direct]
XRL A, @Ri	[A]	$< - - -$	[A] EX-OR [Ri{M}]
XRL A, #data	[A]	$< - - -$	[A] EX-OR data
XRL direct, A	[direct]	$< - - -$	[direct] EX-OR [A]
XRL direct, #data	[direct]	$< - - -$	[direct] EX-OR data
CLR A	[A]	$< - - -$	0
CPL A	[A]	$< - - -$	[/A]
RL A	$[A_{n+1}]$	$< - - -$	$[A_n]$, n = 0 – 6
	$[A_0]$	$< - - -$	$[A_7]$
RLC A	$[A_{n+1}]$	$< - - -$	$[A_n]$, n = 0 – 6
	$[A_0]$	$< - - -$	C*
	C*	$< - - -$	$[A_7]$
RR A	$[A_n]$	$< - - -$	$[A_{n+1}]$, n = 0 – 6
	$[A_7]$	$< - - -$	$[A_0]$
RRC A	$[A_n]$	$< - - -$	$[A_{n+1}]$, n = 0 – 6
	$[A_7]$	$< - - -$	C*
	C*	$< - - -$	$[A_0]$
SWAP A	$[A_{3-0}]$	$\leftarrow - \rightarrow$	$[A_{7-4}]$

A.5 Boolean variable manipulation instructions

CLR C	C*	$< - - -$	0
CLR bit	bit	$< - - -$	0
SETB C	C*	$< - - -$	1
SETB bit	bit	$< - - -$	1
CPL C	C*	$< - - -$	/C*
CPL bit	bit	$< - - -$	/bit
ANL C, bit	C*	$< - - -$	C* AND bit
ANL C,/bit	C*	$< - - -$	C* AND /bit
ORL C, bit	C*	$< - - -$	C* OR bit
ORL C,/bit	C*	$< - - -$	C* OR /bit
MOV C, bit	C*	$< - - -$	bit
MOV C,/bit	C*	$< - - -$	/bit

JC rel   [PC]   < − − −   [PC] + 2
    if C* = 1   [PC]   < − − −   [PC] + rel
JNC rel   [PC]   < − − −   [PC] + 2
    if C* = 0   [PC]   < − − −   [PC] + rel
JB bit, rel   [PC]   < − − −   [PC] + 3
    if bit = 1   [PC]   < − − −   [PC] + rel
JNB bit, rel   [PC]   < − − −   [PC] + 3
    if bit = 0   [PC]   < − − −   [PC] + rel
JBC bit, rel   [PC]   < − − −   [PC] + 3
    if bit = 1   bit   < − − −   0
                            [PC]   < − − −   [PC] + rel

A.6   Program branching instructions

ACALL addr 11   [PC]   < − − −   [PC] + 2
                            [SP]   < − − −   [SP] + 1
                            [SP{M}]   < − − − $[PC_{7-0}]$
                            [SP]   < − − −   [SP] + 1
                            [SP{M}]   < − − − $[PC_{15-8}]$
                            $[PC_{10-0}]$ < − − −   addr 11
LCALL addr 16   [PC]   < − − −   [PC] + 3
                            [SP]   < − − −   [SP] + 1
                            [SP]{M}]   < − − − $[PC_{7-0}]$
                            [SP]   < − − −   [SP] + 1
                            [SP{M}]   < − − − $[PC_{15-8}]$
                            $[PC_{15-0}]$ < − − −   addr 16
RET $[PC_{15-8}]$ < − − −   [SP{M}]
                            [SP]   < − − −   [SP] − 1
                            $[PC_{7-0}]$ < − − −   [SP{M}]
                            [SP]   < − − −   [SP] − 1
RETI $[PC_{15-8}]$ < − − −   [SP{M}]
                            [SP]   < − − −   [SP] − 1
                            $[PC_{7-0}]$ < − − −   [SP{M}]
                            [SP]   < − − −   [SP] − 1
AJMP addr 11   [PC]   < − − −   [PC] + 2
                            [PC]   < − − −   addr 11
LJMP addr 16   [PC]   < − − −   [PC] + 3
                            [PC]   < − − −   addr 16
SJMP rel   [PC]   < − − −   [PC] + 2
                            [PC]   < − − −   [PC] + rel
JMP @A + DPTR   [PC]   < − − −   [A] + [DPTR]
JZ rel   [PC]   < − − −   [PC] + 2
    if [A] = 0   [PC]   < − − −   [PC] + rel
JNZ rel   [PC]   < − − −   [PC] + 2
    if [A] = 0   [PC]   < − − −   [PC] + rel
CJNE A, direct, rel   [PC]   < − − −   [PC] + 3
    if A <>[direct]
                            [PC]   < − − −   [PC] + rel

```
        if A < [direct]
                           C*          < - - -   0
        else               C*          < - - -   0
CJNE A, #data, rel         [PC]        < - - -   [PC] + 3
        if A <> data       [PC]        < - - -   [PC] + rel
        if A < data        C*          < - - -   1
        else               C*          < - - -   0
CJNE Rn, #data, rel        [PC]        < - - -   [PC] + 3
        if [Rn] <> data
                           [PC]        < - - -   [PC] + rel
        if [Rn] < data     C*          < - - -   1
        else               C*          < - - -   0
CJNE @Ri, #data, rel       [PC]        < - - -   [PC] + 3
        if [Ri{M}] <> data
                           [PC]        < - - -   [PC] + rel
        if [Ri{M}] <> data
                           C*          < - - -   1
        else               C*          < - - -   0
DJNZ Rn, rel               [PC]        < - - -   [PC] + 2
                           [Rn]        < - - -   [Rn] - 1
        if [Rn] = 0        [PC]        < - - -   [PC] + rel
DJNZ direct, rel           [PC]        < - - -   [PC] + 2
                           [direct]    < - - -   [direct] - 1
        if [Rn] = 0        [PC]        < - - -   [PC] + rel
```

Appendix B

Philips XA Microcontroller – XA and 8051 Instruction Set Differences

B.1 Arithmetic

8051 INSTRUCTIONS

INC   ADD   ADDC   DA   DEC   SUBB   MUL   DIV

ADDITIONAL INSTRUCTIONS FOR THE XA

ADDS

ADD Short signed value (4-bit: $+7$ to -8) to destination.
Example:
ADDS Rd, #data4

$$[Rd] \; < --- \; [Rd] + data4$$

SUB (.b, .w)

SUBtract without borrow.
Example:
SUB Rd, Rs

$$[Rd] \; < --- \; [Rd] - [Rs]$$

MULU (.b, .w)

MULtiply Unsigned (8×8, 16×16).
Example:
MULU.b Rd, Rs

$$[RdH] \; < --- \; \text{most significant byte of } [Rd] \times [Rs]$$
$$[RdL] \; < --- \; \text{least significant byte of } [Rd] \times [Rs]$$

Example:
MULU.W Rd, Rs

$$[Rd + 1] \; < --- \; \text{most significant byte of } [Rd] \times [Rs]$$
$$[Rd] \; < --- \; \text{least significant byte of } [Rd] \times [Rs]$$

DIVU (.b, .w, .d)

DIVide Unsigned (8/8, 16/8, 32/16).

Example:

DIVU.b Rd, Rs

[RdL] < – – –   8-bit integer portion of [Rd] / [Rs]

[RdH] < – – –   8-bit remainder of [Rd] / [Rs]

Example:

DIVU.w Rd, Rs

[RdL] < – – –   8-bit integer portion of [Rd] / [Rs]

[RdH] < – – –   8-bit remainder of [Rd] / [Rs]

Example:

DIVU.d Rd, Rs

[Rd] < – – –   16-bit integer portion of [Rd] / [Rs]

[Rd + 1] < – – –   16-bit remainder of [Rd] / [Rs]

SEXT (.b, .w)

Sign EXTend N flag (sign bit) into destination register.

Example:

SEXT.b Rd

[Rd] < – – –   FF   if   N = 1

[Rd] < – – –   00   if   N = 0

Example:

SEXT.w Rd

[Rd] < – – –   FFFF   if   N = 1

[Rd] < – – –   0000   if   N = 0

B.2 Logical

8051 INSTRUCTIONS

CLR bit   SETB bit   CPL   CLR   RL   RR   RLC   RRC   ANL   OR   XOR

ADDITIONAL INSTRUCTIONS FOR THE XA

NEG (.b, .w)

NEGate destination register (two's complement).

Example:

NEG   Rd

$$[Rd] < – – – \overline{[Rd]} + 1$$

LSR (.b, .w, .d)

Logical Shift Right destination register, 1–31 number of bits.

Example:

LSR   Rd, Rs (see Figure B.1)

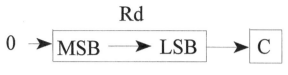

Figure B.1

ASR (.b, .w, .d)

Arithmetic Shift Right destination register, 1–31 number of bits.

Example:
ASR   Rd, Rs (see Figure B.2)

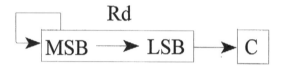

Figure B.2

ASL (.b, .w, .d)

Arithmetic Shift Left destination register, 1–31 number of bits.

Example: ASL Rd, Rs (see Figure B.3)

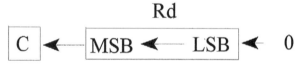

Figure B.3

NORM (.b, .w, .d)

Logically shifts left the contents of the destination register until MSB is set, storing the number of shifts performed in the source register.

Example: NORM   Rd, Rs (see Figure B.4)

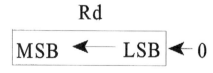

Figure B.4

CMP (.b, .w)

CoMPares the source with the destination by performing a two's complement binary subtraction of source from destination. Some flags are affected.

Example: CMP   Rd, Rs
              [Rd] – [Rs]

AND (.b, .w)

ANDs bitwisely the contents of the source to the destination.

Example: AND   Rd,Rs
              [Rd] < – – – [Rd] • [Rs]

B.3   Control transfer

8051 INSTRUCTIONS (UNCONDITIONAL)

SJMP rel LJMP addr16 AJMP addrll LCALL addr16 ACALL addr11

ADDITIONAL INSTRUCTIONS FOR THE XA (UNCONDITIONAL)

FJMP

Far JuMP absolute causes an unconditional branch to the absolute memory location. The target address is always forced to be EVEN.

Example:
FJMP   addr24
            [PC(23 – 0)]   < – – –   addr24
            [PC(0)]   < – – –   0

CALL

CALL subroutine relative branches unconditionally in the range of + 65 534 bytes to – 65 536 bytes.

Example:
CALL   rel26
            [PC]   < – – –   [PC] + 3
            [SP]   < – – –   [SP] – 4
            [SP(mem)]   < – – –   [PC(23 – 0)]
            [PC]   < – – –   [PC] + rel16
            [PC(0)]   < – – –   0

FCALL

Far CALL subroutine absolute causes an unconditional branch to an absolute location in the 16M bytes of XA address.

Example:
FCALL   addr24
            [PC]   < – – –   [PC] + 4
            [SP]   < – – –   [SP] – 4
            [SP(mem)]   < – – –   [PC(23 – 0)]
            [PC]   < – – –   addr24
            [PC(0)]   < – – –   0

BR

Unconditional BRanch subroutine causes an unconditional branch to a location in the range of + 254 bytes to – 256 bytes.

Example:
BR   rel8

[PC]	< – – –	[PC] + 2
[PC]	< – – –	[PC] + rel8
[PC(0)]	< – – –	0

8051 INSTRUCTIONS (CONDITIONAL)

JB   JC   JNC   JNZ   JZ   JBC   CJNE   DJNZ

ADDITIONAL INSTRUCTIONS FOR THE XA (CONDITIONAL)

BOV

Branch if OVerflow flag is set to a location in the range of + 254 bytes to – 256 bytes.

Example:
BOV   rel8

[PC]	< – – –	[PC] + 2
If [V-flag] = 1 then		
[PC]	< – – –	[PC] + rel8
[PC(0)]	< – – –	0

BNV

Branch No oVerflow, branches if overflow flag is not set, to a location in the range of + 254 bytes to – 256 bytes.

Example:
BNV   rel8

[PC]	< – – –	[PC] + 2
If [V-flag] = 0 then		
[PC]	< – – –	[PC] + rel8
[PC(0)]	< – – –	0

BPL

Branch PLus, branch to a location in the range of + 254 bytes to – 256 bytes if N flag is not set.

Example:
BPL   rel8

[PC]	< – – –	[PC] + 2
If [N-flag] = 0 then		
[PC]	< – – –	[PC] + rel8
[PC(0)]	< – – –	0

BCC

Branch if Carry Clear, branches to a location in the range of + 254 bytes to – 256 bytes if Carry flag is not set.

Example:
BCC   rel8

[PC]   < – – –   [PC] + 2
If [C-flag] = 0 then
[PC]   < – – –   [PC] + rel8
[PC(0)]   < – – –   0

BCS

Branch if Carry Set, branches to a location in the range of + 254 bytes to – 256 bytes if Carry flag is set.

Example:
BCS   rel8

[PC]   < – – –   [PC] + 2
If [C-flag] = 1 then
[PC]   < – – –   [PC] + rel8
[PC(0)]   < – – –   0

BEQ

Branch if EQual, branches to a location in the range of + 254 bytes to – 256 bytes if Zero flag is set.

Example:
BEQ   rel8

[PC]   < – – –   [PC] + 2
If [Z-flag] = 1 then
[PC]   < – – –   [PC] + rel8
[PC(0)]   < – – –   0

BNE

Branch if Not Equal, branches to a location in the range of + 254 bytes to – 256 bytes if Zero flag is reset.

Example:
BNE   rel8

[PC]   < – – –   [PC] + 2
If [Z-flag] = 0 then
[PC]   < – – –   [PC] + rel8
[PC(0)]   < – – –   0

BG

Branch Greater, branches to a location in the range of + 254 bytes to – 256 bytes if the last 'compare' instruction had a destination value that was greater than the source value in an 'unsigned operation'.

Example:
BG   rel8

          [PC]   < – – –   [PC] + 2
          If [Z-flag] OR [C-flag] = 0 then
          [PC]   < – – –   [PC] + rel8
          [PC(0)]   < – – –   0

BGE

Branch Greater Than or Equal to, branches to a location in the range of + 254 bytes to
– 256 bytes if the last 'compare' instruction had a destination value that was greater than
or equal to the source value in a 'signed operation'.

Example:
BGE   rel8

          [PC]   < – – –   [PC] + 2
          If [N-flag] XOR [V-flag] = 0 then
          [PC]   < – – –   [PC] + rel8
          [PC(0)]   < – – –   0

BGT

Branch Greater Than, branches to a location in the range of + 254 bytes to – 256 bytes if
the last 'compare' instruction had a destination value that was greater than the source value
in a 'signed operation'.

Example:
BGT   rel8

          [PC]   < – – –   [PC] + 2
          If ([Z-flag] OR [N-flag]) XOR [V-flag] = 0 then
          [PC]   < – – –   [PC] + rel8
          [PC(0)]   < – – –   0

BLE

Branch Less than or Equal to, branches to a location in the range of + 254 bytes to
– 256 bytes if the last 'compare' instruction had a destination value that was less than or
equal to the source value in a 'signed operation'.

Example:
BLE   rel8

          [PC]   < – – –   [PC] + 2
          If ([Z-flag] OR [N-flag]) XOR [V-flag] = 1 then
          [PC]   < – – –   [PC] + rel8
          [PC(0)]   < – – –   0

BLT

Branch Less Than, branches to a location in the range of + 254 bytes to – 256 bytes if the
last 'compare' instruction had a destination value that was less than the source value in a
'signed operation'.

Example:
BLT   rel8

> [PC]   < – – –   [PC] + 2
> If [N-flag] OR [V-flag] = 1 then
> [PC]   < – – –   [PC] + rel8
> [PC(0)]   < – – –   0

BMI

Branch MInus, branches to a location in the range of + 254 bytes to – 256 bytes if N-flag is set.

Example:
BMI   rel8

> [PC]   < – – –   [PC] + 2
> If [N-flag] = 1 then
> [PC]   < – – –   [PC] + rel8
> [PC(0)]   < – – –   0

BL

Branch Less than or equal to, branches to a location in the range of + 254 bytes to – 256 bytes if the last 'compare' instruction had a destination value that was less than or equal to the source value in an 'unsigned operation'.

Example:
BL   rel8

> [PC]   < – – –   [PC] + 2
> If [Z-flag] OR [C-flag] = 1 then
> [PC]   < – – –   [PC] + rel8
> [PC(0)]   < – – –   0

B.4   Data transfer

8051 INSTRUCTIONS

MOV   MOVC   MOVX

ADDITIONAL INSTRUCTIONS IN THE XA

MOVS (.b, .w)
   MOVe Short, moves signed value (4-bit: + 7 to – 8) to destination.

Example:
MOVS   Rd, #data4

> [Rd]   < – – –   data4

LEA

Load Effective Address, adds the contents of the source register to the offset value (8/16-bit), and stores the result into destination register.

Example:
LEA Rd, Rs + offset 8/16

        [Rd]   < − − −   [Rs] + offset 8/16

B.5 Miscellaneous

8051 INSTRUCTIONS

POP   PUSH   SWAP   XCHD

ADDITIONAL INSTRUCTIONS FOR THE XA

POPU

POP User multiple, pops specified registers (one or more) from the stack (from 1 to 8 times). Any combination of bytes registers in group R0L to R3H or the group R4L to R7H may be popped in a single instruction. Also any combination of word registers in the group R0 to R7 may be popped in a single instruction.

Example:
POPU   Rlist

        [Ri]   < − − −   [SP(mem)]
        [SP]   < − − −   [SP] + 2
        Repeat for all selected Ri registers

PUSHU

PUSH User multiple, pushes specified registers (one or more) into the stack (from 1 to 8 times). Any combination of bytes registers in group R0L to R3H or the group R4L to R7H may be pushed in a single instruction. Also any combination of word registers in the group R0 to R7 may be pushed in a single instruction.

Example:
PUSHU   Rlist

        [SP]   < − − −   [SP] − 2
        [SP(mem)]   < − − −   [Ri]
        Repeat for all selected Ri registers

RESET

The chip is internally RESET without any external effects, when the RESET instruction is executed.

Example:
RESET

        [PC]   < − − −   vector (0) bytes 2 and 3
        [PSW]   < − − −   vector (0) bytes 0 and 1
        [SFRs]   < − − −   reset values into SFRs

TRAP

This causes a specified software trap. The invoked routine is determined by branching to the specified vector entry point. The RETI, return from interrupt, instruction is used to resume execution after the trap routine has been completed.

Example:
RESET

[PC]	< – – –	[PC] + 2
[SSP]	< – – –	[SSP] – 6
[SSP(mem)]	< – – –	[PC]
[SSP(mem)]	< – – –	[PSW]
[PSW]	< – – –	trap vector
[PC (0–15)]	< – – –	trap vector
[PC(23–16, 0)]	< – – –	0

BKPT

This causes a BreaK PoinT trap. The break point trap acts like an Immediate interrupt, using a vector call to a specific piece of code that will be executed in System mode.

Example:
RESET

[PC]	< – – –	[PC] + 1
[SSP]	< – – –	[SSP] – 6
[SSP(mem)]	< – – –	[PC]
[SSP(mem)]	< – – –	[PSW]
[PSW]	< – – –	bkpt vector
[PC (0–15)]	< – – –	bkpt vector
[PC(23–16, 0)]	< – – –	0

Some examples of specific applications using the XA instructions are as follows:

add.b r0h,r0h	add.b r1l, [r2]	add.b r1h, [r3 +]
add.b r2l, [r4 + $44]	add.b r2h, [r5 + $5555]	add.b r3l,$066
add.b r0h,#$11	add.b [r2],#$22	add.b [r3 +],#$33
add.b [r4 + $44],#$44	add.b [r5 + $5555],#5	add.b $066,#$66
add.w r9,r9	add.w R10, [R0]	add.w R11, [R0 +]
add.w R12, [R0 + $0C]	add.w R13, [R0 + $0DDD]	add.w R14,$EE
add.w r9,#$9999	add.w [R0],#$AAAA	add.w [R0 +],#$BBBB
add.w [R0 + $0C],#$CCCC	add.w [R0 + $0DDD],#$0DDD	add.w $EE,#$EEEE
adds.b r0h,#$1	adds.b [r2],#$2	adds.b [r3 +],#$3
adds.b [r4 + $44],#$4	adds.b [r5 + $5555],#$5	adds.b $066,#$6
adds.w r9,#–7		
adds.w [R0],#–6	adds.w [R0 +],#–5	adds.w [R0 + $0C],#–4
adds.w [R0 + $0DDD],#–3	adds.w $EE,#–2	
addc.b R0h,R0h	addc.b R1l, [R2]	addc.b R1h, [R3 +]
addc.b R2l, [R4 + $44]	addc.b R2h, [R5 + $5555]	addc.b R3l,$66

addc.w R9,r9
addc.w r12, [r0 + $0C]

addc.w r10, [r0]
addc.w r13, [r0 + $0DDD]

addc.w r11, [r0 +]
addc.w r14,$ee

sub.b r0h,r0h
sub.b r2l, [r4 + $44]

sub.b r1l, [r2]
sub.b r2h, [r5 + $5555]

sub.b r1h, [r3 +]
sub.b r3l,$066

sub.w r9,r9
sub.w R12, [R0 + $0C]

sub.w R10, [R0]
sub.w R13, [R0 + $0DDD]

sub.w R11, [R0 +]
sub.w R14, $EE

subb.b r0h,r0h
subb.b r2l, [r4 + $44]

subb.b r1l, [r2]
subb.b r2h, [r5 + $5555]

subb.b r1h, [r3 +]
subb.b r3l, $066

subb.w r9,r9
subb.w R12, [R0 + $0C]
movc.b r0l, [r0 +]
mov.b r1h, [r3 +]
mov.b r3l, $066
mov.b 00, [R0]

subb.w R10, [R0]
subb.w R13, [R0 + $0DDD]
mov.b r0h, r0h
mov.b r21, [r4 + $44]
mov.b [r0 +], [r0 +]

subb.w R11, [R0 +]
subb.w R14,$EE
mov.b r1l, [r2]
mov.b r2h, [r5 + $5555]
mov.b [r0], 00

movc.w R8, [R0 +]
mov.w R11, [R0 +]
mov.w R14, $EE
mov.w $88, [R0]

mov.w r9, r9
mov.w R12, [R0 + $0C]
mov.w [r0 +], [r0 +]

mov.w R10, [R0]
mov.w R13, [R0 + $0DDD]
mov.w [r0], $88

movx.b r3h, [r7]

movx.w r15, [r0]

movs.b r0h,#$1
movs.b [r4 + $44],#$4
movs.w r9,#−7
movs.w [R0 + $0C],#−4

movs.b [r2],#$2
movs.b [r5 + $5555],#$5
movs.w [R0],#−6
movs.w [R0 + $0DDD],#−3

movs.b [r3 +],#$3
movs.b $066,#$6
movs.w [R0 +],#−5
movs.w $EE,#−2

and.b r0h, r0h
and.b r21, [r4 + $44]

and.b r1l, [r2]
and.b r2h, [r5 + $5555]

and.b r1h, [r3 +]
and.b r3l, $066

and.w r9, r9
and.w R12, [R0 + $0C]

and.w R10, [R0]
and.w R13, [R0 + $0DDD]

and.w R11, [R0 +]
and.w R14, $EE

or.b r0h, r0h
or.b r21, [r4 + $44]

or.b r1l, [r2]
or.b r2h, [r5 + $5555]

or.b r1h, [r3 +]
or.b r3l, $066

or.w r9, r9
or.w R12, [R0 + $0C]

or.w R10, [R0]
or.w R13, [R0 + $0DDD]

or.w R11, [R0 +]
or.w R14, $EE

xor.b r0h, r0h
xor.b r21, [r4 + $44]

xor.b r1l, [r2]
xor.b r2h, [r5 + $5555]

xor.b r1h, [r3 +]
xor.b r3l, $066

xor.w r9, r9
xor.w R12, [R0 + $0C]

xor.w R10, [R0]
xor.w R13, [R0 + $0DDD]

xor.w R11, [R0 +]
xor.w R14, $EE

rr.b r0l,#00
rlc.b R4h,#7
asl.b r0h,#1
lsr.b r0l,#0

rl.b r1h,#3
sl.b r0h, r0h
asr.b r1l,#2

rrc.b r4h,#$7
asr.b r1l, r1l
lsr.b r0l,r0l

rr.w r8,#$8
rlc.w R7,#15

rl.w R11,#11
asl.w R9,R0l

rrc.w r15,#$f
asr.w R10,R0l

asl.w R9,#9
lsr.w R8,#8

asr.w R10,#10

lsr.w R8,R0l

asl.d R3,R0l
asr.d R5,#14

asr.d R5,R0l
lsr.d R1,#12

asl.d R3,#13
lsr.d R1,R0l

mulu.b R0l,R0l
mulu.b R4l,#$88

mulu.w R4,R4
mulu.w R9,#$99

mul.w R6,R6
mul.w R9,#$99

divu.b R0h,R0h
divu.b R4l,#$88

divu.w R5,R2h
divu.w R8,#88

div.w R7,R3h
div.w R8,#88

divu.d R9,#$99
div.d R15,R15

div.d R9,#$99

divu.d R13,R13

clr my_bit
mov my_bit,C
orl C,my_bit

setb my_bit
anl C,my_bit
orl C,/my_bit

mov C,my_bit
anl C,/my_bit

xch.w r8, [R0]
xch.b R0l, [R0]

xch.w R8,$88
xch.b R0l,R0l

xch.b r0l,0
xch.w r8,R8

lea R0,R0 + 0

lea r0,R0 + $88

norm.b r1h,r1h

norm.w R11,R0l

norm.d R7,R0l

fcall $443322

call $5566

call [R6]

pushu.b R7l,r6h,r6l,r5l,r4h,r4l
pushu.w R15,R14,R13,R12,R11,R10,R9,R8

push.b R3l,r2h,r2l,r1l,r0h,r0l
push.w R7,R6,R5,R4,R3,R2,R1,R0

popu.b R7l,r6h,r6l,r5l,r4h,r4l
popu.w R15,R14,R13,R12,R11,R10,R9,R8

pop.b R7l,r6h,r6l,r5l,r4h,r4l
pop.w R15,R14,R13,R12,R11,R10,R9,R8

cmp.b r0h, r0h
cmp.b r2l, [r4 + $44]
cmp.w r9, r9
cmp.w R14, $EE

cmp.b r11, [r2]
cmp.b r2h, [r5 + $5555]
cmp.w R10, [R0]
cmp.w R11, [R0 +]

cmp.b r1h, [r3 +]
cmp.b r3l, $066
cmp.w R13, [R0 + $0DDD]
cmp.w R12, [R0 + $0C]

cjne.b R1l, $22, dummy1
cjne.w R10, $1AA, dummy1
cjne.w [R0], #$BBBB, dummy1

cjne.b R1h, #$33, dummy1
djnz.w $1AA, dummy1

cjne.b [R3], #$33, dummy1
cjne.w R11, #$BBBB, dummy1

djnz.w r15, dummy

djnz.b $222, dummy1

jz dummy1
jbc my_bit, $

jnz dummy1

jb my_bit, $

jnb my_bit, $

bcc dummy2
bnv dummy2
bg dummy2
bgt dummy2

bcs dummy2
bov dummy2
bl dummy2
ble dummy2

bne dummy2
bpl dummy2
bge dummy2
br dummy2

beq dummy2
bmi dummy2
blt dummy2

jmp [a + dptr]
jmp $5566

jmp [[R0 +]]

jmp [R6]

fjmp $443322

trap #0
trap #4
trap #8
trap #12

trap #1
trap #5
trap #9
trap #13

trap #2
trap #6
trap #10
trap #14

trap #3
trap #7
trap #11
trap #15

da r0l
cpl.w r8
reset

cpl.b r0l
neg.w r8
bkpt

neg.b r0l
ret

sext r8
reti

Appendix C
80C51 Features

Details of packages, pin functions, logic symbol, block diagram and SFRs are reproduced here with the kind permission of Philips Semiconductors. (N.B. The pin configuration is shown as Figure 2.2 and the block diagram is shown as Figure 2.3 in Chapter 2. For details of these features reference should be made to Chapter 2.)

CERAMIC AND PLASTIC LEADED CHIP CARRIER PIN FUNCTIONS

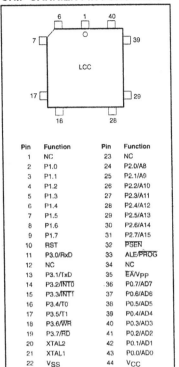

Pin	Function	Pin	Function
1	NC	23	NC
2	P1.0	24	P2.0/A8
3	P1.1	25	P2.1/A9
4	P1.2	26	P2.2/A10
5	P1.3	27	P2.3/A11
6	P1.4	28	P2.4/A12
7	P1.5	29	P2.5/A13
8	P1.6	30	P2.6/A14
9	P1.7	31	P2.7/A15
10	RST	32	PSEN
11	P3.0/RxD	33	ALE/PROG
12	NC	34	NC
13	P3.1/TxD	35	EA/Vpp
14	P3.2/INT0	36	P0.7/AD7
15	P3.3/INT1	37	P0.6/AD6
16	P3.4/T0	38	P0.5/AD5
17	P3.5/T1	39	P0.4/AD4
18	P3.6/WR	40	P0.3/AD3
19	P3.7/RD	41	P0.2/AD2
20	XTAL2	42	P0.1/AD1
21	XTAL1	43	P0.0/AD0
22	Vss	44	Vcc

SU00002

PLASTIC QUAD FLAT PACK PIN FUNCTIONS

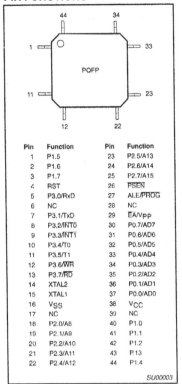

Pin	Function	Pin	Function
1	P1.5	23	P2.5/A13
2	P1.6	24	P2.6/A14
3	P1.7	25	P2.7/A15
4	RST	26	PSEN
5	P3.0/RxD	27	ALE/PROG
6	NC	28	NC
7	P3.1/TxD	29	EA/Vpp
8	P3.2/INT0	30	P0.7/AD7
9	P3.3/INT1	31	P0.6/AD6
10	P3.4/T0	32	P0.5/AD5
11	P3.5/T1	33	P0.4/AD4
12	P3.6/WR	34	P0.3/AD3
13	P3.7/RD	35	P0.2/AD2
14	XTAL2	36	P0.1/AD1
15	XTAL1	37	P0.0/AD0
16	Vss	38	Vcc
17	NC	39	NC
18	P2.0/A8	40	P1.0
19	P2.1/A9	41	P1.1
20	P2.2/A10	42	P1.2
21	P2.3/A11	43	P.13
22	P2.4/A12	44	P1.4

SU00003

LOGIC SYMBOL

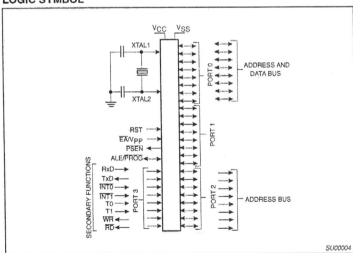

SU00004

Figure C.1 80C51 package pin functions and logic symbol

SYMBOL	DESCRIPTION	DIRECT ADDRESS	BIT ADDRESS, SYMBOL, OR ALTERNATIVE PORT FUNCTION MSB							LSB	RESET VALUE
ACC*	Accumulator	E0H	E7	E6	E5	E4	E3	E2	E1	E0	00H
B*	B register	F0H	F7	F6	F5	F4	F3	F2	F1	F0	00H
DPTR	Data pointer (2 bytes)										
DPH	Data pointer high	83H									00H
DPL	Data pointer low	82H									00H
			AF	AE	AD	AC	AB	AA	A9	A8	
IE*	Interrupt enable	A8H	EA	–	–	ES	ET1	EX1	ET0	EX0	0x000000B
			BF	BE	BD	BC	BB	BA	B9	B8	
IP*	Interrupt priority	B8H	–	–	–	PS	PT1	PX1	PT0	PX0	xx000000B
			87	86	85	84	83	82	81	80	
P0*	Port 0	80H	AD7	AD6	AD5	AD4	AD3	AD2	AD1	AD0	FFH
			97	96	95	94	93	92	91	90	
P1*	Port 1	90H	–	–	–	–	–	–	T2EX	T2	FFH
			A7	A6	A5	A4	A3	A2	A1	A0	
P2*	Port 2	A0H	A15	A14	A13	A12	A11	A10	A9	A8	FFH
			B7	B6	B5	B4	B3	B2	B1	B0	
P3*	Port 3	B0H	$\overline{RD}$	$\overline{WR}$	T1	T0	$\overline{INT1}$	$\overline{INT0}$	TxD	Rxd	FFH
PCON[1]	Power control	87H	SMOD	–	–	–	GF1	GF0	PD	IDL	0xxxxxxxB
			D7	D6	D5	D4	D3	D2	D1	D0	
PSW*	Program status word	D0H	CY	AC	F0	RS1	RS0	OV	–	P	00H
SBUF	Serial data buffer	99H									xxxxxxxxB
			9F	9E	9D	9C	9B	9A	99	98	
SCON*	Serial controller	98H	SM0	SM1	SM2	REN	TB8	RB8	TI	RI	00H
SP	Stack pointer	81H									07H
			8F	8E	8D	8C	8B	8A	89	88	
TCON*	Timer control	88H	TF1	TR1	TF0	TR0	IE1	IT1	IE0	IT0	
TH0	Timer high 0	8CH									00H
TH1	Timer high 1	8DH									00H
TL0	Timer low 0	8AH									00H
TL1	Timer low 1	8BH									00H
TMOD	Timer mode	89H	GATE	C/T	M1	M0	GATE	C/T	M1	M0	00H

NOTES:
* Bit addressable
1. Bits GF1, GF0, PD, and IDL of the PCON register are not implemented on the NMOS 8051/8031.

Figure C.2 80C51 special function registers

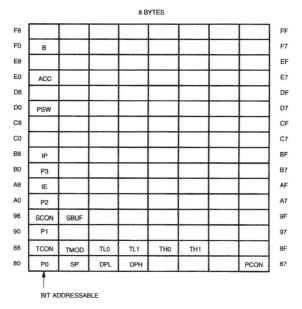

Figure C.3 80C51 SFR memory map

Appendix D

8XC552 Features

Details of packages, pin functions, logic symbol, block diagram and SFRs are reproduced here with the kind permission of Philips Semiconductors.

PIN CONFIGURATIONS

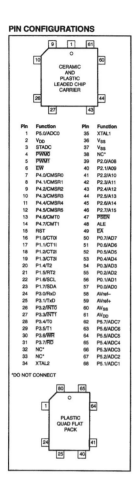

Pin	Function	Pin	Function
1	P5.0/ADC0	35	XTAL1
2	V_DD	36	V_SS
3	STADC	37	V_SS
4	PWM0	38	NC*
5	PWM1	39	P2.0/A08
6	EW	40	P2.1/A09
7	P4.0/CMSR0	41	P2.2/A10
8	P4.1/CMSR1	42	P2.3/A11
9	P4.2/CMSR2	43	P2.4/A12
10	P4.3/CMSR3	44	P2.5/A13
11	P4.4/CMSR4	45	P2.6/A14
12	P4.5/CMSR5	46	P2.7/A15
13	P4.6/CMT0	47	PSEN
14	P4.7/CMT1	48	ALE
15	RST	49	EA
16	P1.0/CT0I	50	P0.7/AD7
17	P1.1/CT1I	51	P0.6/AD6
18	P1.2/CT2I	52	P0.5/AD5
19	P1.3/CT3I	53	P0.4/AD4
20	P1.4/T2	54	P0.3/AD3
21	P1.5/RT2	55	P0.2/AD2
22	P1.6/SCL	56	P0.1/AD1
23	P1.7/SDA	57	P0.0/AD0
24	P3.0/RxD	58	AVref−
25	P3.1/TxD	59	AVref+
26	P3.2/INT0	60	AV_SS
27	P3.3/INT1	61	AV_DD
28	P3.4/T0	62	P5.7/ADC7
29	P3.5/T1	63	P5.6/ADC6
30	P3.6/WR	64	P5.5/ADC5
31	P3.7/RD	65	P5.4/ADC4
32	NC*	66	P5.3/ADC3
33	NC*	67	P5.2/ADC2
34	XTAL2	68	P5.1/ADC1

*DO NOT CONNECT

PLASTIC QUAD FLAT PACK PIN FUNCTIONS

Pin	Function	Pin	Function
1	P4.1/CMSR1	41	P2.3/A11
2	P4.2/CMSR2	42	P2.4/A12
3	NC*	43	NC*
4	P4.3/CMSR3	44	NC*
5	P4.4/CMSR4	45	P2.5/A13
6	P4.5/CMSR5	46	P2.6/A14
7	P4.6/CMT0	47	P2.7/A15
8	P4.7/CMT1	48	PSEN
9	RST	49	ALE
10	P1.0/CT0I	50	EA
11	P1.1/CT1I	51	P0.7/AD7
12	P1.2/CT2I	52	P0.6/AD6
13	P1.3/CT3I	53	P0.5/AD5
14	P1.4/T2	54	P0.4/AD4
15	P1.5/RT2	55	P0.3/AD3
16	P1.6/SCL	56	P0.2/AD2
17	P1.7/SDA	57	P0.1/AD1
18	P3.0/RxD	58	P0.0/AD0
19	P3.1/TxD	59	AVref−
20	P3.2/INT0	60	AVref+
21	NC*	61	AV_SS
22	NC*	62	NC*
23	P3.3/INT1	63	AV_DD
24	P3.4/T0	64	P5.7/ADC7
25	P3.5/T1	65	P5.6/ADC6
26	P3.6/WR	66	P5.5/ADC5
27	P3.7/RD	67	P5.4/ADC4
28	NC*	68	P5.3/ADC3
29	NC*	69	P5.2/ADC2
30	NC*	70	P5.1/ADC1
31	XTAL2	71	P5.0/ADC0
32	XTAL1	72	V_DD
33	IC	73	IC
34	V_SS	74	STADC
35	V_SS	75	PWM0
36	V_SS	76	PWM1
37	NC*	77	EW
38	P2.0/A08	78	NC*
39	P2.1/A09	79	NC*
40	P2.2/A10	80	P4.0/CMSR0

* DO NOT CONNECT
IC = internally connected (do not use)

LOGIC SYMBOL

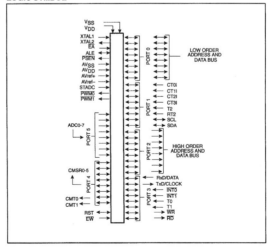

Figure D.1 8XC552 package pin functions and logic symbol

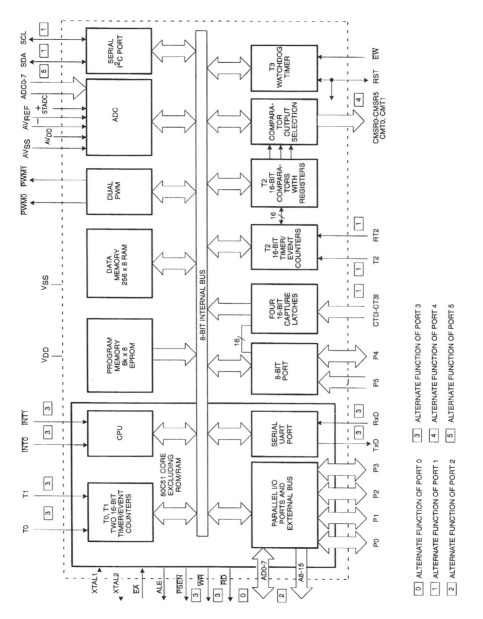

Figure D.2 8XC552 block diagram

SYMBOL	DESCRIPTION	DIRECT ADDRESS	BIT ADDRESS, SYMBOL, OR ALTERNATIVE PORT FUNCTION MSB							LSB	RESET VALUE
ACC*	Accumulator	E0H	E7	E6	E5	E4	E3	E2	E1	E0	00H
ADCH#	A/D converter high	C6H									xxxxxxxxB
ADCON#	Adc control	C5H	ADC.1	ADC.0	ADEX	ADCI	ADCS	AADR2	AADR1	AADR0	xx000000B
B*	B register	F0H	F7	F6	F5	F4	F3	F2	F1	F0	00H
CTCON#	Capture control	EBH	CTN3	CTP3	CTN2	CTP2	CTN1	CTP1	CTN0	CTP0	00H
CTH3#	Capture high 3	CFH									xxxxxxxxB
CTH2#	Capture high 2	CEH									xxxxxxxxB
CTH1#	Capture high 1	CDH									xxxxxxxxB
CTH0#	Capture high 0	CCH									xxxxxxxxB
CMH2#	Compare high 2	CBH									00H
CMH1#	Compare high 1	CAH									00H
CMH0#	Compare high 0	C9H									00H
CTL3#	Capture low 3	AFH									xxxxxxxxB
CTL2#	Capture low 2	AEH									xxxxxxxxB
CTL1#	Capture low 1	ADH									xxxxxxxxB
CTL0#	Capture low 0	ACH									xxxxxxxxB
CML2#	Compare low 2	ABH									00H
CML1#	Compare low 1	AAH									00H
CML0#	Compare low 0	A9H									00H
DPTR:	Data pointer (2 bytes)										
DPH	Data pointer high	83H									00H
DPL	Data pointer low	82H									00H
			AF	AE	AD	AC	AB	AA	A9	A8	
IEN0*#	Interrupt enable 0	A8H	EA	EAD	ES1	ES0	ET1	EX1	ET0	EX0	00H
			EF	EE	ED	EC	EB	EA	E9	E8	
IEN1*#	Interrupt enable 1	E8H	ET2	ECM2	ECM1	ECM0	ECT3	ECT2	ECT1	ECT0	00H
			BF	BE	BD	BC	BB	BA	B9	B8	
IP0*#	Interrupt priority 0	B8H	–	PAD	PS1	PS0	PT1	PX1	PT0	PX0	x0000000B
			FF	FE	FD	FC	FB	FA	F9	F8	
IP1*#	Interrupt priority 1	F8H	PT2	PCM2	PCM1	PCM0	PCT3	PCT2	PCT1	PCT0	00H
P5#	Port 5	C4H	ADC7	ADC6	ADC5	ADC4	ADC3	ADC2	ADC1	ADC0	xxxxxxxxB
			C7	C6	C5	C4	C3	C2	C1	C0	
P4#	Port 4	C0H	CMT1	CMT0	CMSR5	CMSR4	CMSR3	CMSR2	CMSR1	CMSR0	FFH
			B7	B6	B5	B4	B3	B2	B1	B0	
P3*	Port 3	B0H	RD	WR	T1	T0	INT1	INT0	TXD	RXD	FFH
			A7	A6	A5	A4	A3	A2	A1	A0	
P2*	Port 2	A0H	A15	A14	A13	A12	A11	A10	A9	A8	FFH
			97	96	95	94	93	92	91	90	
P1*	Port 1	90H	SDA	SCL	RT2	T2	CT3I	CT2I	CT1I	CT0I	FFH
			87	86	85	84	83	82	81	80	
P0*	Port 0	80H	AD7	AD6	AD5	AD4	AD3	AD2	AD1	AD0	FFH
PCON#	Power control	87H	SMOD	–	–	WLE	GF1	GF0	PD	IDL	00xx0000B
			D7	D6	D5	D4	D3	D2	D1	D0	
PSW*	Program status word	D0H	CY	AC	F0	RS1	RS0	OV	F1	P	00H

* SFRs are bit addressable.
# SFRs are modified from or added to the 80C51 SFRs.

Figure D.3 8XC552 special function registers

8XC552 Special Function Registers (Continued)

SYMBOL	DESCRIPTION	DIRECT ADDRESS	BIT ADDRESS, SYMBOL, OR ALTERNATIVE PORT FUNCTION MSB							LSB	RESET VALUE
PWMP#	PWM prescaler	FEH									00H
PWM1#	PWM register 1	FDH									00H
PWM0#	PWM register 0	FCH									00H
RTE#	Reset/toggle enable	EFH	TP47	TP46	RP45	RP44	RP43	RP42	RP41	RP40	00H
SP	Stack pointer	81H									07H
S0BUF	Serial 0 data buffer	99H									xxxxxxxxB
			9F	9E	9D	9C	9B	9A	99	98	
S0CON*	Serial 0 control	98H	SM0	SM1	SM2	REN	TB8	RB8	TI	RI	00H
S1ADR#	Serial 1 address	DBH	—————— SLAVE ADDRESS ——————							GC	00H
S1DAT#	Serial 1 data	DAH									00H
S1STA#	Serial 1 status	D9H	SC4	SC3	SC2	SC1	SC0	0	0	0	F8H
			DF	DE	DD	DC	DB	DA	D9	D8	
SICON#*	Serial 1 control	D8H	CR2	ENS1	STA	STO	SI	AA	CR1	CR0	00H
STE#	Set enable	EEH	TG47	TG46	SP45	SP44	SP43	SP42	SP41	SP40	C0H
TH1	Timer high 1	8DH									00H
TH0	Timer high 0	8CH									00H
TL1	Timer low 1	8BH									00H
TL0	Timer low 0	8AH									00H
TMH2#	Timer high 2	EDH									00H
TML2#	Timer low 2	ECH									00H
TMOD	Timer mode	89H	GATE	C/T	M1	M0	GATE	C/T	M1	M0	00H
			8F	8E	8D	8C	8B	8A	89	88	
TCON*	Timer control	88H	TF1	TR1	TF0	TR0	IE1	IT1	IE0	IT0	00H
TM2CON#	Timer 2 control	EAH	T2IS1	T2IS0	T2ER	T2B0	T2P1	T2P0	T2MS1	T2MS0	00H
			CF	CE	CD	CC	CB	CA	C9	C8	
TM2IR#*	Timer 2 int flag reg	C8H	T20V	CMI2	CMI1	CMI0	CTI3	CTI2	CTI1	CTI0	00H
T3#	Timer 3	FFH									00H

* SFRs are bit addressable.
\# SFRs are modified from or added to the 80C51 SFRs.

Figure D.3 *continued*

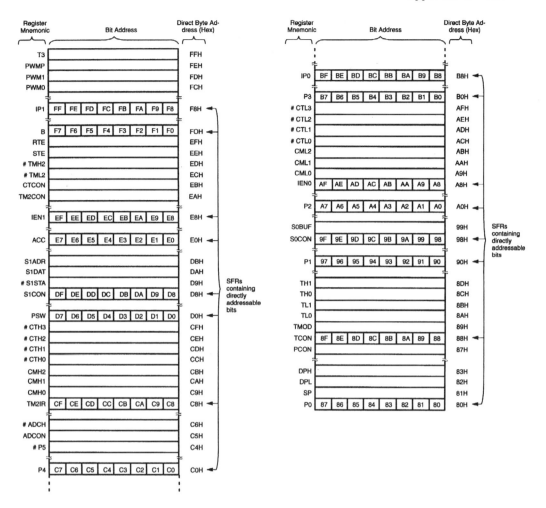

Figure D.4 8XC552 SFR memory map

Appendix E

8XC750 Features

Details of packages, pin functions, block diagram and SFRs are reproduced here with the kind permission of Philips Semiconductors.

PIN CONFIGURATIONS

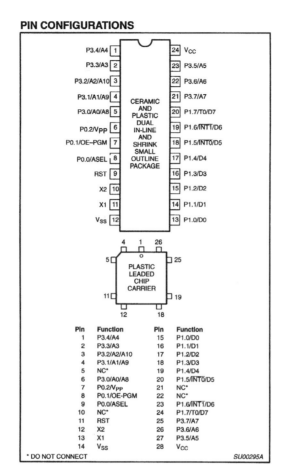

Figure E.1 8XC750 package pin functions

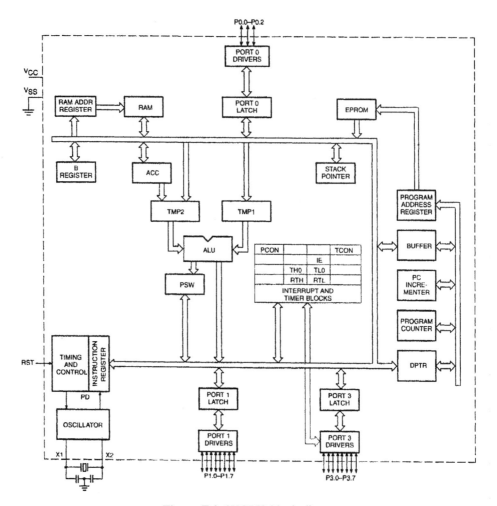

Figure E.2 8XC750 block diagram

SYMBOL	DESCRIPTION	DIRECT ADDRESS	BIT ADDRESS, SYMBOL, OR ALTERNATIVE PORT FUNCTION MSB							LSB	RESET VALUE
ACC*	Accumulator	E0H	E7	E6	E5	E4	E3	E2	E1	E0	00H
B*	B register	F0H	F7	F6	F5	F4	F3	F2	F1	F0	00H
DPTR:	Data pointer (2 bytes)										
DPH	High byte	83H									00H
DPL	Low byte	82H									00H
			AF	AE	AD	AC	AB	AA	A9	A8	
IE*#	Interrupt enable	A8H	EA	–	–	–	–	EX1	ET0	EX0	00H
									82	81	80
P0*#	Port 0	80H	–	–	–	–	–	–	–	–	xxxxx111B
			97	96	95	94	93	92	91	90	
P1*	Port 1	90H	T0	$\overline{\text{INT1}}$	$\overline{\text{INT0}}$	–	–	–	–	–	FFH
P3*	Port 3	B0H	B7	B6	B5	B4	B3	B2	B1	B0	FFH
PCON#	Power control	87H	–	–	–	–	–	–	PD	IDL	xxxxxx00B
			D7	D6	D5	D4	D3	D2	D1	D0	
PSW*	Program status word	D0H	CY	AC	F0	RS1	RS0	OV	–	P	00H
SP	Stack pointer	81H									07H
			8F	8E	8D	8C	8B	8A	89	88	
TCON*#	Timer/counter control	88H	GATE	C/T	TF	TR	IE0	IT0	IE1	IT1	00H
TL#	Timer low byte	8AH									00H
TH#	Timer high byte	8CH									00H
RTL#	Timer low reload	8BH									00H
RTH#	Timer high reload	8DH									00H

* SFRs are bit addressable.
\# SFRs are modified from or added to the 80C51 SFRs.

Figure E.3 8XC750 special function registers

Appendix F

80C51 XA-G3 Features

Details of packages, pin functions, logic symbol, block diagram and SFRs of the XA microcontrollers are reproduced here with the kind permission of Philips Semiconductors. Devices available are the XA-G1, XA-G2 and XA-G3 and they differ only in the amount of ROM/EPROM available on-chip.

PIN CONFIGURATIONS

44-Pin PLCC Package

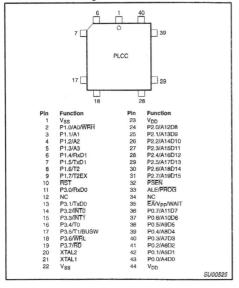

Pin	Function	Pin	Function
1	V$_{SS}$	23	V$_{DD}$
2	P1.0/A0/WRH	24	P2.0/A12D8
3	P1.1/A1	25	P2.1/A13D9
4	P1.2/A2	26	P2.2/A14D10
5	P1.3/A3	27	P2.3/A15D11
6	P1.4/RxD1	28	P2.4/A16D12
7	P1.5/TxD1	29	P2.5/A17D13
8	P1.6/T2	30	P2.6/A18D14
9	P1.7/T2EX	31	P2.7/A19D15
10	RST	32	PSEN
11	P3.0/RxD0	33	ALE/PROG
12	NC	34	NC
13	P3.1/TxD0	35	EA/Vpp/WAIT
14	P3.2/INT0	36	P0.7/A11D7
15	P3.3/INT1	37	P0.6/A10D6
16	P3.4/T0	38	P0.5/A9D5
17	P3.5/T1/BUSW	39	P0.4/A8D4
18	P3.6/WRL	40	P0.3/A7D3
19	P3.7/RD	41	P0.2/A6D2
20	XTAL2	42	P0.1/A5D1
21	XTAL1	43	P0.0/A4D0
22	V$_{SS}$	44	V$_{DD}$

SU00525

44-Pin LQFP Package

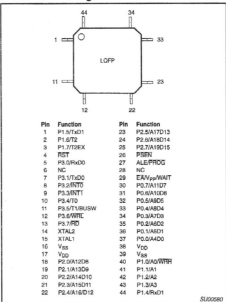

Pin	Function	Pin	Function
1	P1.5/TxD1	23	P2.5/A17D13
2	P1.6/T2	24	P2.6/A18D14
3	P1.7/T2EX	25	P2.7/A19D15
4	RST	26	PSEN
5	P3.0/RxD0	27	ALE/PROG
6	NC	28	NC
7	P3.1/TxD0	29	EA/Vpp/WAIT
8	P3.2/INT0	30	P0.7/A11D7
9	P3.3/INT1	31	P0.6/A10D6
10	P3.4/T0	32	P0.5/A9D5
11	P3.5/T1/BUSW	33	P0.4/A8D4
12	P3.6/WRL	34	P0.3/A7D3
13	P3.7/RD	35	P0.2/A6D2
14	XTAL2	36	P0.1/A5D1
15	XTAL1	37	P0.0/A4D0
16	V$_{SS}$	38	V$_{DD}$
17	V$_{DD}$	39	V$_{SS}$
18	P2.0/A12D8	40	P1.0/A0/WRH
19	P2.1/A13D9	41	P1.1/A1
20	P2.2/A14D10	42	P1.2/A2
21	P2.3/A15D11	43	P1.3/A3
22	P2.4/A16/D12	44	P1.4/RxD1

SU00580

LOGIC SYMBOL

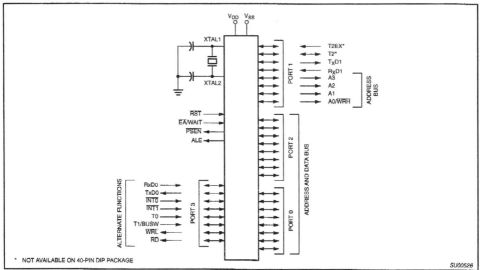

* NOT AVAILABLE ON 40-PIN DIP PACKAGE

SU00526

Figure F.1 XA-G3 pin configurations (44-pin PLCC and 44-pin LQFP) and logic symbol. (Also applicable to the XA-G1 and XA-G2 devices)

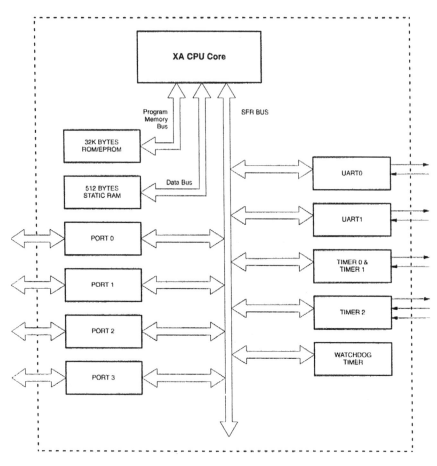

Figure F.2 XA-G3 block diagram. (Applicable also to the XA-G1 and XA-G2 devices except that the XA-G1 has 8k bytes of ROM/EPROM while the XA-G2 has 16k bytes of ROM/EPROM)

NAME	DESCRIPTION	SFR ADDRESS	BIT FUNCTIONS AND ADDRESSES MSB							LSB	RESET VALUE
BCR	Bus configuration register	46A	—	—	—	WAITD	BUSD	BC2	BC1	BC0	Note 1
BTRH	Bus timing register high byte	469	DW1	DW0	DWA1	DWA0	DR1	DR0	DRA1	DRA0	FF
BTRL	Bus timing register low byte	468	WM1	WM0	ALEW	—	CR1	CR0	CRA1	CRA0	EF
CS	Code segment	443									00
DS	Data segment	441									00
ES	Extra segment	442									00
			33F	33E	33D	33C	33B	33A	339	338	
IEH*	Interrupt enable high byte	427	—	—	—	—	ETI1	ERI1	ETI0	ERI0	00
			337	336	335	334	333	332	331	330	
IEL*	Interrupt enable low byte	426	EA	—	—	ET2	ET1	EX1	ET0	EX0	00
IPA0	Interrupt priority 0	4A0	—	PT0		—		PX0			00
IPA1	Interrupt priority 1	4A1	—	PT1		—		PX1			00
IPA2	Interrupt priority 2	4A2	—	—		—		PT2			00
IPA4	Interrupt priority 4	4A4	—	PTI0		—		PRI0			00
IPA5	Interrupt priority 5	4A5	—	PTI1		—		PRI1			00
			387	386	385	384	383	382	381	380	
P0*	Port 0	430	AD7	AD6	AD5	AD4	AD3	AD2	AD1	AD0	FF
			38F	38E	38D	38C	38B	38A	389	388	
P1*	Port 1	431	T2EX	T2	TxD1	RxD1	A3	A2	A1	WRH	FF
			397	396	395	394	393	392	391	390	
P2*	Port 2	432	P2.7	P2.6	P2.5	P2.4	P2.3	P2.2	P2.1	P2.0	FF
			39F	39E	39D	39C	39B	39A	399	398	
P3*	Port 3	433	RD	WR	T1	T0	INT1	INT0	TxD0	RxD0	FF
P0CFGA	Port 0 configuration A	470									Note 5
P1CFGA	Port 1 configuration A	471									Note 5
P2CFGA	Port 2 configuration A	472									Note 5
P3CFGA	Port 3 configuration A	473									Note 5
P0CFGB	Port 0 configuration B	4F0									Note 5
P1CFGB	Port 1 configuration B	4F1									Note 5
P2CFGB	Port 2 configuration B	4F2									Note 5
P3CFGB	Port 3 configuration B	4F3									Note 5
			227	226	225	224	223	222	221	220	
PCON*	Power control register	404	—	—	—	—	—	—	PD	IDL	00
			20F	20E	20D	20C	20B	20A	209	208	
PSWH*	Program status word (high byte)	401	SM	TM	RS1	RS0	IM3	IM2	IM1	IM0	Note 2
			207	206	205	204	203	202	201	200	
PSWL*	Program status word (low byte)	400	C	AC	—	—	—	V	N	Z	Note 2
			217	216	215	214	213	212	211	210	
PSW51*	80C51 compatible PSW	402	C	AC	F0	RS1	RS0	V	F1	P	Note 3
RTH0	Timer 0 extended reload, high byte	455									00
RTH1	Timer 1 extended reload, high byte	457									00
RTL0	Timer 0 extended reload, low byte	454									00
RTL1	Timer 1 extended reload, low byte	456									00
			307	306	305	304	303	302	301	300	
S0CON*	Serial port 0 control register	420	SM0_0	SM1_0	SM2_0	REN_0	TB8_0	RB8_0	TI_0	RI_0	00
			30F	30E	30D	30C	30B	30A	309	308	
S0STAT*	Serial port 0 extended status	421	—	—	—	—	FE0	BR0	OE0	STINT0	00
S0BUF	Serial port 0 buffer register	460									x
S0ADDR	Serial port 0 address register	461									00
S0ADEN	Serial port 0 address enable register	462									00
			327	326	325	324	323	322	321	320	
S1CON*	Serial port 1 control register	424	SM0_1	SM1_1	SM2_1	REN_1	TB8_1	RB8_1	TI_1	RI_1	00
			32F	32E	32D	32C	32B	32A	329	328	
S1STAT*	Serial port 1 extended status	425	—	—	—	—	FE1	BR1	OE1	STINT1	00
S1BUF	Serial port 1 buffer register	464									x
S1ADDR	Serial port 1 address register	465									00
S1ADEN	Serial port 1 address enable register	466									00
			21F	21E	21D	21C	21B	21A	219	218	
SCR	System configuration register	440	—	—	—	—	PT1	PT0	CM	PZ	00
SSEL*	Segment selection register	403	ESWEN	R6SEG	R5SEG	R4SEG	R3SEG	R2SEG	R1SEG	R0SEG	00
SWE	Software Interrupt Enable	47A	—	SWE7	SWE6	SWE5	SWE4	SWE3	SWE2	SWE1	00

Figure F.3 XA-G3 special function registers. (Also applicable to the XA-G1 and XA-G2 devices)

NAME	DESCRIPTION	SFR ADDRESS	BIT FUNCTIONS AND ADDRESSES								RESET VALUE
			MSB							LSB	
			357	356	355	354	353	352	351	350	
SWR*	Software Interrupt Request	42A	—	SWR7	SWR6	SWR5	SWR4	SWR3	SWR2	SWR1	00
			2C7	2C6	2C5	2C4	2C3	2C2	2C1	2C0	
T2CON*	Timer 2 control register	418	TF2	EXF2	RCLK0	TCLK0	EXEN2	TR2	C/T2	CP/RL2	00
			2CF	2CE	2CD	2CC	2CB	2CA	2C9	2C8	
T2MOD*	Timer 2 mode control	419	—	—	RCLK1	TCLK1	—	—	T2OE	DCEN	00
TH2	Timer 2 high byte	459									00
TL2	Timer 2 low byte	458									00
T2CAPH	Timer 2 capture register, high byte	45B									00
T2CAPL	Timer 2 capture register, low byte	45A									00
			287	286	285	284	283	282	281	280	
TCON*	Timer 0 and 1 control register	410	TF1	TR1	TF0	TR0	IE1	IT1	IE0	IT0	00
TH0	Timer 0 high byte	451									00
TH1	Timer 1 high byte	453									00
TL0	Timer 0 low byte	450									00
TL1	Timer 1 low byte	452									00
TMOD	Timer 0 and 1 mode control	45C	GATE	C/T	M1	M0	GATE	C/T	M1	M0	00
			28F	28E	28D	28C	28B	28A	289	288	
TSTAT*	Timer 0 and 1 extended status	411	—	—	—	—	—	T1OE	—	T0OE	00
			2FF	2FE	2FD	2FC	2FB	2FA	2F9	2F8	
WDCON*	Watchdog control register	41F	PRE2	PRE1	PRE0	—	—	WDRUN	WDTOF	—	Note 6
WDL	Watchdog timer reload	45F									00
WFEED1	Watchdog feed 1	45D									x
WFEED2	Watchdog feed 2	45E									x

NOTES:
* SFRs are bit addressable.
1. At reset, the BCR register is loaded with the binary value 0000 0a11, where "a" is the value on the BUSW pin. This defaults the address bus size to 20 bits since the XA-G3 has only 20 address lines.
2. SFR is loaded from the reset vector.
3. All bits except F1, F0, and P are loaded from the reset vector. Those bits are all 0.
4. Unimplemented bits in SFRs are X (unknown) at all times. Ones should not be written to these bits since they may be used for other purposes in future XA derivatives. The reset value shown for these bits is 0.
5. Port configurations default to quasi-bidirectional when the XA begins execution from internal code memory after reset, based on the condition found on the EA pin. Thus all PnCFGA registers will contain FF and PnCFGB registers will contain 00. When the XA begins execution using external code memory, the default configuration for pins that are associated with the external bus will be push-pull. The PnCFGA and PnCFGB register contents will reflect this difference.
6. The WDCON reset value is E6 for a Watchdog reset, E4 for all other reset causes.

Figure F.3 *continued.*

Appendix G
80C51 Development System

G.1 Introduction

Many firms offer development systems to support the 80C51 microcontroller and its family derivatives. The equipment described in this appendix is produced by CEIBO and is reproduced here with their kind permission. The CEIBO DS-51 In-Circuit Emulator is shown in Figure G.1.

The DS-51 is a real-time in-circuit emulator dedicated to the 8051 family of microcontrollers. It can be serially linked to a PC or compatible system and can perform a transparent emulation on the target microcontroller. Emulation is possible with almost all of the 8051 derivatives over the voltage and frequency range specified by the device

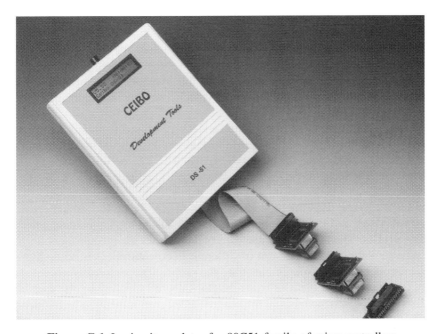

Figure G.1 In-circuit emulator for 80C51 family of microcontrollers

manufacturers. The system also supports the newer low-power and low-voltage micro-controllers providing emulation with a built-in 5 V power supply or any voltage applied to the target circuit. The allowed voltage range is from 1.5 V to 6 V or higher. The software includes Source-Level Debugger for PLM and C, a unique Assembler Debugger, Performance Analyser, On-Line Assembler and Disassembler, Conditional Breakpoints and other features.

Standard systems are provided with 128k bytes of internal memory, 64 k hardware breakpoints, 32 k real-time trace memory and logic analyser with external test points.

G.2   Specifications

Emulator memory. The DS-51 provides 128k bytes of code memory, expandable to 512k bytes, with software mapping and banking capabilities.

Hardware Breakpoints. Breakpoints allow real-time program execution until an opcode is executed at a specified address. Breakpoints on data read or write and an AND/OR combination of two external signals are also implemented. For the latter the logic operator commands allow both signals to be low, any one low, both high, any one high, both leading edge, etc.

Conditional Breakpoints. A complete set of Conditional Breakpoints allow program emulation to be halted on code addresses, source code lines, access to external and on-chip memory, port and register contents.

Software Analyser. A 64k byte buffer records any software and hardware events of the user's program. Details stored include executed code, memory accesses, port and internal register states, external and on-chip memory, etc.

Languages and file formats. The system accepts files with Intel OMF51 object or hex format. Assemblers and high level languages such as C with OMF51 format (Intel, Franklin, Archimedes, IAR, MCC, BSO/Tasking, etc.) are also supported.

Source-Level Debugger. The system software includes a Source-Level Debugger. This may be used to debug code written in Assembler, PLM and C. Commands are included which allow the user to obtain all the information necessary for testing the programs and hardware in real-time. The commands allow the setting of breakpoints on high level language lines, adding a Watch window with the symbols and variables of interest, modifying variables, displaying floating point values, showing the trace buffer, executing assembly steps and many more functions.

Trace and Logic Analyser. The 32k byte trace memory is used to record the microprocessor activities. Eight lines are user selectable test points. Trigger inputs and conditions are available for starting/stopping the trace recording. The Trace Buffer can be viewed in disassembled instructions or high level language lines embedded with the related instructions.

Performance Analyser. This function checks the software Trace Buffer and provides time statistics on modules and procedures as a percentage of the total execution time.

Personality probes. The DS-51 uses standard and bond-out microcontrollers for hardware and software emulation. The selection of different microcontrollers is made by replacing the microcontroller on the probe or changing the probe. The personality probes run at the frequency of the crystal on them or from the clock source supplied by the user hardware. Thus, the same probe may be adapted to user frequency requirements. The frequency range limits are determined by the emulated chip characteristics while the emulator maximum frequency is 42 MHz.

Options.

- Personality probes for different microcontrollers.
- Memory bank set-up.
- Adapter for 44 pin PLCC devices.

Command set. Available functions include:

- FILE (load, save);
- VIEW (watches, variables, module, CPU, dump, registers, trace, file);
- RUN (run, go, trace into, step over, execute, animate, halt, reset);
- BREAKPOINTS (toggle, expression true global, hardware breakpoint, delete all);
- DATA (inspect, evaluate, add watch);
- OPTIONS (environment, path, communications, architecture, mode, save, load);
- WINDOW (zoom, next, size, move, close);
- HELP (index, previous topic).

Input power. 5 V dc at 1.5 A.

DS-51 Debugger. C51D is a menu-driven program supplied with the DS-51. The Debugger runs either under DOS or Windows. The Debugger can be used to load a program and execute it in real-time or as a stand-alone simulator to test user software even without any hardware, although not in real-time and at a speed depending on the user's PC. Functions include the following.

- **Tracing**. Programs may be executed one line at a time. Programs may be traced using high level language lines or assembly instructions.
- **Stepping**. Similar to tracing but program execution steps over CALL instructions without leaving the current procedure.
- **Viewing**. Special windows may be opened showing the program state from various perspectives. The program state includes: variables and their values; breakpoints; a text file; a source file; CPU registers; memory; peripheral registers; etc.
- **Changing**. The current value of a variable can be changed with a user specified value.
- **Watching**. Program variables can be isolated and their values tracked while the program runs.
- **Global and Local menus**. A Global menu lists the commands and is accessible through a menu bar that runs along the top of the window. From there pull-down menus are available for every item on the menu bar. The Debugger is context sensitive and uses Local menus tailored to the particular window in use.
- **Input Boxes**. Many of the Windows Debugger Command Options are available in Input Boxes. An Input Box prompts the user to type in a string, i.e. the name of a file; all entries are recorded in a History Buffer so that the user can pick up any entry just by selecting it with the arrow keys.
- **Toolbar**. The buttons on the Toolbar are the commands needed to operate the most useful functions. See Figure G.2.

Status Line. The Status Line on the bottom of the main application window displays messages related to the cursor position in the Module window, chip type, operating mode (Simulation, Emulation or In-circuit simulation) and current status (program running, ready, error). It also provides on-line help information on selected menus. See Figure G.3.

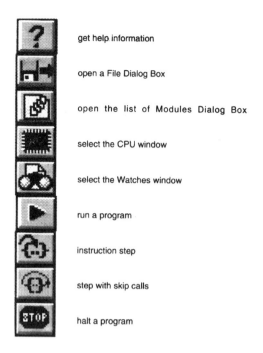

get help information

open a File Dialog Box

open the list of Modules Dialog Box

select the CPU window

select the Watches window

run a program

instruction step

step with skip calls

halt a program

Figure G.2 Toolbar buttons and their functions

Trace options. A selection of source code, disassembled instruction or mixed source and disassembled code is available to display the Trace Memory without stopping the

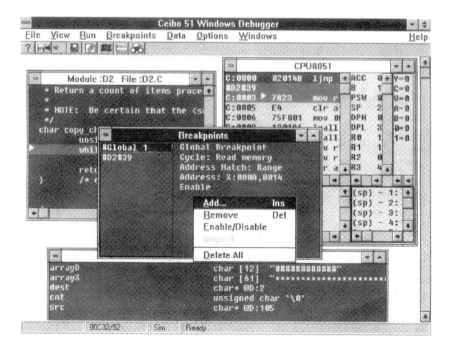

Figure G.3 View of Breakpoint window

emulation. Time stamps can be used to display absolute or relative cycles or time. Filters may be defined to specify which instructions or sequences are of interest. The software also has the capability of saving the Trace Buffer in a disk file.

- **External Trace Start/Stop Triggers**. DS-51 has two External Trigger signals that allow starting and stopping of the trace recording upon external events.
- **Stop Trace when Full or Continuous Recording mode**. There are two Trace Recording modes, Cyclic and Trace Full. In the former the trace is continuously filled with recorded data while in the latter the recording stops when the trace is full.
- **Selectable Trace Trigger levels**. The trigger state allows selection of the way the trigger signals behave. The active mode may be either level or edge for the external start and stop trigger signals.
- **Trace Status on the Fly**. This allows viewing information without stopping emulation. The Trace status includes buffer full, buffer empty, length, etc.
- **Trace filtering on address ranges**. Up to 10 different ranges are allowed to filter the recorded data into the trace memory. The start and stop addresses of modules and procedures can be entered using special prefixes.

Figure G.4 shows an example of a Trace Window.

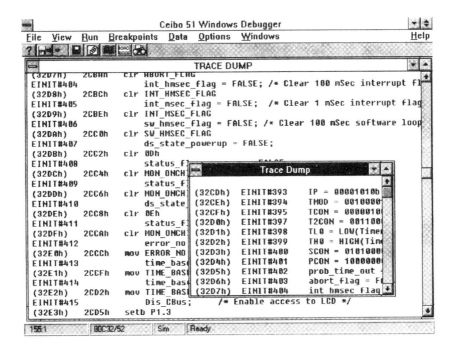

Figure G.4 View of Trace window

Appendix H
80C51 Development Board

H.1 Introduction

Many firms offer development boards to support the 80C51 microcontroller and its family derivatives. The equipment described in this appendix is produced by CEIBO and is reproduced here with their kind permission. The CEIBO DB-51 Development Board is shown in Figure H.1.

The DB-51 is a high performance system design board dedicated to the Philips 80C51 family of microcontrollers. It allows the user to build a primary prototype, analyse, change design and debug. The board is designed to be serially linked to a PC or compatible system. It is not designed for full emulation in complex microcontroller systems and for such circuits the full emulator system is recommended (see Appendix G).

H.2 Specifications

System memory. The DB-51 provides 32k bytes of user code memory. This RAM memory allows downloading and modifying of users' programs.

Breakpoints. Breakpoints allow real-time program execution until an opcode is executed at a specified address.

Conditional Breakpoints. A complete set of Conditional Breakpoints allow program emulation to be halted on code addresses, source code lines, access to on-chip memory, ports and register contents.

User software. There are three software packages available namely C51DB, DW51 and DB51.

C51DB is the most advanced debugger and is the recommended software package for working with the development board. The DW51 program is based on pull-down menus and runs under DOS, although it may be installed to run under Windows as a DOS application. This debugger has three working modes.

- **Real-time emulation**. The user can run and test code without affecting the execution time. The source-level debugger allows a check of a program written in Assembler or in a high level language.
- **In-circuit emulation**. This mode enables the trace and complex breakpoints. Although this is not a real-time mode, all the input/output operations interact with hardware,

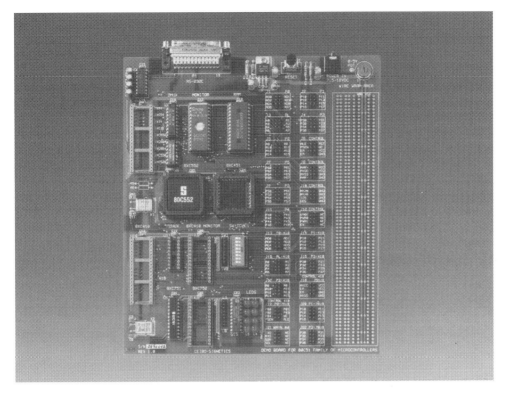

Figure H.1 Development board for the 80C51 family of microcontrollers

while the debugger records the sequence of instructions in a PC buffer for further analysis.
- **Simulation**. The C51DB can be used in this mode without any hardware. This allows software routines to be checked before trying them with the hardware.

The DW51 debugger is also based on pull-down menus but with less functionality and is easier to use. There is a choice of menus which are shown on the upper line of the screen namely: File, View, Debug, Modify, Analyser, Setup, Tools and Quit. Each menu contains a set of commands.

The DB51 program consists of line commands and these are shown on the bottom of the screen.

An on-line Assembler and Disassembler are provided together with upload and download facilities of hexadecimal and object files. Additionally the DB-51 includes the following functions:

- Source-Level Debugger for PLM and C
- Software Trace
- Conditional Breakpoints
- Performance Analyser
- Assembler Debugger

Languages and file formats. The system accepts files generated by Intel software (Assembler, PLM) or compatibles in object or hex format. Other assemblers and high level languages such as C with OMF51 format (Franklin, Archimedes, IAR, MCC, BSO/ Tasking, etc.) are also supported.

Source-Level Debugger. The system software includes a source-level debugger used to debug directly code written in PLM and C. From the code source the user can specify a breakpoint, execute a line step or an Assembly instruction, open a flexible-in-size watch window to display any variable, use the Function keys to display the trace memory, registers and data, redefine the PC and reset the microcontroller.

Software analyser. A 64k byte buffer is used to record any software and hardware events of the user program, such as executed code, memory accesses, port and internal register states, on-chip memory and others. The trace buffer can be viewed in disassembled symbolic or high level language source code.

Input power. 7.5 V dc to 12 V dc.

Limitations. Microcontrollers such as the 8X31/51, 8X32/52, 8XC31/51, 8XC51FA/FB/ FC, 8XC32/52/54/58, 8XC552 and others with external memory addressing and a UART are fully supported. Devices such as the 8XC751 and 8XC752 have limited support. The fully supported microcontrollers are self-debugging on the DB-51. This means that some of the chip resources are used by the board:

- the monitor program uses the bottom 32k byte of program memory;
- chips are always operated in the external memory mode;
- the UART is used to communicate with the PC and is not normally available to the user program;
- interrupt response is slightly slowed by re-vectoring from the monitor program to the user program;
- use of Watchdog Timers and power-down and idle modes of operation are limited due to interaction with the monitor program.

Limited support microcontrollers do not have on-chip UARTS and most do not support external program memory. Therefore downloading of programs to these parts is not supported on the DB-51. An 87C751 or 87C752 microcontroller is supplied with the board and this is pre-programmed with a 'micro' monitor program. Also these parts use the I^{2}C bus to communicate with the PC, limiting the use of the I^{2}C bus for other purposes.

Appendix I
87C750 Development Board

I.1 Introduction

Many firms offer development boards to support the 87C750 microcontroller and its derivatives. The equipment described in this appendix is produced by CEIBO and is reproduced here with their kind permission. The CEIBO DS-750 Development Board is shown in Figure I.1.

The DS-750 is a development tool that supports the Philips 87C750 family of microcontrollers over the frequency range 3.5 MHz to 40 MHz. It is designed to be serially linked to a PC or compatible system with 640 bytes of RAM, one floppy disk drive and an RS-232C interface card for the PC. Emulation is achieved by programming an 87C752 microcontroller with an embedded monitor program and user software. The DS-750 has

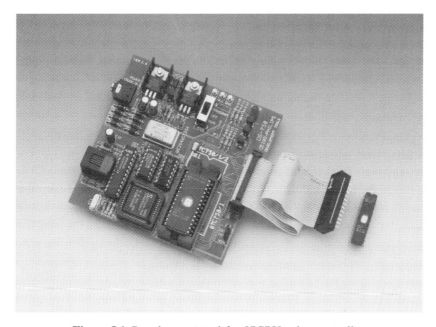

Figure I.1 Development tool for 87C750 microcontrollers

provision for on-board programming capabilities and places the monitor program in the upper 1k byte of memory that is unavailable on the 87C750. Three working modes are available:

- Real-time
- Simulator
- Simulator plus

In real-time operation the user software is executed transparently at the normal operating speed. Breakpoints can be added to stop program execution at a specified address.

For the simulator modes of operation an additional microprocessor is used for the control of the 87C750 lines to simulate its action. The hardware may thus be checked under the control of the software, although at a reduced speed. The software includes C, PLM and Assembler Source-Level Debugger, On-line Assembler and Disassembler, Software Trace, Conditional Breakpoints and more. The software is based on DOS pull-down menus and runs also under MS-Windows. The system is supplied with user's manual, microcontroller documentation, two samples of the 87C752 and one of the 87C750 (all windowed EPROM microcontrollers) and a power supply.

I.2   Specifications

Monitor Program. The Monitor Program provides the link between the microcontroller and the host PC and controls the emulation of application software in real-time. The monitor code is transparent for the 87C750 and does not affect the 1k byte of memory available for application software.

Breakpoints. Breakpoints allow real-time program execution until an opcode is executed at a specified address. Breakpoints are set when an EPROM device is programmed with a user's code. Breakpoints can be disabled although this would add a few cycles to the program execution sequence.

Conditional Breakpoints. Such breakpoints may be set but will not operate in real-time. The program operation will stop at the breakpoint value in Simulation mode

User software. The source-level debugger used allows the use of multiple overlapping windows and a combination of pull-down and pop-up menus. The source-level debugger operates using assembler or a high level language (C, PLM, etc.) and is capable of executing lines of the program while simultaneously displaying the state of any chosen variable.

Symbolic Debugger. The system permits symbolic debugging of Assembler or high level languages using symbols contained in the absolute file generated by the most common Assemblers and high level language compilers.

Software Trace. A 64k byte buffer of the host computer can be used to record program execution. The user is able to define events and variables can be added to the Software Trace as required. The Software Trace is not a real-time function and operates at reduced speed.

Frequency. The system includes a crystal oscillator that can operate at clock frequencies of 5 MHz, 10 MHz, 16 MHz, 20 MHz and 40 MHz. Alternatively the user may operate at a selected frequency by the use of an external clock source connected through application hardware. Frequency selection is achieved through the use of jumpers.

Simulator Debug mode. The Simulator permits breakpoints to be set at any address and condition even though the user software is actually programmed in the 87C752 EPROM.

The Simulator Debug mode will automatically activate in the event of a breakpoint being enabled and not programmed in the device.

Built-in programmer. The system is able to program the 87C748/49/50/51/52 microcontrollers. The maximum programmable memory is limited to that of the 87C752 which is 2k bytes. Program features such as encryption and security are fully supported.

Emulation restrictions. The following restrictions apply to the system.

- Some of the microcontroller resources are used for real-time emulation: one user selectable interrupt (either $\overline{\text{INT0}}$ or $\overline{\text{INT1}}$) and three bytes of the internal stack.
- For a specified breakpoint not programmed in the device the Simulator will slow down program execution.
- Deletion of a breakpoint will cause a Simulator speed reduction.

Input power. 15 V dc to 18 V dc.

DS-750 Debugger. C750D is a menu-driven program supplied with the system. The Debugger can be used to load a program and execute it in real-time or as a stand-alone simulator to test user software, program the microcontroller and other functions. Functions include the following.

- **Tracing**. Programs may be executed one line at a time. Programs may be traced using high level language lines or assembly instructions.
- **Stepping**. Similar to tracing but program execution steps over CALL instructions without leaving the current procedure.
- **Viewing**. Special windows may be opened showing the program state from various perspectives. The program state includes variables and their values; breakpoints; a text file; a source file; CPU registers; memory; peripheral registers etc.
- **Inspecting**. The Debugger can delve deeper into the program and display the variable contents.
- **Changing**. The current value of a variable can be changed with a user specified value.
- **Watching**. Program variables can be isolated and their values tracked while the program runs.

Global and Local menus. A global menu lists the commands and is accessible through a menu bar that runs along the top of the window. From there pull-down menus are available for every item on the menu bar. The debugger is context sensitive and uses Local menus tailored to the particular window in use. Figure I.2 shows the initial screen window with the menu headings at the top of the screen.

The pull-down menu for each item on the menu bar allows the following.

- Open a pop-up menu. Pop-up menus appear when a menu item is chosen followed by a menu icon (▶).
- Open a dialogue box. Dialogue boxes appear when a menu item is chosen followed by a dialogue box icon (. . .).

The global menu commands may be activated by using the Function keys or by simultaneously pressing the ALT key and the command first letter key. As an example to open the View command ALT-V would be pressed. This would give the window shown in Figure I.3.

The View menu commands open windows that display different aspects of the program being debugged. Commands such as Watches (to open a Watch window to show the value

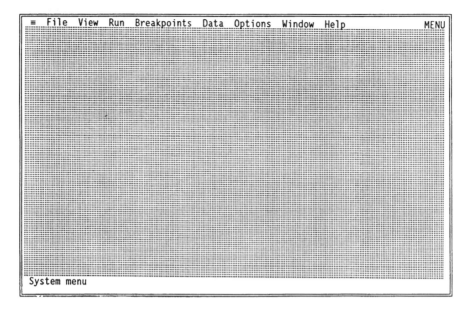

Figure I.2 Screen view of System menu

of specified variables), Variables (to open a Variables window to display a list of the global and local symbols and their values), etc. can be accessed. The CPU command opens a CPU window which displays the disassembled instructions of a user program. Figure I.4 shows the effect of selecting the CPU command.

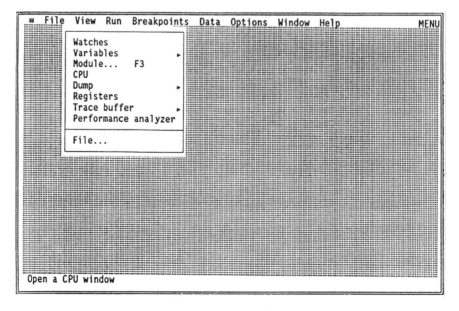

Figure I.3 View menu commands

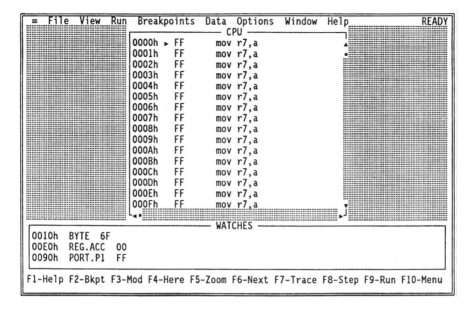

```
 ≡  File   View   Run   Breakpoints   Data   Options   Window   Help                        READY
                                            ── CPU ──
                            0000h ► FF         mov  r7,a                             ▲
                            0001h   FF         mov  r7,a                             ▪
                            0002h   FF         mov  r7,a
                            0003h   FF         mov  r7,a
                            0004h   FF         mov  r7,a
                            0005h   FF         mov  r7,a
                            0006h   FF         mov  r7,a
                            0007h   FF         mov  r7,a
                            0008h   FF         mov  r7,a
                            0009h   FF         mov  r7,a
                            000Ah   FF         mov  r7,a
                            000Bh   FF         mov  r7,a
                            000Ch   FF         mov  r7,a
                            000Dh   FF         mov  r7,a
                            000Eh   FF         mov  r7,a
                            000Fh   FF         mov  r7,a                             ▼
                           ◄▪                                                     ►
                                        ── WATCHES ──
   0010h   BYTE   6F
   00E0h   REG.ACC   00
   0090h   PORT.P1   FF

 F1-Help F2-Bkpt F3-Mod F4-Here F5-Zoom F6-Next F7-Trace F8-Step F9-Run F10-Menu
```

Figure I.4 Use of the CPU and Watches windows

Figure I.4 also shows the effect of opening a Watches window and shows specified variables which in this case are locations 0010h (byte), 00E0h (Accumulator), 0090h (port, pin 1) and their contents.

Also shown in Figure I.4 are the commands at the bottom of the screen. These commands may be actioned by pressing an appropriate Function key (See Table I.1).

A program may be loaded from disk or entered directly, using the on-line assembler, into the lines displayed in the CPU window. The program being debugged may be run using the Run menu with various options as shown in Figure I.5.

The Run command for example would cause the program to execute continuously until halted with the Halt key, or a breakpoint is reached.

Table I.1 CEIBO development system function key commands

Function key		Function operation
F1	Help	On item under current cursor position
F2	Breakpoints	Installs breakpoints at cursor toggling them on or off
F3	Module	Shows list file of selected module; used by the debugger
F4	Here	Moves to current cursor position
F5	Zoom	Makes current window fill the screen; toggles on or off
F6	Next	Moves cursor to the next window
F7	Trace	Single steps through the program (including sub-routines)
F8	Step	Single steps through the program (excluding sub-routines)
F10	Menu	Provides access to Global menu

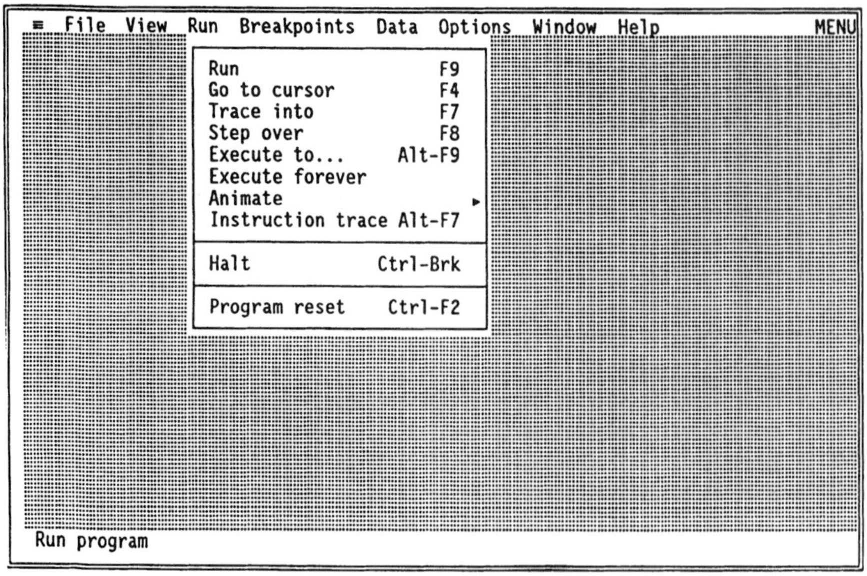

```
≡  File  View  Run  Breakpoints  Data  Options  Window  Help                    MENU
              ┌──────────────────────────────────┐
              │ Run                          F9   │
              │ Go to cursor                 F4   │
              │ Trace into                   F7   │
              │ Step over                    F8   │
              │ Execute to...           Alt-F9    │
              │ Execute forever                   │
              │ Animate                      ▶    │
              │ Instruction trace Alt-F7          │
              ├──────────────────────────────────┤
              │ Halt                    Ctrl-Brk  │
              ├──────────────────────────────────┤
              │ Program reset           Ctrl-F2   │
              └──────────────────────────────────┘



  Run program
```

Figure I.5 Screen view of Run menu

The above gives only an outline of the DS-750 system and for detailed information reference should be made to the CEIBO user's manual. An application using the DS-750 development system can be found in Chapter 11.

Appendix J
80C51XA Development System

J.1 Introduction

The system described in this appendix is produced by CEIBO and is reproduced here with their kind permission. The CEIBO EB-XA Emulation Board is shown in Figure J.1.

The EB-XA is an emulation board dedicated to the Philips 80C51XA microcontroller derivatives. It can be serially linked to a PC or compatible system and can emulate the microcontroller using a variety of external clock sources or the built-in clock oscillator. The built-in clock oscillator can generate 6 MHz, 12 MHz, 14.7456 MHz and 24 MHz. Emulation is provided for a microcontroller with or without ROM as required. A special Philips' bond-out chip is used to emulate the microcontroller transparently and in real-time without affecting port or register states.

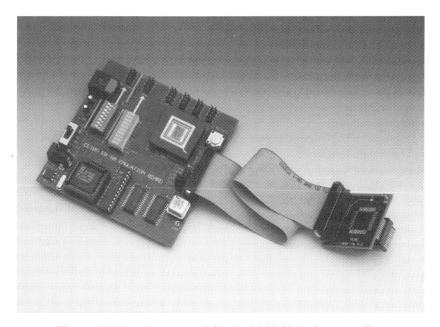

Figure J.1 Development tool for the 80C51XA microcontrollers

Three working modes are possible:

- Real-time
- Simulation
- In-circuit Simulation

In Real-time mode the user software is executed transparently and at the microcontroller speed. Breakpoints can be added to stop program execution at a specified address.

In Simulation mode the software may be debugged without any hardware. Thus the system may be disconnected while using this mode.

In the In-Circuit Simulation mode an additional microprocessor is used to take control of the microcontroller lines and to simulate its operation, but not in real-time. Using this mode allows access to all of the microcontroller functions and interacts with the hardware according to the user software execution or directly by means of emulator commands from the host computer. The Trace, Complex Breakpoints, Performance Analyser and many other functions are enabled in this mode.

The software includes Source-Level Debugger for C and Assembler, On-Line Assembler and Disassembler, Software Trace, Conditional Breakpoints and other features. The code memory allows the downloading and modification of users' programs and breakpoints allow real-time execution up to a specified address or line of source code. All I/O lines are easily accessible and may be connected to on-board switches and LEDs for test purposes.

J.2   Specifications

System memory. The EB-XA provides 64k bytes of user code memory which allows downloading and modification of user programs and variables. The code memory boundaries may be defined to partially map the memory as belonging to the emulation board or to the target circuit. Software control sets the boundaries to 4k, 8k, 16k, 32k or 64k.

Hardware Breakpoints. Breakpoints allow real-time program execution until an opcode is executed at a specified address. Breakpoints may be set to any address of the system code memory. Breakpoints on user RAM addresses are possible if this memory can be written by the microcontroller.

User software. The system runs only under MS-Windows 3.x or MS-Windows 95.

Symbolic Debugger. The system allows symbolic debugging of Assembler or high level languages. The Symbolic Debugger uses symbols contained in the absolute file generated by the most commonly used Assemblers and high level language compilers.

Source-Level Debugger. The system software includes a Source-Level Debugger. This may be used to debug code written in Assembler, C and others, with the capability of executing lines of the program while displaying the state of any variable.

Software Trace. Program execution can be recorded in a 64-byte buffer. Conditional Breakpoints may be defined to stop program execution. The user may define events and variables to be added to the software trace. The software trace is not a real-time function and is performed by slowing down the emulation speed. This function is enabled in Simulation or In-circuit Simulation modes.

Simulation Debug mode. This allows the software to be tested without any hardware. All emulation functions are supported by this powerful emulation debugger.

Supported microcontrollers. The supported microcontrollers are all the Philips XA derivatives functional compatible with the current bond-out devices and with up to 64k bytes internal code memory.

Microcontroller selection. The EB-XA uses the Philips bond-out chip for hardware and software emulation. The selection of a supported microcontroller is done by software. The Debugger menu is used to choose the desired emulated derivative. The minimum and maximum frequencies are determined by the bond-out chip characteristics, while the emulator maximum frequency is 30 MHz.

Frequency. The system includes a crystal oscillator that can supply clock frequencies of 6 MHz, 12 MHz, 24 MHz together with a fixed frequency of 14.7456 MHz. Also, the user may select any other frequency by connecting an external clock source through the application hardware. The crystal oscillator itself is mounted on a socket and may be replaced by another oscillator with a different frequency value. Frequency selection is achieved by means of jumper leads.

Emulation voltage. The system emulates the microcontrollers at 3.3 V or 5 V. The voltage selection is achieved by the position of a slide switch mounted on the emulator board.

Host characteristics. PC or compatible systems with 2 M bytes of RAM, one RS-232C interface card for the PC, DOS or Windows 3.x or later.

Input power. 5 V DC at 1.5 A.

EB-XA Debugger. The Debugger is a menu-driven program used to load a program, execute it in real-time, simulate the software, etc. Functions include the following.

- **Tracing**. Programs may be executed one line at a time. Programs may be traced using high level language lines or assembly instructions.
- **Stepping**. Similar to tracing but program execution steps over CALL instructions without leaving the current procedure.
- **Viewing**. Special windows may be opened showing the program state from various perspectives. The program state includes variables and their values; breakpoints; a source file; CPU registers, memory; peripheral registers, etc.
- **Changing**. The current value of a variable can be changed with a user specified value.
- **Watching**. Program variables can be isolated and their values tracked while the program runs.

Global and Local menus. A Global menu lists the commands and is accessible through a menu bar that runs along the top of the window. See Figure J.2.

From there, pull-down menus are available for every item on the menu bar and allow the following:

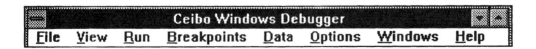

Figure J.2 EB-XA Global menus

- execute a command;
- open a pop-up menu; these appear when a menu item is selected followed by the menu icon (▶);
- open a dialogue box; these appear when a menu item is selected and they are indicated as (. . .);
- check an option to select it.

The Debugger is context sensitive and uses Local menus tailored to the particular window in use. As an example, if the Options menu is selected, a list of options appears, as indicated in Figure J.3, where Mode has been accessed giving the types of Mode available to the system.

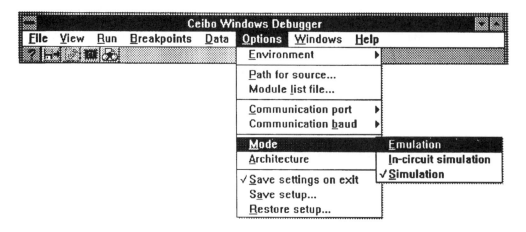

Figure J.3 Selecting an operating mode via the Options menu

Input Boxes. Many of the Windows Debugger Command options are available in Input Boxes. An Input Box prompts the user to type in a string, i.e. the name of a file; all entries are recorded in a History Buffer so that the user can pick up any entry just by selecting it with the arrow keys.

Toolbar. The buttons on the toolbar are the commands needed to operate the most useful functions. The Toolbar is shown in Figure J.4.

Status Line. The Status Line on the bottom of the main application window displays messages related to the cursor position in the Module window, chip type, operating mode (Simulation, Emulation or In-circuit Simulation) and current status (program running, ready, error). It also provides on-line help information on selected menus. See Figure J.5.

As an example of the use of the menu and commands, Figure J.6 shows the result of selecting the View menu. The available commands are: Breakpoints, Variables, Module, Watch, CPU, Registers, Performance Analyser, Trace, Memory Space and Target.

If the Trace command were to be selected, the Trace window could be opened and the Trace Status could be viewed. The Trace functions are enabled in Simulation modes only. The Trace menu is shown in Figure J.7.

The Trace options are: Trace Dump, Trace Triggers and Trace Status.

Trace Dump. The Trace Buffer Dump command opens a Trace window allowing the current Trace Buffer to be viewed, different display formats for the trace selected, data

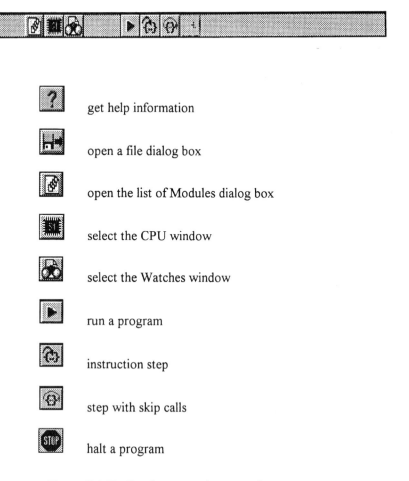

get help information

open a file dialog box

open the list of Modules dialog box

select the CPU window

select the Watches window

run a program

instruction step

step with skip calls

halt a program

Figure J.4 Toolbar buttons and commands

Figure J.5 EB-XA Status Line

from the trace display filtered and data patterns in the buffer searched. This is shown in Figure J.8.

The Local menu of the Trace Dump windows provides many useful functions to set up the operation of the trace and manipulate the accumulated information.

Trace Triggers. This command sets the trace control to the selected option to start and stop the recording. The Trace Triggers window is shown in Figure J.9.

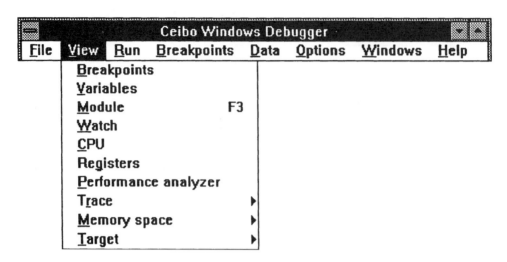

Figure J.6 View menu

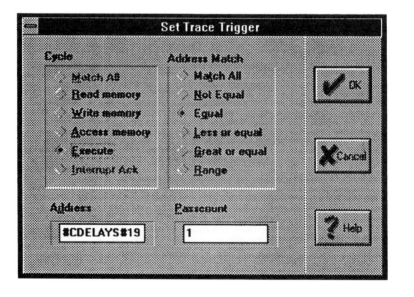

Figure J.7 Trace menu

The different buttons and functions can be seen in the window of Figure J.9. As an example, the function of the **Run begin** button is, when execution commences, to allow the Trace Buffer to capture data from the start program execution until the Trace Buffer is full. This mode automatically selects the **Stop when full** option.

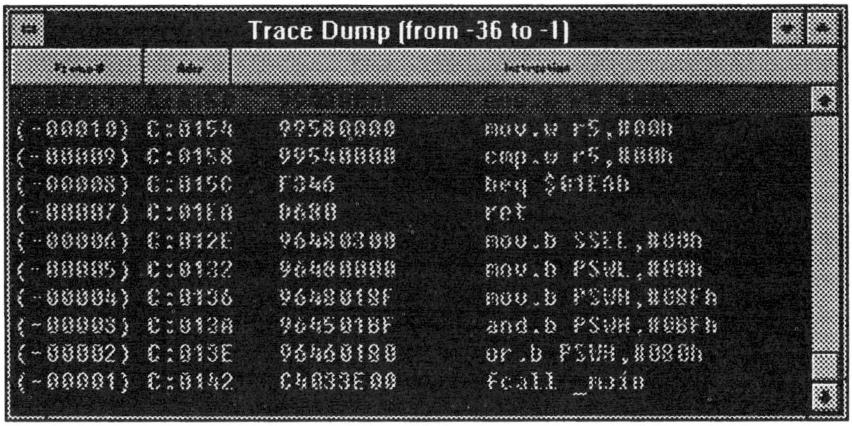

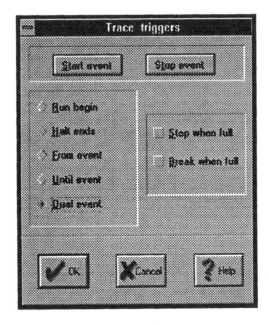

Figure J.8 Trace Dump

Figure J.9 Trace Triggers

A Trace Trigger is the means for selecting the criteria for capturing an execution trace in the target system Trace Buffer.

Trace Status. The Trace Status command displays a window showing the current state of the trace which includes: trace state (recording/halted), trace overflow indication and the number of frames currently in the Trace Buffer. A Trace Status window is shown in Figure J.10.

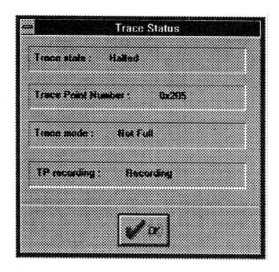

Figure J.10 Trace Status

This appendix is intended to give no more than an indication of the development system offered for the XA device. Full information may be obtained from the user's manual for the system.

Appendix K

The Philips XA-S3 CMOS Single-Chip 16-Bit Microcontroller

Advanced information on this CMOS 16-bit microcontroller is reproduced here with the kind permission of Philips Semiconductors. The XA-S3 is one of the proposed derivatives of the XA device which will possess extra features compared to its first generation predecessor. Just as the 8XC552 is the advanced version of the basic 8XC50 in the 8-bit range, the XA-S3 is likely to be the 16-bit advanced version of the XA-G3. A comparison of the specification of the XA-S3 with that of the XA-G3 can be seen by glancing at the details on the first of the following data sheets. Extra features of the XA-S3 compared to the XA-G3 include:

- 24 address lines
- enhanced on-chip data RAM
- extra ports with up to 50 I/O pins
- programmable counter array
- ADC
- I^2C interface.

The proposed device shows the likely evolution of microcontroller development towards more functions being available on a single chip, albeit with a larger pin-out.

The move towards 16-bit devices is gaining in momentum and, provided cost is not a high priority, they are likely to be the preferred choice for system designers requiring sophisticated solutions for their design requirements using a single microcontroller.

INTEGRATED CIRCUITS

XA-S3
CMOS single-chip 16-bit microcontroller

Objective Specification

1997 Oct 22

IC25 Data Handbook

**Philips
Semiconductors**

PHILIPS

Philips Semiconductors

Advance Information - Subject to Change

Single-chip 16-bit microcontroller

XA-S3

GENERAL DESCRIPTION

The XA-S3 device is a member of Philips' 80C51 XA (eXtended Architecture) family of high performance 16-bit single-chip microcontrollers.

The XA-S3 device combines many powerful peripherals on one chip. With its high performance A/D converter, timers/counters, watchdog, Programmable Counter Array (PCA), I^2C interface, dual UARTs, and multiple general purpose I/O ports, it is suited for general multipurpose high performance embedded control functions.

SPECIFIC FEATURES OF THE XA-S3
- 2.7V to 5.5V operation.
- 32K bytes of on-chip EPROM/ROM program memory.
- 1024 bytes of on-chip data RAM.
- Supports off-chip addressing up to 16 megabytes (24 address lines). A clock output reference is added to simplify external bus interfacing.
- High performance 8-channel 10-bit A/D converter with automatic channel scan and repeated read functions. Completes a conversion in 5 microseconds at 20 MHz (100 clocks per conversion). Operates down to 3V.
- Three standard counter/timers with enhanced features (same as XA-G3 T0, T1, and T2). All timers have a toggle output capability.
- Watchdog timer.
- 5-channel 16-bit Programmable Counter Array (PCA).
- I^2C-bus serial I/O port with byte-oriented master and slave functions. Supports the 100 kHz I^2C operating mode at rates up to 400kHz.
- Two enhanced UARTs with independent baud rates.
- Seven software interrupts.
- Active low reset output pin indicates all reset occurrences (external reset, watchdog reset and the RESET instruction). A reset source register allows program determination of the cause of the most recent reset.
- 50 I/O pins, each with 4 programmable output configurations.
- 30 MHz operating frequency at 2.7 - 5.5V V_{DD} over commercial operating conditions.
- Power saving operating modes: Idle and Power-Down. Wake-Up from power-down via an external interrupt is supported.
- 68-pin PLCC and 80-pin PQFP packages.

Philips Semiconductors

CMOS single-chip 16-bit microcontroller

XA-S3

ORDERING INFORMATION

ROMless	ROM	EPROM	TEMPERATURE RANGE °C AND PACKAGE	FREQ (MHz)	DRAWING NUMBER
P51XAS	XAS	P51XAS OTP	0 to +70, 68-pin Plastic Leaded Chip Carrier	30	SOT188-3
P51XAS30xB	P51XAS xB BD	XAS xB BD	0 to +70, 80-pin Plastic Quad Flat Pkg. 30		SOT315-1

TBD

Philips Semiconductors

Advance Information - Subject to Change

CMOS single-chip 16-bit microcontroller

XA-S3

PIN CONFIGURATIONS

68-Pin PLCC Package

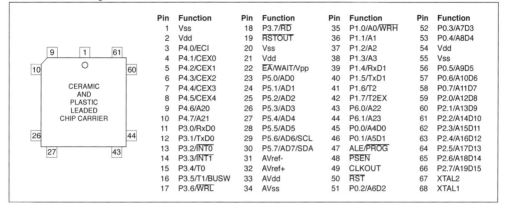

Pin	Function	Pin	Function	Pin	Function	Pin	Function
1	Vss	18	P3.7/$\overline{\text{RD}}$	35	P1.0/A0/$\overline{\text{WRH}}$	52	P0.3/A7D3
2	Vdd	19	$\overline{\text{RSTOUT}}$	36	P1.1/A1	53	P0.4/A8D4
3	P4.0/ECI	20	Vss	37	P1.2/A2	54	Vdd
4	P4.1/CEX0	21	Vdd	38	P1.3/A3	55	Vss
5	P4.2/CEX1	22	$\overline{\text{EA}}$/WAIT/Vpp	39	P1.4/RxD1	56	P0.5/A9D5
6	P4.3/CEX2	23	P5.0/AD0	40	P1.5/TxD1	57	P0.6/A10D6
7	P4.4/CEX3	24	P5.1/AD1	41	P1.6/T2	58	P0.7/A11D7
8	P4.5/CEX4	25	P5.2/AD2	42	P1.7/T2EX	59	P2.0/A12D8
9	P4.6/A20	26	P5.3/AD3	43	P6.0/A22	60	P2.1/A13D9
10	P4.7/A21	27	P5.4/AD4	44	P6.1/A23	61	P2.2/A14D10
11	P3.0/RxD0	28	P5.5/AD5	45	P0.0/A4D0	62	P2.3/A15D11
12	P3.1/TxD0	29	P5.6/AD6/SCL	46	P0.1/A5D1	63	P2.4/A16D12
13	P3.2/$\overline{\text{INT0}}$	30	P5.7/AD7/SDA	47	ALE/$\overline{\text{PROG}}$	64	P2.5/A17D13
14	P3.3/$\overline{\text{INT1}}$	31	AVref-	48	$\overline{\text{PSEN}}$	65	P2.6/A18D14
15	P3.4/T0	32	AVref+	49	CLKOUT	66	P2.7/A19D15
16	P3.5/T1/BUSW	33	AVdd	50	$\overline{\text{RST}}$	67	XTAL2
17	P3.6/$\overline{\text{WRL}}$	34	AVss	51	P0.2/A6D2	68	XTAL1

80-Pin QFP Package

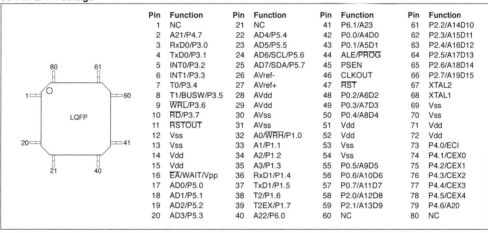

Pin	Function	Pin	Function	Pin	Function	Pin	Function
1	NC	21	NC	41	P6.1/A23	61	P2.2/A14D10
2	A21/P4.7	22	AD4/P5.4	42	P0.0/A4D0	62	P2.3/A15D11
3	RxD0/P3.0	23	AD5/P5.5	43	P0.1/A5D1	63	P2.4/A16D12
4	TxD0/P3.1	24	AD6/SCL/P5.6	44	ALE/$\overline{\text{PROG}}$	64	P2.5/A17D13
5	$\overline{\text{INT0}}$/P3.2	25	AD7/SDA/P5.7	45	$\overline{\text{PSEN}}$	65	P2.6/A18D14
6	$\overline{\text{INT1}}$/P3.3	26	AVref-	46	CLKOUT	66	P2.7/A19D15
7	T0/P3.4	27	AVref+	47	$\overline{\text{RST}}$	67	XTAL2
8	T1/BUSW/P3.5	28	AVdd	48	P0.2/A6D2	68	XTAL1
9	$\overline{\text{WRL}}$/P3.6	29	AVdd	49	P0.3/A7D3	69	Vss
10	$\overline{\text{RD}}$/P3.7	30	AVss	50	P0.4/A8D4	70	Vss
11	$\overline{\text{RSTOUT}}$	31	AVss	51	Vdd	71	Vdd
12	Vss	32	A0/$\overline{\text{WRH}}$/P1.0	52	Vdd	72	Vdd
13	Vss	33	A1/P1.1	53	Vss	73	P4.0/ECI
14	Vdd	34	A2/P1.2	54	Vss	74	P4.1/CEX0
15	Vdd	35	A3/P1.3	55	P0.5/A9D5	75	P4.2/CEX1
16	$\overline{\text{EA}}$/WAIT/Vpp	36	RxD1/P1.4	56	P0.6/A10D6	76	P4.3/CEX2
17	AD0/P5.0	37	TxD1/P1.5	57	P0.7/A11D7	77	P4.4/CEX3
18	AD1/P5.1	38	T2/P1.6	58	P2.0/A12D8	78	P4.5/CEX4
19	AD2/P5.2	39	T2EX/P1.7	59	P2.1/A13D9	79	P4.6/A20
20	AD3/P5.3	40	A22/P6.0	60	NC	80	NC

Philips Semiconductors   Advance Information - Subject to Change

CMOS single-chip 16-bit microcontroller   XA-S3

LOGIC SYMBOL

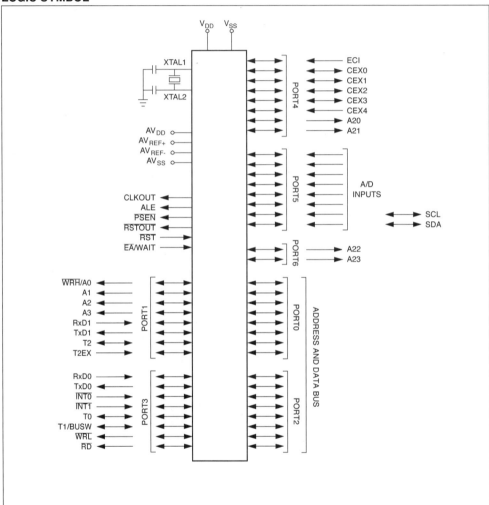

Philips Semiconductors   Advance Information - Subject to Change

CMOS single-chip 16-bit microcontroller   XA-S3

BLOCK DIAGRAM

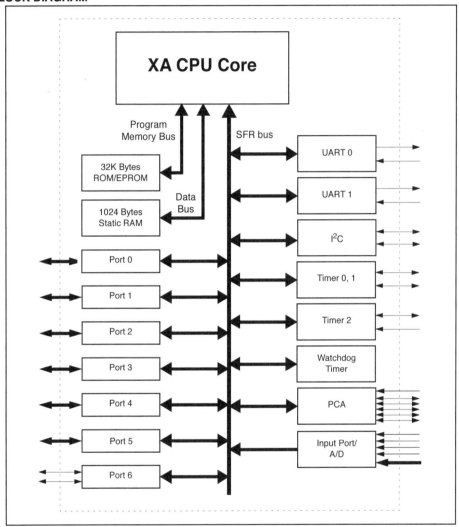

Philips Semiconductors

Advance Information - Subject to Change

CMOS single-chip 16-bit microcontroller

XA-S3

PIN DESCRIPTIONS

MNEMONIC	PIN NO. PLCC	PIN NO. PQFP	TYPE	NAME AND FUNCTION
V_{SS}	1, 20, 55		I	**Ground:** 0V reference.
V_{DD}	2, 21, 54		I	**Power Supply:** This is the power supply voltage for normal, idle, and power down operation.
RST	50		I	**Reset:** A low on this pin resets the microcontroller, causing I/O ports and peripherals to take on their default states, and the processro to begin execution at the address contained in the reset vector.
RSTOUT	19		O	**Reset Output:** This pins outputs a low whenever the XA-S3 processor is reset for any reason. This includes an external reset via the RST pin, watchdog reset, and the RESET instruction.
ALE/PROG	47		I/O	**Address Latch Enable/Program Pulse:** A high output on the ALE pin signals external circuitry to latch the address portion of the multiplexed address/data bus. A pulse on ALE occurs only when it is needed onn order to process a bus cycle. During EPROM programming, this pin is used as the program pulse input.
PSEN	48		O	**Program Store Enable:** The read strobe for external program memory. When the microcontroller accesses external program memory, PSEN is driven low in order to enable memory devices. PSEN is only active when external code accesses are performed.
EA/WAIT/ V_{PP}	22		I	**External Access/Bus Wait/Programming Supply Voltage:** The EA input determines whether the internal program memory of the microcontroller is used for code execution. The value on the EA pin is latched as the external reset input is released and applies during later execution. When latched as a 0, external program memory is used exclusively. When latched as a 1, internal program memory will be used up to its limit, and external program memory used above that point. After reset is released, this pin takes on the function of bus WAIT input. If WAIT is asserted high during an external bus access, that cycle will be extended until WAIT is released. During EPROM programming, this pin is also the programming supply voltage input.
XTAL1	68		I	**Crystal 1:** Input to the inverting amplifier used in the oscillator circuit and input to the internal clock generator circuits..
XTAL2	67		I	**Crystal 2:** Output from the oscillator amplifier.
CLKOUT	49		O	**Clock Output:** This pin outputs a buffered version of the internal CPU clock. The clock output may be used in conjunction with the external bus to synchronize WAIT state generators, etc. The clock output may be disabled by software.
AV_{DD}	33		I	**Analog Power Supply:** Positive power supply input for the A/D converter.
AV_{SS}	34		I	**Analog Ground:** Ground return for the A/D converter.
$+V_{REF}$	32		I	**A/D Positive Reference Voltage.**
$-V_{REF}$	31		I	**A/D Negative Reference Voltage.**
P0.0 - P0.7	45, 46, 51-53, 56-58		I/O	**Port 0:** Port 0 is an 8-bit I/O port with a user-configurable output type. Port 0 latches have 1s written to them and are configured in the quasi-bidirectional mode during reset. The operation of port 0 pins as inputs and outputs depends upon the port configuration selected. Each port pin is configured independently. Refer to the section on I/O port configuration and the DC Electrical Characteristics for details. When the external program/data bus is used, Port 0 becomes the multiplexed low data/ instruction byte and address lines 4 through 11.

Philips Semiconductors

Advance Information - Subject to Change

CMOS single-chip 16-bit microcontroller

XA-S3

MNEMONIC	PIN NO. PLCC	PIN NO. PQFP	TYPE	NAME AND FUNCTION
P1.0 - P1.7	35-42		I/O	**Port 1:** Port 1 is an 8-bit I/O port with a user-configurable output type. Port 1 latches have 1s written to them and are configured in the quasi-bidirectional mode during reset. The operation of port 1 pins as inputs and outputs depends upon the port configuration selected. Each port pin is configured independently. Refer to the section on I/O port configuration and the DC Electrical Characteristics for details.
				Port 1 also provides various special functions as described below.
			O	A0/WRH (P1.0): — Address bit 0 of the external address bus when the external data bus is configured for an 8-bit width. When the external data bus is configured for a 16-bit width, this pin becomes the high byte write strobe.
			O	A1 (P1.1): — Address bit 1 of the external address bus.
			O	A2 (P1.2): — Address bit 2 of the external address bus.
			O	A3 (P1.3): — Address bit 3 of the external address bus.
			I	RxD1 (P1.4): — Serial port 1 receiver input.
			O	TxD1 (P1.5): — Serial port 1 transmitter output.
			I/O	T2 (P1.6): — Timer/counter 2 external count input or overflow output.
			I	T2EX (P1.7): — Timer/counter 2 reload/capture/direction control.
P2.0 - P2.7	59-66		I/O	**Port 2:** Port 2 is an 8-bit I/O port with a user-configurable output type. Port 2 latches have 1s written to them and are configured in the quasi-bidirectional mode during reset. The operation of port 2 pins as inputs and outputs depends upon the port configuration selected. Each port pin is configured independently. Refer to the section on I/O port configuration and the DC Electrical Characteristics for details.
				When the external program/data bus is used in 16-bit mode, Port 2 becomes the multiplexed high data/instruction byte and address lines 12 through 19. When the external data/address bus is used in 8-bit mode, the number of address lines that appear on port 2 is user programmable in groups of 4 bits.
P3.0 - P3.7	11-18		I/O	**Port 3:** Port 3 is an 8-bit I/O port with a user-configurable output type. Port 3 latches have 1s written to them and are configured in the quasi-bidirectional mode during reset. The operation of port 3 pins as inputs and outputs depends upon the port configuration selected. Each port pin is configured independently. Refer to the section on I/O port configuration and the DC Electrical Characteristics for details.
				Port 1 also provides various special functions as described below.
			I	RxD0 (P3.0): — Receiver input for serial port 0.
			O	TxD0 (P3.1): — Transmitter output for serial port 0.
			I	INT0 (P3.2): — External interrupt 0 input.
			I	INT1 (P3.3): — External interrupt 1 input.
			I/O	T0 (P3.4): — Timer/counter 0 external count input or overflow output.
			I/O	T1/BUSW (P3.5): — Timer/counter 1 external count input or overflow output. The value on this pin is latched as an external chip reset is completed and defines the default external data bus.
			O	WRL (P3.6): — External data memory low byte write strobe.
			O	RD (P3.7): — External data memory read strobe.

Philips Semiconductors   Advance Information - Subject to Change

CMOS single-chip 16-bit microcontroller   XA-S3

MNEMONIC	PIN NO. PLCC	PIN NO. PQFP	TYPE	NAME AND FUNCTION
P4.0 - P4.7	3-10		I/O	**Port 4:** Port 4 is an 8-bit I/O port with a user-configurable output type. Port 4 latches have 1s written to them and are configured in the quasi-bidirectional mode during reset. The operation of port 4 pins as inputs and outputs depends upon the port configuration selected. Each port pin is configured independently. Refer to the section on I/O port configuration and the DC Electrical Characteristics for details. Port 4 also provides various special functions as described below.
			I	**ECI (P4.0):** PCA External clock input.
			I/O	**CEX0 (P4.1):** Capture/compare external I/O for PCA module 0.
			I/O	**CEX1 (P4.2):** Capture/compare external I/O for PCA module 1.
			I/O	**CEX2 (P4.3):** Capture/compare external I/O for PCA module 2.
			I/O	**CEX3 (P4.4):** Capture/compare external I/O for PCA module 3.
			I/O	**CEX4 (P4.5):** Capture/compare external I/O for PCA module 4.
			O	**A20 (P4.6):** Address bit 20 of the external address bus.
			O	**A21 (P4.7):** Address bit 21 of the external address bus.
P5.0 - P5.7	23-30		I/O	**Port 5:** Port 5 is an 8-bit I/O port with a user-configurable output type. Port 5 latches have 1s written to them and are configured in the quasi-bidirectional mode during reset. The operation of port 5 pins as inputs and outputs depends upon the port configuration selected. Each port pin is configured independently. Refer to the section on I/O port configuration and the DC Electrical Characteristics for details. Port 5 also provides various special functions as described below. Port 5 pins used as A/D inputs must be configured by the user to the high impedance mode.
			I	**AD0 (P5.0):** A/D channel 0 input.
			I	**AD1 (P5.1):** A/D channel 1 input.
			I	**AD2 (P5.2):** A/D channel 2 input.
			I	**AD3 (P5.3):** A/D channel 3 input.
			I	**AD4 (P5.4):** A/D channel 4 input.
			I	**AD5 (P5.5):** A/D channel 5 input.
			I/O	**AD6/SCL (P5.6):** A/D channel 6 input. I^2C serial clock input/output.
			I/O	**AD7/SDA (P5.7):** A/D channel 7 input. I^2C serial data input/output.
P6.0 - P6.1	43, 44		I/O	**Port 6:** Port 6 is an 8-bit I/O port with a user-configurable output type. Port 6 latches have 1s written to them and are configured in the quasi-bidirectional mode during reset. The operation of port 6 pins as inputs and outputs depends upon the port configuration selected. Each port pin is configured independently. Refer to the section on I/O port configuration and the DC Electrical Characteristics for details. Port 6 also provides special functions as described below.
			O	**A22 (P6.0):** Address bit 22 of the external address bus.
			O	**A23 (P6.1):** Address bit 23 of the external address bus.

Philips Semiconductors

Advance Information - Subject to Change

CMOS single-chip 16-bit microcontroller   XA-S3

SPECIAL FUNCTION REGISTERS

NAME	DESCRIPTION	SFR Address	BIT FUNCTIONS AND ADDRESSES								RESET VALUE
			MSB							LSB	
			3F7	3F6	3F5	3F4	3F3	3F2	3F1	3F0	
ADCON#*	A/D control register	43E	-	-	-	ADCAL	ADRES	ADMOD	ADSST	ADINT	00h
			3FF	3FE	3FD	3FC	3FB	3FA	3F9	3F8	
ADCS#*	A/D channel select register	43F	ADCS7	ADCS6	ADCS5	ADCS4	ADCS3	ADCS2	ADCS1	ADCS0	00h
ADCFG#	A/D timing configuration	4B9	-	-	-	-	A/D Timing Configuration				00h
ADRSH0#	A/D high byte result, channel 0	4B0									xx
ADRSH1#	A/D high byte result channel 1	4B1									xx
ADRSH2#	A/D high byte result, channel 2	4B2									xx
ADRSH3#	A/D high byte result, channel 3	4B3									xx
ADRSH4#	A/D high byte result, channel 4	4B4									xx
ADRSH5#	A/D high byte result, channel 5	4B5									xx
ADRSH6#	A/D high byte result, channel 6	4B6									xx
ADRSH7#	A/D high byte result, channel 7	4B7									xx
ADRSL#	A/D low 2 bits of result	4B8									xx
BCR	Bus configuration register	46A	-	-	CLKD	WAITD	BUSD	BC2	BC1	BC0	Note 1
BTRH	Bus timing register high byte	469	DW1	DW0	DWA1	DWA0	DR1	DR0	DRA1	DRA0	FFh
BTRL	Bus timing register low byte	468	WM1	WM0	ALEW	-	CR1	CR0	CRA1	CRA0	EFh
			2D7	2D6	2D5	2D4	2D3	2D2	2D1	2D0	
CCON#*	PCA counter control	41A	CF	CR	-	CCF4	CCF3	CCF2	CCF1	CCF0	00h
CMOD#	PCA mode control	490	-	WDTE	-	-	-	CPS1	CPS0	ECF	00h
CH#	PCA counter high byte	48B									00h
CL#	PCA counter low byte	48A									00h
CCAPM0#	PCA module 0 mode	491	-	ECOM	CAPP	CAPN	MAT	TOG	PWM	ECCF	00h
CCAPM1#	PCA module 1 mode	492	-	ECOM	CAPP	CAPN	MAT	TOG	PWM	ECCF	00h
CCAPM2#	PCA module 2 mode	493	-	ECOM	CAPP	CAPN	MAT	TOG	PWM	ECCF	00h
CCAPM3#	PCA module 3 mode	494	-	ECOM	CAPP	CAPN	MAT	TOG	PWM	ECCF	00h
CCAPM4#	PCA module 4 mode	495	-	ECOM	CAPP	CAPN	MAT	TOG	PWM	ECCF	00h
CCAP0H#	PCA module 0 capture high byte	497									xx
CCAP1H#	PCA module 1 capture high byte	499									xx
CCAP2H#	PCA module 2 capture high byte	49B									xx
CCAP3H#	PCA module 3 capture high byte	49D									xx
CCAP4H#	PCA module 4 capture high byte	49F									xx
CCAP0L#	PCA module 0 capture low byte	496									xx
CCAP1L#	PCA module 1 capture low byte	498									xx
CCAP2L#	PCA module 2 capture low byte	49A									xx
CCAP3L#	PCA module 3 capture low byte	49C									xx
CCAP4L#	PCA module 4 capture low byte	49E									xx
CS	Code segment	443									00h
DS	Data segment	441									00h
ES	Extra segment	442									00h
			367	366	365	364	363	362	361	360	
I2CON#*	I²C control register	42C	CR2	ENA	STA	STO	SI	AA	CR1	CR0	00h
I2STAT#	I²C status register	46C	I²C Status Code / Vector					0	0	0	F8h
I2DAT#	I²C data register	46D									xx
I2ADDR#	I²C address register	46E	I²C Slave Address							GC	00h

Philips Semiconductors

Advance Information - Subject to Change

CMOS single-chip 16-bit microcontroller

XA-S3

NAME	DESCRIPTION	SFR Address	BIT FUNCTIONS AND ADDRESSES (MSB ... LSB)								RESET VALUE
IEH*	Interrupt enable high byte	427	33F	33E	33D	33C	33B	33A	339	338	00h
			-	-	-	-	ETI1	ERI1	ETI0	ERI0	
IEL#*	Interrupt enable low byte	426	337	336	335	334	333	332	331	330	00h
			EA	EAD	EPC	ET2	ET1	EX1	ET0	EX0	
IELB#*	Interrupt enable B low byte	42E	377	376	375	374	373	372	371	370	00h
			-	-	EI2	EC4	EC3	EC2	EC1	EC0	
IPA0	Interrupt priority A0	4A0	PT0				PX0				00h
IPA1	Interrupt priority A1	4A1	PT1				PX1				00h
IPA2	Interrupt priority A2	4A2	PPC				PT2				00h
IPA3#	Interrupt priority A3	4A3	-				PAD				00h
IPA4	Interrupt priority A4	4A4	PTI0				PRI0				00h
IPA5	Interrupt priority A5	4A5	PTI1				PRI1				00h
IPB0#	Interrupt priority B0	4A8	PC1				PC0				00h
IPB1#	Interrupt priority B1	4A9	PC3				PC2				00h
IPB2#	Interrupt priority B2	4AA	PI2				PC4				00h
P0*	Port 0	430	387	386	385	384	383	382	381	380	FFh
			A11D7	A10D6	A9D5	A8D4	A7D3	A6D2	A5D1	A4D0	
P1*	Port 1	431	38F	38E	38D	38C	38B	38A	389	388	FFh
			T2EX	T2	TxD1	RxD1	A3	A2	A1	A0/WRH	
P2*	Port 2	432	397	396	395	394	393	392	391	390	FFh
			A19D15	A18D14	A17D13	A16D12	A15D11	A14D10	A13D9	A12D8	
P3*	Port 3	433	39F	39E	39D	39C	39B	39A	399	398	FFh
			RD	WRL	T1	T0	INT1	INT0	TxD0	RxD0	
P4#*	Port 4	434	3A7	3A6	3A5	3A4	3A3	3A2	3A1	3A0	FFh
			A21	A20	CEX4	CEX3	CEX2	CEX1	CEX0	ECI	
P5#*	Port 5	435	3AF	3AE	3AD	3AC	3AB	3AA	3A9	3A8	FFh
			AD7/SDA	AD6/SCL	AD5	AD4	AD3	AD2	AD1	AD0	
P6#*	Port 6	436	-	-	-	-	-	-	3B1	3B0	FFh
									A23	A22	
P0CFGA	Port 0 configuration A	470									Note 5
P1CFGA	Port 1 configuration A	471									Note 5
P2CFGA	Port 2 configuration A	472									Note 5
P3CFGA	Port 3 configuration A	473									Note 5
P4CFGA#	Port 4 configuration A	474									Note 5
P5CFGA#	Port 5 configuration A	475									Note 5
P6CFGA#	Port 6 configuration A	476	-	-	-	-	-	-			Note 5
P0CFGB	Port 0 configuration B	4F0									Note 5
P1CFGB	Port 1 configuration B	4F1									Note 5
P2CFGB	Port 2 configuration B	4F2									Note 5
P3CFGB	Port 3 configuration B	4F3									Note 5
P4CFGB#	Port 4 configuration B	4F4									Note 5
P5CFGB#	Port 5 configuration B	4F5									Note 5
P6CFGB#	Port 6 configuration B	4F6	-	-	-	-	-	-			Note 5
PCON*	Power control register	404	227	226	225	224	223	222	221	220	00h
			-	-	-	-	-	-	PD	IDL	
PSWH*	Program status word (high byte)	401	20F	20E	20D	20C	20B	20A	209	208	Note 2
			SM	TM	RS1	RS0	IM3	IM2	IM1	IM0	
			207	206	205	204	203	202	201	200	

Philips Semiconductors

Advance Information - Subject to Change

CMOS single-chip 16-bit microcontroller

XA-S3

NAME	DESCRIPTION	SFR Address	\	\	\	BIT FUNCTIONS AND ADDRESSES	\	\	\	\	RESET VALUE
			MSB							LSB	
PSWL*	Program status word (low byte)	400	C	AC	-	-	-	V	N	Z	Note 2
			217	216	215	214	213	212	211	210	
PSW51*	80C51 compatible PSW	402	C	AC	F0	RS1	RS0	V	F1	P	Note 3
RSTSRC#	Reset source register	463	-	-	-	-	-	R_WD	R_CMD	R_EXT	Note 7
RTH0	Timer 0 reload register, high byte	455									00h
RTH1	Timer 1 reload register, high byte	457									00h
RTL0	Timer 0 reload register, low byte	454									00h
RTL1	Timer 1 reload register, low byte	456									00h
			307	306	305	304	303	302	301	300	
S0CON*	Serial port 0 control register	420	SM0_0	SM1_0	SM2_0	REN_0	TB8_0	RB8_0	TI_0	RI_0	00h
			30F	30E	30D	30C	30B	30A	309	308	
S0STAT#*	Serial port 0 extended status	421	-	-	-	ERR0	FE0	BR0	OE0	STINT0	00h
S0BUF	Serial port 0 data buffer register	460									xx
S0ADDR	Serial port 0 address register	461									00h
S0ADEN	Serial port 0 address enable	462									00h
			327	326	325	324	323	322	321	320	
S1CON*	Serial port 1 control register	424	SM0_1	SM1_1	SM2_1	REN_1	TB8_1	RB8_1	TI_1	RI_1	00h
			32F	32E	32D	32C	32B	32A	329	328	
S1STAT#*	Serial port 1 extended status	425	-	-	-	ERR1	FE1	BR1	OE1	STINT1	00h
S1BUF	Serial port 1 data buffer register	464									xx
S1ADDR	Serial port 1 address register	465									00h
S1ADEN	Serial port 1 address enable	466									00h
SCR	System configuration register	440	-	-	-	-	PT1	PT0	CM	PZ	00h
			21F	21E	21D	21C	21B	21A	219	218	
SSEL*	Segment selection register	403	ESWEN	R6SEG	R5SEG	R4SEG	R3SEG	R2SEG	R1SEG	R0SEG	00h
SWE	Software interrupt enable	47A	-	SWE7	SWE6	SWE5	SWE4	SWE3	SWE2	SWE1	00h
			357	356	355	354	353	352	351	350	
SWR*	Software interrupt request	42A	-	SWR7	SWR6	SWR5	SWR4	SWR3	SWR2	SWR1	00h
			2C7	2C6	2C5	2C4	2C3	2C2	2C1	2C0	
T2CON*	Timer 2 control register	418	TF2	EXF2	RCLK0	TCLK0	EXEN2	TR2	C/T2	CP/RL2	00h
			2CF	2CE	2CD	2CC	2CB	2CA	2C9	2C8	
T2MOD*	Timer 2 mode control	419	-	-	RCLK1	TCLK1	-	-	T2OE	DCEN	00h
TH2	Timer 2 high byte	459									00h
TL2	Timer 2 low byte	458									00h
T2CAPH	Timer 2 capture, high byte	45B									00h
T2CAPL	Timer 2 capture, low byte	45A									00h
			287	286	285	284	283	282	281	280	
TCON*	Timer 0 and 1 control register	410	TF1	TR1	TF0	TR0	IE1	IT1	IE0	IT0	00h
TH0	Timer 0 high byte	451									00h
TH1	Timer 1 high byte	453									00h
TL0	Timer 0 low byte	450									00h
TL1	Timer 1 low byte	452									00h
TMOD	Timer 0 and 1 mode control	45C	GATE	C/T	M1	M0	GATE	C/T	M1	M0	00h
			28F	28E	28D	28C	28B	28A	289	288	
TSTAT*	Timer 0 and 1 extended status	411	-	-	-	-	-	T1OE	-	T0OE	00h

Philips Semiconductors

CMOS single-chip 16-bit microcontroller

XA-S3

NAME	DESCRIPTION	SFR Address	BIT FUNCTIONS AND ADDRESSES MSB							LSB	RESET VALUE
			2FF	2FE	2FD	2FC	2FB	2FA	2F9	2F8	
WDCON*	Watchdog control register	41F	PRE2	PRE1	PRE0	-	-	WDRUN	WDTOF	-	Note 6
WDL	Watchdog timer reload	45F									00h
WFEED1	Watchdog feed 1	45D									XX
WFEED2	Watchdog feed 2	45E									XX

NOTES:
  * SFRs are bit addressable.
1. At reset, the BCR is loaded with the binary value 0000 0a11, where "a" is the value on the BUSW pin. This defaults the address bus size to 24 bits.
2. SFR is loaded from the reset vector.
3. All bits except F1, F0, and P are loaded from the reset vector. Those bits are all 0.
4. Unimplemented bits in SFRs are X (unknown) at all times. Ones should not be written to these bits since they may be used for other purposes in future XA derivatives. The reset value shown for these bits is 0.
5. Port configurations default to quasi-bidirectional when the XA begins execution from internal code memory after reset, based on the condition found on the EA pin. Thus all PnCFGA registers will contain FF and PnCFGB register will contain 00. When the XA begins execution using external code memory, the default configuration for pins that are associated with the external bus will be push-pull. The PnCFGA and PnCFGB register contents will reflect this difference.
6. The WDCON reset value is E6 for a Watchdog reset, E4 for all other reset causes.
7. The RSTSRC register reflects the cause of the last XA-S3 reset. One bit will be set to 1, the others will be cleared to 0.
8. The XA guards writes to certain bits (typically interrupt flags) that may be altered directly by a peripheral function. This prevents loss of an interrupt or other status if a bit was written directly by a peripheral action during the time between the read and write portions of an instruction that performs a read-modify-write operation. Examples of such instructions are:

```
        and     s0con,#$fb
        clr     tr0
        setb    ti_0
```

   XA-S3 SFR bits that are guarded in this manner are: ADINT (in ADCON); CF, CCF4, CCF3, CCF2, CCF1, and CCF0 (in CCON); SI (in I2CON); TI_0 and RI_0 (in S0CON); TI_1 and RI_1 (in S1CON); FE0, BR0, and OE0 (in S0STAT); FE1, BR1, and OE1 (in S1STAT); TF2 (in T2CON); TF1, TF0, IE1, and IE0 (in TCON); and WDTOF (in WDCON).
9. The XA-S3 implements an 8-bit SFR bus, as stated in Chapter 8 of the XA User Guide. All SFR accesses must be 8-bit operations. Attempts to write 16 bits to an SFR will actually write only the lower 8 bits. Sixteen bit SFR reads will return undefined data in the upper byte.

Philips Semiconductors

Advance Information - Subject to Change

CMOS single-chip 16-bit microcontroller

XA-S3

FUNCTIONAL DESCRIPTION

Details of XA-S3 functions will be described in the following sections.

ANALOG TO DIGITAL CONVERTER

The XA-S3 has an 8-channel, 10-bit A/D converter with 8 sets of result registers, single scan and multiple scan operating modes. The A/D input range is limited to 0 to AV_{DD} (3.3V max.). The A/D inputs are on Port 5. Analog Power and Ground (AVref+ and AVref-) must be supplied in order for the A/D converter to be used. Prior to enabling the A/D converter or driving analog signals into the A/D inputs, the port configurations for the pins being used as A/D inputs must be set to the "off" (high impedance, input only) mode.

When 10 result bits are not needed, the A/D may be set up to perform 8-bit conversions at a higher speed than that required for 10-bit results. Further, the A/D timing can be adapted to the application clock frequency in order to provide the fastest possble conversion.

A/D converter operation is controlled through the ADCON (A/D Control) register, see Figure 1. Bits in ADCON start and stop the A/D, flag conversion completion, and select the converter operating modes.

ADCON   Address: 43Eh

Bit addressable

Reset Value: 00h

MSB   LSB

| - | - | - | ADCAL | ADRES | ADMOD | ADSST | ADINT |

BIT	SYMBOL	FUNCTION
ADCON.7	-	Reserved for future use. Should not be set to 1 by user programs.
ADCON.6	-	Reserved for future use. Should not be set to 1 by user programs.
ADCON.5	-	Reserved for future use. Should not be set to 1 by user programs.
ADCON.4	-	Reserved for future use. Should not be set to 1 by user programs.
ADCON.3	ADRES	Selects 8-bit (0) or 10-bit (1) mode of the A/D.
ADCON.2	ADMOD	A/D mode select. 1 = continuous scan of selected inputs after a start of the A/D. 0 = single scan of selected inputs after a start of the A/D.
ADCON.1	ADSST	A/D start and status. Setting this bit by software starts the A/D conversion of the selected A/D inputs. ADSST remains set as long as the A/D is in operation. In continuous conversion mode, ADSST will remain set unless the A/D is stopped by software. While ADSST is set, new start commands are ignored. An A/D conversion in progress may be aborted by software clearing ADSST.
ADCON.0	ADINT	A/D conversion complete/interrupt flag. This flag is set when all selected A/D channels are converted in either the single scan or continuous scan modes. Must be cleared by software.

Figure 1: A/D Control Register (ADCON)

A/D Conversion Modes

The resolution of the A/D converter is selected by the ADRES bit in ADCON. The A/D converter also supports a single scan mode and a continuous scan mode. In either mode, one or more A/D channels may be converted. The ADCS register determines which channels are converted. If the corresponding bit in the ADCS register is set, that channel is selected for conversions, otherwise that channel is skipped. The ADCS register is detailed in Figure 2.

For any A/D conversion, the most significant 8 bits of A/D conversion results are stored in ADRSHn, corresponding to the A/D channel just converted. Register ADRSL contains the 2 least significant bits corresponding to the last read ADRSH register. The two result bits appear in the two highest bits of ADRSL.

A/D conversions are begun by setting the A/D Start and STatus bit in ADCON. In the single scan mode, all of the channels selected by bits in the ADCS register will be converted once. The ADINT flag is set when the last channel is converted. In the

Philips Semiconductors

Advance Information - Subject to Change

CMOS single-chip 16-bit microcontroller

XA-S3

continuous scan mode, the A/D converter continuously converts all A/D channels selected by bits in the ADCS register. The ADINT flag is set when all channels have been converted once.

ADCS   Address: 43Fh

Bit addressable

Reset Value: 00h

MSB   LSB

ADCS7	ADCS6	ADCS5	ADCS4	ADCS3	ADCS2	ADCS1	ADCS0

BIT	SYMBOL	FUNCTION
ADCS.7	ADCS7	A/D channel 7 select bit.
ADCS.6	ADCS6	A/D channel 6 select bit.
ADCS.5	ADCS5	A/D channel 5 select bit.
ADCS.4	ADCS4	A/D channel 4 select bit.
ADCS.3	ADCS3	A/D channel 3 select bit.
ADCS.2	ADCS2	A/D channel 2 select bit.
ADCS.1	ADCS1	A/D channel 1 select bit.
ADCS.0	ADCS0	A/D channel 0 select bit.

Figure 2: A/D Channel Select Register (ADCS)

The A/D converter can generate an interrupt when the ADINT flag is set. This will occur if the A/D interrupt is enabled (via the EAD bit in IEL), the interrupt system is enabled (via the EA bit in IEL), and the A/D interrupt priority (specified in IPA3 bits 3 to 0) is higher than the currently running code (PSW bits IM3 through IM0) and any other pending interrupt. ADINT must be cleared by software.

A/D Timing Configuration

The A/D sampling and conversion timing may be optimized for the particular oscillator frequency and input drive characteristics of the application. Because A/D operation is mostly dependant on real-time effects (charging time of sampling capacitors, settling time of the comparator, etc.) A/D conversion times are not necessarily much longer at slower clock frequencies. The A/D timing is controlled by the ADCFG register, as shown in Figure 3 and Table 2.

The primary effect of ADCFG settings is to adjust the A/D sample and hold time to be relatively constant over various clock frequencies. Two settings (value 6 and B) are provided to allow fast conversions with a lower external source driving the A/D inputs. These settings provide double the sample time at the same frequency. Of course, settings intended for lower frequencies may also be used at higher frequencies in order to increase the A/D sampling time, but this method has the side effect of significantly increasing A/D conversion times.

Philips Semiconductors

Advance Information - Subject to Change

CMOS single-chip 16-bit microcontroller

XA-S3

ADCFG   Address: 4B9h

Not bit addressable

Reset Value: 00h

MSB

LSB

-	-	-	-	A/D Timing Configuration

BIT	SYMBOL	FUNCTION
ADCFG.7	-	Reserved for future use. Should not be set to 1 by user programs.
ADCFG.6	-	Reserved for future use. Should not be set to 1 by user programs.
ADCFG.5	-	Reserved for future use. Should not be set to 1 by user programs.
ADCFG.4	-	Reserved for future use. Should not be set to 1 by user programs.
ADCFG.3-0	ADCFG	A/D timing configuration (see text and table).

Figure 3: A/D Timing Configuration Register (ADCFG)

Table 1: A/D Timing Configuration

ADCFG.3-0	Max. Oscillator Frequency (MHz)	10-bit A/D conversion time (osc. clocks)	10-bit A/D conversion time (μsec at max osc)	8-bit A/D conversion time (osc. clocks)	8-bit A/D conversion time (μsec at max osc)	Sampling time (osc. clocks)
0h (0000)	6.66	90	13.51	70	11.11	4
1h (0001)	10	94	9.4	78	7.8	6
2h (0010)	11.11	98	8.82	82	7.38	8
3h (0011)	13.33	118	8.85	98	7.35	8
4h (0100)	16.66	122	7.32	102	6.12	10
5h (0101)	20	126	6.3	106	5.3	12
6h (0110)*	20	138	6.9	118	5.9	24
7h (0111)	22.2	130	5.85	102	4.95	14
8h (1000)	23.3	150	6.43	126	5.4	14
9h (1001)	26.6	146	5.78	130	4.88	16
Ah (1010)	30	158	5.26	134	4.46	18
Bh (1011)*	30	172	5.73	148	4.93	32
Ch (1100)	32	162	5.06	138	4.31	20
Dh (1101)	33.3	180	5.4	152	4.56	20
Eh (1110)	36.6	204	5.57	172	4.69	22
Fh (1111)	40	208	5.2	176	4.4	24

* = These settings provide additional A/D input sampling time, in order to allow accurate readings with a higher external source impedance.

I²C INTERFACE

The I²C interface on the XA-S3 is identical to the standard byte-style I²C interface found on devices such as the 8xC552 except for the rate selection. **The I²C interface conforms to the 100 kHz I²C specification, but may be used at rates up to 400 kHz**

Philips Semiconductors   Advance Information - Subject to Change

CMOS single-chip 16-bit microcontroller   XA-S3

(non-conforming).

Important: Before the I²C interface may be used, the port pins P5.6 and P5.7, which correspond to the I²C functions SCL and SDA respectively, must be set to the open drain mode.

The processor interfaces to the I²C logic via the following four special function registers: I2CON (I²C control register), I2STA (I²C status register), I2DAT (I²C data register), and I2ADR (I²C slave address register). The I²C control logic interfaces to the external I²C bus via two port 1 pins: P5.6/SCL (serial clock line) and P5.7/SDA (serial data line).

The Control Register, I2CON: This register is shown in Figure 4. Two bits are affected by the I²C hardware: the SI bit is set when a serial interrupt is requested, and the STO bit is cleared when a STOP condition is present on the I²C bus. The STO bit is also cleared when ENA = "0".

I2CON   Address: 42Ch

Bit addressable

Reset Value: 00h

	MSB							LSB
	CR2	ENA	STA	STO	SI	AA	CR1	CR0

BIT	SYMBOL	FUNCTION
I2CON.7	CR2	I²C Rate Control, with CR1 and CR0. See text and table.
I2CON.6	ENA	Enable I²C port. When ENA = 1, the I²C port is enabled.
I2CON.5	STA	Start flag. Setting STA to 1 causes the I²C interface to attempt to gain mastership of the bus by generating a Start condition.
I2CON.4	STO	Stop flag. Setting STO to 1 causes the I²C interface to attempt to generate a Stop condition.
I2CON.3	SI	Serial Interrupt. SI is set by the I²C hardware when a new I²C state is entered, indicating that software needs to respond. SI causes an I²C interrupt if enabled and of sufficient priority.
I2CON.2	AA	Assert Acknowledge. Setting AA to 1 causes the I²C hardware to automatically generate acknowledge pulses for various conditions (see text).
I2CON.1	CR1	I²C Rate Control, with CR2 and CR0. See text and table.
I2CON.0	CR0	I²C Rate Control, with CR2 and CR1. See text and table.

Figure 4: I²C Control Register (I2CON)

ENA, THE I²C ENABLE BIT
ENA = "0": When ENA is "0", the SDA and SCL outputs are in a high impedance state. SDA and SCL input signals are ignored, SIO1 is in the "not addressed" slave state, and the STO bit in I2CON is forced to "0". No other bits are affected. P1.6 and P1.7 may be used as open drain I/O ports.

ENA = "1": When ENA is "1", SIO1 is enabled. The P1.6 and P1.7 port latches must be set to logic 1.

ENA should not be used to temporarily release the I²C bus since, when ENA is reset, the I²C bus status is lost. The AA flag should be used instead (see description of the AA flag in the following text).

In the following text, it is assumed that ENA = "1".

STA, THE START FLAG
STA = "1": When the STA bit is set to enter a master mode, the I²C hardware checks the status of the I²C bus and generates a START condition if the bus is free. If the bus is not free, the I²C interface waits for a STOP condition (which will free the bus) and generates a START condition after a delay of a half clock period of the internal serial clock generator.

Philips Semiconductors
Advance Information - Subject to Change

CMOS single-chip 16-bit microcontroller

XA-S3

If STA is set while the I²C interface is already in a master mode and one or more bytes are transmitted or received, the hardware transmits a repeated START condition. STA may be set at any time. STA may also be set when the I ²C interface is an addressed slave.

STA = "0": When the STA bit is reset, no START condition or repeated START condition will be generated.

STO, THE STOP FLAG

STO = "1": When the STO bit is set while the I²C interface is in a master mode, a STOP condition is transmitted to the I²C bus. When the STOP condition is detected on the bus, the hardware clears the STO flag. In a slave mode, the STO flag may be set to recover from an error condition. In this case, no STOP condition is transmitted to the I²C bus. However, the hardware behaves as if a STOP condition has been received and switches to the defined "not addressed" slave receiver mode. The STO flag is automatically cleared by hardware.

If the STA and STO bits are both set, the a STOP condition is transmitted to the I ²C bus if the I²C interface is in a master mode (in a slave mode, the hardware generates an internal STOP condition which is not transmitted). The I²C interface then transmits a START condition.

STO = "0": When the STO bit is reset, no STOP condition will be generated.

SI, THE SERIAL INTERRUPT FLAG

SI = "1": When the SI flag is set, then, if the EA (interrupt system enable) and EI2 (I²C interrupt enable) bits are also set, an I²C interrupt is requested. SI is set by hardware when one of 25 of the 26 possible I²C interface states is entered. The only state that does not cause SI to be set is state F8H, which indicates that no relevant state information is available.

While SI is set, the low period of the serial clock on the SCL line is stretched, and the serial transfer is suspended. A high level on the SCL line is unaffected by the serial interrupt flag. SI must be reset by software.

SI = "0": When the SI flag is reset, no serial interrupt is requested, and there is no stretching of the serial clock on the SCL line.

AA, THE ASSERT ACKNOWLEDGE FLAG

AA = "1": If the AA flag is set, an acknowledge (low level to SDA) will be returned during the acknowledge clock pulse on the SCL line when:

- The "own slave address" has been received.
- The general call address has been received while the general call bit (GC) in I2ADR is set.
- A data byte has been received while the I²C interface is in the master receiver mode.
- A data byte has been received while the I²C interface is in the addressed slave receiver mode.

AA = "0": if the AA flag is reset, a not acknowledge (high level to SDA) will be returned during the acknowledge clock pulse on SCL when:

- A data has been received while the I²C interface is in the master receiver mode.
- A data byte has been received while the I²C interface is in the addressed slave receiver mode.

When the I²C interface is in the addressed slave transmitter mode, state C8H will be entered after the last serial is transmitted. When SI is cleared, the I²C interface leaves state C8H, enters the not addressed slave receiver mode, and the SDA line remains at a high level. In state C8H, the AA flag can be set again for future address recognition.

When the I²C interface is in the not addressed slave mode, its own slave address and the general call address are ignored. Consequently, no acknowledge is returned, and a serial interrupt is not requested. Thus, the hardware can be temporarily released from the I²C bus while the bus status is monitored. While the hardware is released from the bus, START and STOP conditions are detected, and serial data is shifted in. Address recognition can be resumed at any time by setting the AA flag. If the AA flag is set when the part's own slave address or the general call address has been partly received, the address will be recognized at the end of the byte transmission.

1997 Oct 22

Philips Semiconductors

Advance Information - Subject to Change

CMOS single-chip 16-bit microcontroller

XA-S3

CR0, CR1, AND CR2, THE CLOCK RATE BITS

These three bits determine the serial clock frequency when the I²C interface is in a master mode. An I²C rate of 100kHz or lower is typical and can be derived from a many oscillator frequencies. The various serial rates are shown in Table 2. A variable bit rate may also be used if Timer 1 is not required for any other purpose while the I²C hardware is in a master mode. The frequencies shown in Table 2 are unimportant when the I²C hardware is in a slave mode. In the slave modes, the hardware will automatically synchronize with the incoming clock frequency.

Table 2: I²C Rate Control

Frequency Select (CR2, CR1, CR0)	Clock Divisor	Example I²C Rates at Specific Oscillator Frequencies					
		8 MHz	12 MHz	16 MHz	20 MHz	24 MHz	30 MHz
0h (0000)		(400) [1]	-	-	-	-	-
1h (0001)		(200) [1]	(300) [1]	(400) [1]	-	-	-
2h (0010)		(116.65) [1]	(176.46) [1]	(235.29) [1]	(294.12) [1]	(352.94) [1]	-
3h (0011)		90.91	(136.36) [1]	(181.82) [1]	(227.27) [1]	(272.73) [1]	(340.91) [1]
4h (0100)		50	75	100	(125) [1]	(150) [1]	(187.5) [1]
5h (0101)		29.41	44.12	58.82	73.53	88.24	(110.29) [1]
6h (0110)		22.73	34.09	45.45	56.82	68.18	85.23
7h (0111)	(Timer 1) [2]	(Timer 1) [2]	(Timer 1) [2]	(Timer 1) [2]	(Timer 1) [2]	(Timer 1) [2]	(Timer 1) [2]

Notes:
1. The XA-S3 I²C interface does not conform to the 400kHz I²C specification (which applies to rates greater than 100kHz) in all details, but may be used with care where higher rates are required by the application.
2. The timer 1 overflow is used to clock the I²C interface. The resulting bit rate is 1/2 of the timer overflow rate.

The I²C Status Register, I2STA

I2STA is an 8-bit read-only special function register. The three least significant bits are always zero. The five most significa nt bits contain the status code. There are 26 possible status codes. When I2STA contains F8H, no relevant state information is available and no serial interrupt is requested. All other I2STA values correspond to defined hardware interface states. When each of these states is entered, a serial interrupt is requested (SI = "1").

Note: A detailed I²C interface description and usage informationincluding example drver code will be provided in a separate document.

XA-S3 TIMER/COUNTERS

The XA-S3 has three general purpose counter/timers, two of which may also be used as baud rate generators for either or both of the UARTs.

Timer 0 and 1

Standard XA-G3 timer 0 and 1.

Timer 2

Standard XA-G3 timer 2.

Philips Semiconductors

Advance Information - Subject to Change

CMOS single-chip 16-bit microcontroller

XA-S3

PCA
Standard 80C51FC-style PCA counter/timer. **The XA uses TCLK (the global peripheral clock which is Osc/4, Osc/16, or Osc/64), Timer 0 overflow, and External (ECI pin). When the ECI input is used, the falling edge clocks the PCA counter. The maximum rate for the counter in this mode on the XA is Osc/4. Each PCA module has its own interrupt (in addition to the standard global PCA interrupt).**

WATCHDOG TIMER
Standard XA-G3 watchdog timer. This watchdog timer always comes up running at reset. The watchdog acts the same on EPROM, ROM, and ROMless parts, as in the XA-G3.

UARTS
Standard XA-G3 UART0 and UART1 with double buffered transmit register. A flag has been added to SnSTAT that is set if any of the status flags (BRn, FEn, or OEn) is set for the corresponding UART channel. This allows polling for UART errors quickly at the interrupt service routine. Baud rate sources may be timer 1 or timer 2.

Clocking /Baud Rate Generation
Same as for the XA-G3.

I/O PORT OUTPUT CONFIGURATION
Port output configurations are the same as for the XA-G3: open drain, quasi-bidirectional, push-pull, and off.

EXTERNAL BUS
The external bus will operate in the same manner as the XA-G3, **but all 24 address lines will be brought out to the outside world**. This allows for a maximum of 16 Mbytes of code memory and another 16 Mbytes of data memory.

CLOCK OUTPUT
The CLKOUT pin allows easier external bus interfacing in some situations. This output reflects the X1 clock input to the XA, but delayed to match the external bus outputs and strobes. The default is for CLKOUT to be on at reset, but it may be turned off via the CLKD bit that has been added to the BCR register.

RESET
Active low reset input, the same as the XA-G3.

The associated RSTOUT pin provides an external indication via an active low open drain output when an internal reset occurs. The RSTOUT pin will be driven low when the RST pin is driven low, when a Watchdog reset occurs or the RESET instruction is executed. This signal may be used to inform other devices in a system that the XA-S3 has been reset.

The latched values of EA and BUSW are NOT automatically updated when an internal reset occurs. RSTOUT may be used to apply an external reset to the XA-S3 in order to update the previously latched EA and BUSW values. However, since RSTOUT reflects ALL reset sources, it cannot simply be fed back into the RST pin without other logic.

The reset source identification register (RSTSRC) indicates the cause of the most recent XA reset. The cause may have been an externally applied reset signal, execution of the RESET instruction, or a Watchdog reset. Figure 5 shows the fields in the RSTSRC register.

1997 Oct 22

19

Philips Semiconductors

Advance Information - Subject to Change

CMOS single-chip 16-bit microcontroller

XA-S3

RSTSRC   Address: 463h

Not bit addressable

Reset Value: see below

MSB   LSB

| - | - | - | - | - | R_WD | R_CMD | R_EXT |

BIT	SYMBOL	FUNCTION
RSTSRC.7	-	Reserved for future use. Should not be set to 1 by user programs.
RSTSRC.6	-	Reserved for future use. Should not be set to 1 by user programs.
RSTSRC.5	-	Reserved for future use. Should not be set to 1 by user programs.
RSTSRC.4	-	Reserved for future use. Should not be set to 1 by user programs.
RSTSRC.3	-	Reserved for future use. Should not be set to 1 by user programs.
RSTSRC.2	R_WD	Indicates that the last reset was caused by a watchdog timer overflow.
RSTSRC.1	R_CMD	Indicates that the last reset was caused by execution of the RESET instruction.
RSTSRC.0	R_EXT	Indicates that the last reset was caused by the external RST input.

Figure 5: Reset source register (RSTSRC)

POWER REDUCTION MODES

The XA-S3 supports Idle and Power Down modes of power reduction. The idle mode leaves some peripherals running in order to allow them to activate the processor when an interrupt is generated. The power down mode stops the oscillator in order to absolutely minimize power. The processor can be made to exit power down mode via a reset or one of the external interrupt inputs (INT0 or INT1). This will occur if the interrupt is enabled and its priority is higher than that defined by IM3 through IM0. In power down mode, the power supply voltage may be reduced to the RAM keep-alive voltage V_{RAM}. This retains the RAM, register, and SFR contents at the point where power down mode was entered. V_{DD} must be raised to within the operating range before power down mode is exited.

INTERRUPTS

XA-S3 interrupt sources include the following:

- External interrupts 0 and 1 (2)
- Timer 0, 1, and 2 interrupts (3)
- PCA: 1 global and 5 channel interrupts (6)
- A/D interrupt (1)
- UART 0 transmitter and receiver interrupts (2)
- UART 1 transmitter and receiver interrupts (2)
- I^2C interrupt (1)
- Software interrupts (7)

There are a total of 17 hardware interrupt sources, enable bits, priority bit sets, etc.

Philips Semiconductors

Advance Information - Subject to Change

CMOS single-chip 16-bit microcontroller

XA-S3

EXCEPTION/TRAPS PRECEDENCE

DESCRIPTION	VECTOR ADDRESS	ARBITRATION RANKING
Reset (h/w, watchdog, s/w)	0000-0003	0 (High)
Breakpoint	0004-0007	1
Trace	0008-000B	1
Stack Overflow	000C-000F	1
Divide by 0	0010-0013	1
User RETI	0014-0017	1
TRAP 0-15 (software)	0040-007F	1

EVENT INTERRUPTS

DESCRIPTION	FLAG BIT	VECTOR ADDRESS	ENABLE BIT	INTERRUPT PRIORITY	ARBITRATION RANKING
External Interrupt 0	IE0	0080-0083	EX0	IPA0.3-0	2
Timer 0 Interrupt	TF0	0084-0087	ET0	IPA0.7-4	3
External Interrupt 1	IE1	0088-008B	EX1	IPA1.3-0	4
Timer 1 Interrupt	TF1	008C-008F	ET1	IPA1.7-4	5
Timer 2 Interrupt	TF2 (EXF2)	0090-0093	ET2	IPA2.3-0	6
PCA Interrupt	CCF0-CCF4, CF	0094-0097	EPC	IPA2.7-4	7
A/D Interrupt	ADINT	0098-009B	EAD	IPA3.3-0	8
Serial Port 0 Rx	RI_0	00A0-00A3	ERI0	IPA4.3-0	9
Serial Port 0 Tx	TI_0	00A4-00A7	ETI0	IPA4.7-4	10
Serial Port 1 Rx	RI_1	00A8-00AB	ERI1	IPA5.3-0	11
Serial Port 1 Tx	TI_1	00AC-00AF	ETI1	IPA5.7-4	12
PCA channel 0	CCF0	00C0-00C3	EC0	IPB0.3-0	17
PCA channel 1	CCF1	00C4-00C7	EC1	IPB0.7-4	18
PCA channel 2	CCF2	00C8-00CB	EC2	IPB1.3-0	19
PCA channel 3	CCF3	00CC-00CF	EC3	IPB1.7-4	20
PCA channel 4	CCF4	00D0-00D3	EC4	IPB2.3-0	21
I²C Interrupt	SI	00D4-00D7	EI2	IPB2.7-4	22

SOFTWARE INTERRUPTS

DESCRIPTION	FLAG BIT	VECTOR ADDRESS	ENABLE BIT	INTERRUPT PRIORITY
Software Interrupt 1	SWR1	0100-0103	SWE1	(fixed at 1)
Software Interrupt 2	SWR2	0104-0107	SWE2	(fixed at 2)
Software Interrupt 3	SWR3	0108-010B	SWE3	(fixed at 3)
Software Interrupt 4	SWR4	010C-010F	SWE4	(fixed at 4)
Software Interrupt 5	SWR5	0110-0113	SWE5	(fixed at 5)
Software Interrupt 6	SWR6	0114-0117	SWE6	(fixed at 6)
Software Interrupt 7	SWR7	0118-011B	SWE7	(fixed at 7)

Philips Semiconductors

CMOS single-chip 16-bit microcontroller

XA-S3

ABSOLUTE MAXIMUM RATINGS

PARAMETER	RATING	UNIT
Operating temperature under bias	-55 to +125	°C
Storage temperature range	-65 to +150	°C
Voltage on EA/V_{PP} pin to V_{SS}	0 to +13.0	V
Voltage on any other pin to V_{SS}	-0.5 to V_{DD}+0.5V	V
Maximum I_{OL} per I/O pin	15	mA
Power dissipation (based on package heat transfer, not device power consumption)	1.5	W

DC ELECTRICAL CHARACTERISTICS

Vdd = 5.0V +/- 10% or 3.0V +/- 10% unless otherwise specified;
Tamb = 0 to +70°C for commercial, -40°C to +85°C for industrial, unless otherwise specified.

SYMBOL	PARAMETER	TEST CONDITIONS	LIMITS			UNIT
			MIN	TYP	MAX	
I_{DD}	Power supply current, operating	5.0V, 30 MHz			100	mA
I_{ID}	Power supply current, Idle mode	5.0V, 30 MHz			25	mA
I_{PD}	Power supply current, Power Down mode	5.0V, 3.0V		5	50	μA
V_{RAM}	RAM keep-alive voltage		1.5			V
V_{IL}	Input low voltage		-0.5		$0.22V_{DD}$	V
V_{IH}	Input high voltage, except Xtal1, RST		2.2			V
V_{IH1}	Input high voltage to Xtal1, RST	For both 3.0 & 5.0V	$0.7 V_{DD}$			V
V_{OL}	Output low voltage all ports, ALE, PSEN [4]	I_{OL} = 3.2mA, V_{DD} = 5.0V			0.5	V
		I_{OL} = 1.0mA, V_{DD} = 3.0V			0.4	V
V_{OH1}	Output high voltage, all ports, ALE, PSEN [2]	I_{OH} = -100μA, V_{DD} = 4.5V	2.4			V
		I_{OH} = -30μA, V_{DD} = 2.7V	2.0			V
V_{OH2}	Output high voltage, all ports, ALE, PSEN [3]	I_{OH} = 3.2mA, V_{DD} = 4.5V	2.4			V
		I_{OH} = 1.0mA, V_{DD} = 2.7V	2.2			V
C_{IO}	Input/Output pin capacitance [1]				15	pF
I_{IL}	Logical 0 input current, all ports [7]	V_{IN} = 0.45V			-50	μA
I_{LI}	Input leakage current, all ports [6]	V_{IN} = V_{IL} or V_{IH}			±10	μA
I_{TL}	Logical 1 to 0 transition current, all ports [5]	At V_{DD} = 5.5V			-650	μA
		At V_{DD} = 2.7V			-250	μA

NOTE:
1. Max. 15pF for EA/V_{PP}.
2. Ports in quasi-bidirectional mode with weak pullup (applies to ALE, PSEN only during RESET).
3. Ports in PUSH-PULL mode, both pullup and pulldown assumed to be the same strength.
4. In all output modes.
5. Port pins source a transition current when used in quasi-bidirectional mode and externally driven from 1 to 0. This current is highest when V_{IN} is approximately 2V.
6. Measured with port in high impedance mode.
7. Measured with port in quasi-bidirectional mode.
8. Under steady state (non-transient) conditions, I_{OL} must be externally limited as follows:

   Maximum I_{OL} per port pin: 15mA (*NOTE: This is 85°C specification for V_{DD} = 5V.)
   Maximum I_{OL} per 8-bit port: 26mA
   Maximum total I_{OL} for all outputs: 71mA

   If I_{OL} exceeds the test condition, V_{OL} may exceed the related specification. Pins are not guaranteed to sink current greater than the listed test conditions.

Philips Semiconductors   Advance Information - Subject to Change

CMOS single-chip 16-bit microcontroller   XA-S3

A/D CONVERTER DC ELECTRICAL CHARACTERISTICS

Tamb = 0 to +70°C for commercial, -40°C to +85°C for industrial, unless otherwise specified.

SYMBOL	PARAMETER	TEST CONDITIONS	LIMITS MIN	LIMITS MAX	UNIT
AV_{DD}	Analog supply voltage	A_{VDD} = VDD ±0.2	2.7	3.3	V
AI_{DD}	Analog supply current (operating)	Port 5 = 0 to A_{VDD}		tbd	mA
AI_{ID}	Analog supply current (Idle mode)			tbd	µA
AI_{PD}	Analog supply current (Power-Down mode)	2V < AV_{PD} < A_{VDD} max		tbd	µA
AV_{IN}	Analog input voltage		AV_{SS} - 0.2	AV_{DD} + 0.2	V
R_{REF}	Resistance between $+V_{REF}$ and $-V_{REF}$		tbd	tbd	kΩ
C_{IA}	Analog input capacitance			15	pF
-	A/D input slew rate			tbd	mV/µs
DL_e	Differential non-linearity [1, 2, 3]			±1	LSB
IL_e	Integral non-linearity [1, 4]			±2	LSB
OS_e	Offset error [1, 5]			±2	LSB
G_e	Gain error [1, 6]			±0.5	LSB
A_e	Absolute voltage error [1, 7]			±3	LSB
M_{CTC}	Channel-to-channel matching			±1	LSB
C_t	Crosstalk between inputs of port [8]	0 - 100kHz		-60	dB

NOTES:
1. Conditions: AV_{REF-} = 0V; AV_{REF+} = 3.0V.
2. The differential non-linearity (DL_e) is the difference bewtween the actual step width and the ideal step width.
3. The ADC is monotonic, there are no missing codes.
4. The integral non-linearity (IL_e) is the peak difference between the center of the steps of the actual and the ideal transfer curve after appropriate adjustments of gain and offset error.
5. The offset error (OS_e) is the absolute difference between the straight line which fits the actual transfer curve (after removing gain error), and the straight line which fits the ideal transfer curve.
6. The gain error (G_e) is the relative difference in percent between the straight line fitting the actual transfer curve (after removing offset error), and the straight line which fits the ideal transfer curve. Gain error is constant at every point on the transfer curve.
7. The absolute voltage error (A_e) is the maximum difference between the center of the steps of the actual transfer curve of the non-calibrated ADC and the ideal transfer curve.
8. Thjis should be considered when both analog and digital signals are input simultaneoulsy to Port 5.

Philips Semiconductors

Advance Information - Subject to Change

CMOS single-chip 16-bit microcontroller

XA-S3

AC ELECTRICAL CHARACTERISTICS

V_{dd} = 5V +/- 5%; T_{amb} = 0 to +70°C for commercial, -40°C to +85°C for industrial.

SYMBOL	FIGURE	PARAMETER	LIMITS		UNIT
			MIN	MAX	
External Clock					
f_C	12	Oscillator frequency	0	30	MHz
t_C	12	Clock period and CPU timing cycle	$1/f_C$		ns
t_{CHCX}	12	Clock high-time	$t_C * 0.5$		ns
t_{CLCX}	12	Clock low time	$t_C * 0.4$		ns
t_{CLCH}	12	Clock rise time		5	ns
t_{CHCL}	12	Clock fall time		5	ns
Address Cycle					
t_{LHLL}	6, 8, 10	ALE pulse width (programmable)	$(V1 * t_C) - 4$		ns
t_{AVLL}	6, 8, 10	Address valid to ALE de-asserted (set-up)	$(V1 * t_C) - 12$		ns
t_{LLAX}	6, 8, 10	Address hold after ALE de-asserted	$(t_C/2) - 10$		ns
Code Read Cycle					
t_{PLPH}	6	$\overline{PSEN}$ pulse width	$(V2 * t_C) - 10$		ns
t_{LLPL}	6	ALE de-asserted to $\overline{PSEN}$ asserted	$(t_C/2) - 5$		ns
t_{AVIVA}	6	Address valid to instruction valid, ALE cycle (access time)		$(V3 * t_C) - 30$	ns
t_{AVIVB}	7	Address valid to instruction valid, non-ALE cycle (access time)		$(V4 * t_C) - 25$	ns
t_{PLIV}	6	$\overline{PSEN}$ asserted to instruction valid (enable time)		$(V2 * t_C) - 25$	ns
t_{PHIX}	6	Instruction hold after $\overline{PSEN}$ de-asserted	0		ns
t_{PHIZ}	6	Bus 3-State after $\overline{PSEN}$ de-asserted		$t_C - 8$	ns
t_{UAPH}	6	Hold time of unlatched part of address after $\overline{PSEN}$ de-asserted	0		ns
Data Read Cycle					
t_{RLRH}	8	$\overline{RD}$ pulse width	$(V7 * t_C) - 10$		ns
t_{LLRL}	8	ALE de-asserted to $\overline{RD}$ asserted	$(t_C/2) - 5$		ns
t_{AVDVA}	8	Address valid to data input valid, ALE cycle (access time)		$(V6 * t_C) - 30$	ns
t_{AVDVB}	9	Address valid to data input valid, non-ALE cycle (access time)		$(V5 * t_C) - 25$	ns
t_{RLDV}	8	$\overline{RD}$ low to valid data in (enable time)		$(V7 * t_C) - 25$	ns
t_{RHDX}	8	Data hold time after $\overline{RD}$ de-asserted	0		ns
t_{RHDZ}	8	Bus 3-State after $\overline{RD}$ de-asserted (disable time)		$t_C - 8$	ns
t_{UARH}	8	Hold time of unlatched part of address after $\overline{RD}$ is de-asserted	0		ns
Data Write Cycle					
t_{WLWH}	10	$\overline{WR}$ pulse width	$(V8 * t_C) - 10$		ns
t_{LLWL}	10	ALE falling edge to $\overline{WR}$ asserted	$(V9 * t_C) - 7$		ns
t_{QVWX}	10	Data valid before WR asserted (data setup time)	$(V9 * t_C) - 25$		ns
t_{WHQX}	10	Data hold time after $\overline{WR}$ de-asserted	$(V11 * t_C) - 5$		ns
t_{AVWL}	10	Address valid to WR asserted (setup time) [5]	$(V9 * t_C) - 20$		ns
t_{UAWH}	10	Hold time of unlatched part of address after $\overline{WR}$ is de-asserted	$(V11 * t_C) - 5$		ns
Wait Input					
t_{WTH}	11	WAIT stable after bus strobe ($\overline{RD}$, $\overline{WR}$, or $\overline{PSEN}$) asserted		$(V10 * t_C) - 25$	ns
t_{WTL}	11	WAIT hold after bus strobe ($\overline{RD}$, $\overline{WR}$, or $\overline{PSEN}$) asserted	$(V10 * t_C) - 10$		ns

Philips Semiconductors

Advance Information - Subject to Change

CMOS single-chip 16-bit microcontroller

XA-S3

AC ELECTRICAL CHARACTERISTICS (CONTINUED)

This set of parameters is referenced to the XA-S3 clock input.

SYMBOL	FIGURE	PARAMETER	LIMITS		UNIT
			MIN	MAX	
Address Cycle					
t_{KHLH}	6	Delay from CLKOUT rising edge to ALE rising edge	10	40	ns
t_{KLLL}	6	Delay from CLKOUT falling edge to ALE falling edge			ns
t_{KHAV}	6	Delay from CLKOUT rising edge to address valid			ns
t_{KHAX}	6	Address hold after CLKOUT rising edge			ns
Code Read Cycle					
t_{KHPL}	6	Delay from CLKOUT rising edge to $\overline{PSEN}$ asserted			ns
t_{KHPH}	6	Delay from CLKOUT rising edge to $\overline{PSEN}$ de-asserted			ns
t_{IVKH}	6	Instruction valid to CLKOUT rising edge			ns
t_{KHIX}	6	Instruction hold from CLKOUT rising edge			ns
t_{KHIZ}	6	Bus 3-State after CLKOUT rising edge (code read)			ns
Data Read Cycle					
t_{KHRL}	8	Delay from CLKOUT rising edge to $\overline{RD}$ asserted			ns
t_{KHRH}	8	Delay from CLKOUT rising edge to $\overline{RD}$ de-asserted			ns
t_{DVKH}	8	Data valid to CLKOUT rising edge			ns
t_{KHDX}	8	Data hold from CLKOUT rising edge			ns
t_{KHDZ}	8	Bus 3-State after CLKOUT rising edge (data read)			ns
Data Write Cycle					
t_{KHWL}	10	Delay from CLKOUT rising edge to $\overline{WR}$ asserted			ns
t_{KHWH}	10	Delay from CLKOUT rising edge to $\overline{WR}$ de-asserted			ns
t_{QVKH}	10	Data valid to CLKOUT rising edge			ns
t_{KHQX}	10	Data hold after CLKOUT rising edge			ns
t_{KHQZ}	10	Bus 3-State after CLKOUT rising edge (data write)			ns
Wait Input					
t_{KHWTH}	11	WAIT stable before CLKOUT rising edge			ns
t_{KHWTL}	11	WAIT hold after CLKOUT rising edge			ns

NOTES:
1. Load capacitance for all outputs = 80pF.
2. Variables V1 through V11 reflect programmable bus timing, which is programmed via the Bus Timing registers (BTRH and BTRL). Refer to the XA User Guide for details of the bus timing settings. Please note that the XA-S3 requires that extended data bus hold time (WM0 = 1) to be used with external bus write cycles.
   - V1) This variable represents the programmed width of the ALE pulse as determined by the ALEW bit in the BTRL register. V1 = 0.5 if the ALEW bit = 0, and 1.5 if the ALEW bit = 1.
   - V2) This variable represents the programmed width of the $\overline{PSEN}$ pulse as determined by the CR1 and CR0 bits or the CRA1, CRA0, and ALEW bits in the BTRL register.
     - For a bus cycle with **no** ALE, V2 = 1 if CR1/0 = 00, 2 if CR1/0 = 01, 3 if CR1/0 = 10, and 4 if CR1/0 = 11. Note that during burst mode code fetches, $\overline{PSEN}$ does not exhibit transitions at the boundaries of bus cycles. V2 still applies for the purpose of determining peripheral timing requirements.
     - For a bus cycle **with** an ALE, V2 = the total bus cycle duration (2 if CRA1/0 = 00, 3 if CRA1/0 = 01, 4 if CRA1/0 = 10, and 5 if CRA1/0 = 11) minus the number of clocks used by ALE (V1 + 0.5).
       Example: if CRA1/0 = 10 and ALEW = 1, the V2 = 4 - (1.5 + 0.5) = 2.
   - V3) This variable represents the programmed length of an entire code read cycle **with** ALE. This time is determined by the CRA1 and CRA0 bits in the BTRL register. V3 = the total bus cycle duration (2 if CRA1/0 = 00, 3 if CRA1/0 = 01, 4 if CRA1/0 = 10, and 5 if CRA1/0 = 11).
   - V4) This variable represents the programmed length of an entire code read cycle with **no** ALE. This time is determined by the CR1 and CR0 bits in the BTRL register. V4 = 1 if CR1/0 = 00, 2 if CR1/0 = 01, 3 if CR1/0 = 10, and 4 if CR1/0 = 11.
   - V5) This variable represents the programmed length of an entire data read cycle with **no** ALE. this time is determined by the DR1 and DR0 bits in the BTRH register. V5 = 1 if DR1/0 = 00, 2 if DR1/0 = 01, 3 if DR1/0 = 10, and 4 if DR1/0 = 11.

Philips Semiconductors   Advance Information - Subject to Change

CMOS single-chip 16-bit microcontroller   XA-S3

V6) This variable represents the programmed length of an entire data read cycle **with** ALE. The time is determined by the DRA1 and DRA0 bits in the BTRH register. V6 = the total bus cycle duration (2 if DRA1/0 = 00, 3 if DRA1/0 = 01, 4 if DRA1/0 = 10, and 5 if DRA1/0 = 11).

V7) This variable represents the programmed width of the $\overline{RD}$ pulse as determined by the DR1 and DR0 bits or the DRA1, DRA0 in the BTRH register, and the ALEW bit in the BTRL register. Note that during a 16-bit operation on an 8-bit external bus, $\overline{RD}$ remains low and does not exhibit a transition between the first and second byte bus cycles. V7 still applies for the purpose of determining peripheral timing requirements. The timing for the first byte is for a bus cycle with ALE, the timing for the second byte is for a bus cycle with no ALE.
  - For a bus cycle with **no** ALE, V7 = 1 if DR1/0 = 00, 2 if DR1/0 = 01, 3 if DR1/0 = 10, and 4 if DR1/0 = 11.
  - For a bus cycle **with** an ALE, V7 = the total bus cycle duration (2 if DRA1/0 = 00, 3 if DRA1/0 = 01, 4 if DRA1/0 = 10, and 5 if DRA1/0 = 11) minus the number of clocks used by ALE (V1 + 0.5).
    Example: if DRA1/0 = 00 and ALEW = 0, then V7 = 2 - (0.5 + 0.5) = 1.

V8) This variable represents the programmed width of the $\overline{WRL}$ and/or $\overline{WRH}$ pulse as determined by the WM1 bit in the BTRL register. V8 1 if WM1 = 0, and 2 if WM1 = 1.

V9) This variable represents the programmed write setup time as determined by the data write cycle duration (defined by DW1 and DW0 or the DWA1 and DWA0 bits in the BTRH register), the WM0 and ALEW bits in the BTRL register, and the value of V8.
  - For a bus cycle with **no** ALE, V9 = the total bus write cycle duration (2 if DW1/0 = 00, 3 if DW1/0 = 01, 4 if DW1/0 = 10, and 5 if DW1/0 = 11) minus the number of clocks used by the $\overline{WRL}$ and/or $\overline{WRH}$ pulse (V8) minus the number of clocks used for data hold time (0 if WM0 = 0 and 1 if WM0 = 1).
    Example:if DW1/0 = 11, WM0 = 0, and WM1 = 0, then V9 = 5 - 0 - 1 = 4.
  - For a bus cycle **with** an ALE, there are two cases:
    1. For the parameter t AVWL , V9 = the total bus cycle duration (2 if DWA1/0 = 00, 3 if DWA1/0 = 01, 4 if DWA1/0 = 10, and 5 if DWA1/0 = 11) minus the number of clocks used by the $\overline{WRL}$ and/or $\overline{WRH}$ pulse (V8), minus the number of clocks used by data hold time (0 if WM0 = 0 and 1 if WM0 = 1).
    2. For other parameters, V9 = the above value minus the width of the ALE pulse (V1).
    Example: if DWA1/0 = 11, WM0 = 1, WM1 = 1, and V1 = 0.5, then V9 = 5 - 1 - 2 - 0.5 = 1.5.

V10) This variable represents the length of a bus strobe for calculation of WAIT setup and hold times. The strobe may be $\overline{RD}$ (for data read cycles), $\overline{WRL}$ and/or $\overline{WRH}$ (for data write cycles), or $\overline{PSEN}$ (for code read cycles), depending on the type of bus cycle being widened by WAIT. V10 = V2 for WAIT associated with a code read cycle using $\overline{PSEN}$. V10 = V8 for a data write cycle using $\overline{WRL}$ and/or $\overline{WRH}$. V10 = V7 - 1 for a data read cycle using $\overline{RD}$. This means that a single clock data read cycle cannot be stretched using WAIT. If WAIT is used to vary the duration of data read cycles, the $\overline{RD}$ strobe width must be set to be at least two clocks in duration. Also see Note 4.

V11) This variable represents the programmed write hold time as determined by the WM0 bit in the BTRL register. V11 = 0 if the WM0 bit = 0, and 1 if the WM0 bit = 1.

3. Not all combinations of bus timing configuration values result in valid bus cycles. Please refer to the XA User Guide section on the External Bus for details.

4. When code is being fetched for execution on the external bus, a burst mode fetch is used that does not have $\overline{PSEN}$ edges in every fetch cycle. This would be A3-A0 for an 8-bit bus, and A3-A1 for a 16-bit bus. Also, a 16-bit read operation conducted on an 8-bit wide bus similarly does not include two separate $\overline{RD}$ strobes. So, a rising edge on the low order address line (A0) must be used to trigger a WAIT in the second half of such a cycle.

5. This parameter is provided for peripherals that have the data clocked in on the falling edge of the $\overline{WR}$ strobe. This is not usually the case and in most applications this parameter is not used.

Index